MARX'S EXPERIMENTS
AND MICROSCOPES

Studies in Critical Social Sciences Book Series

Haymarket Books is proud to be working with Brill Academic Publishers (www.brill.nl) to republish the *Studies in Critical Social Sciences* book series in paperback editions. This peer-reviewed book series offers insights into our current reality by exploring the content and consequences of power relationships under capitalism, and by considering the spaces of opposition and resistance to these changes that have been defining our new age. Our full catalog of *SCSS* volumes can be viewed at https://www.haymarketbooks .org/series_collections/4-studies-in-critical-social-sciences.

Marx's Experiments and Microscopes

Modes of Production, Religion, and the Method of Successive Abstractions

Paul B. Paolucci

Haymarket Books
Chicago, IL

First published in 2019 by Brill Academic Publishers, The Netherlands.
© 2019 Koninklijke Brill NV, Leiden, The Netherlands

Published in paperback in 2020 by
Haymarket Books
P.O. Box 180165
Chicago, IL 60618
773-583-7884
www.haymarketbooks.org

ISBN: 978-1-64259-368-6

Distributed to the trade in the US through Consortium Book Sales and
Distribution (www.cbsd.com) and internationally through Ingram Publisher
Services International (www.ingramcontent.com).

This book was published with the generous support of Lannan Foundation and
Wallace Action Fund.

Special discounts are available for bulk purchases by organizations and
institutions. Please call 773-583-7884 or email info@haymarketbooks.org for
more information.

Cover design by Jamie Kerry and Ragina Johnson.

Printed in United States.

10 9 8 7 6 5 4 3 2 1

Library of Congress Cataloging-in-Publication Data is available.

Contents

Acknowledgements

Authors such as myself enjoy and rely on a support network. Though many of the names below the reader will not find in my references, it is only right and proper that I give credit where it is due.

I first want to thank Dr. Jen Koslow, Department of Biology, Eastern Kentucky University. Her input, emotional support, and patience were invaluable at every stage of my writing process. Audience for my bad humor and test subject for more than one poorly executed recipe, I could not have finished this book without her. Love and appreciation to you, Jen Jen!

I would like to thank Dr. David Fasenfest, Department of Sociology at Wayne State University, Acquisitions Editor for Brill International Publishers, and Editor for *Critical Sociology*. David has supported my work over the years and his advice, direction, and encouragement have been invaluable.

I would also like to thank my colleagues at Eastern Kentucky University, several of whom I am sure I bored with my discussions about my various projects over the years. Thanks also goes to Dean Sara Zeigler, EKU College of Letters, Arts, and Social Sciences, for affording me the time needed to see this book through to its end.

Speaking of boring others with my conversation, apologies and thanks to long-time friend, Bryan Swearinger, for being a patient listener and humoring me with his professed anticipation for my final product. It means a lot when friends ask you about your work, express interest in your ideas, and say they are eager to see your results. Friends having faith in you makes it easier to press forward to the finish line.

Finally, though he finds a place within this book's pages, I must nevertheless thank Dr. Bertell Ollman, Department of Politics at New York University. Though our conversations have dwindled in recent times, the sort of work I do is only possible because of his insights and generosity over the years. My understanding of Marx goes through his work and I will always consider myself his student, though I never was involved in one of his classes. I hope you and Paule are doing well.

Illustrations

Figures

List

Tables

Introduction

1   A Provocation and a Challenge

Some readers may find my chosen title provocative or even dismiss it as an analogy that has overreached. There are no experimental tables in Marx's works. How could he possibly have used microscopes? Moreover, the title makes him sound like a positivist. Did not Marx (1936: 210) dismiss Comte's work as "positivist rot"? Such observations notwithstanding, I believe Marx was more favorably inclined toward a positivist philosophy of science—or at least certain aspects of it—than is often assumed and that he was correct in that supposition.

While Marx's biography and lifetime of writings reveal a clear commitment to scientific values, how he adopted conventional scientific methods is easy to overlook, for reasons that often come from Marx himself. With his personal life and political activity regularly interfering with his projects, we have no indication that he ever started the work on method he hoped to complete and this left many of his directives on these matters scattered across his writings.[1] Marx's narrative style and language use often obscure his analytical procedures and he regularly presents his results in ways unfamiliar to scientific protocols both then and now. These barriers are so deeply embedded in his work that many readers—especially new ones and those from non-Marxian traditions—are not cognizant of ways of handling the interpretive challenges they bring. "What scientific method? *Capital* does not seem to follow *any* method I am familiar with. Dialectics? That is philosophy, not science. As a matter of fact, Marx follows no method at all as far as I can tell, especially with his terribly unsystematic writing," scoffs the dismissive analytical philosopher. Such criticisms do not arise without a reason.

Grasping the relationship between Marx's use of scientific and dialectical principles is stubbornly elusive. On the one side, Marx states his embrace of dialectical reason on multiple occasions and we find its language from his early writings to his last notebooks. However, there is no one essay, chapter, or book where Marx expounds upon this issue directly, systematically, and

---

1   Marx's biography is replete with instances of instability (expulsion from Germany, France, and Belgium because of his political activities), family troubles (e.g., poverty, death of children, illnesses and death of his wife, Jenny), his own health problems, involvement in political organizations (the International Working Men's Association), and even slanderous accusations that motivated him to put aside current projects to write lengthy rebuttals few would read and history would hardly remember (e.g., *Herr Vogt*).

thoroughly. This absence has birthed many schools on his "dialectical method" that range from simplistic caricatures, to unhelpful formulaic models, to sophisticated and insightful elucidations. Despite these varying degrees of mastery, all schools agree that dialectical reason is a cornerstone of Marx's methodology. On the other side, multiple inquirers have questioned if "Marxism" is in fact "a science," particularly whether his theories—e.g., the falling rate of profit or workers overthrowing capitalism and installing a socialist-communist system—meet science's customary predictive standards (e.g., see Eastman 1935; Popper 1963; Burawoy 1990; Kitching 1994; Sheehan 2017; David 2018). While Marx thought such "predictions" were theoretically and empirically sound, this question is not my immediate concern. Instead, my concern is with how Marx brought dialectical and scientific principles together into one coherent epistemological framework.

Perhaps I should clarify what I mean by this. If I argued that Marx used both inductive and deductive reasoning, the experienced Marxian scholar would not find the claim novel, and rightly so. Nor would they find it revealing if my thesis is that Marx used historical data and statistics, as that should be obvious to anyone who reads him.[2] But with scant literature on what he termed "scientific dialectics" (Marx 1985: 29), each new generation of intellectuals is unlikely to learn both *that* and *how* Marx bridged dialectics and conventional science, much less how this approach translated into his use of the experimental model, sociological microscopes, and even taxonomic methods. My challenge in this book is to explain just this.[3]

2   The Nature of the Evidence

I do not forge my thesis out of thin air. Marx *did tell us* that his method in *Capital* employed an experimental model and honed in on objects of inquiry as if using a microscope. There are several reasons why the social sciences have left knowledge of how he accomplished this underdeveloped. If one interprets Marx's comments on these matters as analogies instead of methodological statements, then it is easy to give them too little weight. After introducing these ideas early in *Capital*, Marx never returns to them later to say, "Remember

---

2   In the Preface to the First German Edition of *Capital*, Marx ([1867] 1992c: 20) tells us some of his data sources include legislation ("the Factory Acts"), "social statistics" often from "commissions of inquiry," and historical events and developments, e.g., "the American Civil War."

3   I have previously published works that address Marx's relation to positivism and science (Paolucci 2003) and Marx's method of abstraction addressed in this current book (Paolucci 2007: 161–173). The discussions on the topics found in both, however, suffer from lack of sufficient depth and explication.

the Preface? This is an example of a sociological experiment. In the next section, I increase the intensity of my microscopic lens." Marx only on occasion explicitly refers to "variables" and "constants," so it is easy to miss how he uses them or to assume he uses these terms casually. Marx's employment of these tools, as a result, is not at all obvious on first, second, or even third readings. These are not the only reasons for the elusive nature of his method, however.

By the time he wrote *Capital*, Marx had clearly concluded that combining scientific method with a dialectical sensibility was the proper approach. The seductive song of his dialectic, however, can make his pronouncements on science go right past us. One place to experience this is in his Introduction to the *Grundrisse*. Reading it is not an easy undertaking, as he composed these preparatory notes for self-clarification and not for a popular audience. The meaning normally taken from them is as a series of meditations on using dialectical reason in the service of political economy. This interpretation is accurate in many ways. Still, Marx's narrative there does not state every assumption or methodological principle as it goes along (though he highlights several) and we only encounter passing nods to science but without him explicitly elaborating on it. Perhaps Marx believed he understood scientific method sufficiently enough by then that he felt reflecting on it was unnecessary. Perhaps.

Another possibility is that Marx assumed that certain scientific rules and elements of dialectical reason were indistinguishable—with elements of the former embedded in the latter. In his Introduction, for example, Marx addresses building abstract concepts upon observations of the concrete and the need to move analytically from general categories to more specific explanatory frameworks. While both the natural scientist and the dialectician should recognize these principles, it is likely that Marxian scholars are more familiar with the language of "the abstract" and "the concrete." The terms "the general" and "the specific," however, are probably so prosaic that they usually do not command much attention, even though how Marx connected them with the abstract and the concrete and manipulated these connections are crucial procedures in his scientific practice. Moreover, the techniques he used to do this tend to be opaque until one learns to recognize them.

3   Uncovering the Evidence

In working on my dissertation many years ago, I composed several chapters that fell into familiar Marxian categories—i.e., dialectics, the materialist conception of history, political economy, class analysis, and so on. In trying to demonstrate how these moments of inquiry reflected Marx's scientific practices, I grew frustrated when I realized that I had not provided any new insight to these issues. If I were both to answer my research questions and to satisfy my intellectual curiosity, I would have to strike out in a new direction.

I had been reading as much as I could about Marx's dialectical method and felt I understood Bertell Ollman's internal relations approach fairly well. His books and essays provided me the most insight I had encountered yet on Marx's ideas. Nevertheless, Ollman focuses more on Marx's dialectic than on how he used tools common to scientific practice. Marx, it seemed to me, believed his work satisfied criteria *any* scientist in *any* field would recognize. I had encountered little literature that explained how and why that was the case, from Ollman or from anyone else.[4]

As I puzzled over my stalled dissertation, I began to wonder if trying to show how Marx's approach to dialectics was scientific was misplaced. Instead, I thought, perhaps I should examine how his approach to science was dialectical. This brought me to investigate if I could divide my work along conventional scientific lines, rather than traditional Marxian ones. I started with asking, "What do all sciences have in common *as sciences*?" My answer was that they all have assumptions, specific language and concepts, and epistemological procedures. To test my hypothesis, I restarted my work with new chapters—Marx's Ontological Assumptions, Marx's Language and Concepts, Marx's Epistemological Procedures. I found that I could place every subtopic from each of my prior chapters into one of these new ones. I also saw how many of Marx's principles elegantly led from one to another, e.g., why a social ontology that assigns a primary role to labor must epistemologically prioritize historical and materialist concerns. Enthused with these results, I concluded that if I wanted to learn more about Marx the *social scientist*, this was the path forward.

Though it felt like a great advance in my studies, I predictably encountered new problems. If the relations between the abstract, the concrete, the general, and the specific did not require Marx's contemplative attention, then these concepts would not have made the appearance they did in the *Grundrisse*'s Introduction. Convinced this meant something important, I also noticed that

---

4 One exception I encountered at the time was Daniel Little's, *The Scientific Marx*. There, Little (1986) addresses several traditional issues in science found in Marx's approach, such as induction, deduction, falsification, hypothesis testing, and so on. Similarly, journals such as *Science & Society*, *Rethinking Marxism*, *Critical Sociology*, and *Historical Materialism* (among others) regularly publish articles that address Marx's concepts, methods, and forms of analysis. But all of the above also lack an explicit analysis of how Marx adopted the experimental model, used techniques similar to microscopes, and employed a form of taxonomic analysis, the central issues I address here.

he would sometimes connect these terms together. I concluded that this language reflected a core conceptual scheme for Marx and that his epistemological procedures forged these terms together into the (what I termed) "conceptual doublets" of the general abstract, the specific abstract, the general concrete, and the specific concrete. I now needed to see if this framework was useful for interpreting him.

As I re-read *Capital* and used these four categories for interpreting his observations, concepts, and models, my progress came in fits and starts. While I became increasingly comfortable with and adept at applying each doublet, I found certain issues more difficult than others. Some of Marx's topics appeared to be observations of the *general concrete* one moment, while I interpreted him using the same subject matter elsewhere as *specific abstract* concepts. I protested, "It has to be one or the other, it can't be both!" Flummoxed with the discrepancy and flip-flopping in my conclusions multiple times, if I could not use these four categories to interpret Marx consistently, I would have to admit that this avenue was a dead end. Not only that, I would also have consider whether or not Marx was haphazard in his use of concepts and language.

In puzzling over this matter, I had slipped into being a non-dialectical thinker for a moment, like an Aristotle disciple requiring that A equals A and A does not equal non-A and never the twain shall meet. Scientifically, Marx would be on shaky ground if he used words and filled concepts with meaning absent considerations of consistency and precision. This seemed to me to be quite un-Marx-like, too. Reading Ollman led me to understand that Marx only appears this way at times but there usually was a sound logic behind everything he did.[5] Nevertheless, it was true that the meanings and function of his concepts none-too-seldom change in his analyses. I eventually figured out that certain subject matter in Marx's work function as *both* concrete observations and elsewhere as abstract concepts *because they can function as both* and *because he needs them to function as both* (for reasons I later explain). Once I mentally reconstructed the method through which Marx was altering his analytical frameworks, I returned to *Capital* to see if I could discern that method there and I found it everywhere.

Though later chapters explain in detail what this method is, how it works, and the justification for it, here I will provide a brief preview of those discussions. Ollman stresses several meanings designated by the term

5 See Ollman's ([1971] 1976) discussion of Pareto's claim that Marx's words appear as if like bats, where one can see both mice and birds in them; also see his discussion of Marx's internal relations philosophy and his use of abstractions of vantage point (Ollman 2003).

"abstraction" in Marx's work.[6] First, something that is "too abstract" is something poorly conceptualized, overly complicated, or unnecessarily distorted. Second, during analysis there is the mental practice of carving out objects of study, i.e., "to abstract" parts out of a whole. Third, there are "abstractions," or the thinking units that result from the act of abstraction itself. These latter two uses are important here. Marx's method involves using observations to carve out objects of study and developing a series of analytical concepts—or abstractions—that result from those mental acts. While we do this in everyday thinking, scientific inquiry does it more systemically. And compared to how science is often practiced, Marx's approach involves a certain reflexive consciousness of and sensitivity to the act of abstraction, especially in how to actively manipulate abstractions within multiple analytical frameworks.

One of the ways Marx manipulates his abstractions is by carving them from what Ollman calls different "vantage points." As useful and important as this insight is, I came to conclude that we needed an explanation of Marx's method that connects these dialectical roots with the recognized scientific protocols he often used to change such vantage points. Marx constructs abstract concepts based on similarities shared among empirical observations and from these he carves out new categories based on their differences—or what scientists refer to as "lumping" and "splitting" in taxonomic analysis. Dialectically, Marx will *re-abstract* his categories and concepts and alter their meanings for different historical and structural contexts. Consequently—and because of his lack of systematic methodological exposition—readers unaware of this practice often become flustered, confused, or discouraged when reading *Capital*. From a mainstream sociological point of view, it appears as if Marx assembled his material there haphazardly and dialectics is simply a philosophical worldview accompanied by whimsical and other seemingly imprecise linguistic stylings. Without the right interpretive tools to recognize how Marx constructs, uses, and manipulates his abstractions, such conclusions seem entirely reasonable to his critics.[7]

6 In addition to his works just referenced, see Ollman's webpage that provides an excerpt of his writings on the topic of abstraction: "Putting Dialectics to Work: The Process of Abstraction in Marx's Method." Retrieved November 16, 2018: https://www.nyu.edu/projects/ollman/docs/dd_ch05a.php.

7 For example, when one examines the commentary on Marx they often find observers referring to him as an economic philosopher. While Marx would have readily admitted that his work related to economics, to call him a philosopher is a significant misunderstanding of his scholarly mission, especially as far as his mature studies in political economy are concerned. True, Marx's doctoral work was in philosophy and many elements of his early writings deal directly with philosophical questions. But to assume he maintained a philosophical bent over his lifetime and then read and interpret his later work as part of that philosophical project is not only to grossly misunderstand his intellectual goal and program. This interpretation

As Marx did not give this analytical procedure a name despite the consistency with which he used it, I decided it needed one as a reference point. Though Paul Sweezy's phraseology, "the method of successive approximations," came closest to the issue, I thought the estimable economist did not get it totally right.[8] While Marx was certainly doing something successively and his method does involve approximating, what he really was using was *a method of successive abstractions*. I concluded, and continue to believe, that if Marx is to remain vital to our overall sociological mission, and if we are to understand him as someone with more than just a philosophical or political outlook, then his value rests upon us grasping and using methodological techniques such as this.

How much fault rests with Marx for several inconsistent and often incomplete readings of his work? Our understanding of his ideas likely would have progressed more rapidly and without so many divergent schools of thought had he taken the time to provide a full, clear, and systematic accounting of his method. In addition, once several formulaic, rigid, and dogmatic readings of dialectics made their way into the literature, it has taken time to criticize such approaches and make room for more promising lines of inquiry. Though this is normal for progress in any science, by now the literature on Marx's dialectic is established in such a way that once one ventures down its path, it is easy to follow that path into blind alleys a novice might not immediately recognize before they encounter more fruitful approaches. These continuing hurdles notwithstanding, the pursuit of Marx's dialectic remains essential for any adequate understanding of his key ideas.

---

also requires that one overlook his criticisms of philosophy over the course of his scholarly output. As for dialectics, the history of Marxist discourse has generally not been successful in penetrating mainstream sociology with a convincing explanation of how Marx transformed Hegel's philosophy into a consistent and coherent research method beyond reductive catch-phrases (often Marx in origin) such as "turning him on his head." It is for such reasons as these that those involved in Analytical Marxism set out on a different path, one outside of Marx's approach in multiple respects (for my discussion on this latter issue, see Paolucci 2011).

8   Sweezy's discussion is a starting-point for this issue but it only provides a partially faithful description of Marx's approach. Sweezy (1964: 11) describes Marx's method as one "which consists in moving from the more abstract to the more concrete in a step-by-step fashion, removing simplifying assumptions at successive stages of the investigation so that theory may take account of and explain an ever wider range of actual phenomena." But Marx's approach starts with concrete observations, moves to general abstract categories as the widest range of conceptualization, and then works its way back to more specific data and concepts targeting our capitalist present. Further, we must understand this method in terms of Marx's adoption of the experimental model. As such, this book attempts to add to Sweezy's discussion by specifying Marx's method of abstraction, steps in concept construction, and the mobilization of these in empirical analysis.

On top of such issues, while the type of scholarship Marx believed fit for a social science requires a range of expertise, today's academy tends to silo scholars into specialized disciplines. Dialectics tends to attract more attention from philosophers, though social science was the locale of Marx's most productive dialectical applications. The time needed for mastering dialectics leaves less time to master traditional scientific procedures, and methodological specialists in the social sciences are often non-Marxists that gravitate toward statistics, surveys, or ethnographic research. Marx's overall project also requires talents of the historian and the economist, which are time-consuming investigations in their own right. And Marx's advanced political economy requires higher math, skills just a few people in the above groups possess. With Marx bequeathing us a collective series of hurdles most of us cannot clear (myself included), and with Marxist scholarship reflecting the silos found in academic disciplines, a Venn diagram of Marx's fields of inquiry is likely to find few scholars today at its center.

I do not mean to imply that I am the only one that has a good grasp of Marx's research method. Far from it. I have shelves of books and stacks of journal articles from authors who have a first-rate understanding of Marx's analytical approach. I learn more all the time from this literature. My point is that after more than 150 years since the publication of *Capital*, the scholarship on Marx has proceeded without an important tool needed for a more complete understanding of his method. This book's goal, then, is to explain just what that tool is, how Marx used it, and how we might use it ourselves.

4   The Method of the Book

A careful dissection of the discussion above reveals that my argument is asking for a certain license. That is, and this I fully admit, we never see Marx map out my four conceptual doublets in any one place nor does he ever thoroughly explain his use of them. More precisely, while we *do* find Marx occasionally using these terms—the abstract, the concrete, the general, the specific—independently, we do not find him *consistently* forging them together in his writing like I have proposed here. This means that my thesis must rely on a degree of interpretation, which always requires certain leaps and leaves room for error. If the proof of the pudding is in the eating, then the reader can render a reasoned verdict after consuming my argument and weighing the evidence I marshal for it. Toward those ends, I provide an outline of that argument below.

First, I show that Marx acknowledged that the experimental model was part of his research approach and that he provided guidelines on its use.

Second, I demonstrate that the conceptual doublets that comprise Marx's method of successive abstractions hang together logically and perform an in-concert analytical function for him.

Third, extending from the second, I explain how to use these concepts in a way that makes coherent scientific sense. It is one thing to identify certain terms or ideas with Marx and to connect those ideas to one another, but I also must demonstrate how his abstractions serve accepted functions in scientific thinking, including the method of controlled comparison and an ability to focus ever more closely on objects of inquiry.

Fourth, I show how Marx's method of analysis connects these concepts to the data he presents to the reader. Showing that and/or how Marx wrote *about* science is not enough. An explanation of how he *practiced* it on empirical matter is also necessary.

Fifth, accomplishing the first four tasks above should demonstrate how Marx used his method of abstracting and re-abstracting subject matter as a way both to make experiments and to approximate sociological microscopes.

Sixth, as one principle in science is that we can explain its methods in such a way that other researchers can use them, my last set of hurdles is to show how to apply Marx's method to topics beyond those on which he used it.

Accomplishing all of the above will, I hope, convincingly reveal how one of Marx's contributions to the social science enterprise is the forging together of dialectical sensibilities and scientific protocols and how we can do so as well.

I have structured the book to meet all of these goals.

Chapter 1 explains the method of successive abstractions in its overall form, beginning with an outline of the basic maneuvers common to scientific categorization of material. It then addresses Marx's conceptual doublets and explains how they can be lumped and split during analysis. Afterwards, I explain Marx's method of re-abstraction. Combined, these discussions reveal how Marx creates categories, constructs variables, uses controlled comparisons, employs taxonomic analysis, and increases the intensity of his investigative lens.

Chapter 2 shows how Marx uses this method in his analysis of modes of production. My primary focus here is on *Capital* (specifically Volumes One and Three), with some additional appeal to *Theories of Surplus-Value*.

Chapter 3 proposes an investigative schedule for using this method to study the practice of slavery as well as the history of capitalist development during and after Marx's time.

Chapter 4 applies the method to a more conventional model for the study of religion.

Chapter 5 takes the study of religion in a decidedly more Marxian direction, where a historical materialist approach conjoins with the methods of inquiry and analysis found in preceding chapters.

Chapter 6 offers a critical look at religion in the context of Marx's methods and theories, some personal observations, and our contemporary historical moment.

Chapter 7 concludes with reflections on the Marxian project, what this might tell us about the subject matter of the book, and the discipline of sociology as a whole.

Before concluding this Introduction, I should comment on my style of presentation. The reader will find multiple figures, lists, and tables throughout the book. Some are likely to find these more helpful than will others. Thinking, reading, and writing about the abstract, the concrete, the general, and the specific can lead one to scratching their head as they try to keep straight where they are in the narrative's flow, pausing to reorient themselves before moving forward. Because of this, I have often found that relying on memory, at least initially, can serve one poorly in mid-analysis as the nature of the abstractions change for new topics. Because Marx can confuse his readers when he changes his abstractions without explaining that, how, and why he has done so, I have concluded that visually depicting the acts of abstraction and their movement helps with expositional clarity and, hopefully, comprehension. While such a presentational style may not be for everyone, I do hope it provides the reader assistance in checking his or her own impression on where in the process of abstraction any particular discussion is. This also helps demonstrate Marx's step-by-step method of abstraction and re-abstraction.

Another presentational issue is my use of footnotes in documenting examples of Marx's procedures. Though I do not leave all such examples relegated to footnotes, there are several instances where I place the evidence of Marx's construction and comparison of concepts and data there. The reader, of course, will be the judge of the efficacy of my decisions in this strategy, too.

It is my goal in this book to reveal a piece of the Marxian methodological puzzle not yet placed on the board. I believe this piece has been hiding in plain sight and, once understood, it will become more apparent what Marx's mature political economy is doing with its concepts and data. However, for reasons I have outlined above, obstacles have blocked our view of this part of Marx's method and until we clear a path, that view will likely remain obscured. I hope this book is one step in that direction.

Material found in Chapters 1, 3, and 5 were previously published in condensed form in *Critical Sociology* (see Paolucci 2018a, 2018b).

Marx's Method of Successive Abstractions

1 Introduction[1]

Credit for introducing model building and the experimental design to sociology usually goes to Max Weber and Emile Durkheim, respectively. Karl Marx's close association with dialectics tends to overshadow his use of both techniques. When a reviewer claimed *Capital*'s analyses "move with rare freedom in empirical matter," Marx (1988: 528) called this "a paraphrase for the *method* of dealing with the material—that is, the *dialectical method*" (emphases in the original). Though he accepts science's requirement of "clearness and precision of ideas and language" (Marx [1867] 1992b: 95, note 2), Marx often alters his words' meanings, an apparent violation of these standards. As a dialectician, however, Marx regularly shifts his "vantage point" to set up "a perspective that colors everything that falls into it, establishing order, hierarchy, and priorities, distributing values, meanings, and degrees of relevance, and asserting a distinctive coherence between the parts," an approach reflected in "the flexible boundaries that characterize all his theories" (Ollman 2003: 100, 105). This analytical tactic, his changing language use, and an unorthodox presentational style tend to mask his sociological models and experimental designs. With his directives on these matters scattered across his publications, unfinished volumes, personal notes, and private letters, we must reconstruct them if we are to better recognize and use them.

2 Marx and the Experimental Model

In *Capital*'s Preface, Marx ([1867] 1992c: 19) tells us that the "force of abstraction" allows him to make "experiments under conditions that assure the occurrence of [a] phenomenon in its normality" and to study the commodity-form just as one would use "microscopes [in the study of] microscopic anatomy." As the experimental model requires turning empirical observations into concepts and variables, if we recognize the guidelines Marx gives us to do this—scattered about his writings as they are—then we can organize them into a coherent methodological narrative.

---

1 Parts of this chapter previously appeared in *Critical Sociology* (see Paolucci 2018b).

Because the real world or "the concrete...is the concentration of many determinations, hence unity of the diverse," it is "the point of departure for observation and conception." This involves "the working-up of observation and conception into concepts," where "abstract determinations lead towards a re-production of the concrete by way of thought...reproduces it as the concrete in the mind" (Marx 1973: 101). In the act of conceptualization, the analyst constructs "abstract categories" (Marx 1973: 105) based on "common characteristics" through a method that "fixes the common element," while "the elements which are not general and common [are] separated out...so that in their unity...their essential difference is not forgotten" (Marx 1973: 85). In using such "general abstractions...one thing appears common to many, to all [and] ceases to be thinkable in a particular form alone" (Marx 1973: 104). The analyst mobilizes general abstractions to organize initial observations categorically around similar traits—though "an explanation which does not provide the *differentia specifica* is *no* explanation," so overly broad frameworks risk leaving objects "uncomprehended" (Marx [1843] 1975a: 12; emphases in the original). For a more satisfactory degree of comprehension, one must systematically develop concepts that reach an appropriate level of specificity related to the subject matter under investigation.

After constructing general abstractions, human activities occurring "within and through a specific form of society" (Marx 1973: 87) must be "sifted out by comparison" in order to construct "categories [that] express...the characteristics...of this specific society" (Marx 1973: 85, 106). When the analyst "single[s] out common characteristics," they should avoid both "bringing things...organically related into an accidental relation" (Marx 1973: 87–88) and constructing a conceptual model that "succeeds seeing differences, [but] does not see unity" or "sees unity, [but] does not see differences" (Marx [1847] 1976b: 320). Should one fail in these tasks, they risk developing variables whose "identity is illusory" (Marx [1843] 1975a: 82).[2] Because it is only by going from more

---

2   "In what Marx calls the commonsense approach, also found in formal logic, things are either the same/identical or different, not both. On this model, comparisons generally stop after taking note of the way(s) any two entities are either identical or different, but for Marx this is only the first step. Unlike the political-economists, for example, who stop after describing the obvious differences between profit, rent, and interest, Marx goes on to bring out their identity as forms of surplus-value (that is, wealth created by workers that is not returned to them in the form of wages). As relations, they all have this quality, this aspect that touches on their origins, in common. The interest Marx takes in delineating the special features of production or of the working class, without neglecting all they have in common with other economic processes and other classes, are good examples of his approaching identity and difference from the side of identity. The relations that stand in for things in Marx's dialectical

general to more specific abstractions that the "definite relations between these different moments" can be examined adequately (Marx 1973: 99), a researcher accomplishes this via sorting out additional empirical observations relevant to the "general-historical relations" (Marx 1973: 97) associated with their initial abstractions and consequent conceptualizations.

Marx uses the procedures above to conceptualize variables and to model their interrelations. In order to uncover their real world effects, he isolates their causal forces through the experimental method of controlled comparison. In controlling and comparing variables, "[v]ery different combinations are clearly possible, according as one of the three factors is constant and two variable, or two constant and one variable, or lastly, all three simultaneously variable. And...when these factors simultaneously vary, the amount and direction of their respective variations may differ" (Marx [1867] 1992b: 487). Therefore, in order to isolate "phenomena where they occur in their most typical form and most free from disturbing influence" (Marx [1867] 1992c: 19), the introduction of variables must, first, "exclude all relations which have nothing to do with the particular object of the analysis" (Marx 1989: 545). Afterwards, "inquiry will confine itself to...the comparison of a fact, not with ideas, but with another fact," with the goal "to find the law of the phenomenon...[as well as] the law of their variation, of their development.... This law once discovered, [one] investigates in detail the effects in which it manifests itself in social life" (Marx [1873] 1992a: 27–28).[3]

So far, we have seen Marx tell us that to uncover sociological laws one must isolate variables relevant to historical-structural social relations and examine their interrelations. This requires beginning inquiry with observation, sorting out the identities and differences among those observations, systematically working them into concepts with clarity and precision, and increasing model specificity as necessary. To achieve these goals, one compares within and between objects and categories, identifies criteria that allow for "lumping and splitting" those objects and categories, and isolates variables that contain hypothesized causal forces for testing through continued use of the controlled comparative method.

---

conception of reality are sufficiently large and complex to possess qualities that—when compared to the qualities of other similarly constituted relations—appear to be identical and others that appear to be different. In investigating what these are and, especially, in paying extra attention to whichever half of this pairing is currently most neglected, Marx can arrive at detailed descriptions of specific phenomena without getting lost in one-sidedness" (Ollman 2003: 15).

3   Marx is quoting a review of *Capital* that he believes accurately reflects his methodology.

2.1   *Comparisons, Lumping, Splitting, and Further Comparisons*

In the acts of lumping and splitting, the analyst makes initial comparisons both *within* and *between* observations and categories (Figure 1.1). In observing a group of objects, one first compares them with each other to see if they cohere around one or more important characteristics. Depending on the research question and the characteristics of objects so observed, the analyst should separate out those that do not cohere in such a manner and either address them via a separate research schedule or exclude them from further investigation. Observed objects that do cohere around a characteristic (or characteristics) of import are lumped categorically together. This lumping may be only temporary, however, as additional splitting may occur, depending on research questions and needs. This practice is something we do both in everyday common sense knowledge—e.g., "food"—and in more precise moments of categorization—e.g., from "low-calorie" to "high-calorie" foods all the way up to the intricacies of nutritional science.

Once conceptualized, though abstract, it is necessary to compare a category *within* itself to inspect it for whether the attributes with which one is filling it require more clarity and precision. Though categories attempt to capture a class of objects based on specified criteria—e.g., uniformly round shapes—it is important that the category is internally logical—e.g., round white things in my neighbor's yard. Here, the former criterion makes more sense for the science of geometry, while the latter would not make sense unless the question is highly specific and likely nonscientific—e.g., Where did my Frisbee go?

In terms of precision, sometimes an initial category allows too many things into it to be useful for the task needed, thus calling for its re-conceptualization.

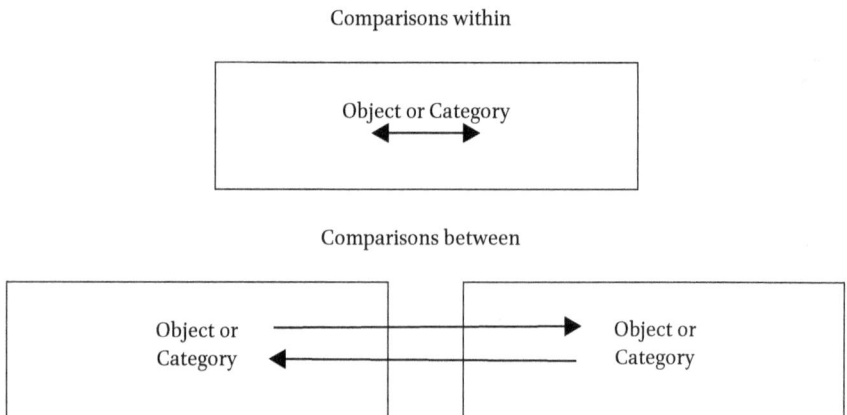

Comparisons within

Comparisons between

FIGURE 1.1   Comparisons within and between objects and categories
SOURCE: CREATED BY AUTHOR

For example, Marx (1973: 102) describes "the family or master-servant relations" as "far more concrete relations" than Hegel's fuzzier and more abstract juridical category of "possession." In this case, Marx's category allows for targeting a narrower set of objects that cohere together under a more precise criterion, while Hegel had carved his category so broadly that one could lump too many possibilities under it, especially those that lack the traits required for relevant comparisons.

After an initial observation, lumped objects may also possess other salient features that differ from one another, which calls for revisiting previous categories in case one needs to create new ones. For example, sometimes the analyst will need to separate a new category out from the original for its own analysis, while maintaining the original one. This is often because one (or more) initial observation(s) may not in fact belong in the original category (Figure 1.2). Someone studying the human practice of "leisure," for example, may at first focus on things like watching movies, listening to live musical performances, participating in amateur sports, and collecting stamps. However, upon reflection, they conclude that the latter two are more active behaviors and would best be, at least for their research purposes, lumped under "hobbies" and placed in a separate research schedule (whether or not they actively pursue that schedule is beside the point here). It is not that playing sports or collecting stamps share no characteristics with watching movies or listening to music, but rather the analyst's vantage point is on activities people engage in as audience members rather than as participants.

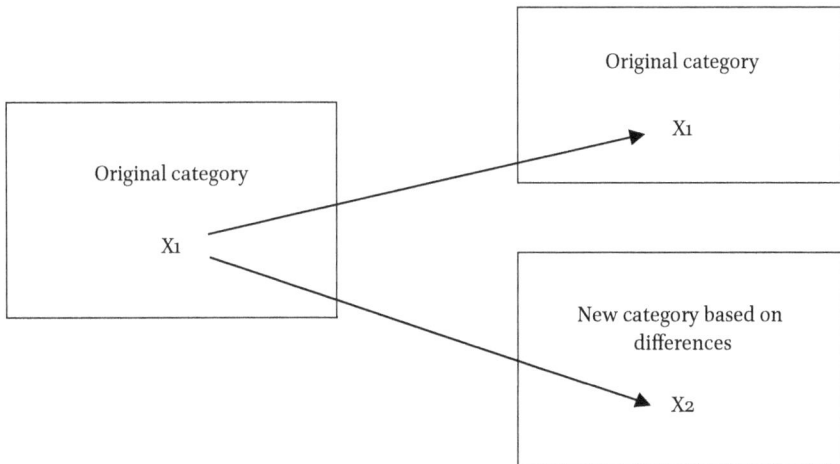

FIGURE 1.2 Separating out a new category because of core differences
SOURCE: CREATED BY AUTHOR

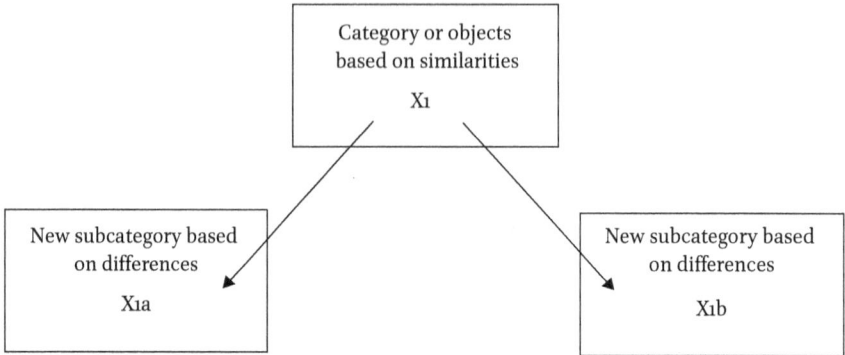

FIGURE 1.3   Splitting a category or set of objects into new subcategories
SOURCE: CREATED BY AUTHOR

Other times, observations lumped together under a category also contain characteristics important enough that they warrant their own subcategory (Figure 1.3). Splitting the once lumped into subcategories means that each new group of objects retains the characteristics previously established categorically among them, while the analyst uses their differing traits to designate new subcategorical groupings. The splitting of "food" into "low calorie" and "high calorie" subcategories above is an example of such a division. Clearly, sometimes subcategories will not have clean and clear distinctions between them. When does a type of food qualify for being "low" or "high" calorie, especially those at the margins of the operational definition? Other times traits used for splitting are more clear-cut, e.g., splitting "sports" into "team sports" versus "individual sports." In any case, the act of splitting allows one to create subcategories underneath an original category and this creates paths that lead from a broader category or observation to more specific subcategories and observations.

Lumping the similar and then splitting them on their differences allows for identifying and isolating variables across multiple levels of generality. In isolating such variables, we examine *within* objects to extract their shared as well as unique properties via the method of controlled comparison, an act that allows one to construct conceptual categories connected to empirical observations. Comparison *between objects* allows one to sort them as different subcategories ready for comparisons between them and objects identified with other categories or subcategories. When comparing *between categories*, one inspects conceptual boundaries carved around objects so that they are internally logical and clearly distinct from other categories. Categorical coherence combined with clearly lumped and split objects associated with them thus facilitates the isolation of relevant differences we can test for causal effects through further controlled comparisons (more on this issue as the discussion continues).

2.2   *General Rules for Taxonomy and Comparisons*

The taxonomic method is the traditional approach for the above concerns and several of its rules apply here. Establishing categories based on shared identities should use criteria that are *meaningful, essential*, and allow for *clear* and *coherent* boundaries. Differentiating trees by the number of leaves they have can create categories for all trees on the planet, but not only is the number of leaves neither a meaningful nor an essential trait, this criterion also would create millions of unusable categories lumped incoherently. Type of leaf blade, on the other hand, would be meaningful and essential as well as usefully coherent for clearly usable categories—e.g., chordate, elliptic, acicula. Both initial categories and the characteristics used for splitting them must meet these criteria.

Once an analyst has created an initial broad class of objects, if observations within more specific subcategories do not fit under the broader one, then they likely need to return to their method of categorizing them. This usually means one of several things. The analyst may have abstracted the broader abstract category poorly—i.e., lacking in meaningful and essential criterion that allow for categorical coherence. They may need to split their initial category into two or more broad categories instead of one. Or, perhaps, both their broader category and their more specific subcategory capture the same phenomenon— possibly because the analyst has split off the narrower subcategory unnecessarily and thus there is no need for both of them.

In using controlled comparison to test causal forces, one first makes observations (or measurements) of objects that are similar, where their similarities should account for similar empirical associations. Next, some variable is changed, where two objects sharing many (or most) characteristics are compared, though they now differ on a characteristic the analyst hypothesizes as having a specified causal influence. Then one makes an observation (or measurement) with and without the presence of that variable. Ideally, if one finds differences—given that the first observation captured relevant similarities— the presence or absence of the changed variable (as the case may be) should account for the differences in the measured results (Figure 1.4).

Let us look at a simple example. Broad categories tend to lump more objects together under criteria shared by many, e.g., all living things on our planet. Because of this broadness, one can split such categories into more detail based on other criteria, just as long as those criteria are non-arbitrary, meaningful, and allow for categorical coherence in relation to the investigative question(s).

General category
or observation

Categories

Observations and comparisons

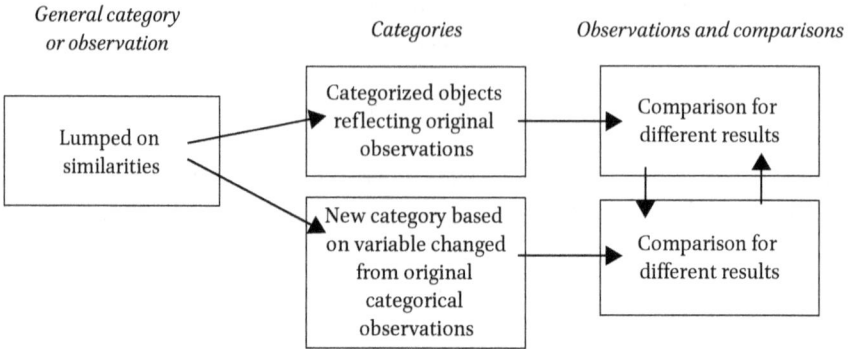

FIGURE 1.4 Controlled comparison
SOURCE: CREATED BY AUTHOR

For all living *green* things on our planet, the criterion of "living" is not arbitrary and is meaningful but when combined with "green things" the category may lose coherence for the biologist, as it allows too many things into it for meaningful comparisons—e.g., certain species of frogs, snakes, birds, grasshoppers, and plants (that said, this sort of lumping could be of interest to an artist or a photographer). While biologists in general might be interested in all living things on planet Earth, many plant biologists tend to focus on all living things on our planet capable of photosynthesis, which adds additional essential meaning and coherence to the categorization. For all living things on our planet capable of photosynthesis observed on Wednesdays by left-handed women, the latter two criteria are arbitrary and not meaningful, even if the category is coherent. By comparison, for all living things on our planet capable of photosynthesis, that produce flowers, and live in tropical saltwater, the latter two criteria are not arbitrary, are meaningful, and bring additional coherence. Continuing this process allows for isolating variables for data collection and testing for causal mechanisms. Do all living green objects capable of photosynthesis, that produce flowers, and live in tropical saltwater live longer [or sustain habitats for a higher number of other species, or have a wider array of reproductive mechanisms, etc.] than do species meeting all of these initial criteria but that live in tropical [or temperate or arctic] freshwater?

Anyone familiar with the scientific method in general will recognize this approach to systematically asking and answering questions. In natural science, researchers usually use a splitting maneuver through identifying one criterion at a time, where the subsequent categories that one splits off do not overlap on that criterion. Many sociological realities, however, we cannot reduce to one or just a few variables, as they hold together through a conglomeration of relationships—i.e., Marx's "the concentration of many determinations." Sociologists often find overlaps in social structures, in their historical development, and in their institutional functions (and so on). Social systems interpenetrate one another and change within themselves and between one and another, though they usually do not do these things with clear breaks and rarely do such changes announce themselves ahead of time. Moreover, contradictions and interactions within and between human social activities can all change the character of objects over time, with some characteristics or causal forces retained, others lost, and/or new ones acquired. While these conditions make drawing boundaries around sociological variables messy and difficult, if our conceptualization of relevant categories focuses on core and essential criteria, then a coherent categorization of complex observations within and between such object boundaries and these dynamic qualities remains possible.[4] Marx used the method of successive abstractions to do just this.

3   The Method of Successive Abstractions

We saw earlier that Marx identified the abstract, the concrete, the general, and the specific as important moments in observation, conceptualization, and analysis. His method of successive abstractions combines these categories into the general abstract, the specific abstract, the general concrete, and the specific concrete (see Paolucci 2007: 159–171; 2018b). The first lesson here is that these terms attain their meaning in relation to one another. They are not "frozen" concepts, defined for finality, isolated from other definitions, concepts, and terms. Dialectical reason rests on relational (not relative) truth and this means that as these categories of abstraction and their attendant objects change, so can the meanings or functions of the terms associated with them

---

4 Marx (1973: 102) explains that "simple categories are the expressions of relations within which the less developed concrete may have already realized itself before having posited the more many-sided connection or relation which is mentally expressed in the more concrete category; while the more developed concrete preserves the same category as a subordinate relation. Money may exist, and did exist historically, before capital existed, before banks existed, before wage-labour existed, etc. Thus in this respect it may be said that the simpler category can express the dominant relations of a less developed whole, or else those subordinate relations of a more developed whole which already had a historic existence before this whole developed in the direction expressed by a more concrete category. To that extent the path of abstract thought, rising from the simple to the combined, would correspond to the real historical process."

change in relation to one another. This general guideline should become more apparent as the discussion below unfolds.[5]

3.1   *The General Abstract, the Specific Abstract, the General Concrete, and the Specific Concrete*

What Marx (1973: 104) calls "general abstractions" are categories constructed based on identities derived from observation, "where one thing appears common to many" (Table 1.1, Cell A). A few rules follow from this. In comparison to the other three categories in an initial model set, the general abstract will be the broadest and most abstract category and all subsequent categories in a pathway will be subsets underneath it.[6] While Marx usually starts with abstractions large enough to encompass a wide range of material, he also breaks down his broader categories into narrower ones in order to focus more intently on objects of interest. As mentioned above, the identities used for this category construction must be essential and meaningful in a way that allows the lumped "many" to cohere with one another, which allows further subdivisions to maintain their own coherence.

Specific abstract categories (Table 1.1, Cell B) are distinct classes contained within the general abstract category. Three elementary rules operate here.

TABLE 1.1   Conceptual doublets in Marx's method of successive abstractions

	The general	**The specific**
The abstract	General abstract (A) ⟶	Specific abstract (B)
The concrete	General concrete (C) ⟶	Specific concrete (D)

SOURCE: CREATED BY AUTHOR

---

5   Recall that in the Introduction, I noted how Ollman (2003) stresses Marx's changing word usage and how this is a key to understanding his overall approach. Ollman provides several frameworks for this understanding, particularly his explanation of "internal relations" and Marx's abstractions of vantage point, extension, and historical generality. In what follows, I examine another, though associated, way of understanding Marx's approach to word use.
6   For the remainder of this chapter and book, a "model set" refers to a group of successive abstractions that attempts to categorize a general phenomenon and break it down into subcategories and observations (e.g., see Table 1.1). A "pathway" refers to the interconnected subcategories that extend from one model set to another, representing increasing internal specificity within that same analytical framework.

First, all categories constructed as the specific abstract should be valid subcategories of the general abstract—meaning they possess the characteristics of the general abstract and share those characteristics with each other. Second, the differences that separate specific abstract categories from each other are meaningful enough to warrant their categorical distinctions, e.g., "language" (general abstract) and "Romance languages," "Germanic languages," and "Slavic languages," among others (specific abstract). Third, though often times there is more than one specific abstract category, this is not always necessarily the case.[7]

The general concrete (Table 1.1, Cell C) refers to empirical domains representative of specific abstract categories, in whole or in part, across a range of real historical conditions, e.g., "language" (general abstract), "Romance languages" (specific abstract), and "Spanish speaking countries" (general concrete). When an initial general abstract category for a model set is very broad, general concrete categories, too, will remain somewhat broad and abstract. When abstracting through more narrow criteria, however, general concrete categories become increasingly empirically identifiable and measurable. For instance, in Chapter 2, we will see how Marx uses economic relations and processes as a general concrete category when abstracting broadly while later focusing more intently on modes of production with different general concrete empirical domains.

The specific concrete includes instances that are more particular, precise measurements or examples, and/or narrower features and observations found within general concrete categories (Table 1.1, Cell D), e.g., "language" (general abstract), "Romance languages" (specific abstract), "Spanish speaking countries" (general concrete), and Spain, Mexico, Peru, Colombia, and so on (specific concrete).

There are few times where Marx works his way through all four successive abstractions in short order. One example comes from the Introduction to the *Grundrisse*. There he brings up the idea of "historical production generally, but of the specific historic mode of production" (Marx 1973: 98). He then discusses how the Mongol "devastations in Russia" were related to "their production, cattle-raising" and how "the Germanic barbarians, who lived in isolation on the land and for whom agriculture with bondsmen was the traditional production, could impose these conditions on the Roman provinces all the more

---

7   For instance, Immanuel Wallerstein (1974) differentiates "world empires" from "world economies." As for the former, there have been many representatives—i.e., the Roman Empire, the Ottoman Empire, the Austro-Hungarian Empire, and so on—for the latter, he argues, we have historically observed only the "capitalist world economy."

easily as the concentration of landed property which had taken place there had already entirely overthrown the earlier agricultural relations." Here, Marx moves quickly from historical production generally (general abstract) to specific historic modes of production (specific abstract) to examples in the general concrete (cattle-raising, agriculture) to specific examples of those (Mongol devastations in Russia, the Germanic impositions on the Roman provinces, respectively). But Marx does not explain *that* and *how* he works through these successive layers of abstraction with any degree of explicitness. Given the purpose of the Introduction as self-reflection, however, it is understandable that he did not feel compelled to do so. On the other hand, this omission often means those who look to his writings for methodological instruction can often remain unaware how his discussion here reflects these crucial steps in his method.

There are several reasons why grasping how Marx sorts out empirical detail and analytical categories in this way is vital for understanding his method to the fullest extent possible. First, the abstract and the concrete and the general and the specific are central analytical units Marx works with to categorically arrange his observations—especially in his mature political economy—even before he gets to issues like value, class, markets, commodities, profits, capital, and so on. Second, with these thinking units linked relationally, we must grasp them both alone and in their interconnections. Third, using these successive abstractions adds complexity to concept construction while also allowing Marx to approximate both experiments and microscopes through manipulating them as variables (as we will see below and in the next chapter). Fourth, the way Marx manipulates these categories is not as straightforward as it at first might seem. If we do not understand how he does this, then we will have a harder time understanding how he mobilizes such frameworks for his political-economic research.

3.2   *Abstracting Successively, Controlled Comparison, Lumping/Splitting*

It will be helpful to visualize how each of Marx's successive abstractions are subject to comparison, lumping, and splitting. The researcher might split an original general abstract category (Figure 1.5, A1) into two (or more) new specific abstract subcategories (Figure 1.5, B1 and B2) that share characteristics with the original general abstract category and with each other. The new specific abstract subcategories will also contain important differences (initially reflected in Figure 1.3). Each specific abstract category (B1 and B2), if carved successfully, should also have identifiable corresponding general concrete conditions (Figure 1.6, C1a, C1b, and C2a, C2b) as well as more particular and measurable details in the specific concrete (Figure 1.7a–1.7b, D1ai,

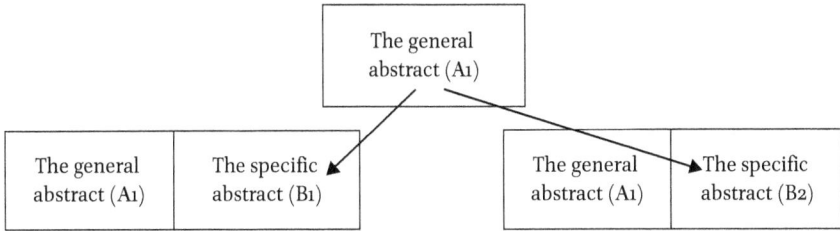

FIGURE 1.5 Abstracting the specific abstract out of the general abstract
SOURCE: CREATED BY AUTHOR

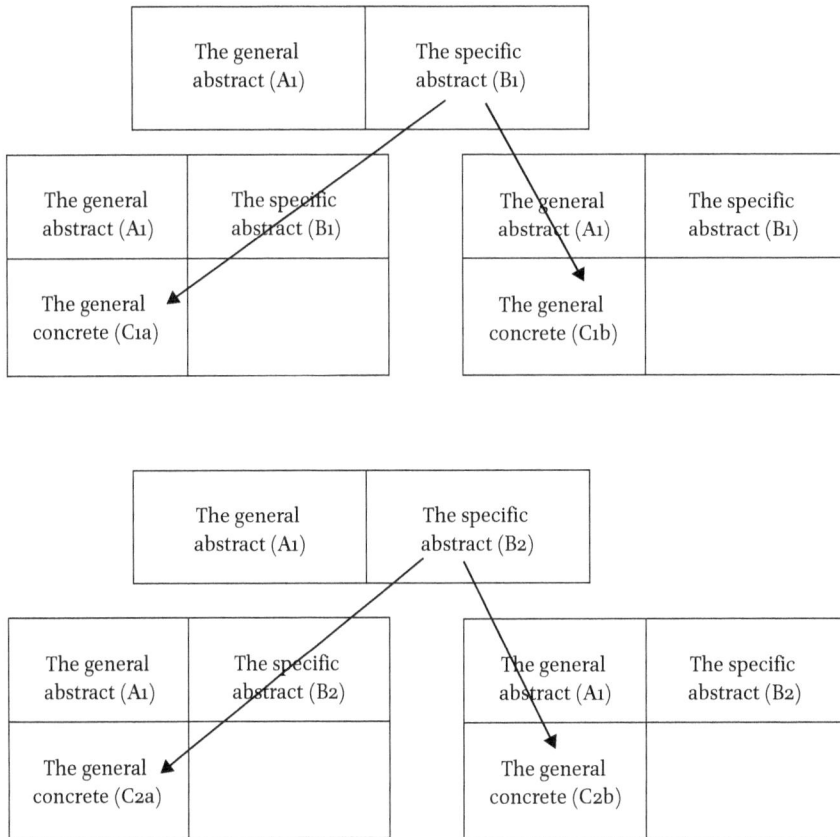

FIGURE 1.6 Identifying general concrete conditions that correspond with specific abstract
categories
SOURCE: CREATED BY AUTHOR

D1aii, D1aiii, D1bi, D1bii, D1biii, and Figure 1.8, D2ai, D2aii, D2aiii, D2bi, D2bii, D2biii).[8]

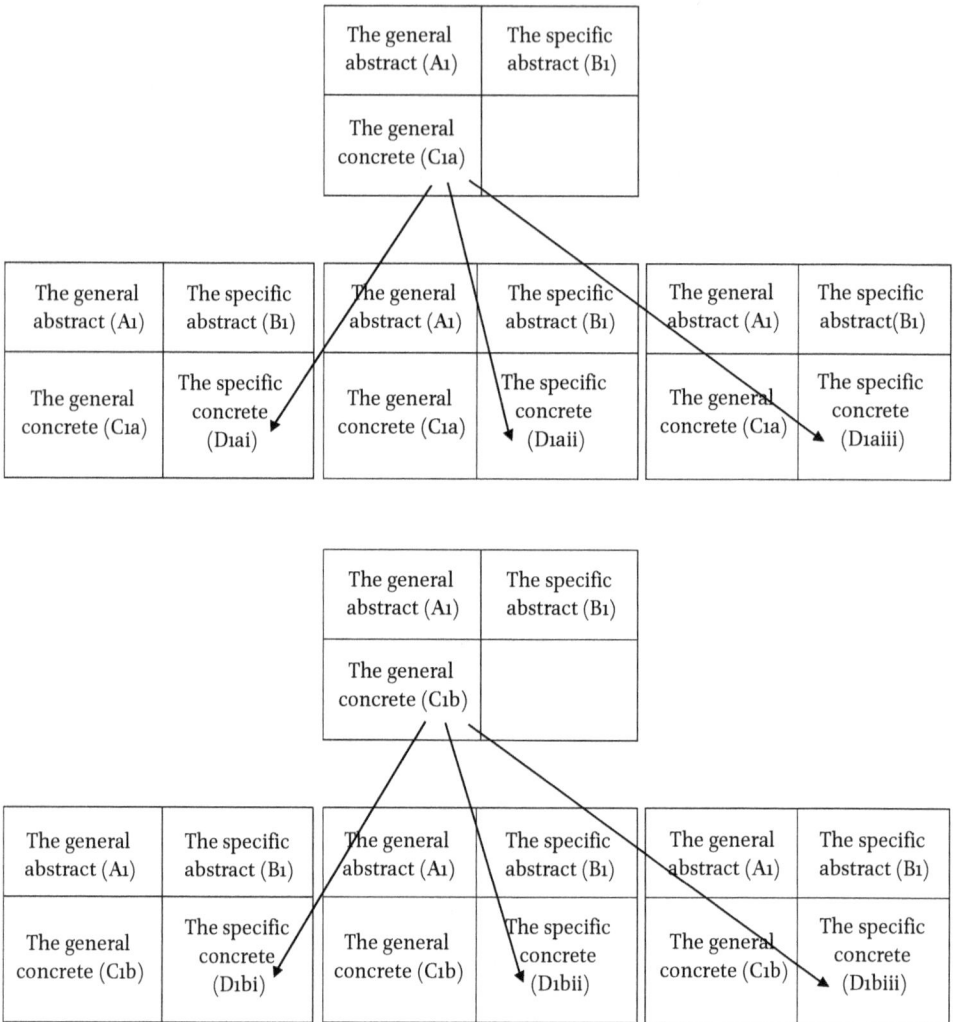

The general abstract (A1)	The specific abstract (B1)
The general concrete (C1a)	

The general abstract (A1)	The specific abstract (B1)	The general abstract (A1)	The specific abstract (B1)	The general abstract (A1)	The specific abstract(B1)
The general concrete (C1a)	The specific concrete (D1ai)	The general concrete (C1a)	The specific concrete (D1aii)	The general concrete (C1a)	The specific concrete (D1aiii)

The general abstract (A1)	The specific abstract (B1)
The general concrete (C1b)	

The general abstract (A1)	The specific abstract (B1)	The general abstract (A1)	The specific abstract (B1)	The general abstract (A1)	The specific abstract (B1)
The general concrete (C1b)	The specific concrete (D1bi)	The general concrete (C1b)	The specific concrete (D1bii)	The general concrete (C1b)	The specific concrete (D1biii)

FIGURE 1.7A   Identifying specific concrete examples within the general concrete (I)
SOURCE: CREATED BY AUTHOR

8   In the figures below, I break down the categories into separate pathways, though this will not always be the case in particular research schedules. For instance, Figures 1.7a and 1.7b show the specific concrete separated out into multiple figures, though very often in practice these are within the same analytical framework. I separate them here for visual purposes to better show how making distinctions across categories has the potential to become increasingly systematic, specific, and precise.

The general abstract (A1)	The specific abstract (B2)
The general concrete (C2a)	

The general abstract (A1)	The specific abstract (B1)	The general abstract (A1)	The specific abstract (B1)	The general abstract (A1)	The specific abstract(B1)
The general concrete (C2a)	The specific concrete (D2ai)	The general concrete (C2a)	The specific concrete (D2aii)	The general concrete (C2a)	The specific concrete (D2aiii)

The general abstract (A1)	The specific abstract (B2)
The general concrete (C2b)	

The general abstract (A1)	The specific abstract (B1)	The general abstract (A1)	The specific abstract (B1)	The general abstract (A1)	The specific abstract (B1)
The general concrete (C2b)	The specific concrete (D2bi)	The general concrete (C2b)	The specific concrete (D2bii)	The general concrete (C2b)	The specific concrete (D2biii)

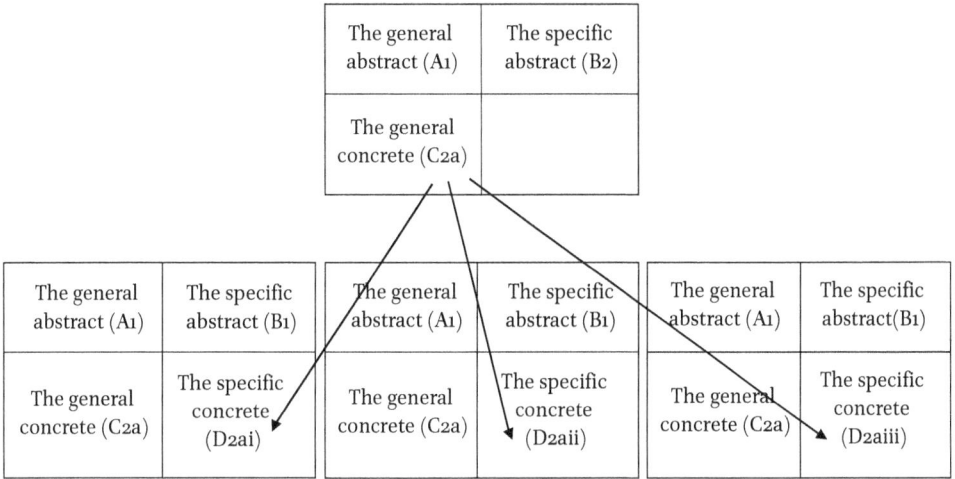

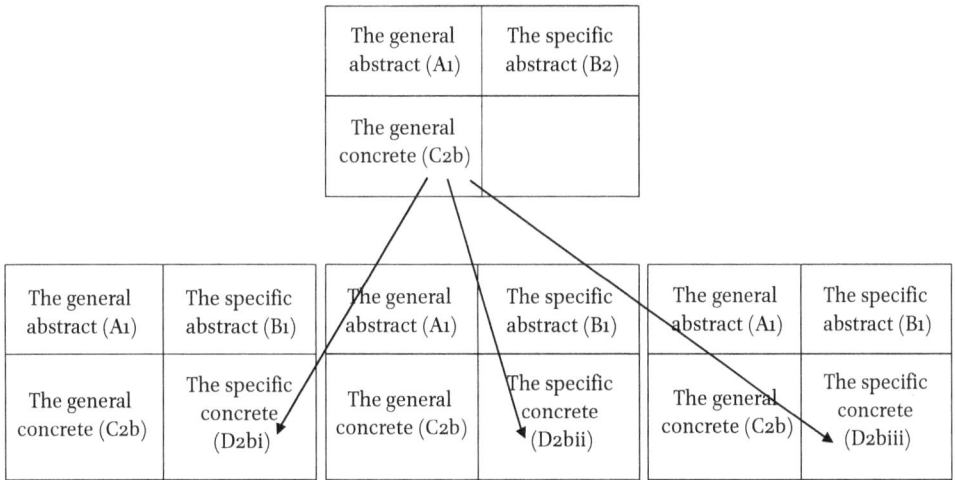

FIGURE 1.7B   Identifying specific concrete examples within the general concrete (II)
SOURCE: CREATED BY AUTHOR

Though this approach to sorting out distinctions between the abstract and the concrete versus the general and the specific should be familiar to any scientist (even if the terminology may not be), this is just the initial stage of the method. Marx's fields of inquiry include the relations between human history and its social structures. Given this, his abstractions recognize that social systems share some variables but not others, that object boundaries within and between systems often overlap and interact, and that processes exist that transform relationships *within* systems and *between* them as well, often across various levels of historical-structural generality. Seeing the world in such a way requires that Marx engage in *re-abstraction*, an act of analysis that accounts for the dialectical freedom he brings to empirical matter.

3.3   Re-abstracting in Marx's Method

We just saw that when a comparison finds salient differences, the analyst often will split objects lumped together previously into either new separate categories or distinct subcategories under the original. Now we come to additional reasons for splitting and new categorization. Because of the interrelationships they contain, social structures (a moment of stability), change both internally and from one system to another across history (moments of transformation), e.g., feudalism's birth of capitalism. In addition, separate systems may share certain features, even though one has not transformed into another, e.g., the role of peasant labor and/or usury in the Asiatic mode of production versus the feudal mode. This means that not only does the analyst need a method for abstracting concepts appropriate for such realities but also that objects previously conceptualized can take on new qualities, sometimes within their original structural contexts as well as, importantly, in new or different ones. Such situations often call for more finely-grained models, especially if the characteristics with which one filled their previous model(s) were abstracted too broadly for the case at hand. Marx's method, therefore, allows for *re-abstracting* previous observations and bringing in new empirical detail, for both comparative analysis and for new conceptualizations.

In this freedom of movement in empirical material, what was previously placed in the specific abstract category (Figure 1.8, Cell B) moves into the general abstract category (Cell A), while what was previously treated as the general abstract is now *assumed* and thus moved to the role of a constant in this pathway. Prior empirical referents and their categories also shift—the

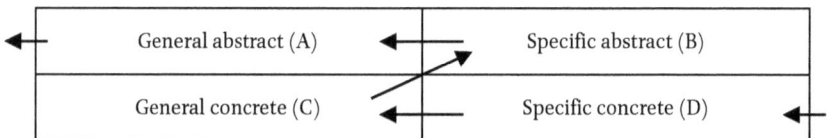

FIGURE 1.8   The act of re-abstracting
SOURCE: CREATED BY AUTHOR

previously general concrete (Cell C) is now treated as the specific abstract (Cell B), the previous specific concrete (Cell D) is now treated as the general concrete (Cell C), and new, more detailed observations move into the specific concrete category (Cell D). During this process, the analyst uses the same methods of comparison, categorization, and potential splitting of categories, which remain available for additional re-abstracting as needed. This method—empirical observation, abstracting, controlled comparison, re-abstracting, and additional empirical investigation—assists in addressing categorical issues, making discoveries—e.g., new functions, causal forces, sociological laws—and/or fixing prior errors in generalizations—i.e., positing equivalencies in data drawn from *multiple* systems but, erroneously, under the same concept or model.

Though each category in a model set is available for re-abstraction—related to one's investigative questions, to the material at hand, to the level of historical generality upon which it falls, and to the level of abstraction one uses to analyze it—some types of re-abstraction tend to predominate. Perhaps the most common type is re-abstracting a specific abstract category into the general abstract, which "pushes" the original general abstract category out of the model set and into the role of a constant. If one has established multiple specific abstract categories, the act of re-abstraction elevates *only one* of them into the general abstract at a time and abstracts the other specific abstract categories out of view—leaving them available for their own re-abstraction under the original model set, for external comparisons, or they can ignored, depending on research needs and questions. This act of re-abstraction also "pulls" the categories below the original specific abstract—i.e., the general and specific concrete—into the specific abstract and the general concrete, respectively, which then makes room for new specific concrete observations brought in behind.

In re-abstracting the specific concrete internal to a model set's pathway, it now takes on the role of the general concrete and pushes the original general concrete associated with it into the specific abstract, while pulling new specific concrete detail in behind. This act also pushes the categories in front of both. Here, the original specific abstract category connected to the specific concrete observation being re-abstracted moves into the general abstract category, pushing the original general abstract category out of the model set and into the role of a constant. And, as a model set has only one general abstract category at a time, this act also relegates all other prior specific abstract categories to external model sets, available for re-abstraction under the original general abstract category, relegated to an external model set for comparison, or ignored if not relevant to a research schedule.

Sometimes in re-abstracting the specific concrete, while at *least one specific concrete observation* is elevated to the general concrete, other original specific concrete elements will move *out* of the model set. This is usually (but not always) done when particular elements in the specific concrete call for closer examination while others do not (which often can be ignored in future analyses). Or this is done when certain specific concrete observations have characteristics that warrant separating them out into a different model set, where they remain useful for external comparisons (note, however, one does not *always* relegate features to external model sets in each act of re-abstraction, as this depends on investigative questions and needs).

Whether one begins re-abstracting by pushing a specific abstract category into the general abstract and thus pulling the other categories behind or by pushing a specific concrete category into the general concrete and thus pushing those in front of both, the model set changes in the same manner, as displayed in Figure 1.9 below.

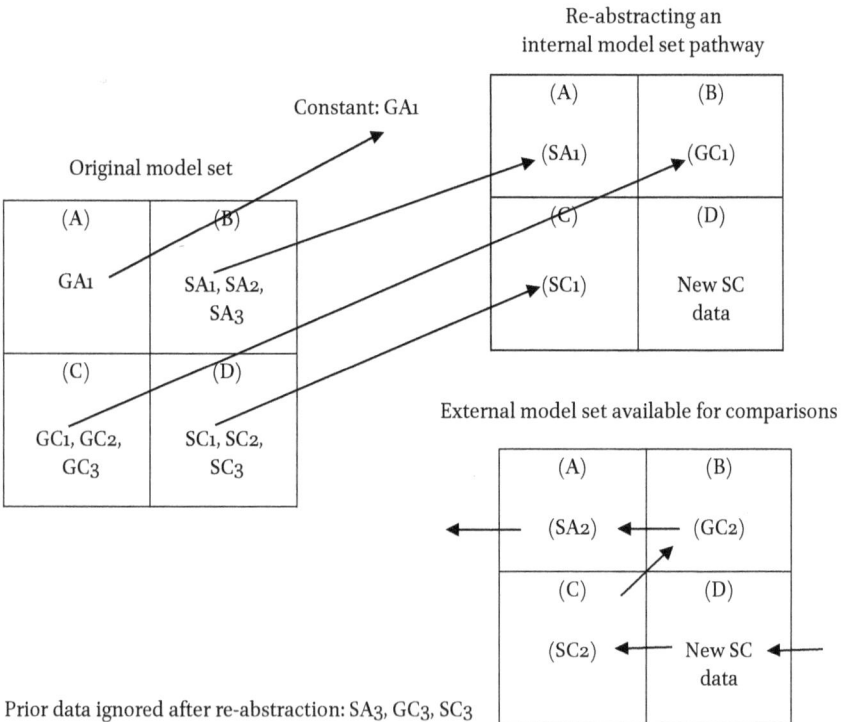

FIGURE 1.9   The push and pull of categories in the act of re-abstracting
SOURCE: CREATED BY AUTHOR

X1 as general concrete in internal model set

X1 and X2 as specific concrete

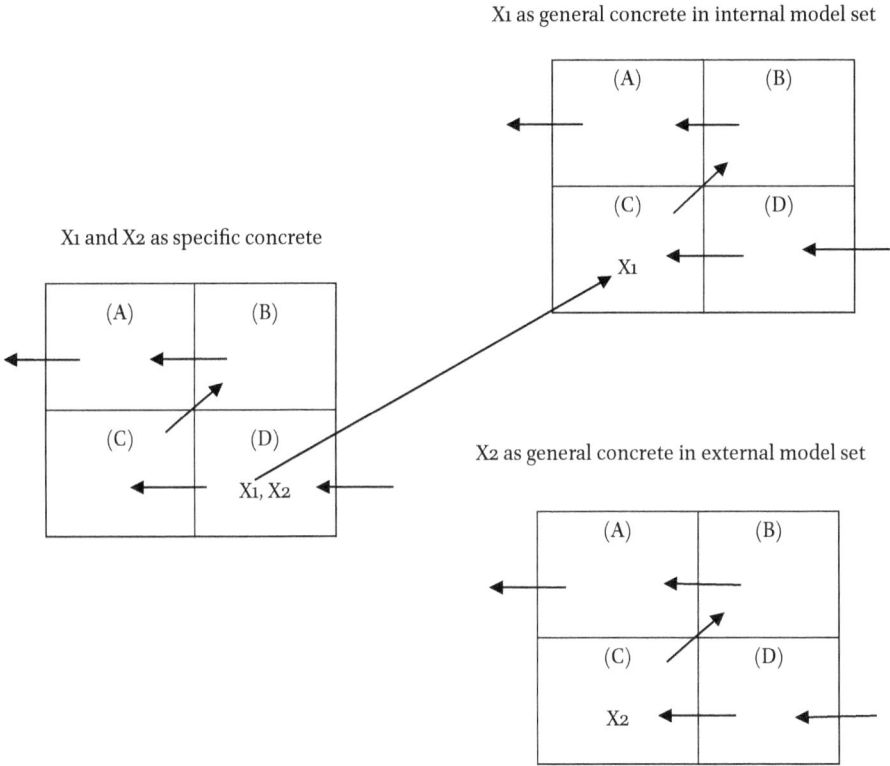

X2 as general concrete in external model set

FIGURE 1.10   Splitting and re-abstracting the specific concrete into general concrete
               categories
               SOURCE: CREATED BY AUTHOR

Figures 1.10–1.11 display a set of original specific concrete observations, X1 and X2, being re-abstracted, where the analyst re-abstracts X1 through the categories in internal model set along the same pathway. Here, the analyst has made an observation of X1 and X2 in the specific concrete (D). The first act of re-abstraction pushes X1 into the general concrete category (C) and abstracts X2 out and into its own external model set (Figure 1.10). For each of these categories, room has been made for new specific concrete empirical observations to be brought in behind. During this process, for X1's model set, the former general concrete category (C) moves into the specific abstract (B) and is isolated for special treatment, while one former specific abstract category (B) is moved into the general abstract (A), and the former general abstract category now is assumed (or held constant). After this initial re-abstraction, X1 can be re-abstracted a successive number of times, moving through the categories of

X1 as general concrete   X1 as specific abstract

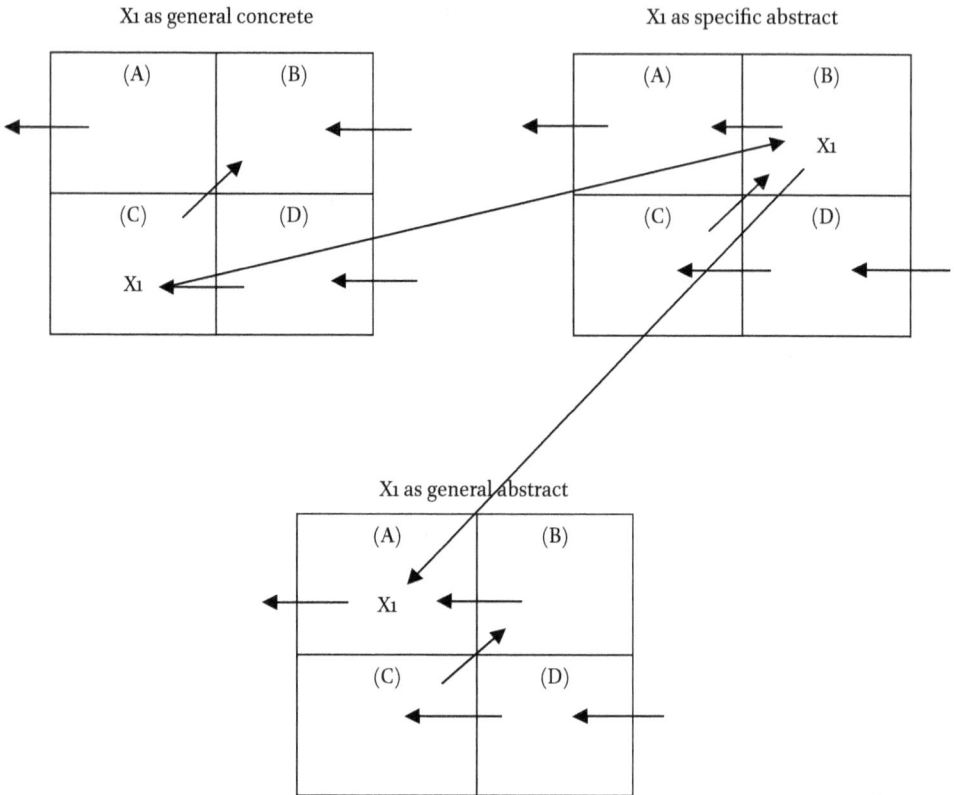

FIGURE 1.11   Re-abstracting the general concrete into the specific abstract and then into the
general abstract
SOURCE: CREATED BY AUTHOR

a model set, becoming more general and abstract as it is progressively treated
as a broader categorical variable while consistently pulling new concrete details into the model's pathway from behind (Figure 1.11). At each stage, the rules
for comparisons remain.

This method is not a rigid formula where either re-abstracting the specific
abstract into the general abstract or moving the specific concrete into the general concrete are the only two possible starting-points. The researcher can re-
abstract in multiple ways. One such way is treating the general concrete as a
general abstract category. In this act, re-abstraction pushes both the previous
general abstract and specific abstract out of the table, with the former and at
most one category of the latter now held constant along this pathway, moving
the other previously specific abstract categories out of the model set and now
ignored or placed into model sets of their own. This also then pulls material
from behind in the main model set in one of two ways.

One version of this involves treating all previous specific concrete observations as specific abstract categories in an internal model set while allowing for new general concrete categories and specific concrete observations (Figure 1.12a). A second version proceeds similarly except now it separates the former specific concrete and pushes only one into the specific abstract category internal to the pathway of interest, while others the analyst may move into distinct external model sets in the specific abstract (Figure 1.12b). Either this or the analyst ignores these original specific concrete observations during further inquiries. Again, the rules for what is/are available for comparison(s) remain at each stage of re-abstraction along this pathway as well as additional ones that might emerge.

3.4   *Marx's Method of Successive Abstractions as a Microscope*

Given that previous specific abstract categories replace initial broad general abstractions (which become assumed in re-abstraction), all new general abstract and specific abstract categories can be re-abstracted again too, similarly pulling their subcategories through the process while incorporating new empirical material. By extension, any additional empirical domains brought into analysis can also move through the re-abstraction process, becoming more categorical and abstract as the act of re-abstraction continues. Across multiple acts of re-abstraction, each category that was the broadest in the prior moment of abstraction—i.e., the general abstract—now becomes a constant, while simultaneously other former categories can be split into variables and

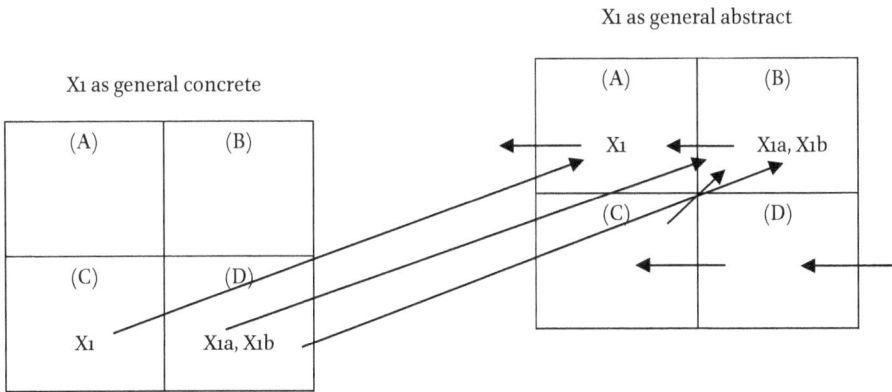

FIGURE 1.12A   Re-abstracting the general concrete into the general abstract with the specific concrete shifting to the specific abstract in an internal model set
SOURCE: CREATED BY AUTHOR

X2 as general abstract
X2a as specific abstract
in an internal model set

X1 as general concrete

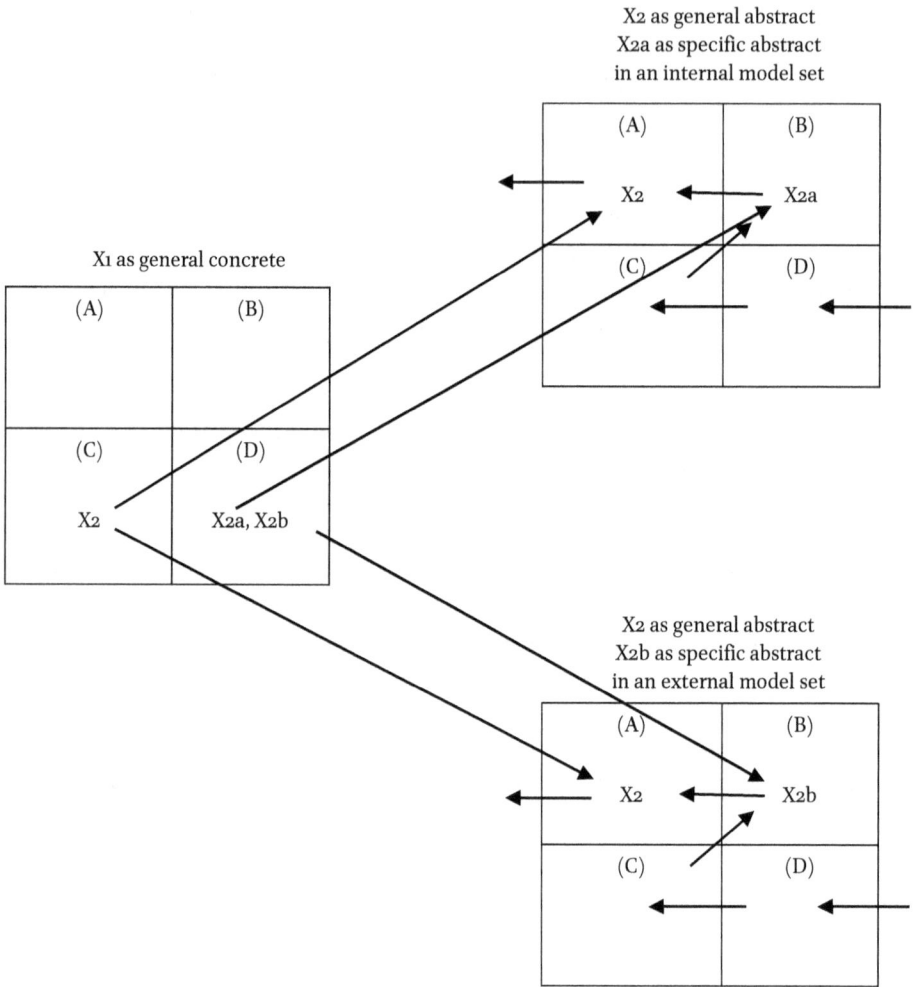

FIGURE 1.12B   Re-abstracting the general concrete into the general abstract with the
specific concrete shifting to separate specific abstract categories in an
external model set
SOURCE: CREATED BY AUTHOR

used for controlled comparison when and as needed. As new observations and
their attendant categories make their way through the re-abstraction process
to become general categories, this procedure increases the focus of the lens on
ever more specific detail while changing investigative slides and controlling
variables along the way. In this way, Marx can increasingly intensify his focus
with more finely-grained observations, embark on new categorizations, and
engage in further observations.

Below I present the method from a more holistic point of view. In this model, I focus only on a few pathways, as displaying every pathway possible results in a level of visual complexity that makes for messy presentation. This depiction follows four phases of abstraction and re-abstraction, where each subsequent phase is contained in the model set that came before it, while contrasting with others in the same phase because of differing characteristics that allow for splitting categories into subcategories at more specific levels of observation. Note, however, I am only presenting four phases because of space limitations. One could continue the process of re-abstraction into ever more finely-grained observations as needed, where the bottom right table is used as a starting-point for additional inquiry and could be broken down even further. This visualization helps reveal why Marx said that he used the force of abstraction to increase his investigative lens in a way comparable to how natural scientists use microscopes.[9]

The table on the far left of Figure 1.13 represents the results of the first act of abstraction (Phase I), where the analyst has established a general abstract category (X_1ga), along with one specific abstract subcategory (X_1sa), located relevant general concrete representations across time and space (X_1gc_1, X_1gc_2, X_1gc_3), and identified specific concrete examples corresponding to each (x_1, x_2, x_3).

The middle three tables (top to bottom) reflect Phase II, where the original general abstract category (X_1ga) is now assumed and all subsequent categories and examples in all remaining tables fall under it. The analyst now treats the previous specific abstract category (X_1sa) as the general abstract category, uses the previous specific concrete categories (x_1, x_2, x_3) as general concrete observations, while bringing in new specific concrete empirical examples (a, b, c) into view for the first time (had there been an X_2sa and X_3sa, there would be similar pathways for each).

Phase III appears in the three tables (top to bottom) on the right of the page. In order to simplify things, the arrows for each of these tables and their pathways represent different moments of re-abstraction, though all three

---

9 Here is the extended quote: "The value-form, whose fully developed shape is the money-form, is very elementary and simple. Nevertheless, the human mind has for more than 2,000 years sought in vain to get to the bottom of it, whilst on the other hand, to the successful analysis of much more composite and complex forms, there has been at least an approximation. Why? Because the body, as an organic whole, is more easy of study than are the cells of that body. In the analysis of economic forms, moreover, neither microscopes or chemical reagents are of use. The force of abstraction must replace both. But in bourgeois society the commodity-form is the economic cell-form. To the superficial observer, the analysis of these forms seems to turn upon minutiae. It does in fact deal with minutiae, but they are of the same order as those dealt with in microscopic anatomy" (Marx [1867] 1992c: 19).

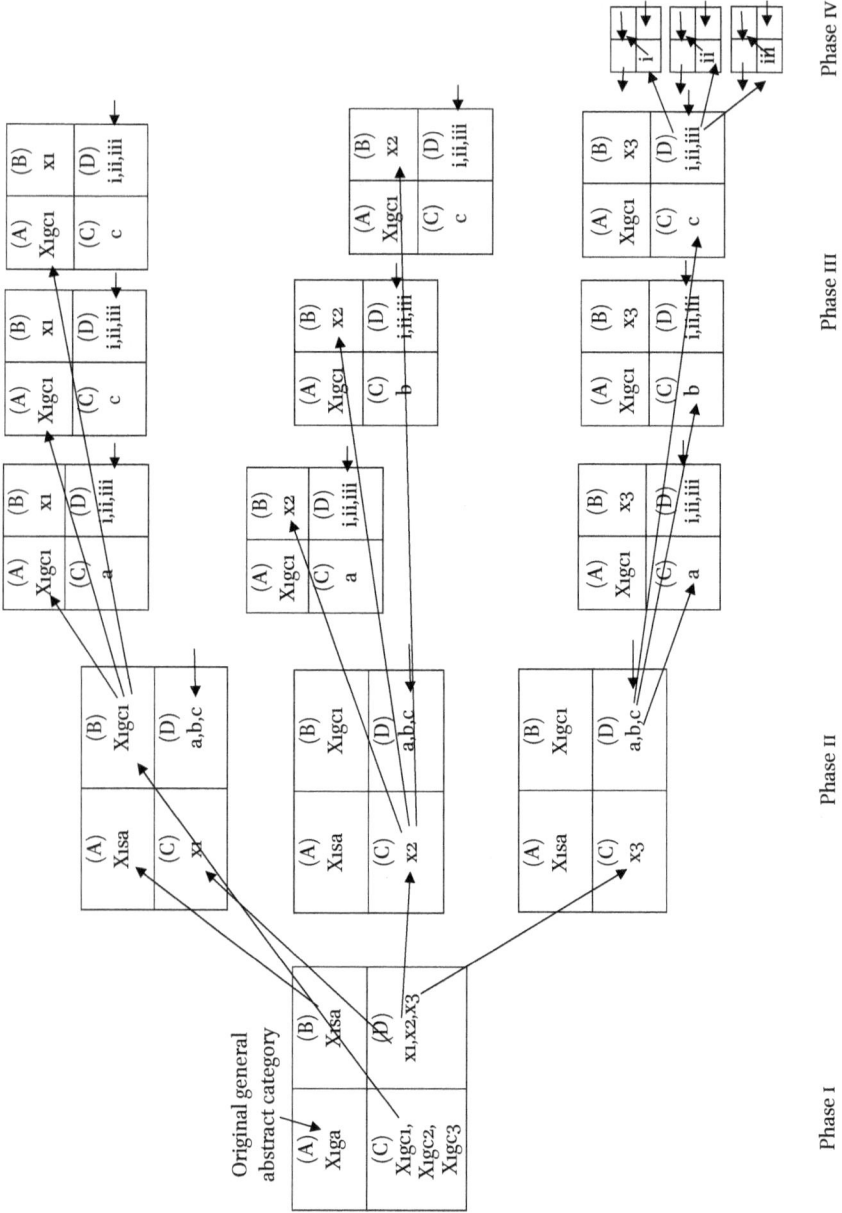

FIGURE 1.13   A model of Marx's successive abstractions along multiple pathways
SOURCE: CREATED BY AUTHOR

tables have gone through the same re-abstracting processes. In the top three on the right, we see how the analyst now treats the specific abstract category from the middle tables (X_1gc_1 and what was originally the general concrete on the far left table) as a general abstract category. In the middle three tables, the analyst treats what was previously the general concrete (x_2 and was the specific concrete in the original table on the far left) as a specific abstract category. For the bottom three tables, we see that previous specific concrete observations (a, b, c and objects not found in the original table at all) are now the general concrete category, making way for new observations (i, ii, iii). Finally, at the far right and very bottom, we see in Phase IV that the analyst can move these new specific concrete observations (i, ii, iii) into the general concrete and make way for new empirical detail (which they can eventually re-abstract all the way up to the general abstract).

As noted in my Introduction, Marx does not explain this practice to us, though he does say that these are mental acts done during inquiry and analysis. Marx also does not present his results in a way that reflects these acts in a linear manner, which is another reason why it is hard to extract this model from his work. At present, it suffices to note that these procedures are not done willy-nilly but rather require intense thought, detailed research, and a careful piecing together of empirical matter. In addition, though Marx did not, there is nothing to prevent other researchers from presenting their work in terms of model sets and pathways as depicted here. That said, this visual presentation allows us to see better how Marx's abstractive practice functions as both microscopic lens as well as a method of controlled comparison, a topic that we return to next.

4   Using Comparisons in the Method of Successive Abstractions

A researcher can make multiple comparisons when using the method of successive abstractions—within one model set, along one of its pathways, along the pathway of interconnected model sets underneath the same initial general abstract category, and between one or more model sets in one pathway compared to other external model sets and their pathways. As this is a complex set of possible comparisons, here I focus on guidelines for the most common ones.

4.1   *Comparisons across Successive Abstractions*
Each category in a set of successive abstractions is subject to comparisons, being lumped and/or split for re-conceptualization, and additional comparisons, both internal and external. The first step is recognizing how to compare categories and observations *within* themselves and *between* each other within a model set (Figure 1.14).

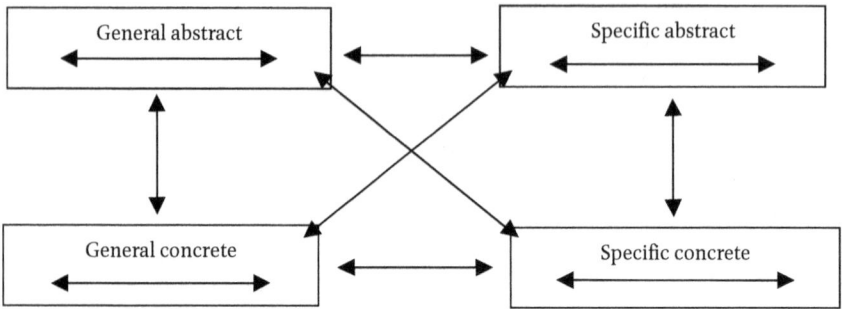

FIGURE 1.14   Points of comparison within a model set
SOURCE: CREATED BY AUTHOR

A few points of clarification before proceeding. First, several of the comparisons below share their overall goals with others, while some have goals particular to them. Second, though we have seen that conceptualization starts with observation of the concrete, my presentation of the acts of comparison below begins with the general abstract. Third, all of the examples in this section reflect comparisons made *within* the same model set. Discussion of comparisons *between* model sets follows in the next section.

4.1.1   General Abstract to General Abstract
Comparing "within" a general abstract category is really comparing a concept to itself. While this might sound tautological, it does not have to be. In this sort of comparison, one is examining a general abstract category for its internal relevance, coherence, logic, and consistency, i.e., does it make sense to abstract out of reality in this way? A few rather extreme examples put the principle in relief. To start one's abstractions with "all physical objects with polysyllabic English-language names" is not only overly broad, but unless the investigative question is quite specific and narrow, it would be hard to see the relevance of such an abstraction, even if it has elements of logic and coherence. Worse yet would be something like "live frogs that talk," which could be coherent and relevant strictly speaking (i.e., imagine the discovery of talking frogs!) but illogical. Perhaps worst of all would be something like "seven-and-a-half dimensional purple sounds," which fails in terms of relevance, coherence, logic, and consistency and, as such, does not even make sense.

Abstraction and analysis require the qualities of internal relevance, coherence, logic, and consistency so that we can break down general abstract categories into subcategories that meet these same requirements. This is necessary so that the variables we construct have clear and commensurate dimensions and precise features, which we need for both controlled comparison and for increasing our focus. In contrast to those in the paragraph above, categories like "sport" or "language" are all relevant (they direct attention to something important about the world), coherent (they collect a group of objects around identifiable and measurable criterion), logical (they do not distort the features of the world we experience unnecessarily), and allow for consistency. This latter requirement relates to subdividing an initial category into new distinct subcategories with reliability and validity, subcategories that also would need to meet the requirements of internal relevance, coherence, logic, and consistency.

4.1.2   General Abstract to Specific Abstract

In comparing a general abstract category with specific abstract ones within a model set, all specific abstract subcategories should meet the criteria of the general abstract, while being at a lower level of generality and providing more specification, e.g., there is "non-animal based food" (general abstract) and there are "fruits," "vegetables," "legumes," "fungi," and so on (specific abstract).

This moment of comparison may double back on the original internal comparison within the general abstract. For instance, it is possible that one initially included too many things in their mental conception of a general abstract category and this may require abstracting out certain things for separate analysis under a different category. Marx tells us, for example, that one can examine "societies" (a general abstract category) from the perspective of their "economic structure" (a specific abstract feature of all of them). When he re-abstracts "economic structure" as a general abstract category, he concludes that he needs to abstract "production" (*Capital, Volume I*) and the "process of circulation" (*Capital, Volume II*) separately for their own analysis (Figure 1.15). This provides each of these moments in an economic structure their specific relevance, internal coherence, logic, and consistency. Consequently, once he has made distinct categories for production and circulation, when Marx places "modes of production" into the general abstract for modeling, this now allows him to subdivide it further into specific abstract categories, first into non-class and class systems and then into sub-forms of each—i.e., primitive communism, ancient society, Asiatic modes, feudalism, and capitalism (Figure 1.16). These more specific categories are all subsumed under "production in general," while each is distinct from the others by the configuration of variables found within them (more on this in Chapter 2). If Marx had left circulation subsumed into his model here, his conceptual framework would lose its coherence and threaten to bog down his analysis with details better placed in a different model set.

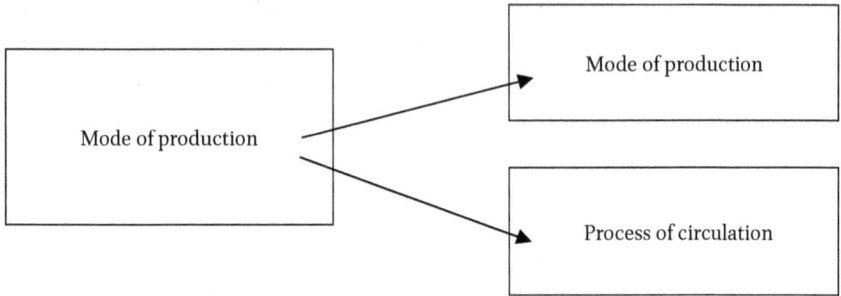

FIGURE 1.15   Distinguishing the mode of production from the process of circulation
SOURCE: CREATED BY AUTHOR

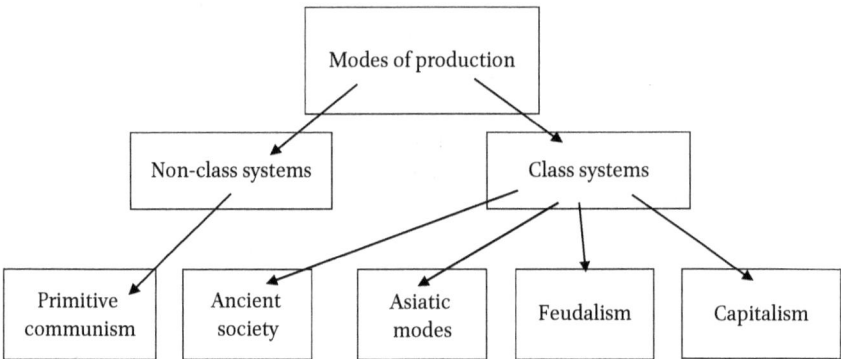

FIGURE 1.16   Splitting the mode of production into subcategories
SOURCE: CREATED BY AUTHOR

4.1.3   General Abstract to General Concrete

Here, the analyst follows a similar path as in the comparison of the general abstract with the specific abstract. In this case, general concrete categories should empirically correspond to a general abstract category but also provide direction for more specific observations and measurable realities grounded in material-historical relations.

4.1.4   General Abstract to Specific Concrete

Comparing the general abstract to the specific concrete follows the same rule above, where a particular empirical field should fit underneath its general concrete, specific abstract, and general abstract categories. However, when research starts with a general abstract category, the analyst usually abstracts that category broadly at first. If one compares a broad general abstract category to the specific concrete, it will be important to attend to how "far" these moments of abstraction are from one another. The broader the initial general abstract category, the less likely it is to contain important information about highly specific things. Though the general abstract is not void in these regards, sometimes several levels of re-abstraction are necessary to more completely model and reveal relevant and needed information about the very specific.

For example, if we start with the broad category "sexual reproduction" (which includes plants and animals), this only tells us so much about why two specific people—with names, ages, gender identities, biographies, and so on—at a particular time and place engage in intercourse. Missing in between the initial category and the particular case are plant versus animal, nonhuman animal versus human, humans in general, humans in cultural contexts (rules about sex, marriage, courtship, etc.), and particular interceding details of the instance (romantic interlude, wedding night, recreation, prostitution, pornography, trying to conceive a child, and so on). Since there are often multiple levels of reality, when one mobilizes an explanatory model abstracted from a very broad category and applies it to a very specific case, they have probably overreached in applying their abstraction. Nevertheless, as abstraction and re-abstraction move steadily towards categories contained in models carved from more specific levels of generality in the same pathway, general abstract categories increasingly close the space between that pathway's initially broad categories and the specific empirical details gained through observation.

4.1.5   Specific Abstract to Specific Abstract

Beginning here starts with the assumption that the general abstract has already been compared with itself and to the specific abstract. Next, one would compare the specific abstract within itself as well. There are two general rules here. First, like the requirements for the general abstract, specific abstract categories should reflect identifiable, essential, and meaningful criteria that meet the requirements of internal relevance, coherence, logic, and consistency.

Second, as subcategories of the general abstract, specific abstract categories should not *significantly* overlap, even though they sometimes share certain characteristics—especially the more narrowly focused research becomes. This is because the analyst needs to construct specific abstract categories in a way that allows for their re-categorization if necessary.[10] For example, returning to

---

10   We will see this principle demonstrated in Marx's taxonomy of modes of production in Chapter 2.

the example of using team sports as general abstract category, an analyst initially may have used baseball, softball, basketball, soccer, football, and team track and field as specific abstract categories. However, if their research is focused on how coaches organize multiple players simultaneously in order to "score" with a "ball" used in a competition, the differences found in team track and field would exclude it from subsequent abstractions within that model set. In considering the matter further, the analyst may also conclude that there is no need to include both softball and baseball as separate abstract categories in the same model set, as their overlap may be as such where the analyst should subsume them into the same category or eliminate one of them.

4.1.6   Specific Abstract to General Concrete

Investigation should be able to match each specific abstract category with a general concrete domain, where one has chosen that domain based on criteria delineated in the specific abstract (as extended from the general abstract). In the case above, the analyst might observe that, in comparison to that played in the United States, Canadian football plays on field of a different size, has several different rules on scoring, and a uses a different number of players. Not wanting to combine it with football in the United States and not needing two data sources on this matter, the analyst decides to exclude Canadian football from their model set (though it could still serve as an external model set for contrasts that might be informative). In addition, depending on the research question and the number of re-abstractions one has gone through, the range of one's general concrete categories may not need to be exhaustive. If football in the United States is the focus, one need not investigate every football team and/or league at every level but could choose among high school, college, or professional football.

4.1.7   Specific Abstract to Specific Concrete

Similar to the comparison just made, each specific concrete example—more specified than the general concrete but still found within it—at the end of model set's pathway should contain clearly articulated elements that correspond to its specific abstract category. In continuing with the example of football, if the analyst has decided in a prior act of abstraction only to include professional teams, then their analysis would exclude American college and high school football teams as domains for data collection. Then, more narrowly, research could focus on the particular number of professional teams relevant to their research question, which could be the entire National Football League or just a sample of a few teams from it—again depending on research questions and needs.

4.1.8 General Concrete to General Concrete

In comparing *within* a general concrete category—and similar to comparing within the general abstract and within the specific abstract—analysis is looking for coherence, logic, relevance, and consistency as well as making sure that each general concrete category corresponds to a specific abstract category in the initial model set. In comparing *between* general concrete categories, each should be distinguishable enough from the others so that identifiable empirical domains can be isolated and one can hold their overlaps in time and space to a minimum. If this is not possible, the analyst should consider collapsing these overlapping categories into one.

4.1.9 General Concrete to Specific Concrete

When one compares the general concrete with the specific concrete, all specific concrete observations should be representative instances within the realm carved by at least one general concrete category. Once one is through the process of re-abstraction several times in a singular pathway and then makes comparisons of the specific concrete representing general concrete categories, the empirical details should show increasingly similar traits, characteristics, and so on—even though they may come from different empirical realms in time/space—as the isolated causal variables are relatively the same. If, after multiple re-abstractions in the same pathway, specific concrete observations are significantly different from one another, this suggests configured variables do not have the causal effects assumed or the presence of some intervening variable. However, if one has carved general concrete categories from *different specific abstract* categories in the same model set that contain different meaningful and essential characteristics, then the comparison of the general concrete to the specific concrete should show different empirical results. If so, this suggests that causal mechanisms have been isolated, which are then subject to additional research for verification via new data collection, re-abstractions, and model set comparisons.

4.1.10 Specific Concrete to Specific Concrete

In comparing *within* a specific concrete category, the primary goal is to make sure they cohere together and to the overall criteria set by the previous three moments of abstraction (which also should cohere with one another). If they do not, then some portion of the specific concrete does not belong within the data set and the analyst likely needs to create new categories or exclude that material. When comparing between specific concrete observations, just as seen above (4.1.9), if they are representative of different general concrete categories identified with different specific abstract categories carved from the

Initial model set   *External model sets*

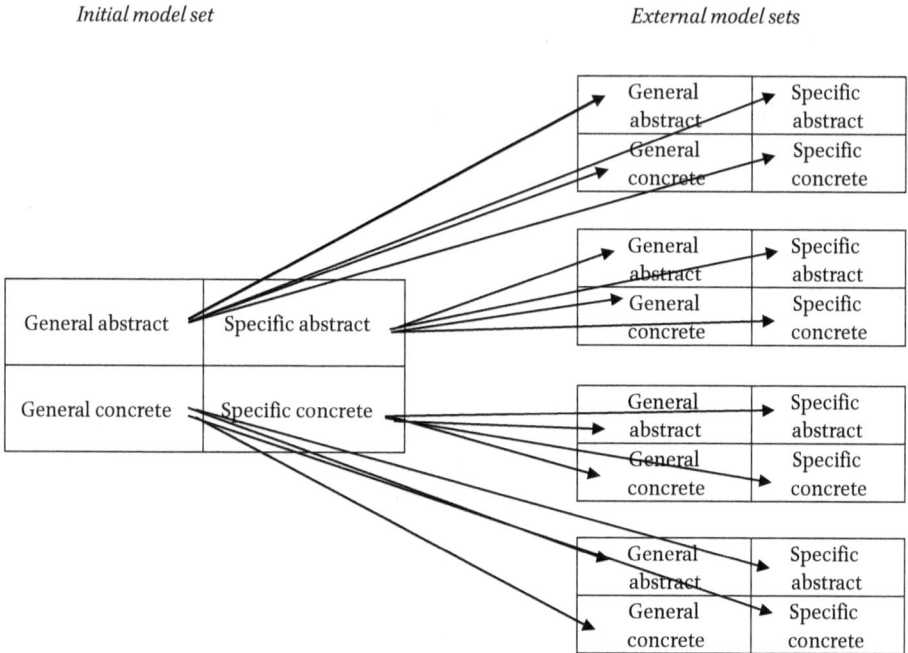

FIGURE 1.17   External comparisons between different model sets
SOURCE: CREATED BY AUTHOR

same general abstract category but have significant differences between them, then a causal mechanism is suggested somewhere along the pathway.

What we see above is that the process of abstraction and re-abstraction allows for developing taxonomic models, isolating causal variables, and testing hypotheses and associated model assumptions. These are not the only possible comparisons, however. One can compare objects and categories externally, to observations and categories made between different model sets (Figure 1.17).

In comparing across two model sets, one might compare *between* their general abstract categories. When initial abstractions are very broad—e.g., food, sport, language—and not yet subdivided, then comparisons between one general abstract category and another are usually external. Here, one should make sure that any comparison that goes forward remains cognizant of several qualifications.

First, comparison is on more solid footing when the categories share some characteristic that allows comparison in the first place. For example, in comparing fruits and vegetables, the analyst is on acceptable ground if they are interested in issues related to vegetarian food. It would not make sense to compare fruits and meat on the same measure, as the question of interest excludes the latter—unless meat is relevant to a research question that requires such a comparison, e.g., health, water/energy use in production, and so on.

Second, comparisons between general abstract categories are usually more fruitful if those categories possess relevant similarities while also contrasting enough so that one can isolate and identify distinct causal forces they might have.

Third, while comparisons between general abstract categories at the same level of generality are often the most useful type, comparison is not restricted to categories and objects from the same moment of abstraction at the same level of generality. If one were interested in "fruit" generally in terms of its average fibrous content, one normally should not then compare this category externally to a specific vegetable, say broccoli, as these are on two different levels of generality. When comparing a broader abstract category in one model set to a more specific concrete observation in another model set, generalizing should only proceed with caution and restraint. In this case, for example, if a doctor advised someone to maximize their fiber intake, he or she might focus on a specific high-fiber vegetable—i.e., broccoli—over the more general category of fruit.

Nevertheless, there are important exceptions to this rule. For example, in examining things from top to bottom of Figure 1.13, if we look at the middle column (Phase II), the central comparison is between the general concrete (x_1, x_2, x_3) and the specific concrete (a, b, c) across these categories. The differences found suggest the possibility of different structural and/or causal mechanisms, thus calling for separate and specific categorization. When either categories or empirical observations share essential salient characteristics that demonstrate causal forces, then one should examine other categories and observations to see if they find such causal forces there. This will often be the case, *but not always*, as this is both a matter of empirical research and the intricacies of modeling. A variable may have the same causal properties across systems, though it also may acquire new properties or lose older features in new structural contexts that include variables not present before.

Important implications for examining similarities also extend from this rule about comparing across different levels of generality. When correctly done, a more abstract category in one model set can provide insightful and revealing comparisons about more concrete observations in other model sets. For example, as we will see in more detail in Chapter 3, one could develop a model of slavery in general and compare its laboring conditions with the more historically specific and concrete laboring conditions of serfs in feudalism and/or wage-laborers in capitalism. Such a comparison allows one to identify how the labor conditions of a feudal serf and/or a wage-laborer share similarities with slavery's extreme forms of exploitation while, at the same time, recognizing relevant differences across all three laboring systems.

Though a complete breakdown of each category available for potential comparisons *between* model sets would be revealing, here I will end my discussion at some general remarks. Between model (or external) comparisons often can allow one to find common functions of different social phenomena. Both sport and art can be vehicles for entertainment or things pursued as hobbies, and so an analyst could fit each underneath a new corresponding model reflecting such characteristics. One also could find empirical examples influenced by other external variables not contained in either model set. For instance, modern society has commodified both sport and art and, as such, one could observe general and specific concrete cases of each that could be re-abstracted as specific abstract examples underneath "commodification" as the general abstract category. It is in such a manner that investigations can lead down multiple paths and uncover multiple interconnections.

4.2   *Additional Guidelines for Re-abstraction and Comparison*

Before concluding this chapter, addressing additional guidelines for the act of re-abstraction and using comparisons relevant to one's investigation as a whole may be helpful.

In the research process, one will go through observation, abstraction and categorization, and re-abstraction and analysis, all before presenting their findings.

Though initial specific abstract categories and general concrete examples should be as exhaustive as possible, this is not always necessary, as there can be many historical examples that demonstrate specific abstract categories. However, the general rule here is that the analyst should address exhaustiveness if it is relevant to a research schedule.

The general concrete need not be *wholly* subsumable under the specific abstract; a general concrete empirical field only needs to possess enough qualities that express what one is trying to capture with their specific abstract category. Other features of a general concrete category may be analyzed underneath a different specific abstract category, though usually one carved from a wholly different general abstract category—and, therefore, a different model set—and thus putting different relevant characteristics into relief.

If a previous act of abstraction created multiple general concrete categories that re-abstraction then pushed (or pulled) in the process, each will become its own specific abstract category with its own general concrete domains. If analysis proceeds by separating specific abstract categories for special treatment, each now becomes a new general abstract category with its own associated model set. One then compares their new general concrete categories, looking for similarities and differences via the specific concrete details associated with them. In both cases, should differences be found, the researcher should closely examine the characteristics that allowed for splitting these categories, as those characteristics often account for those differences. This is how controlled comparison takes place.

Earlier we saw that more general and abstract categories tell us less about more specific and concrete things the farther the distance between them. We also saw that using categories that fail to include meaningful and essential criteria for both our initial abstractions and subsequent re-abstractions leads to poorly conceptualized categories. When combined in the same framework, these two problems compound one another.

For example, if one uses "the economy" to explain the activity of a wage-worker sweeping floors at the local convenience store on Friday night at 11pm, they have omitted several relevant characteristics from their abstraction and stretched the distance between the general category and the specific observation. First, "the economy" is such a general term that it allows too many things into it, such as both production and circulation (which we saw earlier). So, second, the analyst should start with the more precise concept of "production in general," which suggests relationships that inherently entail active labor. While "production in general" has attributes that might tell us something about the activity of a worker in modern society, there are, nevertheless, still several interconnected layers that call for additional acts of re-abstraction:

- After production in general, there are class systems (of which modern capitalism is one), which entail both the appropriation of surplus-value via surplus-labor and a class structure into which an individual is born.
- In capitalism—as in all class systems—there is a need to manage "socially necessary labor-time"—the amount of work and value-production that satisfies the basic needs of laborers—so as to get surplus-value production out of laborers over and above that necessary level, from which business owners generate their profits.
- Capitalism in general is a system that produces "abstract labor," which creates a market on which individual people's labor-power is bought and sold. When there is a supply of laborers higher than the demand for them, a downward pressure on wages ensues, as the need for wages drives many people to accept whatever jobs are available.
- In today's world, capitalism has entered an era of neo-liberalism, which has produced competition among labor markets across global arenas, putting additional downward pressure on wages in some labor markets.

- Also in the neo-liberal era, states have reduced their regulation of said wages, especially in letting minimum wages lag behind inflation.
- Should our store clerk live in the United States, then analysis should include relevant features of American capitalism in the era of neo-liberalism, e.g., the rise of right to work states, the siphoning of the industrial base to lower-wage regions of the world economy, and the decline of unions.
- Perhaps our wage-worker is employed by a business in an urban center, which would then entail all of the above while forcing the worker to struggle with higher costs of living in a de-industrialized metropolis with fewer opportunities for higher-paying waged-work.
- And there may even be a particular incident that created a mess on the floor that required cleaning, which may or may not be associated with carelessness of customers toward wage-workers, defective machinery, and so on.

The explanatory powers of our variables, then, work their way through the categories. "American capitalism in the era of neo-liberalism in an urban center in a right to work state" tells us more about an individual convenience store worker than does "production in general," though production in general is the category upon which the others rest. Moreover, the abstraction of "the economy" unnecessarily distorts the object of inquiry by omitting these essential features of modernity society's political-economic system.

This example reveals why Marx criticized theorists for using abstractions carved at the level of "the economy" for capitalist-specific questions. Starting and ending one's abstractions and analysis there fails to incorporate relevant distinctions among economic forms—i.e., lumping when additional splitting is called for—and leaves out important features from its conceptualization—i.e., structural relations of class and their associated processes of surplus-value appropriation. Such a model disguises capitalism as simply the most recent representative of a sociological universal, i.e., "the economy." In his Afterword to the Second German Edition of *Capital*, Marx rebukes analysts who do this as "schoolboys," "doctrinaire," and even "hired prize fighters" with the "evil intent of apologetic" instead of "disinterested inquirers" pursuing "genuine scientific research."

5   Summary and Discussion

In sum, the method of successive abstractions uses concrete observations to categorize variables at controlled levels of specificity and compares such observations both within and between categories. Via lumping and splitting the interrelations among variables across different levels of generality, one can develop generalizable models conceptualized abstractly. Because interrelations among variables changes their character over time and space, the analyst needs a method to draw and redraw model boundaries in order to capture, compare, and analyze socio-structural variations in their forms of development. If data are unsuitable for a model (or vice-versa)—suggesting a model that is too broad or otherwise ill-fitting—this calls for re-abstracting observations and additional categorical specification of empirical detail.

Marx's narrative is not always explicit about the level of abstraction he is using, when he uses controlled comparison, or when his conclusions result therefrom. This is especially troublesome when he has moved the same concept or observation to another level of abstraction. It bears repeating, then, that knowing and recognizing the method Marx uses for this analytical procedure is vital for understanding his overall method and the conclusions at which he arrives.

A critical reader might argue that this chapter explains nothing other than the scientific method—or at least, a key feature of it. While I would agree, my reply would not end there. If my outline here is simply the basic scientific method, albeit with a healthy dose of Marxian terminology, then I have met my first goal. The analytical approach reviewed in this chapter—at least at the current level of investigation—is a type of analysis that any scientist should recognize. While Marx's method of re-abstracting also stays within conventional scientific protocols, the combined doublets I use to demonstrate this are traditionally associated with his dialectical outlook, suggesting these are not really two different discourses.

Marx's use of successive abstractions reveals that, at least as far as sociology is concerned, a scientific method without a dialectical sensibility limits itself. Marx begins with observations of the historical concrete and constructs concepts on this basis. He systematically controls variables and targets domains for additional data collection, using the interrelations he finds between observations and among concepts for testing causal properties of variables and for subsequent model building. This method of abstraction and re-abstraction provides for the free movement in empirical matter vital for studying historical change and structural complexity, which Marx said was indicative of his dialectical method. In this view, a proper social science is dialectical and without dialectics social science becomes threatened with stasis. Without a scientific basis, dialectical reason remains in the realm of speculative philosophy. Both, each without the other, venture into the apologetic and the uncritical.

One remarkable feature of Marx's method is that it combines the experimental model and the lensing power of a microscope into one epistemological tack. In this way, he can control variables and test hypotheses during research while incorporating ever more finely-grained observations. Note that this is a to-and-fro process. One does not start with a finished model but begins with observations, makes categories, adjusts those categories, and proceeds in careful retesting as they go and re-abstracting as needed. This method provides for developing precise taxonomic categories, isolating causal forces, and, therefore, more focus in generalizing. Should this method be successful, Marx ([1867] 1992c: 28) tells us, the subject matter will appear "reflected as in a mirror" but should not be mistaken for a "mere a priori construction."

While this is a complex set of considerations, I hope that my overview supplies enough instruction so that one can better grasp key aspects of how Marx builds his general categories and subcategories and analytically deploys them. The next step in this reconstruction is demonstrating how Marx used this method to model modes of production.

Marx's Method and Modes of Production

1 Why Marx's Presentation Is a Problem and How to Understand It[1]

Just in the same way he left multiple methodological directives scattered across his writings, Marx provided no systematic or singular exposition on how he modeled modes of production. His commentary on the matter also can seem incomplete and even inconsistent. In his Preface to *A Contribution to the Critique of Political Economy*, for example, Marx (1911: 13) says, "[in] broad outlines we can designate the Asiatic, the ancient, the feudal and the modern bourgeois methods of production as so many epochs in the progress of the economic formation of society." His Preface, however, omits criteria for the list—i.e., What makes *these* modes of production?—as well as primitive communism, one of his known modes of production. While the Preface appears to propose a universal stage model of history, Marx (1847: 128) had earlier argued that "[h]istory does not proceed so categorically." And in *Capital*'s volumes, he writes about "merchant's capital" in multiple pre-capitalist modes of production, yet also states that "[f]or money to be transformed into capital, the prerequisites for capitalist production must exist" (Marx 1971b: 272), conditions he elsewhere emphasizes only existed in feudal society and were absent in both ancient and Asiatic modes of production.

What are we to make of statements such as these? Rather than being inconsistent, haphazard, or even sloppy, Marx's abstractions give facts "form, an order, and a relative value" and he "often redraw[s] the boundaries of [his] units," where the "same relation is being viewed from different sides, or the same process from its different moments" (Ollman 2003: 74, 79, 100). In drawing and redrawing such boundaries, Marx may emphasize historical development, structural relationships, and/or systemic processes. The qualities with which Marx fills such frameworks, "serve individually or collectively as vantage points, just as other vantage points, organized around qualities from other levels of generality, are excluded" (Ollman 2003: 100–101). For instance, the vantage point in Marx's Preface—i.e., "progress of the economic formation of

1 Parts of this chapter previously came out in *Critical Sociology* (see Paolucci 2018b).

society"—excludes history's earliest economic forms—i.e., primitive communism—as they do not represent progress.[2]

In *Capital*, one will not find Marx using a linear universal stage model in his
historical accounts. One also will not find chapters on specific production
modes or even one chapter that compiles them all and outlines the basic structure of each. With the subject and title of his magnum opus being *Capital*—
not *Modes of Production* or *A Taxonomic History of Economic Formations*—
Marx organizes it around features specific to capitalism—e.g., machinery and
modern industry, the general law of capitalist accumulation, etc.—and those
that exist in all systems—e.g., exchange, the working-day, etc. Juxtaposing
these realities provides him a comparative framework for identifying differences and similarities across production systems. For instance, his discussions
of "merchant's capital" for pre-capitalist modes come from the vantage point
of how accumulated money ready for economic use has *parallel* functions in
multiple economic systems without those contexts representing identical
structures.[3]

It is through comparing and contrasting pre-capitalist modes of production
with capitalist society, then, that Marx isolates capitalism's identifying characteristics. Because the latter is his ultimate goal in *Capital*, he seems to feel no
need to systematically layout a catalog of modes of production along with the
explicit characteristics that he identifies with each. Rather, he brings pre-
capitalist production modes into his discussion via comparative analysis when
he needs to shed light on how a particular variable reveals something about
capitalism, whether through sharing this feature with one or more other production modes or through how a certain feature is unique to the capitalist
mode.[4] This does not mean that Marx never settled on the overall criteria for use

---

2 In the *Grundrisse*, Marx (1973: 107) reiterates such a view when he juxtaposes "pastoral peoples" to "mere hunting and fishing peoples," the latter of which "lie outside the point where
   real development begins."
3 Also see Ollman's (2003) discussion of abstractions of extension.
4 "Capital is the all-dominating economic power of bourgeois society. It must form the starting-point as well as the finishing point, and must be dealt with before landed property. After
   both have been examined in particular, their interrelation must be examined. It would therefore be unfeasible and wrong to let the economic categories follow one another in the same
   sequence as that in which they were historically decisive. Their sequence is determined,
   rather, by their relation to one another in modern bourgeois society, which is precisely the
   opposite of that which seems to be their natural order or which corresponds to historic development. The point is not the historic position of the economic relations in the succession
   of different forms of society. Even less is it their sequence 'in the idea' (Proudhon) (a muddy
   notion of historic movement). Rather, their order within modern bourgeois society" (Marx
   1973: 107–108).

in his taxonomic scheme, however. Just the opposite, in fact. Through examining how, in *Capital*, he locates and extracts the structural variables common across modes of production and analyzes both their similar and different expressions in general concrete terms, we can reconstruct his models for different production modes and the taxonomic criteria he uses for modeling them.

Reconstructing Marx in this manner, however, comes with problems that stem from how he views social reality. It bears repeating that he sees a world where "[s]ome determinations belong to all epochs, others only to a few. [Some] determinations will be shared by the most modern epoch and the most ancient," while "[m]utual interaction takes place between the different moments" (Marx 1973: 85, 100). This tells us something important about the content and complexity of his variables, as well as how he uses and writes about them. Some of Marx's variables are *interrelated*, some he places in the *interior* of others, others are *emergent*, others acquire *emergent properties* absent previously, and still others lose their former causal properties in new historical-structural contexts. Unfortunately, Marx usually does not explain that his variables possess such qualities or how he constructs them. Moreover, he often does not refer to his variables *as variables* and sometimes uses different terminology for the same thing or idea. Such practices, in part, explain why Marx's experimental model in *Capital* is difficult to see. Once we do recognize the form of his variables and the content with which he fills them, we can better recognize when and how he employs them in a controlled comparative method through his method of successive abstractions.

Towards those ends, below I present the characteristics Marx isolates and holds constant for all production forms. Next, I look at the variables he uses to initially sort out and categorize modes of production by comparing and contrasting the *productive relations* and *economic processes* that exist across them.[5] I do this by first examining how he mobilizes these variables for pre-capitalist systems, and afterward I turn my attention to how this framework allows him to model capitalism. This work provides me the vantage point needed for presenting a more complete account of the criteria Marx uses for his general taxonomy of modes of production.

---

5   One could hardly overstate the importance of the Marxian conception of fundamental sociological variables as relations and processes. Marx (1983: 354) described *A Contribution to the Critique of Political Economy* as a work where "an important view of social relationships is scientifically expounded for the first time." And Engels ([1888] 1941: 44) remarked that "the world is not to be comprehended as a complex of ready-made things, but as a complex of *processes*, in which the things apparently stable no less than their images in our heads, the concepts, go through an uninterrupted change of coming into being and passing away" (emphasis in the original).

2   Modes of Production through the Method of
         Successive Abstractions

"There are characteristics which all stages of production have in common, and
which are established as general ones by the mind," Marx (1973: 88) writes. Beginning with the abstraction of society in general (Table 2.1, Cell A), societies
across history (Cell B) can be "considered from the standpoint of [their] economic structure" (Marx 1971a: 818).[6] Though all economic structures display
the features of "production in general" (Marx 1973: 85) (Cell C), "in the beginning of civilization...[d]ifferent communities find different means of production, and different means of subsistence in their natural environment. Hence,
their modes of production...are different" (Marx [1867] 1992b: 332) (Cell D).
Here, starting with society in general, Marx carves out historical societies more
specifically, and isolates production as one of their key general concrete features, with different "modes" corresponding to them as specific concrete empirical domains. These categories serve as Marx's general model for arranging
subcategories during and after the act of re-abstracting.

    Holding society in general constant and treating history as a general ab-
straction (Table 2.2, Cell A), Marx focuses on production in general as a specific
abstract element of all societies (Cell B). At the same time, he prepares to differentiate and categorically arrange production modes in the general concrete

TABLE 2.1   From society in general to modes of production

	The general	The specific
The abstract	Society in general (A)	History (B)
The concrete	Production in general (C)	Modes of production (D)

SOURCE: CREATED BY AUTHOR

---

6   "We have seen that the capitalist process of production is a historically determined form of
    the social process of production in general. The latter is as much a production process of
    material conditions of human life as a process taking place under specific historical and eco-
    nomic production relations, producing and reproducing these production relations them-
    selves, and thereby also the bearers of this process, their material conditions of existence and
    their mutual relations, i.e., their particular socio-economic form. For the aggregate of these
    relations, in which the agents of this production stand with respect to Nature and to one
    another, and in which they produce, is precisely society, considered from the standpoint of
    its economic structure" (Marx 1971a: 818–819).

TABLE 2.2   From history to productive relations and economic processes across modes of production

	The general	The specific
The abstract	History (A)	Production in general (B)
The concrete	Modes of production (C)	Productive relations and economic processes (D)

SOURCE: CREATED BY AUTHOR

TABLE 2.3   From production in general to specific relations and processes across them

	The general	The specific
The abstract	Production in general (A)	Modes of production (B)
The concrete	Productive relations and economic processes (C)	Social development of productive forces Subject of production Terms of labor Historical surplus-value relations (D)

SOURCE: CREATED BY AUTHOR

(Cell C) via variations in the productive relations and economic processes constant across them (Cell D). This maneuver is vitally important for his analysis. Recall that part of the taxonomic method is lumping a class of objects under a general criterion, after which one can split or differentiate them within that class. The method to do this is to find (1) the *core, essential* trait(s) they all share that (2) vary in important ways in their specific functions across a series of general concrete examples. Through comparing the specific variability between these general constants, one can construct new categories. Though Marx does not tell us explicitly that this is what he is doing in his analysis of modes of production, we can see that this is the case when we closely examine how he presents his findings to us.

Because "all epochs of production have certain common traits, common characteristics" (Marx 1973: 85), Marx can treat production as a general abstract category (Table 2.3, Cell A), while focusing on the specific abstract commonalities all modes of production share (Cell B): "land...and labour" (Marx 1971a: 816)—with the "elementary factors of the labour-process [being] 1... work itself, 2, the subject of that work, and 3, its instruments" (Marx [1867]

TABLE 2.4   Comparing differences in general constants across historical systems as a method
to build models of modes of production

	Study of similarities	Study of differences
Production in → general	Production in → specific societies over historical development	Social development of productive forces Subject of production Terms of labor Historical surplus-value relations

SOURCE: CREATED BY AUTHOR

1992b: 174)—and the "division of labour in society at large" (Marx [1867] 1992b: 339). Here we see that Marx's initial approximation isolates land, labor, the labor-process—the latter of which interiorizes the subject of work (which he later subdivides) and technological relationships—and the division of labor. Beginning with these assumptions, Marx moves economic relations and processes into the general concrete category (Cell C) and examines the most essential ones in the specific concrete (Cell D). By using controlled comparison, Marx establishes how these variables are configured and interrelated in real historical settings (though he also brings in other variables later, as we shall see) and begins to construct his models of modes of production on this basis (Table 2.4).

Given his nonlinear presentation and the way he interiorizes other variables into those just recounted above, it is easy to miss which variables Marx prioritizes at particular stages of sorting out his categories. If we isolate those that appear across all the modes of production he discusses, we can identify those that comprise his general model. One variable he uses to "distinguish different economic epochs" is "how [things] are made and by what instruments" (Marx [1867] 1992b: 175), or what he often refers to as the *social development of productive forces*.[7] The *subject of production* entails the role of the production of use-values, exchange-values, and surplus-values in a

---

7   This comment from Marx has motivated some of his interpreters to posit a sole technological criterion for differentiating production forms. As we shall see, Marx is not positing a static notion of "level of technological complexity" for identifying modes of production. Rather, Marx is indicating that different modes of production have different *structurally built-in tendencies that encourage or impede technological development* and these structural tendencies thus become a taxonomic criterion. His focus is the dynamic of development, of which technological complexity is an indicator.

system. Interiorized into these categories are systems' relations to nature, the commodity-form, the money-form, hoarding, and merchant's capital as well as different *historical surplus-value relations* (into which he interiorizes rent, taxes, and usury). The division of labor involves *the terms* under which laborers engage in their work.[8] Finally, all of these variables influence the systemic roles of exchange and trade, which reciprocally influence the other variables in turn. Note, however, while exchange and trade return with a new role in Marx's more finalized models, at the initial stage of identifying these variable relationships, he embeds exchange and trade in the category of the subject of production.

Below I first explain Marx's conceptualization of these four variables, the variables he interiorized into them, and interrelations among them. Afterwards, I show how he characterized modes of production through the different configuration of these variables in real concrete societies. The reader here should not interpret the following discussion as a claim that I am the first or only person to notice these concepts in Marx's work, however. One can find most, if not all, of the concepts below in the scholarship. I do nevertheless believe that we do not yet have a satisfactory explanation of how Marx interiorizes some of these concepts inside others and how he mobilizes them as both variables as well as taxonomic criteria through his method of successive abstractions.

2.1   *Social Development of Productive Forces*

Different economic systems have particular ways they shape the technology that is used in productive activities, or what Marx called "the social development of productive forces."

In the "earliest period of human history," humans used their "own limbs" as "instruments of [their] labour" to acquire "ready-made means of subsistence [such] as fruits" and, with "the least development," they created "stone implements and weapons," made tools in the form of "stones, wood, bones, and shells," cultivated "domesticated animals," and hunted "by the chase" (Marx [1867] 1992b: 175, 316). Over time, independent "small-peasant agriculture" and personal "ownership of land" (Marx 1971a: 614) developed and "domestic industry" (Marx 1971b: 445) emerged alongside continued "simple gathering, hunting, fishing and cattle-raising" (Marx 1971a: 632; also see note 11). With increased technological complexity and productive capacity so arise "handicrafts"—e.g., pottery, nail-making, glass-making, baking, or the making

---

8   The phraseology "terms of labor" is my own. I believe it is fitting for how Marx uses a concept
     on which I elaborate more below.

of textiles—which are activities done domestically, by artisans, or in the professions, i.e., "in guilds or not" (Marx [1867] 1992b: 282, 322, 316). The next step in "co-operation...assumes its typical form in manufacture," which had "its growth out of handicrafts," involves the "concentration of workmen," "splitting up the work into a number of heterogeneous processes," and the "assemblage in one workshop...of labourers...in whose hands a given article must pass on its way to completion"—e.g., paper-, needle-, watch-, and glass-making (Marx [1867] 1992b: 318–320, 324, 328). Manufacture, however, "constitutes merely a phase of development leading to" "large-scale industry" (Marx 1968: 583).

It would be easy to mistake these forms of development as constituting a linear model of growth in technological complexity. While history reveals an overall arc of technological growth, this is not a systematic process through which every society or even general history has moved through as if some inexorable force. Forms of development can be mixed and uneven. Modes of production that dominate later, after the emergence of the first societies, may still have things like fishing, herding, and so on. People today still participate in handicrafts. Marx notes that we can find large-scale industry in several societies prior to modernity.[9] What is important is that different systems facilitate a certain momentum (or lack of it) in developing their forces of production, where both *how* that facilitation takes place and the *level* of technological complexity that results are essential features that differentiate modes of production.

2.2   The Subject of Production

All production systems have a primary purpose—or, "the subject of work" (see Marx [1867] 1992b: 174 above). This subject relates to the primary purpose of labor in a production system, i.e., creating use-value, exchange-value, and/or surplus-value. Marx examines the interrelations among these value-forms in terms of (1) the natural economy, (2) the rise of exchange, the commodity-form, the money-form, and trade, (3) hoarding, and (4) merchant's capital.

---

9   It is common to associate the idea of "industry" with the Industrial Revolution, but Marx does not use the term "industry" only to denote mass production using modern complex technology, which he often calls "Modern Industry." Rather, he uses "industry" for large production projects with more complex divisions of labor, whether modern or pre-modern. For example: "It is the necessity of bringing a natural force under the control of society, of economising, of appropriating or subduing it on a large scale by the work of man's hand, that first plays the decisive part in the history of industry. Examples are, the irrigation works in Egypt, Lombardy, Holland, or in India and Persia where irrigation by means of artificial canals, not only supplies the soil with water indispensable to it, but also carries down to it, in the shape of sediment from the hills, mineral fertilisers. The secret of the flourishing state of industry in Spain and Sicily under the domination of the Arabs lay in their irrigation works" (Marx [1867] 1992b: 481).

2.2.1   The Natural Economy

"To the extent that the labour-process is solely a process between man and Nature," Marx (1971a: 833) writes, "its simple elements remain common to all social forms of development." This process, where "the conditions of the economy are...directly replaced and reproduced out of [the economy's] gross product" (Marx 1971a: 795), sets the preconditions for "surplus-value in general"—i.e., "The direct producer must (1) possess enough labour-power and (2) the natural conditions of his labour...must be productive enough to give him the possibility of retaining some surplus-labour over and above that required for the satisfaction of his indispensable needs" (Marx 1971a: 792). Marx refers to the time it takes to produce these needs as "socially necessary labor-time," which includes producing daily survival needs (including those too young to work and those who no longer can) plus a surplus for a social fund for broader concerns (such as unexpected deficits).[10] Thus, "under all modes of production" human labor must produce enough goods for (1) "subsistence," (2) the "reproduction of its own operating conditions," and (2) a "surplus above the indispensable requirements of life," a portion "whose product serves constantly to satisfy general social needs" (Marx 1971a: 790, 877).[11]

---

10   "Of course, if wages are reduced to their general basis, namely, to that portion of the product of the producer's own labour which passes over into the individual consumption of the labourer; if we relieve this portion of its capitalist limitations and extend it to that volume of consumption which is permitted, on the one hand, by the existing productivity of society (that is, the social productivity of his own individual labour as actually social), and which, on the other hand, the full development of the individuality requires; if, furthermore, we reduce the surplus-labour and surplus-product to that measure which is required under prevailing conditions of production of society, on the one side to create an insurance and reserve fund, and on the other to constantly expand reproduction to the extent dictated by social needs; finally, if we include in No. 1 the necessary labour, and in No. 2 the surplus-labour, the quantity of labour which must always be performed by the able-bodied in behalf of the immature or incapacitated members of society, i.e., if we strip both wages and surplus-value, both necessary and surplus labour, of their specifically capitalist character, then certainly there remain not these forms, but merely their rudiments, which are common to all social modes of production" (Marx 1971a: 876).

11   "The natural basis of surplus-labour in general, that is, a natural prerequisite without which such labour cannot be performed, is that Nature must supply—in the form of animal or vegetable products of the land, in fisheries, etc.—the necessary means of subsistence under conditions of an expenditure of labour which does not consume the entire working-day. This natural productivity of agricultural labour (which includes here the labour of simple gathering, hunting, fishing and cattle-raising) is the basis of all surplus-labour, as all labour is primarily and initially directed toward the appropriation and production of food. (Animals also supply at the same time skins for warmth in colder climates; also cave-dwellings, etc.)" (Marx 1971a: 632).

2.2.2   Exchange, the Commodity-Form, the Money-Form, and Trade

In the earliest systems, though production is mainly for use-values for subsistence and general social needs, "the exchange of products springs up at the points where different families, tribes, communities come into contact" (Marx [1867] 1992b: 332). Exchange relations encourage directing some productive activity to the commodity-form and this brings about the primitive money-form, both of which then receive additional focus in production and exchange relations, a dynamic common to multiple systems.[12] In later systems, most domestic agriculture and handicrafts are directed toward subsistence and generally needed use-values as well—though here, too, in addition to production for the social fund, surplus-value is often produced and used for exchange. Marx (1971a: 325–326) explains a sort of interactive dynamic where, "on the basis of every mode of production, trade facilitates the production of surplus-products destined for exchange" and, therefore, "commerce imparts to production a character directed more and more towards exchange-value." In the internal dynamic of exchange relations, "[w]hen production of commodities has sufficiently extended itself, money...becomes the commodity that is the universal subject matter of all contracts" (e.g., rent, taxes, and the like) (Marx [1867] 1992b: 139).

2.2.3   Hoarding

In early systems, exchange of surplus-products transforms them into money-forms and, eventually, precious metals become carriers of wealth. And if trade leads to more production for exchange and these lead to the rise of both the commodity-form and the money-form, then "hoarding necessarily appears

---

12   "Apart from the domination of prices and price movement by the law of value, it is quite appropriate to regard the values of commodities as not only theoretically but also historically *prius* to the prices of production. This applies to conditions in which the labourer owns his means of production, and this is the condition of the land-owning farmer living off his own labour and the craftsman, in the ancient as well as in the modern world. This agrees also with the view we expressed previously that the evolution of products into commodities arises through exchange between different communities, not between the members of the same community. It holds not only for this primitive condition, but also for subsequent conditions, based on slavery and serfdom, and for the guild organisation of handicrafts, so long as the means of production involved in each branch of production can be transferred from one sphere to another only with difficulty and therefore the various spheres of production are related to one another, within certain limits, as foreign countries or communist communities" (Marx 1971a: 177–178; emphasis in the original). "Nomad races are the first to develop the money-form, because all their worldly goods consist of movable objects and are therefore directly alienable; and because their mode of life, by continually bringing them into contact with foreign communities, solicits the exchange of products" (Marx [1867] 1992b: 92).

along with money" (Marx 1971a: 593). In pre-capitalist systems, hoarded money tends to result in over-consumption "beyond the bounds of the necessary means of subsistence" (Marx 1968: 528; also see note 24) but not in the social development of productive forces.

2.2.4   Merchant's Capital

The circulation of commodities, the money-form, and increased trade give rise to merchant's capital, whether or not exchange rests on trade of excess use-values or whether production rests initially on commodity production. While this is a truism for multiple systems, the development of merchant's capital does not require complex social development of productive forces, as "the trading spirit and the development of merchant's capital occur frequently among unsettled nomadic peoples" (Marx 1971a: 332).[13] Given the enriching potential of exploiting price differentials between economic arenas, merchant's capital "gives rise everywhere to the tendency towards production of exchange-values, increases its volume, multiplies it, makes it cosmopolitan, and develops money into world-money," driving commerce with its "dissolving influence" on simpler production forms, especially those "mainly carried on with a view to use-value" (Marx 1971a: 331–332). The rise of merchant's capital among both ancient societies and modern trading nations, consequently, also leads to the spread of raiding and pillaging, piracy, slave trading, and colonization.[14] With slaves "the primitive material of money" (Marx [1867] 1992b: 92),

---

13   "Since merchant's capital is penned in the sphere of circulation, and since its function consists exclusively of promoting the exchange of commodities, it requires no other conditions for its existence—aside from the undeveloped forms arising from direct barter—outside those necessary for the simple circulation of commodities and money. Or rather, the latter is the condition of *its* existence. No matter what the basis on which products are produced, which are thrown into circulation as commodities—whether the basis of the primitive community, of slave production, of small peasant and petty bourgeois, or the capitalist basis, the character of products as commodities is not altered, and as commodities they must pass through the process of exchange and its attendant changes of form. The extremes between which merchant's capital acts as mediator exist for it as given, just as they are given for money and for its movements. The only necessary thing is that these extremes should be on hand as commodities, regardless of whether production is wholly a production of commodities, or whether only the surplus of the independent producers' immediate needs, satisfied by their own production, is thrown on the market. Merchant's capital promotes only the movements of these extremes, of these commodities, which are preconditions of its own existence" (Marx 1971a: 325; emphasis in the original).

14   "So long as merchant's capital promotes the exchange of products between undeveloped societies, commercial profit not only appears as out-bargaining and cheating, but also largely originates from them. Aside from the fact that it exploits the difference between the prices of production of various countries (and in this respect it tends to level and fix

the systemic practice of slavery consequently emerges on the heels of exchange, commodity production, and trade.

2.3   *Terms of Labor: Non-forced and Forced*

Pre-capitalist labor systems differ in their degree of "forced labor" (Marx 1971b: 400). With *non-forced labor*, production is engaged in freely, usually in domestic labor geared toward producing use-values and additional surplus-values for exchange or for the social fund. Laborers here often search for "an independent field of employment," which "must generally be the case in agriculture proper even under pre-capitalist modes of production," modes that still exhibit some degree of "free self-managing peasant proprietorship of land" (Marx 1971a: 676, 807). *Forced labor* exists where, whether by custom, law, or obligation backed by threat of punishment, laborers—e.g., peasants, serfs, slaves—must provide uncompensated labor for others that is over and above the level of their own subsistence. This structural process—i.e., forced labor in the production of surplus-value that is appropriated—has historical origins.

2.4   *Historical Surplus-Value Relations: Rent, Taxes, and Usury*

Surplus-value's origins rest in the natural economy and socially necessary labor-time as preconditions of additional surplus-labor.[15] With these preconditions

---

the values of commodities), those modes of production bring it about that merchant's capital appropriates an overwhelming portion of the surplus-product partly as a mediator between communities which still substantially produce for use-value, and for whose economic organisation the sale of the portion of their product entering circulation, or for that matter any sale of products at their value, is of secondary importance; and partly, because under those earlier modes of production the principal owners of the surplus-product with whom the merchant dealt, namely, the slave-owner, the feudal lord, and the state (for instance, the oriental despot) represent the consuming wealth and luxury which the merchant seeks to trap.... Merchant's capital, when it holds a position of dominance, stands everywhere for a system of robbery, so that its development among the trading nations of old and modern times is always directly connected with plundering, piracy, kidnapping slaves, and colonial conquest; as in Carthage, Rome, and later among the Venetians, Portuguese, Dutch, etc." (Marx 1971a: 330–331).

15   Marx (1971a: 634–635) explains "the general conditions for the existence of surplus-value," which operate for all forms of appropriation, including "profit in general. These conditions are: the direct producers must work beyond the time necessary for reproducing their own labour-power, for their own reproduction. They must perform surplus-labour in general. This is the subjective condition. The objective condition is that they must be able to perform surplus-labour. The natural conditions must be such that a part of their available labour-time suffices for their reproduction and self-maintenance as producers, that the production of their necessary means of subsistence shall not consume their whole labour-power. The fertility of Nature establishes a limit here, a starting-point, a basis. On the other hand, the development of the social productive power of their labour forms the

met and with the development of landed property, some pre-capitalist systems have—in addition to the direct labor exploitation of the slave—corresponding forms of surplus-value appropriation in rent, taxes, and usury.

2.4.1 Landed Property and Rent

Landed property "is based on the monopoly by certain persons over definite portions of the globe, as exclusive spheres of their private will to the exclusion of all others" (Marx 1971a: 615). In such pre-capitalist relations, "[t]he owner may be an individual representing the community, as in Asia, Egypt, etc.; or this landed property may be merely incidental to the ownership of the immediate producers themselves by some individual as under slavery or serfdom; or it may be a purely private ownership of Nature by non-producers, a mere title to land." Wealth extraction here comes from the landowner's "economic realisation" of this "exclusive right" in the form of "ground-rent," where "[a]ll ground-rent is surplus-value, the product of surplus-labour" (Marx 1971a: 634). There are three forms: labor rent, in kind rent, and money-rent.

With labor rent of the corvée, "the direct producer, using instruments of labour (plough, cattle, etc.) which actually or legally belong to him, cultivates soil actually owned by him during part of the week, and works during the remaining days upon the estate of the feudal lord without any compensation," producing "a surplus above his indispensable necessities of life...[whose level] depends...upon the proportion in which his labour-time is divided into labour-time for himself and enforced labour-time" (Marx 1971a: 790).[16] In this

---

other limit. Examined more closely, since the production of means of subsistence is the very first condition of their existence and of all production in general, labour used in this production, that is, agricultural labour in the broadest economic sense, must be fruitful enough so as not to absorb the entire available labour-time in the production of means of subsistence for the direct producers, that is, agricultural surplus-labour and therefore agricultural surplus-product must be possible. Developed further, the total agricultural labour, both necessary and surplus-labour, of a segment of society must suffice to produce the necessary subsistence for the whole of society, that is, for non-agricultural labourers too. This means therefore that the major division of labour between agricultural and industrial must be possible; and similarly between tillers of the soil producing means of subsistence and those producing raw materials. Although the labour of the direct producers of means of subsistence breaks up into necessary and surplus-labour as far as they themselves are concerned, it represents from the social standpoint only the necessary labour required to produce the means of subsistence. Incidentally, the same is true for all division of labour within society as a whole, as distinct from the division of labour within individual workshops."

16 "Finally, labour rent in itself implies that, all other circumstances remaining equal, it will depend wholly upon the relative amount of surplus-labour, or enforced labour, to what extent the direct producer shall be enabled to improve his own condition, to acquire

"brutal form of enforced labour," surplus-value "consists directly in the appropriation of this surplus expenditure of labour-power by the landlord" (Marx
1971a: 792).

With rent in kind—which "presupposes...a higher level of development of
his labour and of society in general," is practiced with the means of production
and land belonging to the laborer, and is "accompanied by survivals...of rent
paid directly in labour corvée-labour"—the laborer is "no longer under the direct supervision and compulsion of the landlord" but "is driven rather by force
of circumstances...through legal enactment rather than the whip" and labor's
products are appropriated, "no matter whether the landlord be a private person or the state." Surplus-product here comes from "combined agricultural and
industrial family labour" and "[c]ompared with labour rent, the producer rather has more room for action to gain time for surplus-labour whose product
shall belong to himself" and, therefore, "it is by no means necessary for rent in
kind...to fully exhaust the entire surplus-labour of the rural family" (Marx
1971a: 794–795).

While in kind rent is "directly the surplus-product itself" (Marx 1971a: 634),
money-rent, or payment in gold, silver, cash or otherwise a money-form, requires further social development of production, where the commodity-form
and a money-economy increasingly dominate. If this is not the case and appropriators introduce money-rent, then they will find accruing that rent difficult and/or the system may be fundamentally changed.[17]

2.4.2   Taxes

Taxes function as rent (labor, in kind, or money) when paid to a state that
serves as a collector for the owning class or is the owning class itself (Marx
1971a: 791).

---

      wealth, to produce an excess over and above his indispensable needs of subsistence, or, if
      we wish to anticipate the capitalist mode of expression, whether he shall be able to
      produce a profit for himself, and how much of a profit, i.e., an excess over this wages
      which have been produced by himself" (Marx 1971a: 793).

17   "[When money becomes the commodity that is the universal subject-matter of all con-
      tracts, r]ent, taxes, and such like payments are transformed from payments in kind into
      money payments. To what extent this transformation depends upon the general condi-
      tions of production, is shown, to take one example, by the fact that the Roman Empire
      twice failed in its attempts to levy all contributions in money" (Marx [1867] 1992b: 139–
      140). "If the foreign trade, forced upon Japan by Europeans, should lead to the substitution
      of money-rents for rents in kind, it will be all up with the exemplary agriculture of that
      country. The narrow economic conditions under which that agriculture is carried on, will
      be swept away" (Marx [1867] 1992b: 140).

2.4.3   Usury

Though "[t]he functions of hoards...arise in part out of the function of money" (Marx [1867] 1992b: 143), "the professional hoarder does not become important until he is transformed into a usurer," a process "bound up with the development of merchant's capital and especially that of money-dealing capital" (Marx 1971a: 593). As appropriation "in the form of interest," usury's influence "depends on the extent, the intensity, etc., of the accumulation process itself, that is, on the *mode of production*" (Marx 1971b: 303–304; emphasis in the original). Where the usurer's capital appropriates all surplus-labor, as in pre-capitalist forms, it "impoverishes the mode of production, paralyses the productive forces instead of developing them, and at the same time perpetuates the miserable conditions in which the social productivity of labour is not developed at the expense of labour itself, as in the capitalist mode of production" (Marx 1971a: 595–596). In these pre-capitalist modes, the usurer "wrecks the forms of property whose constant reproduction in the same form constitutes the stable basis of the political structure...leading to the disintegration of society—apart from the slaves, serfs, etc., and their new masters—into a mob" (Marx 1971b: 531).

Above, Marx treats productive relations and economic processes across systems as a general abstract framework (Table 2.5, Column A), where the social development of productive forces, the subject of production, the terms of labor, and forms of surplus-value appropriation become specific abstract categories (Column B). In this move, Marx shifts previous specific concrete examples into general concrete categories (Column C) and then brings in additional empirical detail (Column D). This systematic sorting provides for structural modeling ready for comparative use through additional observation of real historical data. His analysis is now better prepared to address the division of labor, categorize modes of production, and uncover the interactions among and changes within and between the systems where these productive structures and economic practices predominate. "If one studies each of these developments by itself and then compares them with each other, one will easily find the key to each phenomenon" (Marx [1877] 1979: 321–322), a necessary step for general models to take shape. Marx ([1873] 1992a: 28) states, however, that "the method of presentation must differ in form from that of inquiry.... Only after [one has examined material in detail and traced out their interconnections] can the actual movement be adequately described."

3   Marx's Modes of Production

As he constructs and controls variables through the method of successive abstractions, Marx develops categorical criteria for his taxonomy of modes of

TABLE 2.5   From productive relations and economic processes across historical social
systems to specific concrete examples

The general abstract (A)	The specific abstract (B)	The general concrete (C)	The specific concrete (D)
Productive relations and economic processes across modes of production	Social development of productive forces	Hunting Gathering	The chase, fishing, fruit picking
		Animal husbandry	Domestication of animals
		Agriculture	Small-peasant agriculture, mass agriculture
		Handicrafts	Pottery, nail-making, baking, weaving
		Manufacture	Paper, needles, watches, glass works
		Industry	Irrigation works
	Subject of production	Use-value	Food, tools, clothes, shelter, the social fund
		Exchange-value	Surplus use-values, commodity production, trade
		Surplus-value	Social fund, exchange, hoarding, merchant's capital
	Terms of labor	Non-forced	Hunting-gathering, free peasant proprietorship of land, domestic industry, handicrafts
		Forced	Peasant labor, serf corvée labor, slavery
	Historical surplus-value relations	Rent	Labor, in kind, money
		Taxes	Rent, money
		Usury	Money-interest

production. The subject of production (use-value, exchange-value, surplus-value), labor-terms (unforced, forced), and the social development of productive forces (low, stable, uneven, complex, constant) vary with *other variables, some reconfigured and others now introduced*—i.e., different property relations and their corresponding class relations and value-relations, which include forms of surplus-value appropriation and the systemic role of exchange and trade (Table 2.6).

3.1   *Non-class versus Class Systems*

Marx (1973: 106–107) argues that "[i]n all forms of society there is one specific kind of production which predominates over the rest, whose relations thus assign rank and influence to the others." It is with this sort of rule that he uses observations of real concrete history in conjunction with the variables outlined above to piece together the configuration of variables of different modes of production. Given that "surplus-labour" exists "in any given economic formation of society" (Marx [1867] 1992b: 226) and that "all surplus-value [reduces] to surplus-labour" (Marx 1971b: 254), Marx holds the *existence of surplus-value* constant across all modes of production. For his initial differentiation, "landed property is a historical premise...in all previous modes of production which are based on the exploitation of the masses in one form or another," where there exists the "identity of surplus-value with unpaid labour of others" (Marx 1971a: 617, 792). Marx here models class systems as having a group who controls the means of production (landed property) and who systematically appropriates the surplus-value laborers produce via unpaid forced surplus-labor. By contrast, he characterizes non-class systems as having in-common property relations where labor is unforced in value-production and the surplus-value it produces is not subject to appropriation (Table 2.7).[18]

Once he has made a distinction *between* class systems and non-class systems, Marx next splits class systems based on their different configurations of

---

18   "Capital has not invented surplus-labour. Wherever a part of society possesses the monopoly of the means of production, the labourer, free or not free, must add to the working-time necessary for his own maintenance an extra working-time in order to produce the means of subsistence for the owners of the means of production, whether this proprietor be the Athenian *kalos kagathos*, Etruscan theocrat, civis Romanus, Norman baron, American slave-owner, Wallachian Boyard, modern landlord or capitalist" (Marx [1867] 1992b: 226). "If the labourer wants all his time to produce the necessary means of subsistence for himself and his race, he has no time left in which to work gratis for others. Without a certain degree of productiveness in his labour, he has no such superfluous time at his disposal; without such superfluous time, no surplus-labour and therefore no capitalists, no slave-owners, no feudal lords, in one word, no class of large proprietors" (Marx [1867] 1992b: 479).

TABLE 2.6   From modes of production in general to specific productive relations and
            economic processes

The general abstract	The specific abstract	The general concrete	The specific concrete
Modes of production	Productive relations and economic processes	Class relations	No classes Appropriators and laborers
		Property relations	Communal property Laborer owns their own means of production Landed property Private property
		Subject of production	Use-value (subsistence) Exchange-value (commodity production, merchant's capital) Surplus-value (social fund, exchange, hoarding, accumulation)
		Terms of labor	Unforced, forced
		Forms of surplus-value appropriation	None Slavery Rent (labor, in kind, money) Taxes and tribute Usury Wage-labor
		Role of exchange and trade	Exchange when available National trade Market regulation of exchange Trade on world-market
		Social development of productive forces	Stability, uneven, constant low, moderate, complex

TABLE 2.7   Differentiating non-class and class systems

The general abstract	The specific abstract	The general concrete	The specific concrete
Society in general →	Modes of production →	Non-class systems	Common property Non-forced labor No appropriation of surplus-value
		Class systems	Landed property Appropriation of surplus-value via forced labor

SOURCE: CREATED BY AUTHOR

productive relations and economic processes (while also using non-class systems as a comparative external model set) (Table 2.8). One "essential difference" between class systems "lies only in the mode in which...surplus-labour is in each case extracted from the actual producer, the labourer" (Marx [1867] 1992b: 209). Within their specific forms of appropriation, one "important differentiation" and "a major key for understanding the various economic formations of society" is "between labour that is paid out of capital and labour paid directly from revenue" (Marx 1971b: 414). The "specific economic form" in which this occurs "determines the relationship of rulers and ruled" and thus "reveals... the hidden basis of the entire social structure and with it the political form of the relation of sovereignty and dependence, in short, the corresponding specific form of the state" (Marx 1971a: 791). In this inductive-deductive dialectic, Marx examines specific concrete data, builds a model of each mode, and applies that model to societies representing those modes.

Below, I examine the configuration of variables he identifies with each mode of production and afterwards I present a summary view of that taxonomy.

3.2   Primitive Communism

Society "at the dawn of human development...is based...on ownership in common of the means of production" (Marx [1867] 1992b: 316). These societies are "extremely simple and transparent," where the "productive power of labour has not risen beyond a low stage" and thus display an "immature development of man individually" and where "narrow" "social relations between man and Nature" (Marx [1867] 1992b: 83–84) and "production for the use-value, for immediate

TABLE 2.8   Constants, variables, and constructing models of modes of production via comparisons

Constants	Variables	Modes	Compared to
Society in general	Class relations	Primitive communism	Ancient mode Asiatic mode
Production in general (production of use-value, exchange-value, and surplus-value)	Property relations Subject of production		Feudalism Capitalism
	Terms of labor	Ancient mode	Primitive communism Asiatic mode
Natural economy	Form of appropriation		Feudalism Capitalism
	Role of exchange and trade	Asiatic mode	Primitive communism Ancient mode
	Social development of productive forces		Feudalism Capitalism
		Feudalism	Primitive communism Ancient mode Asiatic mode Capitalism
		Capitalism	Primitive communism Ancient mode Asiatic mode Feudalism

personal requirements, predominates.... In early communal societies in which primitive communism prevailed...it was this communal society itself with its conditions which appeared as the basis of production, and its reproduction appeared as its ultimate purpose" (Marx 1971a: 831). Some portion of surplus-value production in these societies "is directly consumed individually by the producers and their families," a portion "is productively consumed," and a portion "is invariably surplus-labour, whose product serves constantly to satisfy the general social needs" (Marx 1971a: 877–878). Without systemic reinvestment of surplus-value, however, such a mode of production is "unfitted to develop labour as *social* labour and the productive power of social labour" (Marx 1971b: 422–423; emphasis in the original).

Because of common land ownership and the absence of surplus-value appropriation, labor is unforced and primarily geared toward subsistence (small-scale agriculture, household production, fishing, and hunting), though trade might develop among families, tribes, and communities and encourage production of exchange-values as opportunities arise. Common property—therefore no class structure—and lack of forced labor—therefore no surplus-value appropriation—results in relatively egalitarian political relations. Specific concrete instances where Marx refers to primitive communist social forms include "nomad races," "a tribe" (Marx [1867] 1992b: 92, 316), or "primitive Indian communities, or the more ingeniously developed communism of the Peruvians" (Marx 1971a: 877; also see Marx [1867] 1992b: 91). Marx ([1867] 1992b: 82, note 1) also tells us that "common property in its primitive form" can be found among Romans, Teutons, Celts, India, Asia, and even later in Slavonia and Russia, as communal social and property relations survived at times into "ancient communal towns" (Marx 1971a: 831).

3.3   The Ancient Mode of Production

Ancient society's class relations were comprised of landowners (e.g., patricians) and a mix of plebeians/peasants and slaves. In "the best periods of classical antiquity," the "form of free self-managing peasant proprietorship of land parcels as the prevailing, normal form constitutes...the economic foundation of society" (Marx 1971a: 806). "[T]his form of production—in which the conditions of production are the property of the producer—was at the same time the basis of the political relationships, of the independence of the citizen" (Marx 1971b: 531). While there existed the "Egyptian system of castes" (Marx [1867] 1992b: 346) and "Greek society was founded upon slavery, and had, therefore, for its natural basis, the inequality of men" (Marx [1867] 1992b: 65), "[p]easant agriculture on a small scale, and the carrying on of independent handicrafts...form the economic foundation of the classical communities at their best, after the primitive form of ownership of land in common had disappeared, and before slavery had seized on production in earnest" (Marx [1867] 1992b: 316, note 3). Though corvée labor existed "partially in the Ancient World"

TABLE 2.9   From common productive relations and economic processes to primitive
             communism

The general abstract	The specific abstract	The general concrete	The specific concrete
Productive relations and economic processes across modes of production	Class relations Property relations Subject of production	No classes Communal property Use-value Surplus-value (Social fund, exchange)	Early societies, tribes, nomads, primitive Indian communities, Peruvians, communities in Rome, Russia, Slovenia, Asia
	Terms of labor Forms of surplus-value appropriation	Unforced None	
	Role of exchange and trade	Exchange when available	
	Social development of productive forces	Low and stable Simple technology, hunting and gathering, pastoralism, small-scale agriculture	

SOURCE: CREATED BY AUTHOR

(Marx 1971b: 417), slavery eventually predominated and formed "the broad foundation of social production," which was facilitated through merchant's capital and the growth of commodity production and trade (see Marx 1971a: 831, 332; see note 42).

Similar to Asia (particularly India) and feudal society, peasants produced their labor fund for themselves in ancient societies like Greece, though a portion was subject to appropriation.[19] While commodity production and

---

19   After he quotes Richard Jones's list and qualities of "labouring peasants" in ancient Greece, Asia (especially India), and feudal society, Marx (1971b: 416) explains that "[t]he characteristic feature of these groups is that the worker reproduces the labour fund for himself. It is not transformed into capital. Just as the worker directly produces the labour

exchange initially held a "subordinate place," their importance grew, even though "[t]rading nations, properly so called, exist in the ancient world only in its interstices" (Marx [1867] 1992b: 83) where "they acted the middleman" (Marx 1971a: 330). As exchange and trade increased, so arose "widespread" hoarding that went to "unproductive expenditure on art, religious works and public works" and "mad extravagance" (late Rome and Greece). This was because "the ancients never thought of transforming surplus-product into capital" and thus the "development of the material productive forces...by and large...never went beyond handicraft labour," as wealth was "amassed in the hands of a few persons, who, incidentally, did not know what to do with it" (Marx 1968: 528).[20] Under these conditions, systemic over-production tended not to exist and the relation between technology and production developed unevenly. "Ancient Rome, in its later republican days, developed merchant's capital to a higher degree than ever before in the ancient world, without showing any progress in the development of crafts, while in Corinth and other Grecian towns in Europe and Asia Minor the development of commerce was accompanied by highly developed crafts" (Marx 1971a: 332).

---

fund, so he appropriates it directly, although his surplus-labour may be appropriated either wholly or in part by him himself or may be appropriated entirely by other classes, depending on the particular form which his relation to his conditions of production assumes. It is entirely due to economic prejudice that Jones describes this category as wage-labourers. Nothing which characterizes wage-labourers exists among them."

20   Here is the full quote: "This was indeed also the case, and to an even higher degree, in the ancient mode of production which depended on slavery. But the ancients never thought of transforming the surplus-product into capital. Or at least only to a very limited extent. (The fact that the hoarding of treasure in the narrow sense was widespread among them shows how much surplus-product lay completely idle.) They used a large part of the surplus-product for unproductive expenditure on art, religious works and public works. Still less was their production directed to the release and development of the material productive forces—division of labour, machinery, the application of the powers of nature and science to private production. In fact, by and large, they never went beyond handicraft labour. The wealth which they produced for private consumption was therefore relatively small and only appears great because it was amassed in the hands of a few persons, who, incidentally, did not know what to do with it. Although, therefore, there was no *over-production* among the ancients, there was *over-consumption* by the rich, which in the final periods of Rome and Greece turned into mad extravagance. The few trading peoples among them lived partly at the expense of all these essentially poor nations. It is the unconditional development of the productive forces and therefore mass production on the basis of a mass of producers who are confined within the bounds of necessary means of subsistence on the one hand and, on the other, the barrier set up by the capitalists' profit, which [forms] the basis of modern over-production" (Marx 1968: 528; emphases in the original).

Just as in later feudal society, merchant's capital in ancient society facilitat-ed plundering, kidnapping slaves, piracy, and colonial conquest (Marx 1971a: 331; also see note 14). The slave and money economy allowed for additional accumulation through usury. In the last years of the Roman Republic, "manu-facturing stood far below its average level of development" and "merchant's capital, money-dealing capital, and usurer's capital developed to their highest point" (Marx 1971a: 593). However, usury has a "destructive influence on an-cient...wealth and...property...[and] it undermines and ruins small-peasant... production, in short, all forms in which the producer still appears as the owner of his means of production" (Marx 1971a: 596). In addition to the appropriation of surplus-value directly from surplus-labor, "[i]n Rome, as in the entire an-cient world—apart from merchant cities, like Athens and others, which were particularly developed industrially and commercially—[high interest was] a means used by the big landowners not only for expropriating the small propri-etors, the plebeians, but for appropriating their persons" (Marx 1971b: 538). As a result, "class-struggles of the ancient world" were mainly "between debtors and creditors" and, in Rome, this "ended in the ruin of the plebeian debtors" who "were displaced by slaves" (Marx [1867] 1992b: 135).[21]

3.4   The Asiatic Mode of Production

In the Asiatic mode, the class structure was rooted in small village communi-ties, with "common property" in places such as India and Asia (Marx 1971a: 831), land owned by the state elsewhere, and some combination of landed and communal property still in other places. Marx (1971b: 417) places the founda-tion of production here in "the Asiatic communal system with its unity of agri-culture and industry" and home handicrafts, e.g., spinning and weaving. Such communities were often self-sustaining and stable (or even stagnant) across changes in political regimes.[22] Beyond domestic production of use-values, in

---

21   Also: "Moreover, the usury which sucks dry the small producer goes hand in hand with the usury which sucks dry the rich owner of a large estate. As soon as the usury of the Roman patricians had completely ruined the Roman plebeians, the small peasants, this form of exploitation came to an end and a pure slave economy replaced the small-peasant econ-omy" (Marx 1971a: 595).

22   "Those small and extremely ancient Indian communities, some of which have continued down to this day, are based on possession in common of the land, on the blending of ag-riculture and handicrafts, and on an unalterable division of labour, which serves, when-ever a new community is started, as a plan and scheme already cut and dried" (Marx [1867] 1992b: 337). "Japan, with its purely feudal organisation of landed property and its developed *petite culture*, gives a much truer picture of the European middle ages than all our history books, dictated as these are, for the most part, by bourgeois prejudices" (Marx [1867] 1992b: 672, note 1). "The simplicity of the organisation for production in these self-

TABLE 2.10   From common productive relations and economic processes to the ancient mode of production

The general abstract	The specific abstract	The general concrete	The specific concrete
Productive relations and economic processes across modes of production	Class relations	Appropriators (upper castes, patricians) Laborers (plebeians/peasants, slaves)	Greece, Rome, Egypt, Carthage
	Property relations	Landed property Laborers own their own means of production	
	Subject of production	Use-value Exchange-value (commodity production, hoarding) Surplus-value (social fund, exchange, trade)	
	Terms of labor	Mix of independent (unforced) and forced	
	Forms of surplus-value appropriation	Slavery, rent, taxes, usury	
	Role of exchange and trade	Some exchange Trade as intermediaries between nations	
	Social development of productive forces	Moderate and uneven Agriculture, domestic industry, handicrafts industry	

suffing communities that constantly reproduce themselves in the same form, and when accidently destroyed, spring up again on the spot and with the same name—this simplicity supplies the key to the secret of the unchangeableness of Asiatic societies, an unchangeableness in such striking contrast with the constant dissolution and refounding of the Asiatic mode "the conversion of products into commodities...holds a sub-ordinate place, which, however, increases in importance as the primitive communities approach nearer and nearer to their dissolution" (Marx [1867] 1992b: 83). With most production done for domestic consumption or monopolized by a few trades, there was less market competition in exchange relations and thus some appropriation occurred through selling products above the value of the labor contained in them.[23] However, in comparison to later modes, this did not result in almost unlimited extension of the working-day (see notes 28 and 49).

As in ancient society, growth of exchange, money, and commodity production resulted in hoarding and personal consumption, especially in Asia and the East Indies.[24] The general form of Asiatic surplus-value appropriation was rent, practiced on the largest scale historically speaking and resting on "the forcible domination of one section of society over the other" in the form of "slavery, serfdom or political dependence" (Marx 1971b: 400). While some labor was non-forced—i.e., domestic handicrafts and agriculture with laborers in possession of their means of production, sometimes in a "natural production community" such as in India—rent in kind was required (thus, forced labor) and often paid in taxes to the state who served as the landowner.[25] In kind

---

Asiatic states, and the never-ceasing changes of dynasty. The structure of the economic elements of society remains untouched by the storm-clouds of the political sky" (Marx [1867] 1992b: 338–339). Marx (1971a: 333–334) describes India and China as having "internal solidity and organisation of pre-capitalistic, national modes of production" where "[t]he broad basis of the mode of production here is formed by the unity of small-scale agriculture and home industry, to which in India we should add the form of village communities built upon the common ownership of land, which, incidentally, was the original form in China as well.... [In these] small economic communities...the spinning and weaving industries...were an ancient integrating element of this unity of industrial and agricultural production....[where]...the association of agriculture with manufacture...[laid] the economic groundwork of Asiatic production."

23   "Similarly in all countries, as for example the Asiatic, where the principle revenue of the country is in the hands of landlords, princes, etc., in the form of rent, the manufacturers, *few in number* and therefore not restricted by competition, sell them their commodities at monopoly prices, and in this way appropriate a part of their revenue; they enrich themselves not only by selling to them 'unpaid' labour, but by selling the commodities at over the quantity of labour contained in them" (Marx 1969: 277; emphases in the original).

24   "In the early stages of the circulation of commodities, it is the surplus use-values alone that are converted into money. Gold and silver thus become of themselves social expressions for superfluity or wealth. This naïve form of hoarding becomes perpetuated in those communities in which the traditional mode of production is carried on for the supply of a fixed and limited circle of home wants. It is thus with the people of Asia, and particularly of the East Indies" (Marx [1867] 1992b: 131).

25   "Should the direct producers not be confronted by a private landowner, but rather, as in Asia, under direct subordination to a state which stands over them as their landlord

TABLE 2.11   From common productive relations and economic processes to the Asiatic mode of production

The general abstract	The specific abstract	The general concrete	The specific concrete
Productive relations and economic processes across modes of production	Class relations	Appropriators (the state, despots, landlords) Laborers (peasants, serfs, slaves)	India, China, Japan, East Indies
	Property relations	Landed property Laborers own their own means of production	
	Subject of production	Use-value Exchange-value (commodity production, hoarding) Surplus-value (social fund, exchange)	
	Terms of labor	Mix of independent (unforced) and forced	
	Forms of surplus-value appropriation	Slavery, rent, taxes, usury	
	Role of exchange and trade	Some exchange Trade not emphasized	
	Social development of productive forces	Moderate and stable Agriculture, domestic industry, handicrafts	

and simultaneously as sovereign, then rent and taxes coincide, or rather, there exists no tax which differs from this form of ground-rent. Under such circumstances, there need exist no stronger political or economic pressure than that common to all subjection to that state. The state is then the supreme lord. Sovereignty here consists in the ownership of land concentrated on a national scale. But, on the other hand, no private ownership of land exists, although there is both private and common possession and use of land" (Marx 1971a: 791). "The form of rent in kind, by being bound to a definite type of product and production itself and through its indispensable combination of labor rent was not the only form of appropriation in that usury long existed but "without bringing about real disintegration, but merely giving rise to economic decay and political corruption" (Marx 1971b: 531).

3.5   The Feudal Mode of Production

With a class structure rooted in monopoly rights of landed property, "the basis of the feudal mode of production" rested on "the guild-bound handicrafts of the medieval urban industries" (Marx 1971a: 334), "[p]easant agriculture on a small scale, and the carrying on of independent handicrafts" (Marx [1867] 1992b: 316, note 3). Self-managing peasants owning small parcels of land and using their own tools and family handicrafts to produce subsistence was the foundation for personal independence.[26] There also existed communal property alongside personal ownership of land (similar to the Asiatic mode) that was often transferred from peasants to landlords. Such a system of "[p]roprietorship of land parcels by its very nature exclude[d] the development of social productive forces of labour" (Marx 1971a: 807) and gave rise to forced serf labor in the corvée, though in other places the corvée led to serfdom.[27] Though

---

agriculture and domestic industry, through its almost complete self-sufficiency whereby the peasant family supports itself through its independence from the market and the movement of production and history of that section of society lying outside of its sphere, in short owing to the character of natural economy in general, this form is quite adapted to furnishing the basis for stationary social conditions as we see, e.g., in Asia" (Marx 1971a: 796).

26   "The free ownership of the self-managing peasant is evidently the most normal form of landed property for small-scale operation, i.e., for a mode of production, in which possession of the land is a prerequisite for the labourer's ownership of the product of his own labour, and in which the cultivator, be he free owner or vassal, always must produce his own means of subsistence independently, as an isolated labourer with his family. Ownership of the land is as necessary for full development of this mode of production as ownership of tools is for free development of handicraft production. Here is the basis for the development of personal independence" (Marx 1971a: 807).

27   "A survival of the old communal ownership of land, which had endured after the transition to independent peasant farming, e.g., in Poland and Rumania, served there as a subterfuge for effecting a transition to the lower forms of ground-rent. A portion of the land belongs to the individual peasant and is tilled independently by him. Another portion is tilled in common and creates a surplus-product, which serves partly to cover community expenses, partly as a reserve in cases of crop failure, etc. These last two parts of the surplus-product, and ultimately the entire surplus-product including the land upon which it has been grown, are more and more usurped by state officials and private individuals, and thus the originally free peasant proprietors, whose obligation to till this land in common is maintained, are transformed into vassals subject either to corvée-labour or rent in kind; while the usurpers of common land are transformed into owners, not only of the usurped common lands, but even the very lands of the peasants themselves" (Marx 1971a: 803). "In the corvée the surplus-labour is accurately marked off from the necessary labour.... In the Danubian Principalities, the corvée was mixed up with rents in kind and other

most peasant labor went toward subsistence, social reproduction, and surplus-value for the social fund, in the serf labor of the corvée (like slave labor) rent "is paid in labour not in products, still less in money" (Marx 1971b: 401). Such forced labor rent also existed in "the urban craft guild system of the Middle Ages" (Marx 1971b: 417), with "conceptions of professional duty, craftsmanship, etc." that masked its "relations of dominion and servitude" (Marx 1971a: 831). Via in kind rent, landlords' revenues came from agricultural products, domestic handicrafts, manufacturing, and industrial labor, "prerequisites of that mode of production upon which natural economy rests" (Marx 1971a: 786–787). While earlier systems—e.g., Asiatic modes—saw a limited working-day, feudalism stretched it further (only to be increased again under capitalism).[28]

Similar to ancient society, feudalism's combination of exchange, a money-form, and trade led to personal consumption of wealth and luxury and an increasing influence of merchants in piracy, plunder, slavery, and colonial conquest under the Venetians, Portuguese, and Dutch (among others) (Marx 1971a: 331; also note 14). Colonialism of the feudal period, with its forms of trade, usury, money-rent, and the transformation of both landed property and the terms of labor, initiated "[t]he formation process of capital," feudalism's "dissolution process" and served as the capitalist mode of production's "historical genesis" (Marx 1971b: 491).

3.5.1   Trade, Usury, Money-Rent, and the Transition to Capitalism
Trade in feudalism spurred on more commodity production by creating markets for goods and generating a global search for raw materials, both often through force.[29] This colonial expansion of trade in the world-market targeted

---

appurtenances of bondage, but it formed the most important tribute paid to the ruling class. Where this was the case, the corvée rarely arose from serfdom; serfdom much more frequently on the other hand took origin from the corvée" (Marx [1867] 1992b: 227).

28   Marx (1971b: 434) writes: "the continuous labour of the non-agricultural labourers lasting from morning to night is by no means something which arises spontaneously, but is itself a *product* of economic development. In contrast to the Asiatic form and to the Western form of labour (prevailing in former times, partly even today) in the countryside, the urban labour of the Middle Ages already constitutes a great advance and serves as a preparatory school for the capitalist mode of production, as regards the continuity and steadiness of labour" (emphasis in the original).

29   "Originally, trade is the pre-condition for the transformation of guild, rural domestic agricultural production into capitalist production. It develops the product into a commodity, partly by creating a market for it, partly by giving rise to new commodity equivalents and partly by supplying production with new materials and thereby initiating new kinds of production which are based on trade from the very beginning because they depend both on production for the market and on elements of production derived from the world-market.

TABLE 2.12   From common productive relations and economic processes to the feudal mode
of production

The general abstract	The specific abstract	The general concrete	The specific concrete
Productive relations and economic processes across modes of production	Class relations	Appropriators (landowners) Laborers (artisans, peasants, serfs)	Middle Ages, England in 16th century, Romania (Danubian principalities), Poland, Germany, France, Sweden
	Property relations	Landed property Laborers own their own means of production	
	Subject of production	Use-value Exchange-value (commodity production, hoarding) Surplus-value (Social fund, exchange, trade)	
	Terms of labor	Mix of independent (unforced) and forced	
	Forms of surplus-value appropriation	Rent (labor, in kind, money), taxes and tribute, usury	
	Role of exchange and trade	Some exchange Trade	
	Social development of productive forces	Moderate and slow development Agriculture, domestic handicrafts, guilds and manufacture, industry	

SOURCE: CREATED BY AUTHOR

"As soon as manufacture gains strength (and this applies to an even greater extent to large-scale industry), it in turns creates the market, conquers it, opens up, partly by force, markets which it conquers, however, by means of its commodities. From now on, trade is merely a servant of industrial production for which a constantly expanding market has become a very condition of existence, since constantly expanding mass production, surplus-labor extraction, transforming labor conditions in prior systems wherever it inserted itself.[30] Unlike other systems, such as in the Asiatic mode, usury in feudalism led to "the centralisation of the conditions of production in the form of capital" (Marx 1971b: 532).[31] This was because usury in feudalism existed "where the other conditions for capitalist production exist—free labour, a world-market, dissolution of the old social connections, a certain level of the development of labour, development of science, etc." In such conditions, usury "leads to the ruin of feudal wealth and property" and "brings about the ruin of petty-bourgeois, small-peasant production" (Marx 1971b: 530) as the usurer "gradually acquires possession even of his…land, house, etc." (Marx 1971a: 595). For the feudal ruling class, "[i]n the middle ages the contest [between debtors and creditors thus] ended with the ruin of the feudal debtors, who lost their political power together with the economic basis on which it was established" (Marx [1867] 1992b: 135). With increasing commodity production and trade leading to the growth of a money economy, legal contracts codified money-rent, making it easier for both new landowners and better off serfs to exploit

---

    circumscribed not by the existing limits of trade (insofar as trade is only an expression of the existing level of demand), but solely by the amount of capital available and the level of productivity of the workers, always flooding the existing market and consequently seeks constantly to expand and remove its boundaries. Trade is now the servant of industrial capital, and carries out one of the functions emanating from the conditions of production of industrial capital" (Marx 1971b: 470).

30   "But it is only foreign trade, the development of the market to a world-market, which causes money to develop into world money and *abstract labour* into social labour. Abstract wealth, value, money, hence *abstract labour*, develop in the measure that concrete labour becomes a totality of different modes of labour embracing the world-market. Capitalist production rests on the *value* or the transformation of labour embodied in the product into social labour. But this is only [possible] on the basis of foreign trade and of the world-market. This is at once the pre-condition and the result of capitalist production" (Marx 1971b: 253; emphases in the original).

31   "Usury has a revolutionary effect in all pre-capitalist modes of production only in so far as it destroys and dissolves those forms of property on whose solid foundation and continual reproduction in the same form the political organization is based. Under Asian forms, usury can continue a long time, without producing anything more than economic decay and political corruption. Only where and when the other prerequisites of capitalist production are present does usury become one of the means assisting in establishment of the new mode of production by ruining the feudal lord and small-scale producer, on the one hand, and centralizing the conditions of labour into capital, on the other" (Marx 1971a: 597).

propertyless day laborers, all of which facilitated the transfer of land ownership to the incipient capitalist class.[32]

3.5.2   Landed Property and the Transition to Capitalism

With growing capitalist development, the feudal "form of landed property...
does not suit it.... It thus transforms feudal landed property, clan property,
small peasant property...into the economic form corresponding to the requirements of [the capitalist] mode of production" (Marx 1971a: 617).[33] This meant
dissolving landowners' and laborers' legal or customary ties to the land, expropriating them, and transforming the land into a form of property that makes
absentee ownership and agricultural production for profits possible.[34] Larger

---

32   "The transformation of rent in kind into money-rent is furthermore not only inevitably
      accompanied, but even anticipated, by the formation of a class of propertyless day-la-
      bourers, who hire themselves out for money. During their genesis, when this new class
      appears but sporadically, the custom necessarily develops among the more prosperous
      peasants subject to rent payments of exploiting agricultural wage-labourers for their own
      account, much as in feudal times, when the more well-to-do peasant serfs themselves also
      held serfs. In this way, they gradually acquire the possibility of accumulating a certain
      amount of wealth and themselves becoming transformed into future capitalists. The old
      self-employed possessors of land themselves thus give rise to a nursery school for capital-
      ist tenants, whose development is conditioned by the general development of capitalist
      production beyond the bounds of the country-side. This class shoots up very rapidly
      when particularly favourable circumstances come to its aid, as in England in the 16th
      century, where the then progressive depreciation of money enriched them under the cus-
      tomary long leases at the expense of the landlords.
           Furthermore: as soon as rent assumes the form of money-rent, and thereby the rela-
      tionship between rent-paying peasant and landlord becomes a relationship fixed by
      contract—a development which is only possible generally when the world-market, com-
      merce, and manufacture have reached a certain relatively high level—the leasing of land
      to capitalists inevitably also makes its appearance. The latter hitherto stood beyond the
      rural limits and now carry over to the country-side and agriculture the capital acquired in
      the cities and with it the capitalist mode of operation developed—i.e., creating a product
      as a mere commodity and solely as a means of appropriating surplus-value. This form can
      become the general rule only in those countries which dominate the world-market in the
      period of transition from the feudal to the capitalist mode of production" (Marx 1971a:
      798–799).
33   Marx (1971a: 615–616) writes: "the problem is to ascertain the economic value, that is, the
      realisation of this monopoly [of landed property] on the basis of capitalist production....
      The legal view itself only means that the landowner can do with the land what every
      owner of commodities can do with his commodities. And this view, this legal view of free
      private ownership of land, arises in the ancient world only with the dissolution of the
      organic order of society, and in the modern world only with the development of capitalist
      production. It has been imported by Europeans to Asia only here and there."
34   "The form of landed property which we shall consider here is a specifically historical one
      a form *transformed* through the influence of capital and of the capitalist mode of

landowners taking over common land for wealth extraction and smaller farmers losing out to competitive market forces dominated by large producers facilitated the rise of mass agriculture.[35] Older feudal forms of labor remained
for a time, while domestic rural industries gave way to larger ones, depleting
land fertility and transforming peasant land into commercial enterprises.[36]

---

production, either of feudal landownership, or of small-peasant agriculture as a means of
livelihood, in which the *possession* of the land and the soil constitutes one of the prerequisites of production for the direct producer, and in which his *ownership* of land appears
as the most advantageous condition for the prosperity of *his* mode of production. Just as
the capitalist mode of production in general is based on the expropriation of the conditions of labour from the labourers, so does it in agriculture presuppose the expropriation
of the rural labourers from the land and their subordination to a capitalist, who carries on
agriculture for the sake of profit" (Marx 1971a: 614–615; emphases in the original). Expansion of capitalism "transforms agriculture from a mere empirical and mechanical self-
perpetuating process employed by the least developed part of society into the conscious
scientific application of agronomy...divorces landed property from the relations of dominion and servitude...totally separates land as an instrument of production from landed
property and landowner...dissolves the connection between landownership and the land
so thoroughly that the landowner may spend his whole life in Constantinople, while his
estates lie in Scotland...discarding all its former political and social embellishments and
associations...which are denounced...as useless and absurd superfluities by the industrial
capitalists themselves.... The rationalising of agriculture...which makes it for the first
time capable of operating on a social scale, and the reduction *ad absurdum* of property in
land...are the great achievements of the capitalist mode of production" (Marx 1971a:
617–618).

35   "Here, in small-scale agriculture, the price of land, a form and result of private landownership, appears as a barrier to production itself. In large-scale agriculture, and large
estates operating on a capitalist basis, ownership likewise acts as a barrier, because it
limits the tenant farmer in his productive investment of capital, which in the final analysis benefits not him, but the landlord. In both forms, exploitation and squandering of the
vitality of the soil (apart from making exploitation dependent upon the accidental and
unequal circumstances of individual producers rather than the attained level of social
development) takes the place of conscious rational cultivation of the soil as eternal communal property, an inalienable condition for the existence and reproduction of a chain of
successive generations of the human race. In the case of small property, this results from
the lack of means and knowledge of applying the social labour productivity. In the case of
large property, it results from the exploitation of such means for the most rapid enrichment of farmer and proprietor. In the case of both through dependence on the market-
price" (Marx 1971a: 812).

36   "This form of free self-managing peasant proprietorship of land parcels as the prevailing,
normal form...is found among modern nations as one of the forms arising from the dissolution of feudal land ownership. Thus, the yeomanry in England, the peasantry in Sweden, the French and West German peasants. We do not include colonies here, since the
independent peasant there develops under different conditions.... It is a necessary transi-
tional stage for the development of agriculture itself. The causes which bring about its
downfall show its limitations. These are: Destruction of rural domestic industry, which

Thus abolished was the economic relationship at the basis of the natural economy in all systems, up to and including feudalism, alienating humans from this connection to their natural conditions.[37]

3.5.3   The Creation of Free Wage-Laborers and the Transition to Capitalism

As an ascendant ruling class, capitalists extracted land and profits from feudal lords via monopoly pricing and usury.[38] Thus began the "invasion of agriculture

---

forms its normal supplement as a result of the development of large-scale industry; a gradual impoverishment and exhaustion of the soil subjected to this cultivation; usurpation by big landowners of the common lands, which constitute the second supplement of the management of land parcels everywhere and which alone enable it to raise cattle; competition, either of the plantation system or large-scale capitalist agriculture. Improvements in agriculture, which on the one hand cause a fall in agricultural prices and, on the other, require greater outlays and more extensive material conditions of production, also contribute towards this, as in England during the first half of the 18th century" (Marx 1971a: 806–807).

37   "In natural economy proper, when no part of the agricultural product, or but a very insignificant portion, enters into the process of circulation, and then only a relatively small portion of that part of the product which represents the landlord's revenue, as, e.g., in many Roman latifundia, or upon the villas of Charlemagne, or more or less during the entire Middle Ages (see Vinçard, *Histoire du travail*), the product and surplus-product of the large estates consists by no means purely of products of agricultural labour. It encompasses equally well the products of industrial labour. Domestic handicrafts and manufacturing labour as secondary occupations of agriculture, which forms the basis, are the prerequisite of that mode of production upon which natural economy rests—in European antiquity and the Middle Ages as well as in the present-day Indian community, in which the traditional organisation has not yet been destroyed. The capitalist mode of production completely abolishes this relationship; a process which may be studied on a large scale particularly in England during the last third of the 18th century" (Marx 1971a: 786–787).

38   "In the period of the declining Middle Ages and rising capitalist production the rapid enrichment of the industrial capitalist is in part to be explained by the direct fleecing of the landlords. As the value of money fell, as a result of the discoveries in America, the farmers paid them nominally, but not really, the old rent, while the manufacturers sold them commodities above their value—not only on the basis of the higher value of money" (Marx 1969: 276–277). "The high rate of profit in the Middle Ages is not entirely due to the low composition of capital, in which the variable component invested in wages predominates. It is due to swindling on the land, the appropriation of a portion of the landlord's rent and of the income of his vassals. If the country-side exploits the town politically in the Middle Ages, wherever feudalism has not been broken down by exceptional urban development—as in Italy, the town, on the other hand, exploits the land economically everywhere and without exception, through its monopoly prices, its system of taxation, its guild organisation, its direct commercial fraudulence and its usury" (Marx 1971a: 800–801).

by the capitalist mode of production" and the "transformation of independently producing peasants into wage-workers" (Marx 1971a: 650). While part of this process involved "impoverishing the direct producers" (Marx 1971a: 618), it required turning serfs into wage-laborers rather than slaves because "so long as slavery is predominant, the capitalist relationship can only be sporadic and subordinate, never dominant" (Marx 1971b: 419). The comparison to Rome is instructive. Both feudal serfs and Roman plebeians were "deprived of everything," but the former occurred in the midst of not only "large landownership but also in large-scale money capitalism" and the latter did not. As a result, Roman plebeians became an "idle mob," with some turned into slaves, while feudal serfs became wage-workers (Marx [1877] 1979: 321).

3.5.4   Colonialism and the Transition to Capitalism

Though pre-capitalist agricultural communities and home industry present "obstacles" to capitalist development, "the corrosive influence of commerce," the "low prices of its goods," and capitalism's "big industries" destroy these "very gradually," e.g., the English in China and India (Marx 1971a: 333–334). The colonial system further bolstered capitalist development through the discovery of gold and silver in America, enslavement and conquest of original peoples and their lands, and extraction of resources (and people) from the East Indies and Africa. These colonial developments and their protagonists were "the chief momenta of primitive accumulation," "with the globe as their theatre," and "more or less in chronological order...Spain, Portugal, Holland, France, and England" (Marx [1867] 1992b: 703). This historical "expropriation of the mass of the people from the soil [formed] the basis of the capitalist mode of production" (Marx [1867] 1992b: 719).

3.6   *The Capitalist Mode of Production*

"A greater number of labourers working together, at the same time, in one place...in order to produce the same sort of commodity under the mastership of one capitalist, constitutes, both historically and logically, the starting-point of capitalist production" (Marx [1867] 1992b: 305). The capitalist, as "the owner of the conditions of labour," "can undertake the process of exploiting labour" because "the labourer [is] the owner of only labour-power" (Marx 1971a: 41) and not "the land he cultivates nor the tools with which he works" (Marx 1971b: 530). Instead, "the means of production transformed into capital" are "monopolised by a certain section of society" and confront "living labour-power as products and working conditions" (Marx 1971a: 814–815). With the transformation of feudalism into capitalism, land becomes private property, "an idea

[that] could only spring up in a bourgeois society already well-developed" (Marx [1867] 1992b: 92).³⁹

In this transformation, "the capitalist...has taken charge of agriculture just as he has of industry, and has *excluded* the *landowner* from any direct participation in the production process" (Marx 1968: 153; emphases in the original). Capitalism's division of labor transforms manufacture "by combining different handicrafts together under the control of a single capitalist" and, with a "greater number of workmen simultaneously employed by one...individual capital," capital transforms production into "Modern Industry" in "its most highly developed form...in a factory" (Marx [1867] 1992b: 319, 305, 372). Here, a new type of machinery "supersedes the workman," is "able to drive many machines at once," and "becomes a wide-spreading apparatus" with the laborer "a mere appendage" (Marx [1867] 1992b: 355, 357, 364).⁴⁰ With growth in the number of inventions, the "division of labour in these manufactures was more and more developed," a transformation in technological complexity, speed, enormity, and efficiency that further opened up world-markets, often by colonial

---

39   "As James Mill observes, production could therefore continue undisturbed if the landed
      proprietor disappeared and the state took his place. He—the private landowner—is not
      a necessary agent for capitalist production, although it does require that the land should
      belong to someone, so long as it is not the worker, but for instance the state. Far from be-
      ing an error on the part of Ricardo, etc., this reduction of the classes participating directly
      in production, hence also in the value produced and then in the products in which this
      value is embodied, to *capitalists and wage-labourers*, and the *exclusion of landowners*
      (who only enter *post festum*, as a result of conditions of ownership of natural forces that
      have *not grown out* of the capitalist mode of production but have been *passed on* to it) is
      rooted in the nature of the *capitalist mode of production*—as distinct from the feudal,
      ancient, etc. This reduction is an adequate theoretical expression of the capitalist mode
      of production, and reveals its *differentia specifica*.... From the standpoint of capitalist pro-
      duction, *capital property* does in fact appear as the 'original' because capitalist production
      is based on this sort of property and it is a factor of and fulfils a function of *capitalist
      production*; this does not hold good of landed property. The latter *appears* as derivative,
      because modern landed property is in fact *feudal* property, but transformed by the action
      of capital upon it; in its form as modern landed property it is therefore *derived from*, and
      the result of capitalist production" (Marx 1968: 152–153; emphases in the original).
40   "The tool or working machine is that part of the machinery with which the industrial
      revolution of the 18th century started. And to this day it constantly serves as such a start-
      ing-point, whenever a handicraft, or a manufacture, is turned into an industry carried on
      by machinery...under very altered forms, the apparatus and tools used by the handicrafts-
      man or the manufacturing workman; with this difference, that instead of being human
      implements, they are the implements of the mechanism, or mechanical implements"
      (Marx [1867] 1992b: 353).

conquests that increased "gigantically during the infancy of Modern Industry" (Marx [1867] 1992b: 361, 708–709).[41]

In ancient society, commerce and merchant's capital facilitated a slave economy; in modernity, these forces helped bring about the capitalist mode of production, especially as they encouraged commodity production.[42] Compared to previous systems, capitalist production is based on the exploitation of wage-labor in the production of commodities that are sold for a profit, where

---

41   "But more especially, the revolution in modes of production of industry and agriculture made necessary a revolution in the general conditions of the social process of production, i.e., in the means of communication and of transport. In a society whose pivot, to use an expression of Fourier, was agriculture on a small scale, with its subsidiary of domestic industries, and the urban handicrafts, the means of communication and transport were so utterly inadequate to the productive requirements of the manufacturing period, with its extended division of labour, its concentration of the instruments of labour, and of the workmen, and its colonial markets, that they became in fact revolutionised. In the same way the means of communication and transport handed down from the manufacturing period soon became unbearable trammels on Modern Industry, with its feverish haste of production, its enormous extent, its constant flinging of capital and labour from one sphere into another, and its newly-created connexions with the markets of the whole world" (Marx [1867] 1992b: 362–363). "On the one hand, the immediate effect of the machinery is to increase the supply of raw material in the same way, for example, as the cotton gin augmented the production of cotton. On the other hand, the cheapness of the articles produced by machinery, and the improved means of transport and communication furnish the weapons for conquering foreign markets. By ruining handicraft production in other countries, machinery forcibly converts them into fields for the supply of its raw material. In this way, East India was compelled to produce cotton, wool, hemp, jute, and indigo for Great Britain. By constantly making a part of the hands 'supernumerary,' modern industry, in all countries where it has taken root, gives a spur to emigration and to the colonisation of foreign lands, which are thereby converted into the settlements for growing raw material of the mother country; just as Australia, for example, was converted into a colony for growing wool" (Marx [1867] 1992b: 424–425). "During its first stages of development, industrial capital seeks to secure a market and markets by force, by the colonial system (together with the prohibition system). The industrial capitalist faces the world-market; [he] therefore compares and must constantly compare his own cost-price with market prices not only at home, but also on the whole market of the world. He always produces taking this into account. In the earlier period this comparison is carried out only by the merchants, thus enabling merchant capital to dominate over productive [capital]" (Marx 1971b: 470).

42   "In the ancient world the effect of commerce and the development of merchant's capital always resulted in a slave economy; depending on the point of departure, only in the transformation of patriarchal slave system devoted to the production of immediate means of subsistence into one devoted to the production of surplus-value. However, in the modern world, it results in the capitalist mode of production. It follows therefrom that these results spring in themselves from circumstances other than the development of merchant's capital" (Marx 1971a: 332).

such profits are reinvested back into the production process, features that make capitalist production "a particular species of social production" (Marx [1867] 1992b: 85, note 1). In comparison to other systems, the "purpose of capitalist production, however, is self-expansion of capital, *i.e.*, appropriation of surplus-labour, production of surplus-value, of profit" "and the reconversion of a portion of it into capital"—this is "the immediate purpose and compelling motive of capitalist production," i.e., its "specific character" (Marx 1971a: 251, 243–244). With this subject of production, the capitalist is "indifferent" to use-value or social needs but "is only concerned with producing surplus-value" and "realising as much surplus-value, or profit...as any other capital of the same magnitude...at prices which yield the average profit" (Marx 1971a: 195).

This "distinctive feature" of capital accumulation is "the direct aim and determining motive of production" and results in "a special form of development of the social productive powers" "peculiar to the capitalist period" (Marx 1971a: 880–881), which is a "continuous process" (Marx 1971b: 272). While slavery, serf-dom, and capitalism all presuppose "surplus-labour in general" and the "complete idleness of a stratum of society," capitalism's "civilizing aspects" result from how it "enforces surplus-labour" in a way that leads to "the development of the productive forces [and] social relations," "making it possible in a higher form of society to combine this surplus-labour with a greater reduction of time devoted to material labour in general" (Marx 1971a: 819).

In other class systems, where appropriation came in the form of slavery, rent, and usury and "all labour in part still pays itself (like for example the agricultural labour of the serfs) and in part is directly exchanged for revenue (like the manufacturing labour in the cities of Asia), no capital and no wage-labour exists in the sense of bourgeois political economy" (Marx [1963] 1969: 157). With capitalism and wage-labor established, usury spurs on further development of the productive forces—e.g., larger, more centralized workshops, development of technology, etc.—but "usury can no longer separate the producer from his means of production, for they have already been separated" (Marx 1971a: 596).[43] As a class system reliant on this exploitation of laborers separated from the means of production, in wage-labor just as in slavery,

---

43   "Under the developed capitalist mode of production, the labourer is not the owner of the means of production, i.e., the field which he cultivates, the raw materials which he processes, etc. But under this system separation of the producer from the means of production reflects an actual revolution in the mode of production itself. The isolated labourers are brought together in large workshops for the purpose of carrying out separate but interconnected activities; the tool becomes a machine. The mode of production itself no longer permits the dispersion of the instruments of production associated with small property; nor does it permit the isolation of the labourer himself. Under the capitalist

"surplus-value exists as surplus-product. Surplus-labour in general, as labour performed over and above the given requirements, must always remain" (Marx 1971a: 819). In both slavery and capitalism, the owner of the means of production provides the laborer a portion of labor's product previously produced in the form of subsistence (in the former) and wages (in the latter), which are not things *advanced* to the worker (see Marx 1971b: 93).[44] However, in capitalism, the wage paid across working-hours disguises unpaid labor, whereas in feudalism and slavery a clear distinction exists between labor that is or is not compensated (more below).

While the use of large-scale cooperation "in ancient times, in the middle ages, and in modern colonies" often led to slavery (Marx [1867] 1992b: 316), "[w]age-labour on a national scale—and consequently, the capitalist mode of production as well—is only possible where the workers are personally free" (Marx 1971b: 431).[45] Free labor here means several things. First, workers are not tied to land nor are they owned as "slaves, bondsmen, &c, nor do the means of production belong to them, as in the case of peasant proprietors; they are, therefore, free from, unencumbered by, any means of production of their own" (Marx [1867] 1992b: 668). Second, unlike a feudal serf tied to the land, they are "free" to search for employers to whom they sell their labor-power. Here, labor is not forced via legal threats of violence but is, instead, forced by economic circumstance—for one, private ownership of the means of production that divorces laborers from the right to access those means and, for another, the commodification of the means of subsistence and of labor-power. Should the laborer not sell their labor-power to the capitalist, they risk starvation, homelessness, even death.[46] As a result, wage-labor "in essence…always remains

---

mode of production usury can no longer separate the producer from his means of production, for they have already been separated" (Marx 1971a: 596).

44 Also see Chapter 3, note 10.

45 "The sporadic application of co-operation on a large scale in ancient times, in the middle ages, and in modern colonies, reposes on relations of dominion and servitude, principally on slavery. The capitalistic form, on the contrary, pre-supposes from first to last, the free wage-labourer, who sells his labour-power to capital. Historically, however, this form is developed in opposition to peasant agriculture and to the carrying on of independent handicrafts whether in guilds or not. From the standpoint of these, capitalistic co-operation does not manifest itself as a particular historical form of co-operation, but co-operation itself appears to be a historical form peculiar to, and specifically distinguishing, the capitalist process of production" (Marx [1867] 1992b: 316).

46 "Furthermore, already implicit in the commodity, and even more so in the commodity as a product of capital, is the materialisation of the social features of production and the personification of the material foundations of production, which characterises the entire capitalist mode of production" (Marx 1971a: 880).

forced labour—no matter how much it may seem to result from free contractual agreement" (Marx 1971a: 819).

In feudalism's corvée, unforced labor versus forced uncompensated labor
"differ in space and time in the clearest possible way," while "[a]ll the slave's
labour appears as unpaid labour. In wage-labour, on the contrary, even surplus-
labour, or unpaid labour, appears as paid," as capitalism's "wage-form…extin-
guishes every trace of the division of the working-day into necessary labour
and surplus-labour, into paid and unpaid labour" (Marx [1867] 1992b: 505).[47]
The "antithesis between the owner of means of production and the owner of
mere labour-power" results in the "servitude of the direct producers" under
"management and supervision" (Marx 1971a: 385) rather than "political or theocratic rulers as under earlier modes of production" (Marx 1971a: 881).[48] The
goal of (at least) an average profit rate influences levels of surplus-value extraction, where, despite technology's potential for "shortening labour-time," extracting surplus-value "for the purpose of expanding the value of his capital"
"becomes the most unfailing means for placing every moment of the labourer's
time and that of his family, at the disposal of the capitalist" (Marx [1867] 1992b:
384).[49] In colonial domains, landowners from "a conquering commercial

---

47   "We see, further: The value of 3s by which a part only of the working-day—i.e., 6 hours'
      labour—is paid for, appears as the value or price of the whole working-day of 12 hours,
      which thus includes 6 hours unpaid for. The wage form thus extinguishes every trace of
      the division of the working-day into necessary labour and surplus labour, into paid and
      unpaid labour. All labour appears as paid labour. In the corvée, the labour of the worker
      for himself, and his compulsory labour for his lord, differ in space and time in the clearest
      possible way. In slave labour, even that part of the working-day in which the slave is only
      replacing the value of his own means of existence, in which, therefore, in fact, he works
      for himself alone, appears as labour for his master. All the slave's labour appears as unpaid
      labour. In wage-labour, on the contrary, even surplus-labour, or unpaid labour, appears as
      paid. There the property-relation conceals the labour of the slave for himself; here the
      money-relation conceals the unrequited labour of the wage-labourer" (Marx [1867] 1992b:
      505).
48   "Whereas, on the basis of capitalist production, the mass of direct producers is confront-
      ed by the social character of their production in the form of strictly regulating authority
      and a social mechanism of the labour-process organised as a complete hierarchy—this
      authority reaching its bearers, however, only as the personification of the conditions of
      labour in contrast to labour, and not as political or theocratic rulers as under earlier
      modes of production—among the bearers of this authority, the capitalists themselves,
      who confront one another only as commodity-owners, there reigns complete anarchy
      within which the social interrelations of production assert themselves only as an over-
      whelming natural law in relation to individual free will" (Marx 1971a: 881).
49   "Hence that remarkable phenomenon in the history of Modern Industry, that machin-
      ery sweeps away every moral and natural restriction on the length of the working-day.
      Hence, too, the economic paradox, that the most powerful instrument for shortening

nation" can reduce laborers to a "minimum means of subsistence...e.g., the English in India" (Marx 1971a: 796).

The capitalist mode of production transforms previous forms of surplus-value appropriation into its own "special forms—rent, interest of money and industrial profit" (Marx 1971b: 254). In this transformation of all value-forms into commodities, free exchange relations in a competitive market regulate prices. The "ideal average" of market forces operates in conjunction with "the world-market, its conjunctures, movements of market-prices, periods of credit, industrial and commercial cycles, alternations of prosperity and crisis," movements that "appear [to the capitalist] as overwhelming natural laws that irresistibly enforce their will over them, and confront them as blind necessity" (Marx 1971a: 831). "The capitalist system of production, in fact, has this feature—[i.e., that production is not subject to social control]—in common with former systems of production, in so far as they are based on trade in commodities and private exchange" (Marx 1971a: 574). As the social role of markets increases, the capitalist mode of production moves a step further away from active, rational control, where "[i]n the pre-capitalist stages of society commerce ruled industry. In modern society the reverse is true" (Marx 1971a: 330).[50]

In addition to local exchange and intermediate regional trade, one of the "cardinal facts of capitalist production" is the "[c]reation of the world-market," which "itself forms the basis for this mode of production" (Marx 1971a: 266, 333) as a whole. The growth of commodity production "is intrinsically bound up with the expansion of the market, the creation of the world-market, and therefore foreign trade," though with such expansion "it is forced to produce on a scale which has nothing to do with the immediate demand but depends on a constant expansion of the world-market" (Marx 1968: 423, 468). Given capitalism's drive for accumulation and patterns of reinvestment, this search for profit forms "the basis of modern over-production" and leads to "general crises of the world-market, arising out of the production process itself," as this system tends towards over-production of goods and an "over-production of capital" (Marx 1968: 528, 497; also see note 20).

---

labour-time, becomes the most unfailing means for placing every moment of the labourer's time and that of his family, at the disposal of the capitalist for the purpose of expanding the value of his capital" (Marx [1867] 1992b: 384).

50 "Among the effects of the gold drain, then, the fact that production as social production is not really subject to social control, is strikingly emphasised by the existence of the social form of wealth as a thing external to it. The capitalist system of production, in fact, has this feature in common with former systems of production, in so far as they are based on trade in commodities and private exchange" (Marx 1971a: 574).

TABLE 2.13   From common productive relations and economic processes to the capitalist
mode of production

The general abstract	The specific abstract	The general concrete	The specific concrete
Productive relations and economic processes across modes of production	Class relations	Appropriators (capitalists) Laborers (wage-laborers)	England, America, Venice, Portugal, Holland, France
	Property relations	Private ownership of means of production Laborers dispossessed of means of production (free labor)	
	Subject of production	Surplus-value and capital accumulation	
	Terms of labor	Legally unforced Forced by market conditions	
	Forms of surplus-value appropriation	Rent, money-interest, wage-labor	
	Role of exchange and trade	Market regulation of exchange Trade on world-market	
	Social development of productive forces	Complex and constant development Mass agriculture, manufacture, modern industry	

SOURCE: CREATED BY AUTHOR

4   Discussion

In the above observations, we see how Marx isolates variables, builds models
for and compares modes of production, and identifies capitalism as a *differentia specifica*. He abstracts from production in general (Table 2.14, Column A,
below), examines specific historical data (Column D), differentiates non-class
versus class systems (Column B), and from there constructs models of modes

TABLE 2.14   From production in general to modes of production to specific societies

The general abstract (A)	The specific abstract (B)	The general concrete (C)	The specific concrete (D)
Production in general	Non-class systems	Primitive communism	Earliest societies, nomads, tribes, primitive Indian communities, Peruvians, communities in Rome, Russia, Slovenia, Asia
	Class systems	Ancient society	Egypt, Greece, Rome, Carthage
		Asiatic modes	India, China, Japan, East Indies
		Feudalism	Middle Ages, England in 16th century, Romania (Danubian principalities), Poland, Germany, France, Sweden
		Capitalism	Venice, England, Portugal, Holland, France, America

SOURCE: CREATED BY AUTHOR

of production (Column C) based on their class structure (including class relations and property relations), terms of labor, subject of production, forms of appropriation, the role of exchange and trade, and the social development of productive forces. This process of re-abstracting conceivably can (and should) occur again.[51]

Below we can see an overview of Marx's successive abstractions in his identification of modes of production. In Figure 2.1a (far left table), we see society

---

[51]   For instance, after using a variable in a specific concrete category (e.g., the social development of productive forces) it could next be treated in the general abstract, its general concrete types (i.e., hunting-gathering, animal husbandry, agriculture, handicrafts, manufacture, industry) treated as specific concrete categories, and forms of each (i.e., large-scale industry) treated as general concrete examples, while new and very specific analyses are provided for them (e.g., specific cultures, industries, histories, policies, statistics, and etc.). Should one look into Marx's volumes of *Capital*, they would find just this, though space requirements here disallow a detailed elaboration.

Phase III

	The general	The specific
The abstract	Modes of production	Non-class systems
The concrete	Primitive communism	No classes, common property, production for use-value, unforced labor, etc.

	The general	The specific
The abstract	Modes of production	Class systems
The concrete	Ancient society	Patricians, slaves, serfs, landed property, laborers own their own means of production, mixed labor, etc.

	The general	The specific
The abstract	Modes of production	Class systems
The concrete	Asiatic mode	Despots, landlords, the state, serfs, slaves, mixed labor forms, stagnant development, etc.

	The general	The specific
The abstract	Modes of production	Class systems
The concrete	Feudalism	Landed property, peasants, serfs, mixed labor forms, rent, trade, moderate development, etc.

	The general	The specific
The abstract	Modes of production	Class systems
The concrete	Capitalism	Capitalists, wage-laborers, private ownership of means of production, legally unforced labor, world-market, complex development, etc.

Phase II

	The general	The specific
The abstract	Production in general	Modes of production
The concrete	Non-class systems	Primitive communism

	The general	The specific
The abstract	Production in general	Modes of production
The concrete	Class systems	Ancient society, Asiatic mode, Feudalism, Capitalism

Phase I

	The general	The specific
The abstract	Society in general	Production in general
The concrete	Modes of production	Non-class systems, class systems

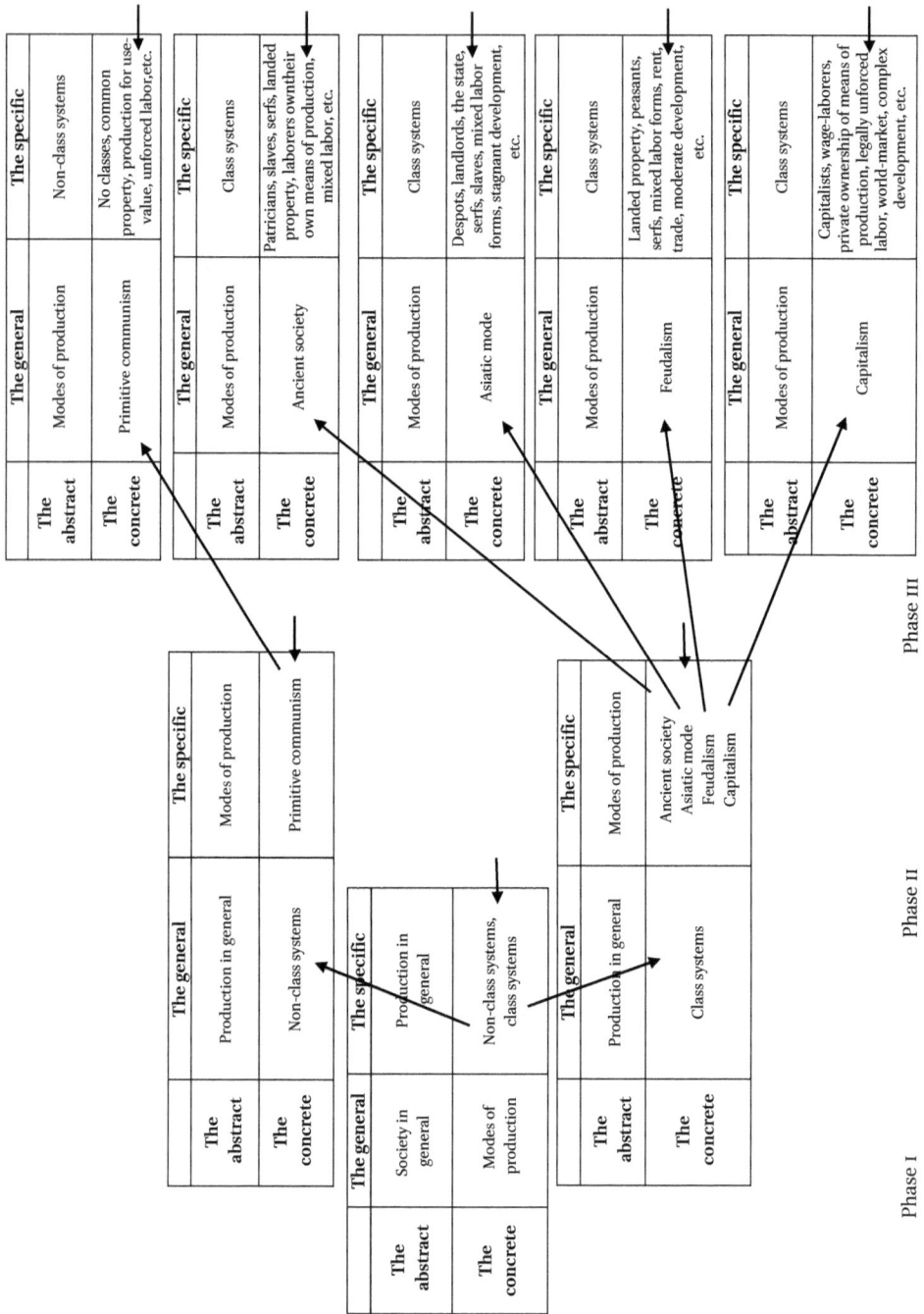

FIGURE 2.1A   Modes of production via successive abstractions (1)

Phase IV

Primitive communism

	The general	The specific
The abstract	Non-class systems	Primitive communism
The concrete	No classes, common property, production for use-value, unforced labor, etc.	Tribes, nomads, primitive Indian communities, etc.

	The general	The specific
The abstract	Class systems	Ancient society
The concrete	Patricians, slaves, serfs, landed property, laborers own their own means of production, mixed labor, etc.	Greece, Rome, Egypt, Carthage

	The general	The specific
The abstract	Class systems	Asiatic mode
The concrete	Despots, landlords, the state, serfs, slaves, mixed labor forms, stagnant development, etc.	India, China, Japan, East Indies

	The general	The specific
The abstract	Class systems	Feudalism
The concrete	Landed property, peasants, serfs, mixed labor forms, rent, trade, moderate development, etc.	Middle Ages, England in 16th century, Romania, Poland, etc.

	The general	The specific
The abstract	Class systems	Capitalism
The concrete	Capitalists, wage-laborers, private ownership of means of production, legally unforced labor, world-market, complex development, etc.	England, America, Venice, Portugal, Holland, etc.

Phase III (from previous page)

	The general	The specific
The abstract	Modes of production	Non-class systems
The concrete	Primitive communism	No classes, common property, production for use-value, unforced labor, etc.

	The general	The specific
The abstract	Modes of production	Class systems
The concrete	Ancient society	Patricians, slaves, serfs, landed property, laborers own their own means of production, mixed labor, etc.

	The general	The specific
The abstract	Modes of production	Class systems
The concrete	Asiatic mode	Despots, landlords, the state, serfs, slaves, mixed labor, stagnant development, etc.

	The general	The specific
The abstract	Modes of production	Class systems
The concrete	Feudalism	Landed property, peasants, serfs, mixed labor, trade, moderate development, etc.

	The general	The specific
The abstract	Modes of production	Class systems
The concrete	Capitalism	Capitalists, wage-laborers, private ownership of means of production, legally unforced labor, world-market, complex development, etc.

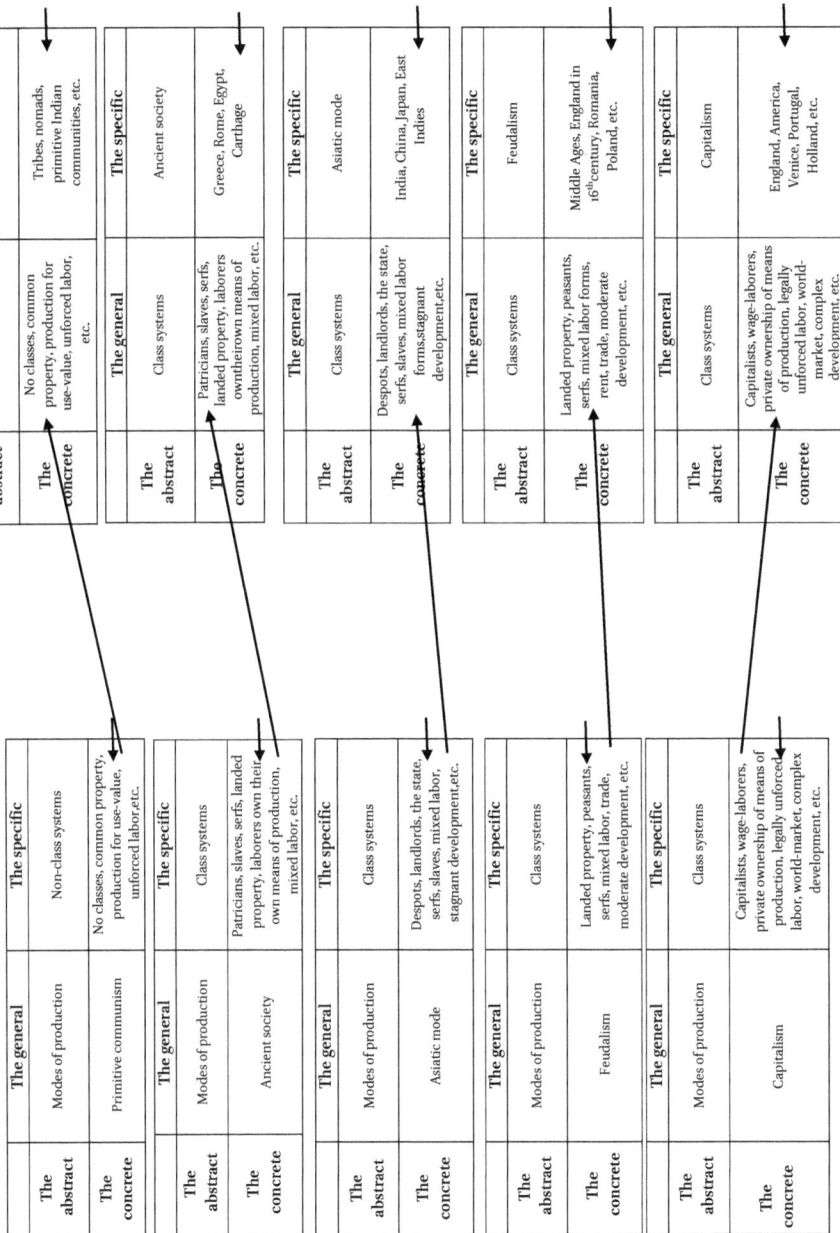

FIGURE 2.1B   Modes of production via successive abstractions (II)

SOURCE: CREATED BY AUTHOR

in general as the broad starting-point, out of which he abstracts production in general, with which he identifies modes of production in the general concrete and non-class and class systems more specifically. When treating production in the general abstract (Figure 2.1a, middle two tables), production "modes" become a specific abstract extension of that idea, represented by non-class (primitive communism) and class systems (ancient, Asiatic, feudal, and capitalist modes). Moving modes of production into the general abstract pulls the other categories along behind. In this movement, non-class and class systems as specific abstract categories are abstracted apart from one another as external model sets based on the configuration of specific concrete variables—productive relations and economic processes—that represent different modes of production in the general concrete (Figure 2.1a, far right five tables). Finally, from here, Marx treats non-class and class systems in the general abstract, where each mode of production becomes a specific abstract category, and the variables for each are general concrete identifiers that connect with specific concrete societies (Figure 2.1b, right five tables). Not shown here would be the next logical act of abstraction, where one treats each mode of production in the general abstract—pulling the other categories through the model—and examines new and more specific events, details, cases, and so on in the specific concrete (a topic picked up in the next chapter).

Table 2.15 summarizes both Marx's finalized taxonomic scheme and how the variations within its categories identify different modes of production, a view that gives us a better understanding of the theoretical and empirical justifications for the models upon which he settled.

Looking for a singular taxonomic criterion in Marx's work foists upon him assumptions that are too simple and thus unrealistic for economic formations.

TABLE 2.15   Marx's taxonomy of modes of production

Variables	Primitive communism	Ancient society	Asiatic modes	Feudalism	Capitalism
Appropriating class	None	Upper castes, patricians	The state, despots, landlords	Landowners	Capitalists
Laboring class	Everyone	plebeians, peasants, slaves	Peasants, serfs, slaves	Artisans/craftsmen, peasants, serfs*	Wage-laborers*

Variables	Primitive communism	Ancient society	Asiatic modes	Feudalism	Capitalism
Property relations	Means of production held in common	Landed property	Landed property	Landed property	Private ownership of means of production
		Laborers own their own means of production	Mix of state ownership and land owned in common	Laborers own their own means of production	Laborers dispossessed of means of production
Subject of production	Use-value (subsistence), surplus-value (social fund, exchange)	Use-value (subsistence), exchange-value (hoarding), surplus-value (social fund, exchange, trade)	Use-value (subsistence), exchange-value (hoarding), surplus-value (social fund, exchange)	Use-value (subsistence), exchange-value (hoarding), surplus-value (social fund, exchange, trade)	Surplus-value and capital accumulation
Terms of labor	Non-forced	Mix of independent and forced	Mix of independent and forced	Mix of independent and forced	Legally unforced, forced by market conditions
Form of surplus-value appropriation	None	Slavery, rent, taxes, usury	Slavery, rent, taxes, usury	Rent, taxes, usury	Rent, money-interest, wage-labor
Role of exchange and trade	Exchange of surplus with external communities when available	Some exchange, trade as intermediaries between nations	Some exchange, trade not emphasized	Some exchange, proto-national trade	Market regulation of prices and production, Trade on world-market

TABLE 2.15   Marx's taxonomy of modes of production (*cont.*)

Variables	Primitive communism	Ancient society	Asiatic modes	Feudalism	Capitalism
Social development of productive forces	Simple technology, hunting, gathering, animal husbandry, agriculture	Agriculture, domestic industry and handicrafts	Agriculture, domestic industry and handicrafts	Agriculture, domestic handicrafts, guilds and manufacture, modern industry	Mass agriculture, manufacturing workshops, modern industry
	Stability, low stage of development	Uneven development	Stability, stagnation	Slow development	Constant and complex development

SOURCE: CREATED BY AUTHOR

This is not Marx's fault. History's social structures, not neat and tidy, are too complex for a classification scheme built upon reductive criteria. But if, as we saw Marx earlier assert, some determinants belong to all epochs, others only a few, and others will be shared by the most modern epoch and the most ancient, then *selectively* isolating *just one* of Marx's criteria produces several different and incompatible taxonomies:

- Isolating *technology* (which Marx interiorizes into the social development of productive forces) produces hunter-gatherers, simple agriculture (including husbandry), handicrafts, mass agriculture, manufacture, and industry, a model similar to Lenski's (see Lenski, Nolan, and Lenski 1970).
- Using the *terms of labor* results in legally non-forced labor systems (primitive communism and capitalism) and legally forced labor systems (ancient society, Asiatic modes, and feudalism).
- Using *class structure* produces common property (primitive communism), landed property (ancient, Asiatic, and feudal modes), and private property (capitalism) systems.
- Choosing *methods of appropriation* results in non-appropriating (primitive communism), slave-rentier (ancient society, Asiatic modes), rentier (feudalism), and wage-labor (capitalism) systems.

Each of these approaches either leaves out essential traits—e.g., using only technology omits class structure and surplus-value appropriation—lumps together modes that are more different than similar—e.g., primitive communism and capitalism—or lumps when additional splitting is needed—e.g., combining ancient, Asiatic, and feudal modes into one category overlooks the lack of slavery structured into feudal society and omits the state as an appropriator in Asiatic systems.

Sometimes Marx's analysis uses just one or two of these vantage points. For example, his use of "agriculture" highlights technology and his use of "slavery" highlights a type of surplus-value appropriation. While technology combined with a division of labor relates to whether agriculture is simple or mass in form, technology and slavery are relatively unrelated (but not always—e.g., with both slaves and technology commodified, as would be the case in capitalism, a situation could arise where purchasing machinery is more cost effective than purchasing a workforce of slaves). Just as agriculture exists across a variety of labor-terms, slavery exists in more than one property system. Though Marx *seems* to discuss slavery and agriculture as modes of production, this is only apparent. Certain characteristics must be in place before Marx applies his concept of "mode of production" and neither slavery nor agriculture fit the *full complement* of those characteristics. As a result, we never find Marx using the term "mode of production" for either agriculture or slavery—nor for serfdom, handicrafts, manufacture, or industry, for that matter. In *Capital*, the consistency with which Marx applied his model of "modes of production" is evidence of the mental clarity he had of it and the conceptual precision with which he used it.

Constructing each mode on its classes (or lack thereof), the property relations at the basis of that class structure (or the lack thereof), the terms of labor, the subject of production, forms of surplus-value appropriation (or lack thereof), the role of exchange and trade, and the social development of productive forces has several methodological and theoretical advantages. First, Marx's variables provide a more complete set of taxonomic criteria and thus could be used to categorize societies he left under-theorized—e.g., the cultures, tribes, city-states of the Americas, including Mesoamerica and South America—recently extinct production systems—such as the Soviet Union—newly discovered ones, and/or even those emergent after capitalism.

Second, Marx's are sort of living-breathing models that can be adapted to new historical and/or scientific developments, as they are *comparative* models and not indemonstrable *universal linear-evolutionary* ones, a claim he never makes and which would leave the Asiatic mode unaccounted for or anomalous.[52] As a tool for comparative analysis, once we have a handle on the general

---

52 In Stalinist Russia, a rigid and doctrinaire reading of Marx's Preface to *A Contribution to the Critique of Political Economy* emerged that depicted his categories as a universal and linear progression of production forms that each society would inherently go through

model, if we cannot imagine any other *structural* criteria that work as variables across modes of production, then we must declare his model satisfactory.[53] If we *can* find criteria that Marx left out, then his general model stands as the starting-point to which we can add new variables and examine them for how they interact with those he has already established.

Third, his taxonomic criteria are both descriptive traits and *explanatory variables*. As explanatory variables, Marx's comparative analysis helps him identify their causal effects within and between systems. Take usury, for example. Usury requires the development of a money-form (which emerges with generalized exchange) but only becomes systemic with the development of merchant's capital, itself made possible because of hoarding. Usury's presence and effects are, therefore, variable across different modes of production. It is not operative in primitive communism, while in ancient, Asiatic, and feudal modes it has a destructive effect on landowners and tends to drive laborers further into debt, often leading to their enslavement and/or social stagnation. Further, merchant's capital results in the trade in slaves, further institutionalizing slavery into these prior modes of production. In capitalism, on the other hand, usury enriches the appropriator class instead of ruining them, encourages development of productive forces, while, like in other systems, it leads to debt among laboring classes and drives wage-labor down to levels that increasingly resemble the forced labor of slavery—thus the popular culture terminology of "wage-slavery." Like all the variables we have seen Marx address in this chapter, then, we could construct a model that displays the causal effects of usury depending on the systemic set of interrelations in which we find it (Tables 2.16–2.20).

Fourth, the method of successive abstractions helps reveal what often remains hidden within the capitalist system. Using abstractions carved from the

---

because of history's inexorable logic. Though Marx never claimed such a thing, nor can such an interpretive model be extracted from his writings in *Capital*, this idea was attractive to Soviet ideologues in that they could place (their version of) socialism as the natural historical progression after capitalism. Not only was this quite a metaphysical argument for an officially atheist doctrine but, moreover, this misinterpretation of Marx's Preface as a universal model left the Asiatic mode anomalous, as it did not seem to fit into a step-by-step linear path from primitive communism to ancient society to feudalism to capitalism. Even outside of Soviet influence, interpreting Marx as making a universal historical claim became a standard reading for many social scientists, Marxist and non-Marxist alike. Successful challenges to this interpretation have emerged within the last several years, even though it still makes its appearance in a variety of literature. It is in such ways that once a standard reading gets set, no matter if accurate or not, it can echo its way down through years and generations.

53   I return to this question in Chapter 7.

TABLE 2.16   The causal effects of usury in primitive communism

Mode of production	Economic relation or process: usury		
	Existence?	*Variables it interacts with*	*Causal effects*
Primitive communism	No	Primitive communism sets preconditions for merchant's capital (which is one precondition for usury): barter and exchange, simple circulation, early money-forms, proto-market development	

SOURCE: CREATED BY AUTHOR

TABLE 2.17   The causal effects of usury in the ancient mode of production

Mode of production	Economic relation or process: usury		
	Existence?	*Variables it interacts with*	*Causal effects*
Ancient mode	Yes	Preconditions: money-form, hoarding, merchant's capital Landed property Laborers own their own means of production Plebeian, serf, and slave labor	Undermines landowners Ruins small-peasant production Paralyzes productive forces Turns plebeians into slaves Rise of the mob

SOURCE: CREATED BY AUTHOR

vantage point of the terms of labor and their interrelations in prior systems puts Marx in position to highlight their unique nature in capitalism. In slavery and serfdom, labor is compulsory. In capitalism, people are "free" to move and to enter contracts, though the impersonal market, not law or custom, compels them to sell their labor-power at risk of personal well-being if failing to do so. In slavery, all of the laborer's efforts are at the bidding of the owner of the means of production, though the slave receives some subsistence product in return. In feudalism, serfs work certain days for the landlord, other days for themselves, and own their own means of production. In capitalism, it only

TABLE 2.18   The causal effects of usury in the Asiatic mode of production

Mode of production	Economic relation or process: usury		
	Existence?	*Variables it interacts with*	*Causal effects*
Asiatic mode	Yes	Preconditions: money-form, hoarding, merchant's capital Landed property The state Laborers own their own means of production Peasant, serf, and slave labor	Undermines landed property Political corruption Paralyzes productive forces Separates laborer from means of production Economic decay

SOURCE: CREATED BY AUTHOR

TABLE 2.19   The causal effects of usury in the feudal mode of production

Mode of production	Economic relation or process: usury		
	Existence?	*Variables it interacts with*	*Causal effects*
Feudalism	Yes	Preconditions: money-form, hoarding, merchant's capital Landed property Laborers own their own means of production Peasant and serf labor	Swindling of feudal landlords, decline of their political power Ruin of petite bourgeoisie and small-peasant production Paralyzes productive forces Separates laborer from means of production Transforms serfs into wage-laborers

SOURCE: CREATED BY AUTHOR

TABLE 2.20   The causal effects of usury in the capitalist mode of production

Mode of production	Economic relation or process: usury		
	Existence?	Variables it interacts with	Causal effects
Capitalism	Yes	Preconditions (from feudalism): free labor, world-market, increased social and scientific development Capitalism's conditions: rise of banking, lending, commodity production, and capital accumulation Commodification of land, subsistence, and the means of production	Profits for capitalist class Centralization of conditions of production Develops productive forces Impoverishes working class

SOURCE: CREATED BY AUTHOR

appears as if the laborer, already dispossessed of the means of production, gets compensated for each hour worked, though they produce, on average, more value per unit worked than is returned to them in wages.[54] Marx thus uncovers how capitalism shares labor exploitation with other class systems but in a form disguised by the capitalist system's structure, where it only seems as if labor is

---

54   "Let us take a peasant liable to do compulsory service for his lord. He works on his own land, with his own means of production, for, say, 3 days a week. The 3 other days he does forced work on the lord's domain. He constantly reproduces his own labour fund, which never, in his case, takes the form of a money payment for his labour, advanced by another person. But in return, his unpaid forced labour for the lord, on its side, never acquires the character of voluntary paid labour. If one fine morning the lord appropriates to himself the land, the cattle, the seed, in a word, the means of production of this peasant, the latter will thenceforth be obliged to sell his labour-power to the lord. He will, cæteris paribus, labour 6 days a week as before, 3 for himself, 3 for his lord, who thenceforth becomes a wages-paying capitalist. As before, he will use up the means of production as means of production, and transfer their value to the product. As before, a definite portion of the product will be devoted to reproduction. But from the moment that the forced labour is changed into wage-labour, from that moment the labour fund, which the peasant himself continues as before to produce and reproduce, takes the form of a capital advanced in the form of wages by the lord. The bourgeois economist whose narrow mind is unable to separate the form of appearance from the thing that appears, shuts his eyes to the fact, that it is but here and there on the face of the earth, that even nowadays the labour fund crops up in the form of capital" (Marx [1867] 1992b: 533–534).

unforced and all working-hours receive compensation. Workers forced to sell their labor this way are less likely to experience their conditions as servitude. Or, if they do perceive their servitude, they are less likely to interpret their problems as systemic in nature—though Marx's prediction of revolution is based on workers coming to this exact realization and organizing on its basis. This revealing of what normally remains hidden is part of the political fallout of a social science done well, i.e., it becomes critical in nature.

When it comes to evaluating any approach to modeling and the conclusions at which an analyst arrives, it is important to keep in mind Ollman's (2003: 74) observation that "[w]hat counts as an explanation is likewise determined by the framework of possible relationships imposed by Marx's initial abstractions." This principle holds for social scientists as a whole, not just Marx. For instance, it is common for sociologists to examine the modern world under the concept of "society" or, somewhat more accurately (though not entirely with the requisite precision) as "industrial society." Economists come closer to an adequate conceptualization when they model the modern world as a "market society." Both approaches, however, make the nature of "capital" disappear as modernity's central organizing mechanism. While many economists understand the modern world as a capitalist one and include capital in their models, they usually omit the "appropriation of surplus-value through exploitation of wage-labor" and the associated "class struggle" from their conceptualization of what makes capital and capitalism what they are. This is something that sociologists outside of Marx's tradition also often do.

Critics could likewise argue that Marx isolated the wrong variables, omitted others, or poorly matched his observations with misconceptualized models. This amounts to saying that Marx misapplied the method but it does not bear on the method itself. Using concrete observations to construct models and holding some variables constant while allowing others to vary and comparing the results in order to isolate causal mechanisms is the classic experimental model. Marx's approach and his resulting work, given the nature of the data he had available, sits somewhere between Einstein's mental experiments and Pasteur's laboratory. His unique contribution to scientific modeling for sociological inquiry comes from using successive abstractions to draw and redraw his categories at levels of specificity appropriate for his data while maintaining the needed degree of precision. By extension, combining both scientific procedures and dialectical sensibility provided Marx the ability to analyze variable interrelations and to further test their causal properties across real history—i.e., the free movement in empirical matter.

This method is not limited to the uses to which Marx put it, though, as we can employ it for wider sociological considerations. The next step is to demonstrate how to do so.

CHAPTER 3

Slavery, Capitalist Development, and the Method of Successive Abstractions

1   Introduction

The first two chapters established the method's overall form and demonstrated Marx's use of it. As it would be instructive to demonstrate its further application, this chapter discusses how to apply the method to investigations of both slavery and the history of capitalist development, while the following chapters address the study of religion. While these chapters do not engage in highly detailed empirical analyses, they provide some particulars for demonstrative purposes. Their modest goals are to provide models for such studies based on the first two chapters, to offer a few new methodological suggestions, and to make additional observations about this approach's overall utility.

2   Slavery and the Method of Successive Abstractions

Because of numerous similarities and differences in slavery's historical practice, we cannot understand it adequately with a singular model. We must analyze slavery at successive levels of generality fit for multiple structural contexts across this historicity—from society in general, to the features of class systems in general, to the features of specific class systems—while controlling variables and comparing models along the way.

Considered from the standpoint of value-producing labor (Table 3.1, Cell A) while disregarding its other characteristics, slave labor shares with all labor systems in all societies in general the production of use-value, exchange-value, and surplus-value (Cell B). Non-class and class systems alike (Cell C) need a certain amount of labor to produce basic subsistence plus an amount of added, or surplus, labor above this level for generational reproduction, the social fund, and additional products to use for exchange (Cell D). When combined, these laboring tasks—embedded in the natural economy—determine an amount of socially necessary labor-time.

In this first model set, what slavery shares with labor in general across history comes into view rather than characteristics associated with labor in any specific society or mode of production. A model carved at this level—even if

TABLE 3.1   Labor from production of value in general to labor's products across modes of production

	The general	The specific
The abstract	Labor in the production of value in general (A)	Production of use-value Production of exchange-value Production of surplus-value (B)
The concrete	Value-producing labor in non-class systems	Production of subsistence Social reproduction Production of exchangeable goods
	Value-producing labor in class systems (C)	Production of the social fund in primitive communism, ancient society, Asiatic modes, feudalism, capitalism (D)

SOURCE: CREATED BY AUTHOR

having the concrete labor of slaves (or serfs or peasants) as its data set—does not place the development of productive forces, the terms of labor, class appropriation of surplus-value—or the political relationships associated with these—within its abstractions. While this limits what such a model tells us, beginning here means that all subsequent re-abstractions in this pathway assume slavery *as a value producing labor system* prior to any other structurally specific traits or qualities it may acquire in historically particular times and places.

Inquiry next uses two analytical acts to train its focus on the essential and meaningful characteristics that make slave labor what it is. First, re-abstraction pushes surplus-value production from the specific abstract category in the previous model set (Table 3.1, Cell B) into the general abstract category (Table 3.2, Cell A). All subsequent re-abstractions in this pathway, therefore, focus on surplus-value production. Second, historical comparison reveals that surplus-value is not appropriated in some systems, while in other systems it is (Cell B), all of which are represented by real production modes in the general concrete (Cell C). Comparison between these systems reveals that, while labor in all modes of production produces surplus-value via surplus-labor, surplus-value *appropriation* occurs through a class structure that rests on control of production relations through forced surplus-labor. Slavery shares these traits with other labor systems—e.g., corvée serf labor of feudalism—while contrasting with labor both in primitive communism and those portions of the working-day

TABLE 3.2   From the production of surplus-value in general to specific labor relations[a]

	The general	The specific
The abstract	Production of surplus-value (A)	Non-class (non-appropriating) systems Class (appropriating) systems (B)
The concrete	Primitive communism	Unforced labor relations: Nomads, tribes, other communal systems
		Mix of unforced and forced labor relations:
	Ancient society	Upper castes, patricians / plebeians, peasants, serfs, slaves
	Asiatic modes	States-despots, landlords / peasants, serfs, slaves
	Feudalism	Landowners / tradesmen and apprentices, peasants, serfs
	Capitalism (C)	Capitalists / wage-laborers (D)

SOURCE: CREATED BY AUTHOR

a   In Table 3.2, the specific abstract, the general concrete, and the specific concrete are internally divided to indicate lumped and split realities within those categories. The arrows used here indicate comparisons being made between the categories and objects but *within* a particular moment of abstraction, e.g., the specific abstract split into non-class and class systems compared with one another. In future tables below, I continue to indicate internal splitting within a category in this way, where multiple splits within categories indicate that comparisons are available on the differences between variables. When a cell has multiple examples that are not split with lines between them, that indicates analysis is examining them on their shared properties within that category.

during which peasants in ancient, Asiatic, and feudal societies use their own means of production for free and independent labor in production of subsistence, the social fund, etc. (Cell D).

In this model set, the analyst compares non-appropriating and appropriating labor relations as a whole and without yet specifically comparing different methods of appropriation. One important difference that emerges is the distinction between the free independent labor relation versus exploitation of forced labor found in the master-servant relation. Exploitation is the act of taking advantage of someone who is vulnerable and/or cannot adequately fight back or defend themselves. Forced labor is working activity that results from threatening another with some form of bodily harm—e.g., withholding food, imprisonment, beating, maiming, torture, death—if they do not perform as demanded. Appropriation is an economic process of wealth transfer that rests on a class relation, where one person or group acquires the value or wealth someone else produces through his or her labor. Understood as such, the concept of surplus-value appropriation interiorizes several things: class relations (which assumes a group that controls production relations), threat or use of force in exploiting the labor of others (who have from limited to no options against this force), and putting laborers to the task of producing surplus-value for appropriating. This model recognizes all three—class exploitation, forced labor, and wealth appropriation—as internally and reciprocally related.

Several relevant historical-structural contrasts are noteworthy. The earliest human systems were non-appropriating, relatively small, and with rudimentary development of productive forces. With the means of production collectively owned, there is no basis for exploited forced labor and, subsequently, political-economic relations remain relatively egalitarian. Though labor here produces surplus-value, that production in itself is not the dominant subject of production, given the lack of class-appropriation.[1] Class systems, on the other hand, have landed property owners whose wealth is reliant on systematic surplus-value appropriation via forced labor. These systems emerge with sedentary societies—particularly city-states and mass agriculture—and develop new political-economic features—more formal state organizations and professional militaries (to secure societal self-defense, to pursue interests of elites, and for expansion), more complex technology and division of labor, and more advanced exchange and trade relations. This latter development directs more labor toward commodity production, and this doubles back by encouraging additional exchange and trade, resulting in the rise of complex money-forms and merchant's capital, i.e., preconditions for the emergence of systemic slavery.[2]

In non-appropriating labor relations, natural circumstance and the level of technological development determine the quality and quantity of labor

---

1   As we saw in Chapter 2, Marx also observed the existence of common property relations that survive into the socio-historical development of more complex systems, though these property relations were not the basis of the mode of production in those societies.

2   See Chapter 2, notes 14 and 42 and the discussion there. Note that this does not mean that people were never enslaved prior to the emergence of these economic forms. Rather, slavery in the sense of a "slave economy" did not develop as a structural feature of a mode of production until these other economic relations and economic processes arose and fell into place as structural features.

required in a working-day to meet the needs of subsistence, generational reproduction, the social fund, and a desired amount of exchange-values. In appropriating labor relations, custom, requirements of law, and/or threat of violence force laborers to produce a surplus of value over and above these needs. For such class systems generally, though production of use-values, exchange-values, and surplus-values remain, the class relation of exploitation centers on the latter. In such a system, forced labor can be put to multiple uses—mass agriculture, extraction of ores and minerals from the ground, building projects (e.g., canals, dams), the pursuit of war (as impressed soldiers), entertainment, utilization of specialized skills, maintenance of an elite household, and/or commodity production for exchange (though not exhaustive, this list is relatively representative). Coercive states play multiple roles in class relations of production and appropriation: acquiring a laboring class and/or securing the conditions of its existence, organizing laboring projects, encoding, regulating, and enforcing property relations and rights, as well as the legal rights and/or laboring obligations of individuals while regulating the rules on force should laborers refuse to work.

Comparing non-class versus class labor relations reveals that five combined variables set a baseline for how labor conditions—i.e., the amount and quality of unforced versus forced labor, the length and intensity of the working-day—shape the health, quality of life, and longevity of laborers:
- the *amount* and *kind* of labor needed for daily subsistence;
- the *amount* and *kind* of surplus-labor needed for producing a desired amount of surplus-value;
  - in non-class systems: the social fund, generational reproduction, exchange needs;
  - in class systems: these above plus surplus-values that can be appropriated as wealth;
- *whether or not* some labor is forced;
- the *ratio* of unforced versus forced labor directed toward the desired amount of surplus-value production;
- *type* of force used as the threat against non-compliance.

With these conditions as a baseline, the type and degree of threat or force should vary with the following:
- different class relations and the role of surplus-value in their subject of production;
- different projects set for laboring classes, including but not limited to the production of surplus-value;
- the degree of labor difficulty involved in those laboring projects, including but not limited to achieving the amount of surplus-value demanded;

– the political structures and relations related to different class systems;
  – degree of formal rights, obligations, and freedom of appropriators and laborers;
  – amount/level of state involvement in enforcing those rights, obligations, and freedoms.

The configuration of these relationships will vary under different modes of production, as well as because of historical events that shape the dynamics of the structural relations in societies shaped by those modes. Understood as such, examination must next focus on the interrelationships between such variables within and between modes of production.

Having compared and contrasted non-appropriating (non-class) and appropriating (class) systems, re-abstraction moves class systems from the specific abstract (Table 3.2, Cell B) to the general abstract category (Table 3.3, Cell A) and non-appropriating systems move out of the model set's pathway (now available for external comparisons). Production in general and surplus-value's

TABLE 3.3   From class systems in general to specific histories of class societies

	The general	The specific
The abstract	Class systems (A)	Ancient society Asiatic modes Feudalism Capitalism (B)
The concrete	Ancient labor (forced and non-forced): plebeians/peasants and slaves	Egypt, Greece, Rome, Carthage
	Asiatic labor (forced and non-forced): peasants, serfs, and slaves	India, China, Japan, East Indies
	Feudal labor (forced and non-forced): tradesmen and apprentices, peasants, serfs, and slaves	The Middle Ages, England in 16th century, Romania (Danubian principalities), Poland, Germany, France, Sweden
	Capitalist labor (forced and non-forced): slaves and wage-labor (C)	England, America, Venice, Portugal, Holland, later France, Germany

SOURCE: CREATED BY AUTHOR

class-appropriation (and its associated variables) are now assumed, while specific class systems (Cell B) are isolated (with their class structure and property relations interiorized). Of particular empirical interest are the general labor forms and the methods of surplus-value appropriation associated with each mode, into which is interiorized the relative mix of unforced versus forced labor across the working-day (Cell C)—using real historical examples for empirical grounds (Cell D). Note here that while structural models for feudalism and capitalism do not contain slavery as fundamental relation (Table 3.2), slavery existed as part of their historical development, which we now abstract into our investigative model (reflected in Table 3.3).

In comparing class systems with one another, one finds that while the nature of appropriation requires that each relies on forced labor, the nature of that force is variable across different labor relations between and within such systems. Force can be the withdrawal of privileges or other forms of privation (forced hunger), force can be threats of violence or even imprisonment, or force can be direct violence, including risk of death. Generally speaking, type and severity of force varies with types of class-labor relations, types of legal relationships, the status of certain laboring roles, and the range of options laborers have for resistance as well as the odds of, and their actual, success. More specifically for this inquiry, when a class system's appropriation form centers on slavery, the role of violence in forced labor tends to predominate.

The abstractive steps above better situate analysis to handle, as necessary, multiple possible comparisons within and between labor systems that include slavery and other forms of forced labor:

- Slavery versus other forms of forced labor *within* the same mode of production, e.g., slavery compared with plebeian/peasant labor within ancient modes of production (Egypt, Greece, Rome, Carthage); comparisons of peasants, serfs, and slaves in feudal societies (The Middle Ages, England in 16th Century, Romania, Poland, Germany, France, Sweden, and so on).
- Comparisons of similarities and differences of slavery as practiced *within* modes of production, e.g., comparing ancient slavery in Egypt, Greece, Rome, and Carthage against one another; comparing Asiatic slavery in India, China, Japan, and East Indies against one another, and so on.
- Comparing the practices of slavery *between* modes of production, e.g., the practices of slavery in Rome compared to China, either or both compared to Holland, Portugal, America, and so on.
- Comparing slavery in one system to other forms of forced labor in another system, e.g., comparing slavery in Rome to wage-labor in England or America.

– Comparing the practice of slavery in general with specific types of labor systems in different modes of production.

Mutually comparing forms of exploited labor helps one clarify their investigative priorities prior to further research. Below I briefly focus on several of these possible comparisons.

2.1   Ancient and Asiatic Labor: Plebeians, Peasants, and Serfs Compared to Slavery

Plebeian/peasant and serf labor in ancient and Asiatic modes contrast with slavery in several ways. First, while some laborers owned their own means of production, landowners related to laboring classes—slaves, serfs, other bondsmen—as if they were "part and parcel of the means of production" (Marx [1867] 1992b: 668).

Second, these systems divided labor between independent work and work for appropriators, with labor, therefore, part unforced and part forced. However, though the form of appropriation shaped how labor was used, as long as forced surplus-value production was at a manageable level—e.g., without systematic wealth accumulation as the subject of production—the Roman plebeian or the Indian serf had a modicum of freedom in dividing their working-day.[3] By contrast, a slave-owner could, in potential, direct and control all of a slave's work. If a slave is forced to expend the entire working-day on the production of surplus-value meant for appropriation, no labor-time remains for their subsistence labor. Because subsistence labor comes from that part of the working-day in which the slave-owner is not forcing them to work, that

---

3 "It is furthermore evident that in all forms in which the direct labourer remains the 'possessor' of the means of production and labour conditions necessary for the production of his own means of subsistence, the property relationship must simultaneously appear as a direct relation of lordship and servitude, so that the direct producer is not free; a lack of freedom which may be reduced from serfdom with enforced labour to a mere tributary relationship. The direct producer, according to our assumption, is to be found here in possession of his own means of production, the necessary material labour conditions required for the realisation of his labour and the production of his means of subsistence. He conducts his agricultural activity and the rural home industries connected with it independently. This independence is not undermined by the circumstance that the small peasants may form among themselves a more or less natural production community, as they do in India, since it is here merely a question of independence from the nominal lord of the manor. Under such conditions the surplus-labour for the nominal owner of the land can only be extorted from them by other than economic pressure, whatever the form assumed may be. This differs from slave or plantation economy in that the slave works under alien conditions of production and not independently. Thus, conditions of personal dependence are requisite, a lack of personal freedom, no matter to what extent, and being tied to the soil as its accessory, bondage in the true sense of the word" (Marx 1971a: 790–791).

subsistence remains a form of forced labor, now done under the threat of starvation.

Third, as a systemic labor relation, slavery developed in ancient society in a variety of ways. In Egypt, Greece, and Rome, slaves initially were, in the main, prisoners captured through warfare, with a slave trade and widespread debt bondage developing only over time. Roman plebeians—free citizens with legal rights—often were independent artisans, though some peasants had labor obligations for the patrician class. The introduction of money-rent and tax increases required an additional portion of labor-time devoted to surplus-labor in the production of surplus-value, which could take the form of producing and selling agricultural or handicraft goods or renting out one's own labor-power. Because both money-rent and usury could lead to debt, non-slave laborers' financial obligations could grow and, when failing to pay these down, they often sold themselves into (hopefully temporary) serfdom or slavery. These processes set the preconditions out of which a system of slave labor in ancient society extended itself further.

The ancient mode displayed multiple forms of slave labor exploitation. Egyptian rulers often used slaves for large building projects and agriculture, slave laborers in Greece mainly engaged in handicraft production, while early Roman slavery commonly was of a "patriarchal" character in a home doing childcare and maintenance. When the product of military victories, Romans also used slaves as sacrificial participants in gladiator battles for public entertainment or put them to work on large construction projects or in the mines. In Rome's later years, slavery shifted to large-scale agriculture and the growth of its money-economy deeply embedded slave labor into its system of commodity production and wealth appropriation.[4]

2.2 Feudal Peasant and Serf-Corvée Labor Compared to Slavery in General

In the feudal labor system, the peasant often owned parcels of land and tools and had a degree of labor independence in small-scale agriculture, domestic industry, and handicrafts for subsistence, the social fund, and social reproduction. They also often owed labor rent (e.g., during harvest season), in kind rent, and money-rent (including taxes) and thus part of their labor was forced and subject to appropriation. Like the nominally freer peasant, serfs experienced

---

4 "In all the forms in which [the] slave economy…of later Grecian and Roman times…serves as a means of amassing wealth," money "is a means of appropriating the labour of others through the purchase of slaves, land, etc." and "can be expanded as capital, i.e., bear interest, for the very reason that it can be so invested" (Marx 1971a: 594).

forced labor but here in the form of the corvée, with the laborer's day or week systematically divided between independent work and work for the appropriator-landowner. Conversely, slaves do not generally own their own means of production, while slave-owners can appropriate all forms of surplus-value as desired and have monopoly control over the division and length of the working-day.[5]

Politically, some feudal peasants remained free (i.e., not serfs), worked as tradesmen and/or apprentices, and could marry and move. Serfs, on the other hand, were in "debt bondage" and tied to the land or manor on which they worked. They could not marry without the lord's permission, who could trade or sell them along with the land they owned, all qualities of legal property. In return for these conditions of servitude, the landlord owed serfs protection, justice, and access to common lands for their subsistence.

Like the legal-class relation that ensnares the serf, a similar one allows the slave-owner to sell them and forbid them from leaving the land and/or the household to which they are tied without permission. Unlike serfs, however, slaves often do not expect that their master owes them protection from physical harm or a measure of justice. The rights of slaves to marry and establish families historically varies across different systems and at different times. In those areas with high importation of slaves and high death rates, slave marriage tends not to develop or remains rudimentary. However, in South American, Caribbean, and North American slavery, as the captured workforce increasingly became long-term with the decline of an external slave trade,

---

5   "We need not further investigate slave economy proper (which likewise passes through a metamorphosis from the patriarchal system mainly for home use to the plantation system for the world-market) nor the management of estates under which the landlords themselves are independent cultivators, possessing all instruments of production, and exploiting the labour of free or unfree bondsmen, who are paid either in kind or money. Landlord and owner of the instruments of production, and thus the direct exploiter of labourers included among these elements of production, are in this case one and the same person. Rent and profit likewise coincide then, there occurring no separation of the different forms of surplus-value. The entire surplus-labour of the labourers, which is manifested here in the surplus-product, is extracted from them directly by the owner of all instruments of production, to which belong the land and, under the original form of slavery, the immediate producers themselves. Where the capitalist outlook prevails, as on American plantations, this entire surplus-value is regarded as profit; where neither the capitalist mode of production itself exists, nor the corresponding outlook has been transferred from capitalist countries, it appears as rent. At any rate, this form presents no difficulties. The income of the landlord, whatever it may be called, the available surplus-product appropriated by him, is here the normal and prevailing form, whereby the entire unpaid surplus-labour is directly appropriated, and landed property forms the basis of such appropriation" (Marx 1971a: 804).

slave-owners increasingly allowed marriage among slaves to facilitate their intergenerational reproduction.

2.3   *Slavery Compared to Wage-Labor*

One can compare slavery to wage-labor on multiple dimensions. In late feudalism, slavery primarily existed in external colonial holdings during the primitive accumulation of capital and thus was a precondition for the emergent mode of production.[6] In this transition, exploitation of pre-capitalist labor forms intensified in a globally competitive search for profits.[7] Capitalism's structure, nevertheless, is not as such that slavery becomes predominant, as capitalism relies on wage-laborers spending their wages on commodities, money-rent, payments of interest, and taxes. Under a regime of capital accumulation, capitalists buy and sell slaves as commodities, transform them into private property, and use them as means of production. There thus emerges a calculating form of exploitation, where "[t]he price paid for a slave is nothing but the anticipated and capitalised surplus-value or profit to be wrung out of the slave" (Marx 1971a: 809).[8]

Even though slavery cannot be predominant under capitalist class relations, given its competitive market and that its subject of production is the extraction of surplus-value to achieve maximum profits, it is a system that can drive labor conditions—i.e., the intensity of work, the length of the working-day, types and amount of coercion, and conditions of survival—to a level that

---

6   "In the second type of colonies—plantations—where commercial speculations figure from the start and production is intended for the world-market...the business in which slaves are used is conducted by *capitalists*. The method of production which they introduce has not arisen out of slavery but is grafted on to it. In this case the same person is capitalist and landowner" (Marx 1968: 303).

7   "But as soon as people, whose production still moves within the lower forms of slave labour, corvée labour, &c, are drawn into the whirlpool of an international market dominated by the capitalistic mode of production, the sale of their products for export becoming their principal interest, the civilised horrors of overwork are grafted on the barbaric horrors of slavery, serfdom, &c. Hence the negro labour in the Southern States of the American Union preserved something of a patriarchal character, so long as production was chiefly directed to immediate local consumption. But in proportion, as the export of cotton became of vital interest to these states, the overworking of the negro and sometimes the using up of his life in 7 years of labour became a factor in a calculated and calculating system. It was no longer a question of obtaining from him a certain quantity of useful products. It was now a question of production of surplus labour itself. So was it also with the corvée, e. g., in the Danubian Principalities (now Rumania)" (Marx [1867] 1992b: 226–227; also see Marx 1971a: 804).

8   "In the same way, the slave-holder considers a Negro, whom he has purchased, as his property, not because the institution of slavery as such entitles him to that Negro, but because he has acquired him like any other commodity, through sale and purchase" (Marx 1971a: 776).

parallels slavery in several ways. Capitalists pay wage-labor per hours worked, though, as a class relation, this involves uncompensated surplus-labor over and above that needed for subsistence, generational reproduction, and the social fund. While this holds true for slavery as well, slave surplus-labor derives from legal and direct enforcement; the force the wage-laborer experiences is indirect and from an impersonal market. For both the slave and the wage-laborer, what their master provides for their survival—subsistence for the former and wages for the latter—comes from value derived from prior acts of production.[9] In both cases, therefore, without access to their own means of production, failure to provide surplus-labor for new appropriation puts each at risk, the slave through direct violence and the wage-laborer through the threat of privation. For the latter, the access to jobs and the wage level available in relation to the cost of commodities shape the boundaries of the threat. These boundaries, in turn, shape how long and under what conditions a laborer needs to and/or will work to secure basic provisioning. These conditions can drive wage-labor to long hours, intense and dangerous work, and barely subsistence-level pay. In comparison, then, "[t]he Roman slave was held by fetters: the wage-labourer is bound to his owner by invisible threads" (Marx [1867] 1992b: 538).

In such a dynamic, a contradiction arises between private property relations (capital) and "free" citizens (labor), as the state backs the rights of both. Unlike the slave-owner, the capitalist does not have a legal claim on the life of the wage-laborer outside the place of employment, so certain social regulations, such as the conditions of marriage, shift to the state. With its commodification of more and more areas of life, private property in the capitalist mode of production includes not only means of production (including land) but also the means of labor's reproduction, i.e., housing, food, clothing, and so on—things

---

9   Marx (1971b: 93) writes: "what the capitalist pays the worker (as well as the part of capital which confronts the worker as constant capital) is nothing but a part of the worker's product itself and, indeed, a part which does not have to be transformed into money, but which has already been sold, has already been transformed into money, since wages are paid in money, not in kind. Under slavery, etc., the false appearance brought about by the previous transformation of the product into money—insofar as it is expended on wages—does not arise; it is therefore obvious that what the slave receives as wages is, in fact, nothing the slave-owner 'advances' him, but simply the portion of the realised labour of the slave that returns to him in the form of means of subsistence. The same applies to the capitalist. He 'advances' something only in appearance. Since he pays for the work only after it has been done, he advances or rather *pays* the worker as wages a part of the product produced by the worker and already transformed into money. A part of the worker's product which the capitalist appropriates, which is *deducted beforehand*, returns to the worker in the form of wages—as an advance on the new product, if you like" (emphases in the original).

capitalists legally own. Though states recognize formal legal rights of laborers-as-citizens, law forbids laborers from appropriating this private property by means other than purchasing it. They must sell their labor to the capitalist for the needed wages at a level the capitalist sets in relation to a labor market and, as such, the free laborer is still dependent on a capitalist who owes no further obligation—and certainly not justice or projection—to the laborer beyond the wage paid for their work. It is with such wages that the laborer must reproduce themselves and pay for the generational reproduction of labor.

2.4   *Comparing Slavery, Serfdom, and Wage-Labor with Each Other*

As understood through a model of the "master-servant" relation, noteworthy distinctions between the slave, the serf, and the wage-laborer extend from the above. This relationship is one both of superordination and subordination and of mutual dependence. All three laboring groups must have access to the minimum means of subsistence to maintain their lives and their laboring capacities. All of them must perform duties their masters command, duties whose general function is the production of surplus-value their masters appropriate. Those duties for the slave may include upkeep on the master's personal living conditions. The slave, in return, receives life-sustaining sustenance and shelter from the master, which enables the slave to continue to execute those duties. A slave-master thus has an interest in the well-being of the slave in that they are dependent on that slave's labor for surplus-value production and their class situation of personal comfort and displays of wealth. Given these conditions, and depending on the slave-owner's overall productive needs and their access to a slave workforce generally, the level of subsistence and material well-being extended to a slave will tend to vary across the following dimensions:

– *relatively* generous (such as a patriarchal house slave);
– enough to produce and reproduce their own labor-power and the subsistence needs of their children (such as in a plantation system without additional introduction of slaves from external sources);
– just enough to sustain their own labor-power but not enough for generational reproduction (such as in a plantation system with extensive importation of slaves);
– relative starvation levels (where slaves are worked to death while the workforce as as a whole is replenished via conquest and/or trade).

Though a feudal lord might want higher rent at times, several variables—natural limits of the working-day, types of rent (labor, in kind, or money), the level of technological development, and the lord's desire to maintain a workforce for current and future rents—produce structural conditions that shape how long and how hard they could force serfs to work. Should the landlord want continued rents, the serf must have enough time for free and independent labor for their own subsistence and that of their family (thus generational reproduction of labor), plus any contribution to the social fund they might need or want to make. If not, if a lord demands rents above a certain level, they risk undermining their own workforce's ability to sustain and reproduce itself. This set of relationships puts a limit on the level and rate of exploitation a lord can enforce without undermining their own interests.

The relation of the wage-laborer to the capitalist is wholly different. The capitalist and the wage-laborer have ostensibly agreed on a payment to the laborer for selling them their labor-power over a period of time (per hour, per day, and so on). The obligation of the capitalist to the wage-laborer, therefore, is only when the worker is "on the clock." If the capitalist finds legal and market conditions—e.g., high levels of unemployment—as such that they can drive down the price of labor to a bare subsistence minimum or even below, there is little preventing them from doing so—other than conscience (which competition can remedy) or state regulation. Once the laborer leaves their place of employment after the agreed upon time, what they do with their remaining time and their long-term survival are not relevant to the capitalist's business calculations. Even slave-owners in certain situations—i.e., if not working slaves to death—had an incentive to keep their labor force in conditions that made future labor possible and likely. The feudal lord even more so.

Under capitalism, however, with a reserve pool of available laborers a constant, the ability of the employer-as-master to replenish their working staff-as-servants usually remains assured. In a relationship such as this, workers' ability to sustain themselves as well as raise a new generation of laborers are their own concern. Like variations in slavery's labor replenishment, the *size* of this unemployed labor pool shapes the relative bargaining position of capitalists and laborers in their struggle over the terms of pay, labor conditions, and length of the working-day. That is, for both capitalist and slave-owner, the ease or difficulty they have in replacing a laborer translates, in part, into the boundaries that shape their treatment of their workforce. If employers have an unlimited supply of laborers divorced from the means of production and in need of wages to secure necessities, there are always potential new laborers at the ready to refill an employer's workforce coffers at wage levels the employer determines. In such a relationship, the level surplus-value extraction any one capitalist will find beneficial to their interests has no theoretical limit.

This dynamic changes when examined from the perspective of capital as a whole versus labor as a whole and in a way qualitatively different from the direct relationship of a lord to their serf workforce. From this vantage point, *capitalists as a class* can appropriate so much social wealth and/or drive the total amount of purchasable goods available via the wage-bill so low that *laborers as a class* cannot sustain their lives and health day-to-day, much less being able to produce and raise a new generation of laborers. However, capitalists usually act at the individual and firm level in pursuit of their own interests, rather than in-concert at the class level. This situation builds a contradiction into capital–labor relations as a whole, where an action that benefits an individual capitalist undermines that class as a whole if/when done by all of them.

A feudal lord generally is dependent on their serfs, not a formal labor market, and this relationship facilitates a legal structure that ties serfs to their master's land. The lord, in turn, has an incentive both to make sure that the conditions of labor and the magnitude of their surplus-value extraction (as related to the working-day) do not completely negate the health and well-being of their labor force. Unlike feudal lords, the actions of capitalists as individuals push in one direction—i.e., maximizing profits—while the needs of their class as a whole—i.e., constant accumulation without limit—push in another—i.e., producing a concentration of wealth that can undermine wage-laborers as a class. In viewing the capital–labor relation from the vantage point of that of the lord–serf relation, we can see *that* and *how* the capitalist mode of production severs this element in the master-servant connection—i.e., the feudal lord must be concerned with the long-term well-being and survival of their laborers, whereas the capitalist does not.

The analysis above suggests that labor relations in slavery will tend to vary across three general models of the master-servant relationship: (1) one like the captured Roman slave worked to death in construction projects or the mines as a matter of course, (2) one like the severed connection between capitalist and the wage-laborer, where the slave-owner extracts the labor needed and leaves the slave's survival to their own devices, and (3) one like the lord–serf relation where the master must take their workforce's conditions of labor, and thus survival, into account.

Several structural-historical variables influence where an exploiter–slave relationship is likely to fall along this continuum. How do the property relations, political structures, and subjects of production associated with different modes of production impact class-labor relations in them? Given that slavery is forced labor, what variables influence the intensity of such labor enforcement so that it drives the slave to or even over the physical limits of their ability to work, of self-preservation, and of intergenerational reproduction? By a similar extension, while slave labor is categorically different from that of peasants, serfs, or wage-workers, structural pressures and dynamics can press on the latter three labor forms and drive them closer in practice toward slavery-like conditions. This suggests investigating how, why, and when does slavery emerge from these non-slave labor relations? For example, in terms of capitalist wage-labor, states can enact and enforce laws that regulate working conditions or fail to, recognize the right of laborers to organize or restrict it, enact minimum laws to support livable wages or decline to do so, and so on. This interconnection between state intervention in the labor market and the drive for capital accumulation accounts for, should a state decline its potential regulating function, how working conditions can gravitate toward those similar to slavery and why slavery often reemerges in market systems.

Other associated questions come up as well. The distinction between forced and non-forced labor and the relative independence of the laborer connects with political relations and their dynamics, such as the obligations of laborers, legal rights of property owners, and the level and extent of certain potential freedoms and rights of citizens. If the threat and reality of force is behind labor exploitation, what options does this provide the laborer? Withdrawing labor is an attempt to leave the relationship, but to what extent can laborers do this and what options do appropriators have to prevent it? What type of force—legal and extra-legal—and how much of it can an appropriator use and how widely? Politics—related to state actors, parties, culture, and social movements—often serve as intervening variables here. States can participate in the slave trade, regulate it, allow it, or ban it and enforce such a ban. States can enact laws that encode obligations—or lack thereof—of slave-owners and/or rights—or lack thereof—of slaves. States can ban slave labor outright and/or work to eliminate it when it again arises, or they can remain inert amid slavery's existence and/or resurgence. Cultural norms and values both within the enslaving class and among the population as a whole can determine what range of violence a slave-master might feel free in using. Social movements that oppose the treatment of slaves or even the institution as a whole can spring up and such movements can work through the state to shape its policies toward slavery as a practice.

These observations suggest a research schedule that targets what variables may intensify or reduce how slaves are subject to different levels of exploitation, violence, and repression. List 3.1 presents potential questions for such a research schedule below (many items of which should not be novel to scholars already steeped in this research and/or the literature related to it).

A sampling of historical observations demonstrate the relevance of such questions. For instance, Jamaican sugar plantations experienced the highest levels of slave importation in the Americas (e.g., see Klein 1978). Slave-owners there enjoyed access to a replenishing labor pool and therefore had fewer concerns over replacing laborers as compared to slave-owners with lower levels of slave importation. As a result, death rates were higher in the former compared

LIST 3.1   Proposed research schedule for the relation between slavery and violence

Variables / areas of investigation	Questions during inquiry
Type and level of advantage to be gained from use of slaves	Are workers needed for labor-intensive projects? As soldiers? As servants in elite households? For commodity production? How many are needed?
Need for the use of slaves for non-specialized versus specialized labor tasks	What type of labor is needed? General labor or specific labor such as iron-smithing or forms of animal husbandry or certain fields of intellectual knowledge? Do specialized labor skills provide some element of protection against violence, in that such a laborer would be difficult to replace? By extension, do non-specialized slave laborers experience a higher threat of violence and/or shorter lives?
Rate of replenishing new laborers into the system	Are slaves sporadic and few and brought into servitude via contingent events? Are slaves regularly captured via war? Is war something used as regular practice to capture slaves? Is there an active slave trade? How large is it? Is reproduction of the slave workforce dependent on their own generational reproduction?
Level of threat of violence against non-cooperation and withdrawal of labor	What options remain to slave-owners in the use of violence? Can slaves be killed if they withdraw their labor? Can they be worked to death? Do slaves have any rights against violence to their persons? To what extent do states enforce them?
Level of slave dependence on slave-owners for subsistence	How much provision is provided? Is it adequate for health? Or just enough to keep a slave alive long enough so that they expend the desired amount of labor? Are provisions enough to produce and raise children? How much time in the working-day is allotted to labor for needed provisioning? What lengthens or shrinks this working-day?

LIST 3.1   Proposed research schedule for the relation between slavery and violence (*cont.*)

Variables / areas of investigation	Questions during inquiry
State policies and practices related to the legal status of slavery and slaves as individuals	Do slaves have any legal rights? If so, how many and what kind? Do states enforce these rights? Do slaves have access to political means by which they can advocate for themselves? What sort of legal rights do slave-owners have over their slaves? To what extent is the state empowered to and actively involved in enforcing those rights?
Social norms generally on the acceptability of slavery as a practice and the social acceptability of violence against slaves	What is the community attitude toward slavery as a practice? In favor, opposed, mixed, indifferent? How does a culture view the status of the enslaved? As the unjustly oppressed? Hated enemies? Unlucky defeated soldiers? Nonhuman beasts of burden? To what extent do wider social norms about slavery and the social status of slaves influence the manner in which a slave-owner treats them? How do norms within the slave owning class compare to wider social norms outside of it?
Level of organization among and resistance of slaves	In terms of the relation between levels of mortality and slave replenishment, do slave workforces constantly in flux have lower ability and lower likelihood to organize resistance? Conversely, are slave workforces whose living conditions are more permanent and last over generations more or less likely to find avenues for organization and resistance? How do geographical conditions influence the possibilities of resistance? Do slaves have access to opportunities to flee, such as a frontier situation? Or are slaving areas relatively enclosed, such as island plantations? What about those in between, areas deep into slave territory though abutting non-slaving areas at some distance? Extending from these points, what is the relationship between resistance and violence? Does violence from slave-owners upfront keep resistance down? Does resistance increase the actual level of violence subsequently then inflicted and how does this in turn shape subsequent odds of additional resistance?

SOURCE: CREATED BY AUTHOR

to the latter. How did the Jamaican situation compare with that of Haiti, which also had one of the highest levels of slave importation and extremely high death rates? Haiti experienced a successful slave revolt that overthrew the slave-owning class (the hemisphere's first) and Jamaica, though experiencing rebellions, did not. Both were island nations, had high levels of slave importation, and were subject to the brutality of colonial overseers. Do any structural conditions account for the different outcomes? To what extent did these different outcomes result from historically contingent factors, such as distinct decisions made by the British in Jamaica and/or the French in Haiti? Did other structural factors shape those decisions? Do any comparisons here allow for deriving successful generalizations?

Construction of the US Transcontinental Railroad (1863–1969) was the country's largest engineering project of its time. In January of 1865, after the Central Pacific railroad company advertised for 5,000 workers and only gained a few hundred, they turned to California's Chinese immigrant population, hoping the Chinese would make for submissive and docile workers. Initial success encouraged Central Pacific to bring laborers in from China, who eventually made up 80–90% of their workforce, with about 8,000 building tunnels and 3,000 laying track. Assigned the most dangerous work (tunnels could collapse and often did), weather running hot and cold, and expected to secure their own tents and food, Chinese laborers frequently faced violence and risk of death (approximately one thousand died during the railroad's construction). With laborers "free" to search for employment in a capitalist system, some railroad workers quit, sometimes lured away by better prospects in Western silver mines. Consequently, Chinese railroad workers were sometimes whipped or restrained to thwart such designs, should they have them. In 1867, after going on strike for equal pay and working conditions (compared to white, mainly Irish, laborers), company bosses halted shipments of supplies to their camps to starve them out, while also sending in a posse of whites to intimidate them (Bain 1999; Ambrose 2000; Fuchs 2017). Though not legal slavery as such, how does this labor dynamic compare to the Roman use of slaves in the mines? How did cultural norms—e.g., racism, the experience with legal slavery, and a civil war—view this labor force, its exploitation, and laborers' rights? How did ostensibly democratic states play a role in such practices?

Perhaps modernity's most extreme form of slave labor came from Nazi use of prisoner labor in World War II—e.g., POWs, Jewish and Roma communities, and other official enemies. Here, the state was powerful, a singular party enjoyed a monopoly on that power, social norms were as such that opposition to such practices (if known at all) was muted, and the number of prisoners brought in were at high enough levels that some were executed immediately while officials sorted others into labor camps. The ability of prisoners-as-slaves to resist, either via pressure on states for intervention or through their own organized efforts, was close to nil (though not totally absent). These conditions of enslavement only ended after Allied forces liberated the camps, demonstrating how far a laboring system can decline when closed off from internal societal forces that can influence it.

An analyst could use the type of inquiry above as a research agenda on its own or use it as a preparatory investigative framework to establish a knowledge base for research on other specific cases. Below I look at additional limited examples through new successive abstractions while keeping the above framework in mind.

2.5   Comparing Slavery between Systems: Rome v. the Americas

If one were interested in examining slavery in multiple historical-structural moments, they could start by comparing slaving practices in the ancient mode of production with modern slavery in the capitalist mode (Table 3.4). With models of both class systems and multiple forms of forced labor in hand, they could skip the steps of re-abstracting every specific production mode found above (Table 3.3, Cell B) and instead move slavery straight into the general abstract category (Table 3.5, Cell A). Carved as such, "slavery" has both master-servant and class-labor relations interiorized into it, particularly the appropriation of surplus-value through forced labor exploitation. From here, the analyst could focus on empirical areas first carved in the specific abstract for comparison—in this case ancient society versus capitalist society (Cell B)—and then identify historical slave systems that existed in the general concrete—e.g., Roman slavery in antiquity and modern slavery in the Americas (Cell C). From there research would hone in on specific empirical examples, facts, events, observations and so on (Cell D).

While slaves in both Rome and in the Americas were part of "the objective conditions of production" (Marx 1971b: 422), there are several comparisons and

TABLE 3.4   Comparing slavery in Rome and the Americas with each other

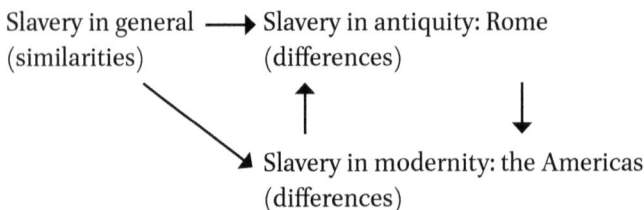

Slavery in general ⟶ Slavery in antiquity: Rome
(similarities)   (differences)

                         Slavery in modernity: the Americas
                         (differences)

SOURCE: CREATED BY AUTHOR

TABLE 3.5   From slavery in general to particular laws, practices, times, places, etc. in Rome and in the Americas

	The general	The specific
The abstract	Slavery (A)	Slavery in the ancient mode of production
		Slavery in the capitalist mode of production (B)
The concrete	Roman slavery Slavery in the Americas (C)	Particular laws, practices, times, places, etc. Particular laws, practices, times, places, etc. (D)

SOURCE: CREATED BY AUTHOR

contrasts after this fact. In both, the purchase of a laborer turned them into an object of possession, even though under different socio-structural relations.[10] In Rome, slavery's origins and institutionalization was multifaceted. The Romans acquired slaves after military victories and through a trade in them due to piracy. Other slaves were born into households, on farms, or on agricultural estates. By the third century, Roman landowners faced a labor shortage and relied on freemen as tenant farmers to make up the difference. Because of a tax system that assessed both land and the peasants on it, the state changed laws to prohibit peasant laborers from leaving the land. By the fourth century, a sort of serf-slave system developed, as debtors sometimes sold themselves and/or their children into slavery to cover their obligations.

Roman slavery thus reflected numerous legal statuses and forms exploitation. Some slaves were owned by the state, working in temples and in public administrative offices as servants to officials, e.g., as accountants or physicians. Their owners often allowed them to earn money for personal use and would sometimes free them by legal declaration. Household slaves often worked as cooks, with children (supervision, teaching), as seamstresses, and so on. Such slaves often enjoyed living conditions better than those of poor peasants.

---

10   "The nature of capital remains the same in its developed as in its undeveloped form. In the code which the influence of the slave-owners, shortly before the outbreak of the American Civil War, imposed on the territory of New Mexico, it is said that the labourer, in as much as the capitalist has bought his labour-power, 'is his (the capitalist's) money.' The same view was current among Roman patricians. The money they had advanced to the plebeian debtor had been transformed *viâ* the means of subsistence into the flesh and blood of the debtor. This 'flesh and blood' were, therefore, 'their money'" (Marx [1867] 1992b: 272–273, note 3).

Other Roman slaves worked in manufacturing professions, such as bakers, shoemakers, engravers, and so on. Some of these slaves lived relatively independent of their masters, though they still had financial obligations to them. Unskilled slaves (often captured in war or sentenced to slavery as punishment) worked on farms, at mills, and in the mines under brutal conditions.

With this complex and layered class-labor relation, so, too, were the political relationships related to slavery's practice complex. While most slaves were legal property without recognized personhood, some slaves could hold property (though legally their master's) and use it for their own ends. Some skilled and educated slaves could earn money and buy their freedom. Nonetheless, slaves had limited legal rights. For example, they could not testify in court unless tortured (under the assumption a slave would be loyal to their master and therefore the truth must be extracted by force). Over time, however, they did receive more legal protections, such as the right to file complaints against masters and prohibitions against being murdered. Freed Roman slaves could become citizens and vote (if male), but were prohibited from holding public office or joining the state priesthood. If a former master deemed them untrustworthy, criminal, and/or a threat to society, however, a freed slave could have citizenship withheld. Children born to freed slaves, nevertheless, did enjoy full rights of Roman citizenship.

The status of Roman slaves left them subject to varying degrees of violence. For laborers who sold themselves to others to cover debts, the period of bondage was often limited and the bonded serf/slave did not lose their legal status as a citizen, which was supposed to afford them some protection from violence. By contrast, Roman non-citizen slaves suffered from legal corporal punishment, sexual exploitation, torture, and mass execution. In a similar contrast, masters of slaves who were born into households or on farms or agricultural estates had a stronger obligation for their care, while the expectation was that captured slaves working in mines and quarries would die there. Rebellion and fleeing were constant concerns. A slave-hunting profession developed to capture runaways, laws prohibited providing them haven, and returned slaves could be legally whipped, burned, branded, or even killed.

In the Americas, slavery went through several changes from its inception in the early period of colonization to its existence within later nation-states birthed by that same colonialism. For the time being, focus here remains primarily on the early colonial period.

Colonial slavery in the Americas originated as a commercial enterprise related to commodity production, particularly sugar (tobacco, rice, coffee, cocoa, and still later cotton would prove influential in its spread). After efforts at sugar cultivation in the Mediterranean, bankers and merchants from Genoa and other parts of what is now Italy established commercial networks in Lisbon and Seville. By the fifteenth century, they developed sugar enterprises on Atlantic islands between Spain and the northwest coast of Africa (Madeira, the Canary Islands) and later further south off of Africa's coast (São Tomé and Principe). These latter areas served as plantation-style models for European merchants interested in the Americas, first in Brazil and later in the Caribbean (e.g., Barbados). European traders and merchants closest to the Mediterranean gateway to the Atlantic and to Africa—i.e., in Portugal and Spain—paved the way for the modern transatlantic slave trade's initial thrust. This enterprise relied on the capture of human beings, though here it was less military conquest of enemies but rather buying slaves from African traders and kingdoms who had defeated their rivals. As the practice grew, other regions of the world entered the trade, including Brazil, Britain, France, and the Netherlands. Trade agreements—e.g., the Asiento de Negros agreements Spain developed with individuals, companies, and countries such as Germany, Portugal, England, and France to supply them with slaves—state chartered monopolies—e.g., England's Company of Royal Adventurers Trading to Africa (1660) and The Royal African Company (1672)—and private trading companies—e.g., Royal African Company (Britain, 1660–1752), the Dutch West India Company (the Netherlands, 1602–1792)—proliferated. These economic developments and ties linked up areas of purchase in Africa with ports of trade in Europe, the Caribbean (Barbados, Jamaica, Guadeloupe, Martinique, Saint-Domingue [later Haiti]), Brazil, and in later North American colonies.

The state was involved in the political relationships surrounding colonial slavery in several other ways. State laws backed rights of slave-owners as any other property owner, making slaves legally personal and private property, with bondage life-long (save for manumission). The designation as property usually negated their status as persons and citizens with legal rights, a legal-economic relation that carried over to slaves' children, who became slaves automatically.

While some slaves worked as seafarers and even on slave ships, slave-owners primarily put slaves to work on plantations, in mines, and in households. Through starting with a mix of free, indentured, and slave labor, plantation owners found slave labor the most profitable, especially for growing sugar, tobacco, and rice. Slaves grew cheaper and easier to acquire as world trade expanded on growing consumer demand, as commodities that were formerly luxuries for the affluent (like sugar) became everyday necessities (for sweetening tea or coffee or for making rum). As the capitalist world economy grew, demand for labor across a variety of specializations—such as masons, distillers, nurses, carpenters, cattlemen, seamstresses, and so on—also grew, as did the need for additional agricultural labor to feed owners and other slaves. House slaves became a way to maintain one's standard of living and as a way to demonstrate one's wealth and prestige.

Superstructural components—as reciprocal effects of beliefs, law, political practice, and culture on one another—also influenced slavery's development in the Americas. A central issue was designations for individual and group legal statuses that ranged from free to unfree, the latter thus eligible for enslavement. In the early colonial period, slaves legally were, in effect, prisoners of war who were also "heathens," a combination of older Roman notions of enslaving captured soldiers and religious notions that forbid Christians from enslaving other Christians. After some slaves converted to Christianity, governments in colonies such as Maryland changed their laws to designate those with heathen ancestry as eligible for enslavement, which shifted the non-free indicator from mindset to physical appearance. In Brazil, cultural attitudes and legal rights and freedoms made distinctions between African-born slaves, African-born ex-slaves, Brazilian-born slaves, and Brazilian-born ex-slaves. These distinctions correlated with skin tone, where the lighter skin color of the "mulatto" (often indicating at least part European ancestry) often afforded them a greater likelihood of manumission and more potential social freedoms and mobility than darker skinned slaves and ex-slaves. In such ways, slavery and its class-culture-legal relations in the Americas developed the dynamics of a racial system.

Violence was a regular component of slavery in the Americas, from slaves being captured in the African interior, shackled on the march to the coast and through the Middle Passage, sold in slave trading ports, and subjected to violent discipline in the labor process. The legal designations of free person, indentured servant, and slave also played a role in such violence. Free persons had more legal rights, though still not extensive ones—e.g., debtor's prisons and the forced labor associated with them. A slave-owner who expected a lifetime of work from a slave might treat them better than would an overseer of an indentured servant, as maiming the latter only meant a few years of diminished labor, while maiming the former meant a potential lifetime of lost work. This was less an issue in plantation situations where there was a high level of slave importation—increasing the likelihood of masters working slaves to death (in contrast to labor environments where owners need to cultivate an internal slave workforce). Institutionalized violence also influenced the rise of anti-slavery sentiments. In England, for example, images of implements of bondage—e.g., shackles, whips, and injured slaves—inspired an abolitionist movement there. After activists won legislative victories that banned the trade and later the practice, the British Royal Navy policed the Caribbean, often freeing the captured from slaving ships.

The discussion above informs us about the intricacies of modeling. While slave systems in Rome and the Americas have similarities, if an analysis proceeds under the concept of "slavery" without controlling for the mode of production and/or the temporal order of material-ideological relationships, the analyst could misapply relevant explanatory variables or miss them altogether. A model set carved from only "class systems in general," for example, may be too broad a framework for more specific observations. While both systems of slavery involved legal servitude, agricultural labor, exploitation, threats of and actual violence, slavery in the Americas existed in a *capitalist* labor system of commodity production for sales in a competitive world-market, accruing profits from such sales, and using such profits for capital accumulation. Slavery in Rome had none of these latter characteristics, which thus explains why elevating slaves to higher order professions such as accountants or physicians existed there but was rare enough in the Americas that one could consider it non-systemic. Instead, when we combine value production in general, the labor exploitation of class systems, and the drive to accumulate capital from profits resting on commodity production and sales, we can better understand how slavery under capitalist auspices became "the meanest and most shameless form of man's enslaving recorded in the annals of history" (Marx [1861] 1984: 30).

Such systemic material relations must be the starting-point for understanding slavery's historical practice, especially prior to investigating conditions in the ideological sphere. An idealist model might target individualistic moral sentiments such as "greed" in accounting for the rise of slavery, though such an explanation does not hold for either case. In Rome, slavery initially was a solution for what to do with prisoners of war, i.e., better to enslave them than kill them. Over time, the maturation of landed property, a money economy, usury, merchant's capital and trade progressively institutionalized slavery as a labor system. While greed probably motivated modern slavery's first practitioners and encouraged more individuals to get involved in the practice, such individual traits must have a structural context—e.g., private property system, a profit-motive hooked into a forced labor system, and forms of surplus-value production associated with both—in order to become generalized economic practices. Once a property system resting on commodity production, sales for profits in a competitive market, and accumulating profits as capital developed, such systemic variables would compel economic actors to participate in its most profitable forms of wealth extraction as a market imperative, regardless of their individual moral dispositions.

Comparison also provides insight into different political relations associated with each system. In both, laws needed to spell out the legal rights and obligations of slaves versus non-slaves. As forms of labor exploitation, neither Rome nor the Americas initiated their slave system upon a racial hierarchy. In Rome, a distinction fell along the lines of (1) the Roman-citizen versus (2) the freed-slave-as-Roman-citizen versus (3) the Roman prisoner-of-war-slave.

In the Americas, free versus non-free status started from historical roots in old Roman law (i.e., captured warriors) combined with a religious justification (i.e., Christian versus heathen) and only later shifted to a racial system. In the Americas, racist ideological designations, that is, arose *after* modern slavery's initial thrusts. This shift—where slavery caused racism, not the reverse—worked itself further into law and culture, thus making race a uniquely modern ordering mechanism that has remained long after slavery's abolition. We find no comparable racial ordering in Roman history.

2.6   Comparing Slavery within Systems: British Slavery v. American Slavery

Given the considerations above, focus now turns to examining slavery as practiced under capitalist auspices specifically. Here, two consecutive acts of re-abstraction are necessary to avoid missing crucial differences *within* the same general system. The first moment of re-abstracting keeps slavery as the general abstract category (Table 3.6 Cell A) and treats slavery under capitalism as a specific example of slavery in general (Cell B), while relegating all other non-capitalist forms of slavery in other modes of production to external model sets (available for comparison as needed). In this model set, the unique features of modern slavery in the Americas are examined in the general concrete (Cell C), thus organizing the investigation of slavery there into a framework that allows for comparing and contrasting specific concrete situations of empirical interest, e.g., British slavery in the Caribbean versus slavery in North America (Cell D). Doing this properly requires another act of abstraction.

If we started and ended with the model set below (Table 3.6), the general labor system initially abstracted is "slavery" and only afterward "labor in the capitalist mode of production." Remaining at this level of abstraction threatens analysis with isolating slavery *outside* its interconnections with wider structural phenomena within that system. This means we must analyze slavery

TABLE 3.6   British slavery in the Caribbean and North American slavery: similarities

	The general	The specific
The abstract	Slavery (A)	Slavery in the capitalist mode of production (B)
The concrete	Capitalist slavery in the Americas (C)	British slavery in the Caribbean, slavery in North America (D)

SOURCE: CREATED BY AUTHOR

through a pathway that goes through models of production in general, class systems, and then the capitalist mode of production. This procedure allows for placing modern slavery in the Americas in its proper structural context: (1) capital–labor class relations; (2) private ownership of the means of production, (3) use of wage-labor in commodity production for sale in a competitive marketplace for profits, (4) the accumulation of profits as capital, (5) reinvestment of profits in labor-saving machinery (and thus the general social development of productive forces), and (6) a world-market as the grounds for resource extraction, labor exploitation, trade, and sales.

As previously noted, while slavery is not internal to the structure of the capitalism mode of production, it is a reality and a variable in its historical development. Reflecting this, Table 3.7 shifts capitalism into the general abstract category and places capitalist slavery in the Americas into the specific abstract category. Analysis then splits capitalist slavery in the Americas into its British forms in the Caribbean and enslaving in North America. Isolating these specific historical-structural conditions allows for greater care in comparing them to each other and to broader realities that may prove informative. This maneuver helps the analyst avoid attributing real empirical differences they might find to what these systems share but at broader levels of generality.

Note that several issues from prior inquiries above inform this study. First, the model set in use has already interiorized the production of use-value, exchange-value, and surplus-value, class exploitation, and forms of forced labor into it. Variables related to the pursuit of appropriation and its levels of violence and repression, as well as how these influence the working-day, similarly are interiorized into class exploitation and forms of forced labor. Second, also already

TABLE 3.7   Comparing British slavery in the Caribbean with North American slavery

The general abstract	The specific abstract	The general concrete	The specific concrete
Capitalist mode of production	Capitalist slavery: the Americas (similarities)	British slavery: the Caribbean ⟋ Slavery in North America	Specific plantations, policies, dates, people, etc. (differences) ↑ ↓ Specific plantations, policies, dates, people, etc. (differences)

SOURCE: CREATED BY AUTHOR

developed is a model of slavery as practiced within the capitalist mode of production, which is here assumed. Third, any comparisons with external model sets proceed with the assumption that the acts of abstraction have controlled the different variables associated with those modes of production versus those of capitalism.

By abstracting modern slavery at its correct level of generality and comparing empirical details in a controlled manner, we can isolate and discover the causal properties that relevant variables had (or did not have) on the use of slave labor for capital accumulation. A salient feature—be it a key variation in a structural constant or a historical development—should drive research questions. Such variables often are interrelated, of course, but one must first break them down during research into distinct parts for analysis before piecing together their interconnections.

The slave trade is one such variable. Modern slavery centered on commodity production, sales, profits, and capital accumulation in a world-market based on international trade. Spain participated in slavery but not its transatlantic trade, being restricted to buying slaves from the Portuguese (among others). In 1807, after pressure from abolitionist movements, Britain officially abolished the slave trade, though not slavery itself. The United States banned the trade a year later. It was not until the 1860s that Brazil, Portugal's main colonial holding, banned importing slaves. Such distinctions suggest comparisons between (1) countries that did not directly participate in the transatlantic trade as well as (2) the practices related to slavery in countries during this trade and after it ceased.[11]

In the transatlantic trade, slave traders in the Middle Passage calculated survival rates of prisoners reaching slave markets in the Americas. For the investor, survival of all those captured would be ideal. For a slaving ship's commander, the total number of slaves that survived for final sale upon reaching markets was a primary concern. Slavers concluded that, despite its higher death rates, the "tight pack" was most efficient and thus most profitable. A slave buyer at the auction block was only concerned with the future survival of those they bought. After purchase, a plantation owner's concern was that a slave produce more value in sellable goods than their cost of purchase plus the value production used for their subsistence needs. More labor output by the slave created more potential profits. This meant that capitalist slave-owners

---

11   Note here that the specific year a country banned the slave trade does not mean that its slave traders and other merchants immediately ceased their involvement that same year. However, such dates could serve to mark periods toward which inquiry directs its attention. Observation may reveal that the actual cessation of slave trading from representatives of such countries required additional incentives to fully withdraw, e.g., interventions by the British Navy.

had to calculate how they doled out violence, as maiming, killing, or working a slave to death meant loss of potential revenue. Moreover, replenishment came from the birth of a slave's children and/or from new purchases, not from victories in war, so the slave-owner managed the maintenance of a labor force via ledger sheet and through cultivating an internal workforce.

How do these variables relate to one another? The slave trade itself could be variable in terms of the quantity and rate of slave importation. In the colonial system in the Caribbean, slave importation was extremely high. To what extent did plantation owners need slave labor for slaves' upkeep and/or the general social fund? If slaves are imported in high numbers and/or with sufficient rapidity and thus are plentiful, they are likely to cost less and be seen as more expendable. Such a situation would lend itself to re-trading them as a commodity when needed, harsher treatment in labor discipline, longer working-days, and therefore higher death rates, and so on.[12] Cutting off trade meant that plantation owners as masters, dependent as they are on a captured and exploitable labor force, would have to allow slaves to live longer. This would require that they improve slaves' living conditions—i.e., more food, less violence—allow them to marry, have children, and maintain families to some extent. Slaves' level of vulnerability and expendability would thus decline in relation to these changing conditions.

To investigate such issues, Table 3.8 below suggests three comparisons between general concrete slaving areas with and without a slave trade:

---

12 "The slave-owner buys his labourer as he buys his horse. If he loses his slave, he loses capital that can only be restored by new outlay in the slave-mart. But 'the rice-grounds of Georgia, or the swamps of the Mississippi may be fatally injurious to the human constitution, but the waste of human life which the cultivation of these districts necessitates, is not so great that it cannot be repaired from the teeming preserves of Virginia and Kentucky. Considerations of economy, moreover, which, under a natural system, afford some security for humane treatment by identifying the master's interest with the slave's preservation, when once trading in slaves is practised, become reasons for racking to the uttermost the toil of the slave; for, when his place can at once be supplied from foreign preserves, the duration of his life becomes a matter of less moment than its productiveness while it lasts. It is accordingly a maxim of slave management, in slave-importing countries, that the most effective economy is that which takes out of the human chattel in the shortest space of time the utmost amount of exertion it is capable of putting forth. It is in tropical culture, where annual profits often equal the whole capital of plantations, that negro life is most recklessly sacrificed. It is the agriculture of the West Indies, which has been for centuries prolific of fabulous wealth, that has engulfed millions of the African race. It is in Cuba, at this day, whose revenues are reckoned by millions, and whose planters are princes, that we see in the servile class, the coarsest fare, the most exhausting and unremitting toil, and even the absolute destruction of a portion of its numbers every year'" (Marx [1867] 1992b: 253–254; cites: Cairnes, "The Slave Power," pp. 110, 111).

TABLE 3.8   Comparing capitalist slavery across regions, times, and policy changes

The specific abstract	The general concrete	→ Comparison group(s)	Specific concrete data
Capitalist slavery: the Americas	Spanish slavery	Portuguese slavery up to 1860s British slavery in the Caribbean up to 1807 American slavery up to 1808	Rates of slave mortality, average lifespan, work hours, gender ratios, birth rates, calorie supply (etc.) for specific states, plantations, dates, people, etc.
	British slavery in the Caribbean, 1807	Brazilian slavery, 1807 US slavery, 1807	
	British slavery up to 1807	British slavery after 1807	
	American slavery up to 1808	American slavery after 1808	

SOURCE: CREATED BY AUTHOR

(1) compare the conditions of Spanish slavery with that of the Portuguese, the British, and the Americans prior to their ban on the trade; (2) compare the differences between British slavery in 1807 and how it was practiced in Brazil as well as the United States at the same time; and (3) compare the real differences within each area before and after each banned the trade, e.g., British slavery in the Caribbean before abolition of the trade versus after and/or the same analysis for the United States. Data collection here (the specific concrete) could focus on differences in mortality rates of slaves, their average lifespan, hours worked per day/week, etc., conditions of family life, gender ratios, birth rates, calorie supply, and so on.

Such analytical maneuvers are but a step in isolating causal variables that might help account for observed historical facts, given research could bring other variables into account. How did a more coherent and ascendant capitalist class and state in Britain, Brazil, or the United States influence slavery's practice, its survival, and/or its abolition as compared to Spain or Portugal? Were different types of agricultural products across these regions and eras— i.e., given levels of global demand and the difficulty or ease in cultivating and/ or harvesting certain crops—influential in the treatment of slaves? Did slaveowners treat slaves with more specialized skills differently in different regions and eras than those without such skills? How did the dynamic of "abstract labor" in capitalist labor relations influence both of these situations for slaves? Did population density in slave numbers influence the practice? How were slave resistance and rebellion related both to population density and to the rate of trade on island plantations—e.g., where high turnover makes rebellion more difficult—versus their relation in those areas where a frontier existed for escape? And so on. Given all previous model sets discussed, we could set up a series of questions-as-variables for interpretation and explanation:

> In a study of slavery in the Americas, what is comparatively accounted for by the characteristics of...
> ...production in general?
> ...class systems of labor exploitation in general?
> ...slavery in general?
> ...capitalist slavery?
> ...capitalist slavery with a slave trade?
> ...capitalist slavery without a slave trade?
> ...capitalist slavery (with and without a slave trade) in sugar, cotton, tobacco, etc.?
> ...capitalist slavery (with and without a slave trade) in sugar, cotton, tobacco, etc. without frontiers?
> ...capitalist slavery (with and without a slave trade) in sugar, cotton, tobacco, etc. in a frontier situation?
> And so on...

To avoid any possible misunderstanding, my argument is not that researchers have yet to ask or answer such questions, nor am I the first to bring up many of the empirical and/or structural observations made here. There is an immense literature on the topic. The point here is to demonstrate how the method of successive abstractions provides a way to systematically introduce concepts at multiple and interconnected levels of abstraction, identify empirical domains fit for analysis at these various levels, and systematically isolate, control, compare, and account for observations while focusing more and more closely on objects of study.

3   Capitalism and the Method of Successive Abstractions

Now we come to abstracting and re-abstracting capitalism as a system. First, to minimize repetition, I will expeditiously move through several of the initial abstractive levels already reflected in Chapter 2.

3.1   *Capitalism and Production in General*

Table 3.9 begins with production in general as the general abstract category (Cell A). While recognizing different historical production configurations allows for later splitting, at this level of abstraction focus starts with the commonalities of all forms of production, i.e., the production of values (use, exchange, and surplus) (Cell B). How value production is structured into systems—i.e., property relations, labor relations (unforced and/or forced), and (non-existence or existence of) appropriation—distinguishes non-class from class systems (Cell C). One can further subdivide the latter by their specific class and property relations, how they develop their productive forces, their subject of production, their modes of appropriation (or lack thereof), their specific configuration of unforced and forced labor-terms, and the roles of exchange and trade in them (Cell D).

This beginning emphasizes how the capitalist mode of production has systemic functions found in all economic systems, i.e., production of subsistence, of useful and needed things, of exchangeable goods, and of values not immediately consumed. Note two things here. First, we saw earlier that the capitalist mode of production is concerned only with the production and appropriation of surplus-value, so these other tasks are either only a byproduct of that end or are produced outside the formal economy. Second, this level of abstraction determines only the *general array of possible options to which surplus-value could be used*—including the reproduction of labor over generations, the social fund, over-consumption, hoarding, and accumulation—but not *how specifically those surplus-values are used and by whom*. The model also contains other variables found in all modes of production, including socially necessary

TABLE 3.9   From production in general to specific modes of production

	The general	The specific
The abstract	Production in general (A)	Modes of producing use-value, exchange-value, and surplus-value (B)
The concrete	Non-class and class systems (C)	Primitive communism Ancient mode of production Asiatic mode of production Feudal mode of production Capitalist mode of production (D)

SOURCE: CREATED BY AUTHOR

labor-time (shaped by the natural economy, levels of technology, class relations), division of labor (with levels and types of social roles and statuses), and the form and role of state structures (e.g., forms of authority, power relations, use of martial force, political rights and obligations). Given that these differences *initially* lay in the distinction between non-class and class systems, and given the focus of the research schedule is capitalism's historical development, analysis would move from this initial focus on capitalism's similarities with all systems and turn to the question of class systems more specifically.

3.2   *Capitalism and Class Systems*

The next step is examining capitalism as a mode of production (Table 3.10a, Cell A) from the standpoint of class systems (Cell B), with non-class systems abstracted out of the model set. Class systems are identified by landed property and the appropriation of surplus-value through the use of forced labor in its production (which interiorizes class-labor relations and processes). For this model set, capitalism is lumped with other class systems on their similarities and their empirical details in general are examined (Cells C and D). Either this or one can contrast them with one another for differences in their class structures and the fallout that extends from them (Table 3.10b).

As far as similarities go, of interest here are those features, processes, activities, and so on, that stem from the structural variables of *class systems in general rather than features unique to any specific class system.* These are things like ruling and laboring classes locked in a "class struggle," a repressive state appa-

TABLE 3.10A   From production in general to similarities among specific class systems

	The general	The specific
The abstract	Modes of production (A)	Class systems (B)
The concrete	Ancient mode	Egypt, Greece, Rome, Carthage
	Asiatic mode	India, China, Japan, East Indies
	Feudal mode	The Middle Ages, England in 16th century, Romania (Danubian principalities), Poland, Germany, France, Sweden
	Capitalist mode (C)	England, America, Venice, Portugal, Holland (D)

TABLE 3.10B   From production in general to differences between specific class systems

	The general	The specific
The abstract	Modes of production (A)	Class systems (B)
The concrete	Ancient mode	Egypt, Greece, Rome, Carthage
	Asiatic mode	India, China, Japan, East Indies
	Feudal mode	The Middle Ages, England in 16th century, Romania (Danubian principalities), Poland, Germany, France, Sweden
	Capitalist mode (C)	England, America, Venice, Portugal, Holland (D)

SOURCE: CREATED BY AUTHOR

ratus that manages the relations of ruling in such a society—building armies, putting down dissent, self-defense and waging war, or even undertaking projects like building canals, mass agriculture, roads, and other forms of infrastructure. Class systems also have divisions of labor that are more complex and a greater level of development of productive forces (which also allows for the aforementioned building projects). Finally, because of their class relations and struggles, the use of force, resistance, and forms of development of productive forces, class societies are subject to revolutions—social, technological, political, and/or economic.

In terms of their differences, class systems have different forms of property, including landed property (e.g., state landowners, individual and family landowners, hereditary landowners, and so on) and private property (private ownership of the means of production). By extension, class systems have different class-labor relations (e.g., patricians, despots, landlords, capitalists / peasants, serfs, artisans, slaves, wage-laborers), different subjects of production (use-value production remains but greater attention is directed toward exchange-value and surplus-value), different forms of appropriation (e.g., slavery, labor rent, usury, taxes, wages), different ways and levels in which technology develops (stagnate/slow/constant development, low/moderate/high complexity), different state forms (e.g., despotism, oligarchs, monarchs, representative democracies) and the ways states support the interests of ruling groups (e.g., law, public discourse, propaganda, policing, use of military), different forms of laboring class political resistance, and different likelihoods of and paths to successful revolutions and/or the ways they are defeated. Though space considerations prevent delineating the possible permutations and combinations of these variables, a model of class systems in general and their specific features would incorporate both what we have learned from Marx on these matters and from our entire history of social research on class systems.

3.3   *Capitalism as a System*

The next step is to hone in more closely on capitalism as a system. At this step, with the features of both production and class systems in general assumed, we next isolate capitalism's unique features as a class system. Reflecting this, Table 3.11 re-abstracts class systems into the general abstract category (Cell A), treats the capitalist mode of production as a specific class system (Cell B), isolates its general concrete history for analysis (Cell C), and trains empirical focus on specific times and places (Cell D). At this point, research undertakes new observations, constructs relevant concepts, and sorts out identifying categories.

This step extracts capitalism's features as a class system by examining its historical representatives and contrasting them to other class systems as external model sets, which guides a research schedule's inquiries. What are capitalism's central and unique classes and property relations? In what way is its subject of production organized around producing use-value versus exchange-value versus surplus-value? What is its form of appropriation? How does it tend to develop its division of labor and productive forces? How do capitalist class-relations shape its state apparatus? What sort of struggles do its classes engage in because of all of these conditions? Such questions prepare analysis for modeling the specific structure of the capitalist mode of production.

Based on investigations reflected in Tables 3.9–3.11, we next derive a structural model of the capitalist system (Table 3.12, Cell A). At this point, what was

TABLE 3.11   From class systems in general to capitalism and its history

	The general	The specific
The abstract	Class systems (A)	Capitalism as a class system (B)
The concrete	England, America, Venice, Portugal, Holland, and later France and Germany, and eventually the world-market (C)	Specific times, places, events, observations, etc. (D)

SOURCE: CREATED BY AUTHOR

TABLE 3.12   From the capitalist mode of production to empirical detail

	The general	The specific
The abstract	The capitalist mode of production (A)	Capitalism's historical stages (B)
The concrete	Societies representing capitalism's historical stages (C)	Specific places, times, policies, organizations, people, etc. (D)

SOURCE: CREATED BY AUTHOR

once treated as its general concrete expressions (Table 3.11, Cell C above) are examined in constructing the specific abstract category with a concern on isolating whether or not this system has more than one form or stage specific to it (Table 3.12, Cell B) (more below). Investigation here is trained on studying its real historical development in its general concrete manifestations (Cell C) in terms of specific places, times, policies, organizations, people, etc. (Cell D).

From such an analysis comes insight to capitalism's basic structure. Its class relations rest on private ownership of the means of production. The subject of production is surplus-value extraction (via unpaid labor) and capital accumulation, with use-value and exchange-value only of interest to the extent that they service these ends. Surplus-value is based on the realization of profits from the sale of commodities produced by wage-laborers. Capitalist commodity production—i.e., the M-C-M'...M'-C-M"...∞ model—sets production in motion by using wage-laborers (who are divorced from possession of their own means of production) to make goods whose full value laborers do not receive in wages. Such structural relations allow for modeling how capitalism's configuration results in predictable tendencies.

Given competitive markets for labor-power, raw materials, and commodity sales, the capitalist must strive for at least average costs and average profits, while dividing their profits in a least three ways: personal gain, accumulation for business coffers (i.e., the capitalist's own social fund), and reinvestment into production (i.e., capital's generational reproduction).[13] The relationship between profits (or capitalist surplus-value) and capital investments—into technology, or constant capital, and labor costs, or variable capital—produces

---

13   The current model set does not include forms of capitalism where a firm has outside investors who have a right to claim returns on profits in the form of interest or dividends.

a rate of profit.[14] This rate can be depicted in a formula: $s / c + v$. Class relationships—especially competition within the capitalist class and the antagonism between them and laboring classes—compel the capitalist to reinvest a portion of their profits into labor-saving technology (lowering their wage-bill and increasing surplus-values available for realization as profits). Over time, the amount of capital outlay for c (machinery, technology, and so on) tends to increase faster than v (wages, pensions, and so on). These relations and processes build multiple interconnected tendencies into the system:

- Continual development of socially productive forces...
- which leads to a division of labor with an increasing relative ratio between technological complexity and the amount of workers needed to staff it (or, an increasing organic composition of capital)...
- which leads to reducing the relative outlay of money going to labor, either in particular businesses or across the capitalist class as a whole...
- which—in combination with wealth appropriation via the wage-system already in place—tends to produce a systematic concentration of wealth...
- which results in a tendency for the rate of profit to fall (relative to other variables that can accelerate or impede this) which, when occurring industry-wide or class-wide, tends to produce...
- economic contractions and systemic crises (i.e., over-production, recessionary boom and bust cycles, financial crises, depressions, and so on).

Other relationships and processes connect with these tendencies. There is a class struggle between capital and labor and a state the capitalist class dominates in this struggle, though one subject to democratic reforms that allow the working class to press for their interests. The system increasingly organizes society around the accumulation of capital, including the commodification of social life, the growth of monopolies, a tendency for capital to centralize wealth, technology, and classes geographically, and, thus, the growth of urban centers that divide town from country.

3.3.1   Capitalism and Its Historical Stages

One researcher might be interested in capitalism's development out of the feudal order, while another might be interested in the development of capitalism over its own history. In a study of how one system developed out of another or of a system's transition from one historical stage to another, the "fixed presuppositions themselves become fluid in the further course of development.

---

14   "When in general we speak about profit or rate of profit, then *surplus-value* is supposed to be *given*. The influences therefore which determine surplus-value *have* all operated. This is the presupposition" (Marx 1971b: 228; emphases in the original).

But only by holding them fast at the beginning is their development possible without confounding everything" (Marx 1973: 817). In such analysis, then, the initial starting-point is asking whether an identifying structure remains in place. If core structural variables of a system are no longer in place, or in the process of dissolution, then the analysis is of changes *between* systems. If an identifying structure remains while changes in its internal variables take place, then analysis is modeling changes *within* that system.

Capitalism's structural configuration produces its constant historical development. To identify its historical stages, one begins with a structural model and views the system's history in reverse, starting from the present. As long as its structural variables—private ownership of the means of production, use of wage-labor (surplus-value extraction assumed), production for the purpose of the accumulation of capital—remain constant, then investigation necessarily involves the capitalist mode of production. And if "the relation between capital and wage-labor determines the entire character of the mode of production" (Marx 1971a: 880), then one can use changes within this relation to demarcate capitalism's distinct historical periods.[15]

Once one has identified different stages, several other questions arise. Should they contextualize data in a model set for one stage or another? What if one's data appears to be from a transitionary period with variable temporal-structural-geographical boundaries? What Marx (1971b: 491) says about the transition from feudalism to capitalism can serve research purposes here: "[t]he process of capital becoming capital or its development *before* the capitalist production process exists, and its realisation in the capitalist process of production itself belong to two historically different periods. In the second, capital is *taken for granted*, and its existence and automatic functioning is presupposed. In the first period, capital is the sediment resulting from the process of dissolution of a different social formation" (emphases in the original). This proviso suggests multiple guidelines for contextualizing investigations:

– Analysis of transitionary periods leading up to capitalism's establishment should remain cognizant of remnant class relations from the prior mode of production, where landed property (some becoming capitalists, some still practicing under feudal auspices) as well as earlier labor forms (such as corvée labor) still exist but with capital and wage-labor gradually taking them over.

---

15   "The existing basis on which capitalist production works is wage-labour, which is however at the same time reproduced continuously by it. It is therefore based also on *capital*, the form assumed by the conditions of labour, as its given prerequisite, a prerequisite however which, like wage-labour, is its continuous presupposition and its continuous product" (Marx 1971b: 492; emphasis in the original).

- In established capitalism, research assumes that wage-laborers and capital-ists predominate—though this assumption about labor may not always ap-ply to capitalism's colonial domains, where its class relations often drove labor down to a slave-like existence and none-too-seldom conditions of ac-tual slavery.
- Depending on their historical-structural location, some data might be best contextualized by a capitalist model in one feature (e.g., monopoly capital-ism in the core), while also connected to separate models in other features (e.g., primitive communism or the Asiatic mode in a periphery), e.g., neo-colonial situations with capital penetration of pre-capitalist societies once outside of global markets.
- Data may need to be placed between stages and thus within mixed capital–labor relations, or even where one geographical area is better understood within one framework (e.g., transnational capitalism) and another geo-graphical area is contextualized in a different one (e.g., manufacture).
- In each case, the researcher should be sensitive to how these relations set in motion additional processes of transformation. For example, if capitalist organizations from the core penetrate a society understood under a model for primitive communism, this will transform that society and, therefore, that previous model of primitive communism breaks down, necessitating its replacement, perhaps with a model comparable to a colonial one.

In such examinations, a researcher incorporates empirical domains in con-junction with interpretive guidelines. Looking backward from present and iso-lating, say, the neo-liberal period of 2000–2020, one could choose multiple modern nation-states as examples of regimes pursuing free trade policies. If one is interested in the Industrial Revolution, they can examine one or all among several countries going through it during a period of interest. If a re-searcher is interested in the earliest forms of capitalist development, they might narrow their attention to the colonial conquests of the Spanish, the Por-tuguese, or the Dutch, while recognizing the feudal relations that still existed in parts of Europe and the Asiatic forms in China, Japan, and so on. In the ta-bles below, then, I try to provide cases that are, arguably, exemplary of the model set's pathway from its initial abstract categories down to more specific ones and their concrete examples.

During European colonial expansion, the emerging new mode of produc-tion (Table 3.13, Cell A) existed primarily at the proto-national level and focused on production of and trade in products from peasant, serf, and slave labor with a growing class of wage-laborers in a period of "agricultural capitalism" (Cell B). In researching this period, one could identify one of the historical form's leading representatives and its associated practices, e.g., the Dutch

TABLE 3.13   From the capitalist mode of production to empirical detail: Dutch Colonial
Empire

	The general	The specific
The abstract	The capitalist mode of production (A)	Capitalism's historical stages: colonialism and agriculture (B)
The concrete	Dutch Colonial Empire, 1500–1700s (C)	Specific places, times, policies, organizations, people, etc. (D)

SOURCE: CREATED BY AUTHOR

TABLE 3.14   From the capitalist mode of production to empirical detail: rise of English
manufacturing

	The general	The specific
The abstract	The capitalist mode of production (A)	Capitalism's historical stages: manufacture (B)
The concrete	England in 1700s (C)	Specific places, times, policies, organizations, people, etc. (D)

SOURCE: CREATED BY AUTHOR

Colonial Empire (Cell C), and examine its specific holdings, e.g., the Dutch East India Company in Indonesia (Cell D). Both the model of capitalism in general (with society in general and class systems assumed) as well as traits associated with this stage provide investigative guides, tools, and explanatory variables. However, during this period—the birth of capitalism—there still existed remnants of feudal class relations in Europe—e.g., conflicts between the Spanish and the Dutch in Holland—as well as class relations from pre-capitalist forms in colonized areas—e.g., the Dutch in Indonesia, the Spanish in the Philippines and the Caribbean.

Colonialism set the stage for further capitalist development. As technology, markets, and local/regional businesses congealed and matured, the capitalist mode of production (Table 3.14, Cell A) entered a stage of "manufacture" (Cell B), destroying the remaining feudal guilds and further raising wage-labor to the norm. Regions of Europe, though England most dramatically, grew rapidly after former serfs, tradesmen, and peasants were expropriated from traditional

TABLE 3.15   From the capitalist mode of production to empirical detail: the Industrial Revolution

	The general	The specific
The abstract	The capitalist mode of production (A)	Capitalism's historical stages: industrial capitalism (B)
The concrete	Great Britain, France, Germany, the United States, 1800–1900s (C)	Specific places, times, policies, organizations, people, etc. (D)

SOURCE: CREATED BY AUTHOR

lands and fled a foundering feudal economy and migrated to cities in search of work. Manufacture sprang from capitalism's continual development of its productive forces, growth of this new workforce that was desperate for wages, and on the fuel of raw materials garnered from both the destruction of the feudal rural economy and colonial conquests. Investigation here would use a fuller model of the capitalist mode of production, with a leading area or country chosen for empirical focus, in this case England of the 1700s (Cells C and D).

With the capitalist mode of production's (Table 3.15, Cell A) competitive market and business profits invested in labor-saving machinery spurring on its productive forces, the "[c]olonial system, public debts, heavy taxes, protection, commercial wars, &c., these true children of the manufacturing period, increase gigantically during the infancy of Modern Industry" (Marx [1867] 1992b: 708–709). These developments facilitated the rise of an "industrial" capitalist period (Cell B) that witnessed intense exploitation in mines and factories, concentration of capital and labor in urban areas, and growing labor unrest—e.g., union organization, party formation, radicalism, rebellions, and so on. Already at the head of capitalist development, Great Britain was the initial major center of industry, though France, Germany, and the United States were not far behind (Cells C and D).

In the capitalist mode of production (Table 3.16, Cell A), leading industries tend to out compete smaller ones and, over time, wealth tends to concentrate and capital increasingly centralizes. As leading capitals grow large and dominate the market, so do their host nation-states and their populations correspondingly grow. With these developments so, too, does the world-market grow, a process that made late industrial capitalism mature into a period of "monopoly capital" (Cell B). In this stage, after the unrest of the industrial period, the state negotiated a détente between capital and labor, with corporate/

TABLE 3.16   From the capitalist mode of production to empirical detail: monopoly capitalism

	The general	The specific
The abstract	The capitalist mode of production (A)	Capitalism's historical stages: monopoly capitalism (B)
The concrete	United States, 1900s–WWII (C)	Specific places, times, policies, organizations, people, etc. (D)

SOURCE: CREATED BY AUTHOR

TABLE 3.17   From the capitalist mode of production to empirical detail: transnational capitalism

	The general	The specific
The abstract	The capitalist mode of production (A)	Capitalism's historical stages: transnational capitalism (B)
The concrete	Europe, United States, Japan, WWII to 2000 (C)	Specific places, times, policies, organizations, people, etc. (D)

SOURCE: CREATED BY AUTHOR

union cooperation in Fordism, welfare-state provisions, and increased state regulation of the economy, which lasted up until (and somewhat during) World War I–II (Sweezy 1966). The United States began taking the lead over Britain in the world economy during this period (Cells C and D).

With the world-market a central feature of the capitalist mode of production (Table 3.17, Cell A), capitals reaching an economy of scale are best placed to further forge international production and trading links and/or take advantage of those already in place. During World War II, the United States went on a wartime economy, leading to significant growth in its air, auto, energy, metals, munitions, and communications industries. After the peace, the United States (along with Britain) assumed leadership in rebuilding the world economy through sponsoring institutions and programs such as the World Bank and International Monetary Fund, the Marshall Plan, subsidized housing and education loans for former soldiers and their families, and building projects focused on things like interstate highways, advanced rail, and airports. With the recovery of Europe and Japan during and after this period, capital became more "transnational" (Cell B), with offices and factories in multiple countries, even greater capital mobility, and a regime of accumulation crossing state lines

TABLE 3.18   From the capitalist mode of production to empirical detail: global capitalism

	The general	The specific
The abstract	The capitalist mode of production (A)	Capitalism's historical stages: global capitalism (B)
The concrete	World-market as a whole (C)	Specific places, times, policies, organizations, people, etc. (D)

SOURCE: CREATED BY AUTHOR

worldwide. This period saw initial growth in global GDP and a rise of the middle classes, though, over time, competing global labor markets and union decline led to a shrinking middle class in many core sectors (Cells C and D).

Despite all of these historical changes and with much of the transnational stage still with us, the key structural features of the capitalist mode of production (Table 3.18, Cell A) have given rise to an era of neo-liberalism (for discussion, see Harvey 2005). This era experienced shifts in the capital–labor relation yet again, bringing in a period of "global" capitalism (Cell B). This era is marked by free trade agreements, privatization policies, the death of Fordism (with declines in unions, dismantling of welfare-states, capital mobility and international competition leading to wage suppression, and general labor disorganization), deregulation of state constraints on capital, the rise of finance capital, an interconnected computerized world, the ascendance of new industrial powers (e.g., China and India), and a rising level of new slavery (Cells C and D).

These observations suggest ways to bring our models together. As "production in general" and "class systems" remain too broad for sufficient model specificity (while still containing relevant information), the examples above require moving toward frameworks that combine models of "capitalism in general" modified by contingencies relative to its stages. Research could use such a framework to study specific industries at specific times and places. Table 3.19 provides an overview of such a possible research schedule.

There are multiple ways for inquiry here to proceed. For instance, one might use a model of agricultural capitalism to study slavery in the American South of the colonial period. Or they could combine multiple models of industry, monopoly, and transnational stages of capitalism to trace changes in the oil industry over time. One could study global commodity chains that connect goods like coffee and/or major international conglomerates and industries like fast food across vast portions of time and space with a model carved at the level global capitalism, while remaining cognizant of uneven development across regions of the world economy. Here one might apply models of

TABLE 3.19   From the capitalist mode of production to its historical stages and specific
organizations, periods, and events

The general abstract	The specific abstract	The general concrete	The specific concrete
The capitalist mode of production (production in general and class systems assumed)	Agriculture	Proto-national capitals, colonialism, corvée, slavery, and wage-labor	Dutch East India Company, feudal landowners as new capitalists, slavery in Caribbean, North America, etc.
	Manufacture	Maturation of businesses, markets, and wage-labor	Rise of powerful banking houses, influence of mining, textile, and sugar industries, etc.
	Industry	Growth of factories, urban concentration of capital, mass labor forces	Industrial Revolution in London, Manchester, New York, etc.
	Monopoly	Concentration of industries, state-regulation, and Fordism	United Steel, Standard Oil, United Autoworkers, welfare-states (e.g. the New Deal)
	Transnational	Multinational corporations, global labor competition, multipolarity, decline of middle classes	Dole, Exxon-Mobil, JP Morgan Chase, US–Europe–Japan centers of commerce and trade
	Global	Transnational capital, neo-liberalism, computerization, global labor disorganization	Berkshire Hathaway, IKEA, Walmart, NAFTA, TTP, Internet commerce (e.g., Amazon, Alibaba)

SOURCE: CREATED BY AUTHOR

globalization for core areas while using models of capitalism fit for colonial or neo-colonial situations in peripheral areas (which is another way to depict the model of world systems analysis, in a sense). Table 3.20 below presents such a research agenda.

TABLE 3.20   From capitalism in general and its historical stages to specific industries

The general abstract	The specific abstract	The general concrete	The specific concrete
Capitalism in general	Capitalist agriculture	American slavery	Colonial plantations of Virginia, Georgia, 1700
	From industrial to transnational capitalism	Oil and gas industries, late 1800s–1990s	Standard Oil, British Petroleum, Royal Dutch Shell, Aramco
	Global capitalism	Global commodities, multinational food corporations, fast food companies	Coffee industry, Archer Daniels Midland, McDonald's

SOURCE: CREATED BY AUTHOR

Sometimes investigators have questions that both are more general but at the same time require more specified concepts and empirical domains. Imagine a researcher is interested in how the oil industry as a whole changed across the transition from industrial to transnational capitalism. They could carve out a schedule that combines multiple oil companies and their practices across such periods. Alternatively, their research may begin with a historically specific case—e.g., British Petroleum in Iran—and piece that company's activities—e.g., the 1953 overthrow of the Shah—together with wider social-historical realities. In either case, the researcher would trace their data and conceptual framework back through the abstractions while targeting relevant historical events and structural variables. As such, Table 3.21 below portrays a re-abstracting process beginning with transitions between stages of capitalism and tracing connections to specific companies at specific times in the same industry.

In a final example, starting with capitalism in general, one could choose a specific company and trace its activities across capitalism's stages (Table 3.22). Such an analysis could reveal how that company responded to capitalism's historical development in a way that facilitated its survival. One would not have to limit their examination to only one company across these periods, as banking may have developed in ways where a long historical past was not a prerequisite for getting into the industry in a more recent stage. By extension, one could also compare a variety of industries and/or companies across these

TABLE 3.21   From the transition from industrial capitalism to transnational capitalism and specific industries and corporations

The general abstract	The specific abstract	The general concrete	The specific concrete
From industrial to transnational capitalism	Oil and gas industries, 1800–1990s	Standard Oil	Standard Oil, 1870–1945
		British Petroleum	British Petroleum, 1909–1954
		Royal Dutch Shell	Royal Dutch Shell, 1907–1990s
		Aramco	Aramco, 1920s/1944–1990s

SOURCE: CREATED BY AUTHOR

TABLE 3.22   From capitalism in general to a specific banking house across stages of capitalist development

The general abstract	The specific abstract	The general concrete	The specific concrete
Capitalism in general	Banking industries	Agricultural capitalism	Barclays, 1690–1700s
		From manufacture to industry	Barclays, 1700s–1800s
		From industry to monopoly capitalism	Barclays, 1800s–1900s
		Monopoly capitalism	Barclays, 1900–WWII
		From monopoly capitalism to transnational	Barclays, WWII–1990s
		From transnational to global capitalism	Barclays, 1990s–present

SOURCE: CREATED BY AUTHOR

stages and isolate those common strategies that aided their survival (e.g., diversification, as well as specific types of it) and/or find other common themes that account for their failure (e.g., slow to innovate, as well as failures in actual attempts at innovation, etc.).

4   Some Methodological Provisos and Observations

There are several useful methodological implications from the discussion above.

Though social scientists study historical development and model structural relationships, they also need tools for bringing those inquiries together. Marx's method provides for bridging both forms of inquiry by using structural models to map empirical data, historical events, and forms of social development over time. That said, a tension always remains between a structural model and real history. This is for three main interconnected reasons. First, just as Max Weber emphasized, though a well-constructed model should have a non-insignificant degree of application, it will often have some distance between its descriptions, predictions, and/or explanations and specific concrete events. Second, a model's variables often interact with other variables external to the model as well as historical events not contained in the main or any other model set. Third, given the fact of historical change, the more temporally narrow one carves their model, the more likely they will need to adjust it over time or develop an entirely new one.

Structural and historical analyses, though often intertwined, reveal different things. The first part of this chapter included slavery in models for both feudalism and capitalism, though it was absent in their models in the previous chapter. The difference is that slavery is not part of the *structure of these systems per se*, but rather was a *historical development within them*. In feudalism, slavery primarily existed as a colonial labor system that underpinned the transition to capitalism. Multiple designations for laborers existed during that transition: slaves, free and half-free persons, indentured servants, etc. Considered as a closed system outside of history, slavery is not a structural variable of the capitalist mode of production, either. Capitalism could neither develop, grow, nor even exist at all with slavery as its base labor relation. Nevertheless, slavery *is* part of its historical reality, particularly when the variables preventing exploitation from driving labor into slavery are not in place, e.g., resistance from working classes and forms of state regulation and intervention. Slavery thus internally relates to capitalism as a historical relation instead of a structural one, though that structure itself impresses upon social conditions in a way where slavery emerges from those social conditions with regularity.[16]

---

16   In both feudalism and capitalism, the labor system and the mechanisms of wealth appropriation rely on labor exploitation, and each contains a dynamic where labor conditions can sink to their lowest form, that of enslavement. Nevertheless, these structures are as such that they could operate with serf and wage-labor respectively, i.e., without the

Because Marx constructed his structural variables for capitalism as a closed system, the system's historical developments and constant expansion into new territories bring counteracting variables into his models—variables Marx (1971b: 232–240) attempted to catalog. Consequently, the empirical grounds available for testing elements of his theories—e.g., the falling rate of profit— have usually contained only a partial identity with the premises of the structural model. It can only be when capitalism is a closed system that such model testing becomes hypothetically realistic. Perhaps today, with the era of globalization, we are reaching such a situation.

Two properties of the method are important to stress before closing. First, the method facilitates connecting causal explanations with variables carved from the appropriate level of generality. Using capitalism as an example, the method assists in addressing which observations are accounted for by relations of production in general, class structures in general, capitalism in general, a stage of capitalism, or perhaps some unique historical situation within that context. For example, things that are capitalist-specific might be poorly modeled under class relations more generally, e.g., the roles that commodity production, world markets and trade, and capital accumulation—realities absent in a general class model—played in modern slavery. The reverse can happen, too, where the observer views sociological phenomena that have origins in class structures as specifically capitalist in nature, e.g., Marx's historical-materialist model provides for class struggles and revolutions under *any* class system, not just under capitalism.

Second, and in a related manner, one could continue re-abstracting and moving categories right down to treating an individual plantation or

---

introduction of slavery. That said, historical events played on these variables in a way resulting in slavery in more than one time or place. In feudalism, this was mainly during its transition period to capitalism, in its colonial domains where the threat (and reality) of violence and the lack of effective political-social barriers, pressures, or pushback amidst the drive for resource extraction allowed slavery and/or slave-like conditions to arise. In capitalism, appropriators could install slavery at different times and in different places— e.g., the American South—just so long as enough wage-laborers exist elsewhere to purchase commodities at a level that provides for the needed profits. We see such relations still in place in the capitalist world-market today. Areas in its periphery—because of reasons accounted above—none-too-seldom experience labor conditions comparable to slavery (and actual slavery), while the system as a whole remains afloat and reliant on paid workers in the core and the semi-periphery for sufficient and necessary levels of commodity purchasing. As capitalism increasingly eliminates all prior external systems globally speaking, we also witness a downward leveling of labor conditions across its regions at the same time as growth in consumptive middle classes across once poor regions.

corporation in the general abstract and then examining its specific abstract, general concrete, and specific concrete developments in just the same way as re-abstracting systems as a whole. For example, one could treat banking industries as a general abstract category (assuming capitalism in general and the transition from transnational to global capitalism), use Barclays as a specific abstract example, examine it in the general concrete between the 1990s and the present, and focus on specific branches, actors, and/or policies as specific concrete data. In continuing to re-abstract, one could move Barclays between the 1990s and the present into the general abstract category (with capitalism in general, banking industries, and the period from transnational to global capitalism all assumed). Beginning here, one could then focus on a specific branch, its actors, and/or policies as specific abstract examples, follow those policies and practices over this period in the general concrete as indicative of behaviors across banking industries, with focus on a singular specific concrete instance that demonstrates them. It is in such a way that Marx's method can put a particular capitalist institution under a microscope.

5   Discussion

Marx's method does not require building models anew each time we embark on research. In the case of slavery, as it is an exploitative labor system for the purpose of surplus-value extraction, we can adapt research on this subject matter to models of class-based modes of production we already have and examine it across and/or between them. While also a research schedule under a previously established model of class systems in general, a study of capitalist development is a study *within* a mode of production for which we also have a model.

By extension, then, the care with which Marx's method imbues empirical investigation, comparative analysis, and the drawing of conclusions is a valuable framework through which to understand and evaluate other theoretical models and claims about human history and society. For example, one of the claims underpinning postmodern theory is that Marx's "grand narrative" is an obsolete model for our contemporary experience. While more grounded ideas from a different direction, multiple theories of "globalization" make a similar claim. For both, today's world is no longer the world upon which Marx founded his political-economic models. What are those foundations?
– Private ownership of the means of production;
– Commodity production for market sales;
– Market sales for profits;

- Profits for the accumulation of capital;
- Accumulation of capital as the central pursuit of the capitalist class;
- The existence of an exploited class of wage-laborers upon which all of the above rest;
- The struggles between the class of accumulators and the class of laborers;
- Constant and complex development of productive forces as capitalists invest in technology to lower labor costs in pursuit of surplus-value production;
- The state as an arena of struggle dominated primarily by the capitalist class;
- A tendency toward a concentration of wealth resulting from the system's inherent operations;
- Periodic crises produced by this concentration of wealth;
- Increasing urbanization and centralization of capital;
- The centralization of financial capital in urban centers;
- The growth of financial capital as the result of how wealth concentration leaves less and less investment opportunities in productive capital.

And so on. The points above reflect the world we live in today, just as they did in Marx's day. Theories of postmodernity and globalization, while pointing to possibly new historical developments, are about a world that has not structurally changed in its fundamentals.

Marx's models of our modern political-economy have stood the test of time, insofar as one uses capitalist development as a marker of that time. Though capitalism was going through an industrializing period during his lifetime, part of his genius was his ability to model the basic structure of the system from the empirically available material he could access. It does not follow, however, that Marx's model of modern society is time-locked, as his conclusions about capitalism as a mode of production were not specific to the industrial world in which he lived. Similarly, if capitalism undergoes a fundamental transformation and a new class system takes its place, Marx's models of production in general and of class systems remain operative. If a non-class system replaces capitalism, his model for production in general still serves as a starting-point of inquiry. Moreover, Marx's method of successive abstractions as a way to study the histories and the structures involved in all of these potential changes remains through it all.

CHAPTER 4

Successive Abstractions and Religion (1): A Conventional Approach

1 Introduction

This chapter begins an investigation of religion by treating it as a form of knowledge that asserts truths about the world, the cosmos, and human relationships to both, where these truths purport to come from a realm outside of our everyday existence. This form of knowledge has existed at both the level of social lore and social institutions across extensive periods of time and space. Given its historicity, its multiple forms, and its changing practices, it is a topic particularly well-suited for the method of successive abstractions. In this chapter, I apply the method to a more conventional sociology of religion, while the next chapter, by way of contrast, uses the method for a more Marxian historical materialist examination of the same subject.

2 Religion and the Method of Successive Abstractions

Below I begin with "knowledge in general," which includes all ideas, beliefs, ideologies and so on that assert truths relevant to the natural world, historical societies as a whole, and human experiences in both (Table 4.1, Cell A).[1] From this general category, I lump together lore, art, religion, historical discourse, political ideology, philosophy, science, and so on (Cell B). From these I isolate one knowledge-form based on its unique and identifying characteristics, i.e., the positing of a sacred realm distinct and separate from the profane one, where the former can influence the latter through special rituals, or "religion in general" (Cell C).[2] Finally, specific concrete examples of this knowledge-form are isolated in terms of what sort of powers and/or entities and their number they posit to exist in that sacred realm, i.e., animism, polytheism, and monotheism (Cell D).

---

1   The approach taken here does not construct "knowledge" as only those claims verified as accurate or true but rather simply as assertions humans make about reality and their experience in it.
2   This conceptualization of religion comes from Durkheim (1915).

TABLE 4.1   Religion as a specific form of knowledge in general

	The general	The specific
The abstract	Knowledge-forms in general (A)	Religion (also lore, art, history, political ideology, philosophy, science, etc.) (B)
The concrete	Religion in general: the sacred, the profane, and ritual (C)	Animism, polytheism, monotheism (D)

SOURCE: CREATED BY AUTHOR

Table 4.2 separates out religious forms in the specific concrete and shifts them into the general concrete category (Cell C), where each of them can receive their own analysis. Here, religion moves from a general concrete example to a specific abstract category (Cell B) of knowledge in general (Cell A). Thus far, this model has treated religion mainly as a social institution and a form of knowledge, identified its basic features and its general forms, and made a place in such a categorization scheme for specific empirical examples that demonstrate subcategories of the concept (Cell D). This initial approximation permits for sorting out detail through a framework to group religions with their shared identities at one moment while later allowing for the identification of their differences. Investigation is now ready for additional research of general concrete forms of religion by examining specific concrete examples of each using the controlled comparative method.

Leaving religion and the characteristics it shares with other knowledge-forms in the same category likely will not provide fine enough specificity as would a study of *religions per se*, i.e., what we observe in particular cases, events, or even overall patterns indicative of the practice or a culture where it predominates. Therefore, for a more concentrated focus, Table 4.3 moves religion into the general abstract category (Column A), where knowledge in general was previously placed. Here, other forms of knowledge (art, history, etc.) are abstracted out of the model set and religion as a knowledge-form asserting a relation between the sacred and the profane remains abstracted in (differences between religion-as-knowledge versus other knowledge-forms can now be contrasted). Analysis here treats animism, polytheism, and monotheism as specific abstract (Column B) forms of religion in general and puts into relief their specific theistic and organizational differences (Column C). Making such distinctions allows for sorting their differences and later bringing into view

TABLE 4.2   From religion as a specific form of knowledge in general to religion's general forms

	The general	The specific
The abstract	Knowledge-forms in general (A)	Religion in general: the sacred, the profane, and ritual (B)
The concrete	Animism	Earliest spiritual beliefs, Native American religions, Buddhism, Shintoism[a]
	Polytheism	Greek and Roman religions, Hinduism
	Monotheism (C)	Zoroastrianism, Judaism, Christianity, Islam (D)

SOURCE: CREATED BY AUTHOR

a   Students of religion often find handling non-theist spiritual traditions in a theological categorization difficult. Though many Shinto and Buddhist traditions are atheistic in outlook, they do share with animism the belief that our existence is filled with forces, energies, and even quasi-spirits that have relevance for how we conduct our affairs. So, even without a godhead, Shintoism and Buddhism are included here as religious beliefs akin to animism, even if how traditional animism has been practiced often bears little institutional resemblance to contemporary societies where Shintoism and Buddhism predominate.

specific concrete examples of any or all of these general concrete religious practices (Column D).

The process of successive abstractions continues as necessary. Having a model of religion in general developed, focus could turn to the particular features of one of its broader forms, such as monotheism. Table 4.4 places monotheism in the general abstract category (Column A), with all forms of shamanism and polytheism abstracted out into an external model set. This requires, at the moment, treating forms of monotheism as specific abstract examples (Column B) of the general abstract category, while, at the same time, holding constant the features of religion in general. With this categorization, research focuses on concrete examples for special attention (Columns C and D). For instance, one might be interested in particular practices of early Orthodox Judaism as a form of monotheism. Or, perhaps, research is focused on Christianity and thus splits it into both Catholicism and Protestantism (just to name two).

TABLE 4.3   From religion in general to types of theisms and their representations

The general abstract (A)	The specific abstract (B)	The general concrete (C)	The specific concrete (D)
Religion in general	Animism	Shamanism	Magic cults of Papua New Guinea, North America, Australia, Congo, etc.
		Denominational Animists	Shintoism in Japan, Buddhism in Japan, China, India, etc.
	Polytheism	Religions of antiquity	Greek Pantheon (Zeus, Poseidon, Hera, and other gods) rites, festivals, etc. Roman Pantheon (Jupiter and other gods), rites, festivals, etc.
		Hinduism	Vaishnavism, Shaivism, Shaktism, Smartism in India
	Monotheism	Zoroastrianism	Pre-Iranian Persia, India
		Judaism	Judaism in ancient Palestine, Orthodox Judaism in Israel, Reform Judaism in America
		Christianity	Roman Catholicism, Eastern Orthodox Church, Protestantism
		Islam	Sunni Islam, Shia Islam

SOURCE: CREATED BY AUTHOR

Afterwards, investigation might turn to specific concrete examples of Catholicism that emerged from the Roman Empire and its fall or modern forms of Protestantism. Their differences can be compared at either the level of the general concrete or the specific concrete, depending on how finely-grained the questions.

ABSTRACTIONS AND RELIGION: A CONVENTIONAL APPROACH

TABLE 4.4   From monotheism in general to specific religious studies

The general abstract (A)	The specific abstract (B)	The general concrete (C)	The specific concrete (D)
Monotheism	Judaism	Orthodox Judaism	Late 18th and early 19th century German Jewry
	Christianity	Roman Catholicism	Roman Catholic Church in 400s–1500s
		Protestantism	Southern Baptists in 1900s

SOURCE: CREATED BY AUTHOR

Differentiating monotheism from animism and polytheism and splitting various monotheisms into general forms with specific representatives is, thus far, only a classification scheme. Recall from Chapter 1 that in proposing investigative questions for additional abstraction, one criterion is that any new subdivision and subsequent research question should be based on a salient feature. For the analysis here, such a feature could be key doctrinal differences.

For instance, while some religious doctrines are exclusionary, others posit that anyone can participate given certain stipulations (and some religions have changed from one to the other over time). As opposed to animism (for which the concept does not really apply), people from any background may convert to Buddhism, Hinduism, Judaism, Christianity, or Islam (Table 4.5, Cells B, C, and D), i.e., they are "universalist" in nature. Among these, only Judaism, Christianity, and Islam are monotheistic (Table 4.6, Cells B, C, and D). To whom does this belief and practice in one god apply? Judaism is "universal" in a limited sense. Initially, Judaism and its god were specific to a tribe or a people (as was commonplace in that period). Over time, Judaism allowed conversion into its ranks after a period of trial, such as tests over doctrine and scripture and a ceremonial initiation (as is similar with Catholicism). For Christianity, after his crucifixion, believers later interpreted Jesus as the incarnation of the one, true god (the old Jewish god, Yahweh) that had dominion over heaven, Earth, and all of humanity. This was a more expansive expression and assertion of universalism, where not only was Jesus's authority applicable to everyone but faith in his divinity was now *required* for entry into heaven. Islam adopted

TABLE 4.5   From religion in general to specific universalistic theisms

	The general	The specific
The abstract	Religion in general: the sacred, the profane, and ritual (A)	Doctrinal theologies (B)
The concrete	Universalist theisms (C)	Buddhism, Hinduism, Judaism, Christianity, and Islam (D)

SOURCE: CREATED BY AUTHOR

an approach to the single Abrahamic god similar to Christianity, though Islam excluded the belief in Jesus-as-Christ. Finally, a key difference between Buddhism, Hinduism, and Judaism versus Christianity and Islam is that the former three do not posit that failure to participate in those belief systems has implications for what happens after death, while the latter two assert that god will punish an individual for their lack of belief and reward them for having it. We might characterize this procession as going from theism to monotheism to universalist monotheism to *required universalist monotheism* (Table 4.7).

Such differentiations assist us in asking, and potentially answering, several questions. To what extent does religious belief shape adherents' behaviors under (1) general theism? (2) doctrinal theistic codification? (3) doctrinal theistic universalism? (4) doctrinal monotheist universalism? (5) doctrinal required monotheist universalism? (6) doctrinal required monotheist universalism applied to reward or punishment in the afterlife? Armed with a model set that has required universalist monotheisms abstracted in, such questions could be addressed both through comparing internally *within* that model set and through an external comparison *between* it and the model sets abstracted out.

For instance, while Buddhism, Hinduism, and Judaism have comparatively mixed ideas on the afterlife, none threaten believers with eternal torment, and none require others to convert. Christianity and Islam do claim that a god-figure has designed a rewarding afterlife for believers and promises punishment to those who their doctrines fail to convince.[3] This difference perhaps

---

3   Christianity has had two traditional forms of a punishing afterlife. The first is more a "lack of reward" sort of punishment, in that individuals requiring additional purifying and/or repentance go to "purgatory" rather than "heaven." In the other, unrepentant sinners and (in some Christian traditions) nonbelievers go to "hell" for eternity. In Islam, though variations exist, everyone goes to "hell" (or "Jahannam") for a level of purification related to the amount and type of evil they have done in their life, though there are variations here as well. In general,

TABLE 4.6   From religion in general to specific universalistic monotheisms

	The general	The specific
The abstract	Doctrinal theologies (A)	Universalist theisms (B)
The concrete	Universalist monotheisms (C)	Judaism, Christianity, and Islam (D)

SOURCE: CREATED BY AUTHOR

explains why Christianity and Islam became proselytizing programs with oc-casional violence against heretics, blasphemers, apostates, and nonbelievers. Such behaviors toward religious outgroups—based on religious affiliation itself—are much less observed (but not completely absent) in cultures where Buddhism, Hinduism, and Judaism predominate.

One possible hypothesis here is that when religions do not require them to convert others, divergence in religious belief becomes less and less a basis for outward conflict with others. However, the use of violence toward nonbeliev-ers among Buddhists, Hindus, and Jews—whose religions are not required uni-versalist monotheisms—is not unknown. Research would need to examine whether or not such violence tended to come from certain subgroups within those religious traditions or if violence was equally likely from any believer in those religious traditions regardless of their sectarian differences. One likely associated hypothesis is that religious believers who are more conservative, fanatical, and/or fundamentalist in their outlook are more likely to engage in hostility toward others. As such, one could now compare moderates and con-servatives within these groups to see if there are differences in behavior be-tween them. Moreover, one could also compare between conservatives among these religions versus conservatives among the required universalist monothe-isms and try to isolate common behavioral traits, while using moderates from each as an additional point of comparison.

There are other associations with required universalist monotheism in which we also might be interested. Do these beliefs within both Christianity and Islam tell us something about why it is *relatively easy* to convert to those

---

the length of stay there will vary on the extent to which an individual requires purifying, with some being there only for a very short time and others being there for (what feels like to hu-mans) thousands of years. For some Islamic believers, punishment for the sinner is eternal, especially for non-Muslims. According to other Islamic beliefs, however, at some point god conquers hell and frees all souls who suffer there.

TABLE 4.7   From religion in general to required universalistic monotheisms

	The general	The specific
The abstract	Doctrinal theologies (A)	Universalist-monotheisms (B)
The concrete	Required universalist monotheisms (C)	Christianity and Islam (D)

SOURCE: CREATED BY AUTHOR

religions as compared to Judaism (or Catholicism)? One *could* simply declare themselves "a Christian" or "a Muslim" or even "a Buddhist," but it would sound peculiar to declare oneself "a Jew" (or "a Catholic") without going through the conversion process. Thus another question: To what extent do the unique properties of Jewish history versus the structural features of its religious doctrine compared to others account for this? What about Catholicism's history? Can we find any shared traits or parallels? Addressing such questions requires careful and systematic analysis, and this means a method is needed to sort out such historical and structural details in order to better establish their interconnections, something the method of successive abstractions is set up to do.

Below, Christianity is treated in its general abstract form (Tables 4.8–4.9, Cell A), where analysis focuses on the overall theological outlook that marks Christianity *as Christianity*. These traits are the beliefs that (1) the one true god sent his son to Earth (2) to redeem human sin (3) who was later executed, (4) rose from the dead, and (5) that belief in these claims is required for entrance into heaven as (6) the sacrifice this represented made heaven available for everyone. Set up as such, forms of Christian theology can be treated as specific abstract forms of the general category, focusing here on the split in Catholicism (Table 4.8, Cell B) after the Protestant Reformation (Table 4.9, Cell B; note that those in this cell are not the only ones that could be there, just examples). Abstracting out just two specific abstract forms of Christianity allows for a focus on the general concrete forms that represent them. In this case, one can choose from a wide variety of specific concrete forms of either Catholicism or Protestantism, e.g., the Roman Catholic Church in the 17th century (Table 4.8, Cell C and D) and the various forms Protestantism has taken (Table 4.9, Cells C and D). While such an examination of Protestant faiths based on their similarities would be revealing, one could gain additional insight by separating them into their various denominations for comparing them with each other (Table 4.10) and with Catholicism and its practices (Table 4.11). For example,

TABLE 4.8   From Christianity in general to Roman Catholic institutions and churches

	The general	The specific
The abstract	Christianity (A)	Roman Catholicism (B)
The concrete	Roman Catholic Church in 1600s (C)	The Vatican, specific churches and congregations (D)

SOURCE: CREATED BY AUTHOR

TABLE 4.9   From Christianity in general to similarities within Protestantism

	The general	The specific
The abstract	Christianity (A)	Protestantism (B)
The concrete	Anglicanism, Calvinism, Lutheranism, Baptists, Methodists, etc. (C)	Specific churches, synods, doctrines, and so on (D)

SOURCE: CREATED BY AUTHOR

Protestants do not recognize the authority of the Pope, do not venerate Mary or the saints, and do not believe that the wafer used in the communion ritual turns into the actual flesh of Jesus.

Similarly, as seen in Table 4.12, one could compare the history of Roman Catholicism with its own evolution over time. Here, one would start with Christianity as the general abstract category (Column A) and isolate Roman Catholicism as one of its specific abstract expressions (Column B). From there one could trace its historical development, such as its early configuration during the Roman Empire, between Rome's fall and before the Protestant Reformation, after that period and up to Vatican II, and finally its features after Vatican II (Columns C and D). One could then move Roman Catholicism into the general abstract category (Table 4.13, Cell A), treat its historical periods as specific abstract categories (Cell B), and then mutually compare them with each other for similarities in the general and specific concrete (Cells C and D). One could also locate other significant events in that church's history or, importantly, graph such changes onto wider historical changes in the social system in which it exists, e.g., political-economic developments in its host countries, world wars, and so on.

TABLE 4.10   From Christianity in general to differences among Protestantism

The general abstract (A)	The specific abstract (B)	The general concrete (C)	Group compared to	The specific concrete (D)
Christianity in general	Protestantism	Anglicanism	Calvinism Lutheranism Baptists Methodists	Specific churches, synods, doctrines, and so on
		Calvinism	Anglicanism Lutheranism Baptists Methodists	
		Lutheranism	Anglicanism Calvinism Baptists Methodists	
		Baptists	Anglicanism Calvinism Lutheranism Methodists	
		Methodists	Anglicanism Calvinism Lutheranism Baptists	

Below, similar to the above, I break down Islam (Table 4.14, Column A) as specific concrete subject matter into Sunni Islam in general and Shia Islam in general (Column B). Starting here, we can focus further by examining the countries where these forms predominate (Column C) and the details of specific individuals, leaders, and congregations (Column D), comparing and contrasting their real world similarities and differences along the way. For instance, Sunni and Shia Islam are both required universalistic monotheisms, accept Mohammad as god's last prophet, and believe that he brought back a pure

TABLE 4.11   Comparing Protestantism with Catholicism

The general abstract (A)	The specific abstract (B)	The general concrete (C)	Group compared to	The specific concrete (D)
Christianity in general	Protestantism	Anglicanism Calvinism Lutheranism Baptists Methodists	Catholicism Catholicism Catholicism Catholicism Catholicism	Specific churches, synods, doctrines, and so on

TABLE 4.12   From Christianity in general to comparing Catholicism in general to its historical changes

The general abstract (A)	The specific abstract (B)	The general concrete (C)	The specific concrete (D)
Christianity in general	Roman Catholicism in general	Catholicism under Rome	Specific churches, synods, doctrines, and so on
		Catholicism after fall of Rome and before the Protestant Reformation	
		Catholicism after the Protestant Reformation and before Vatican II	
		Catholicism after Vatican II	

form of Abrahamic belief. Nevertheless, certain disagreements differentiate them, e.g., they disagree on who was Mohammad's rightful successor. Each of these required monotheistic universalisms stem from a religious tradition forged between warring factions within a class system, with violence and forced conversions observed within and between cultures where these traditions predominate. This also explains, in part, their ongoing animosity

TABLE 4.13   From Catholicism in general to comparison of its historical periods with each other

The general abstract (A)	The specific abstract (B)	The general concrete (C)	The specific concrete (D)
Roman Catholicism in general	Catholicism under Rome	Catholicism after fall of Rome and before the Protestant Reformation Catholicism after the Protestant Reformation and before Vatican II Catholicism after Vatican II	Specific churches, synods, doctrines, and so on
	Catholicism after fall of Rome and before the Protestant Reformation	Catholicism under Rome Catholicism after the Protestant Reformation and before Vatican II Catholicism after Vatican II	
	Catholicism after the Protestant Reformation and before Vatican II	Catholicism under Rome Catholicism after fall of Rome and before the Protestant Reformation Catholicism after Vatican II	
	Catholicism after Vatican II	Catholicism under Rome Catholicism after fall of Rome and before the Protestant Reformation Catholicism after the Protestant Reformation and before Vatican II	

SOURCE: CREATED BY AUTHOR

toward each other. To what other variables might we trace this divide? Culture? Social-structural variables extant at the time of its founding? Some combination thereof? Ties with external political-economic powers? Interference from such powers? Etc.

TABLE 4.14   From religion in general to comparing Sunni and Shia Islam

	The general	The specific
The abstract	Islam in general (A)	Sunni Islam Shia Islam (B)
The concrete	Sunni Islam in Saudi Arabia	Specific imams, mosques, etc.
	Shia Islam in Iran (C)	Specific imams, mosques, etc. (D)

SOURCE: CREATED BY AUTHOR

Observation of the real history of a specific religion-as-denomination could also introduce questions about its organizational structure. How might an organizational structure influence both a religion's history and its connection with wider social realities? For instance, an investigation of Islam reflected above might observe that its authority structure comes from the imam at the mosque level (with some influence from ayatollahs, muftis, and grand muftis). However, Islam does not have a centralized organizational structure that crosses multiple cultures and countries in the same way as the Roman Catholic Church, which is highly centralized. Several Protestant traditions in the United States, too, have bottom-up authority structures, where congregations grant approval or disapproval of their specific church's leader. Given its top-down structure with worldwide authority, the Catholic Church can initiate reforms from above, though the connections between an individual believer and the religion's leadership are more distant and impersonal. In comparing their authority structures, one would predict that Catholicism's history evidences more effective methods of reform and doctrinal adjustment, while one would expect that religious leaders have more influence over individuals' beliefs and behaviors for Islamic and Protestant congregations.

As an extension, bottom-up authority combined with the strict doctrinal interpretations of conservative Protestantism have produced a history of schisms and the proliferation of multiple doctrines, churches, and congregations. Why, while not totally absent, has this been less evidenced in Islam? Such questions, of course, are empirical in nature but the overall point is that such traits could be isolated and controlled systematically. After having moved through all the levels of abstraction, a researcher here would be in a better position to pinpoint the influence of specific variables: (1) from religious belief

TABLE 4.15 From religion in general to a comparison of authority structures across three
different religious traditions

The general abstract	The general concrete	The specific abstract	Group compared to	The specific concrete
Monotheism (religion in general assumed)	Required monotheisms: bottom-up authority	Southern Baptists, Pentecostals	Sunni Islam in Saudi Arabia Global Roman Catholicism	Specific doctrines, people, dates, behaviors, statistical trends, etc.
	Required monotheisms: meso level authority	Sunni Islam in Saudi Arabia	Southern Baptists, Pentecostals Global Roman Catholicism	
	Required monotheisms: macro level authority	Global Roman Catholicism	Southern Baptists, Pentecostals Sunni Islam in Saudi Arabia	

SOURCE: CREATED BY AUTHOR

in general to (2) monotheism to (3) a distinction between required monotheisms to (4) those required monotheisms with a bottom-up authority structure versus (5) those required monotheisms whose authority sit at meso or macro levels. Table 4.15 below reflects such a comparative model.

3   Discussion

The discussion above applies the method of successive abstractions to the question of religion, though with only minimal empirical rigor brought to bear. This method requires that we specify the criteria of inclusion and exclusion in category construction, while focusing on both defining structural characteristics and historical developments across subject matter. In such research, there is no way for us to come up with scientifically sound generalizations unless we have a way to carefully and systematically construct appropriate categories, target their empirical referents, and control and compare our observations. In

ABSTRACTIONS AND RELIGION: A CONVENTIONAL APPROACH

order to increase our overall precision, we must have the facility to re-abstract in this process. Given historical change, various levels of sociological generality, and so on, there are several interconnected benefits to using such a method, whether for the study of religion or other social phenomena.

First, this method helps us avoid applying overly broad conceptualizations of objects to more narrow empirical observations. Recall from Chapter 1 the principle that the further away an observation of the concrete is from an initially broad abstract category the less likely it is that that broad category tells us all we need to know about that observation (though it is not without useful information). Should we observe behaviors of particular devotional groups—say a proclivity toward racism or sexism or the belief in magical spells—how do we account for this? By the beliefs of a particular church or congregation? By a particular tradition for a historical period? By the overall theology of the particular religion as a whole? By religion in general itself as a form of knowledge? All of the above? Maybe it is something else? In respect of such questions, abstracting objects at any one level (usually temporary) allows for carving them with the principle of precision in mind, which is necessary for both clarity and accuracy in concept development and for successful generalizations based on similarities. This is so because the method allows us to isolate relevant historical moments found in empirical detail and decipher whether a causal explanation lies in something unique to those moments, whether causal forces lie at a broader level, or some combination of both.

Second, this method provides the needed flexibility in mobilizing and manipulating conceptual frameworks in a way that respects crucial differences resulting from the cultural, economic, and political changes we observe. This, too, helps us avoid false generalizations, such as treating a specifically constructed historical social form as a sociological constant, an error of reification in scientific analysis and theory. For example, researchers often conceptualize "religion" at this broad level and then apply that model to all cases across history that fit this a priori definition. Very often in such an approach, details external to but influential on religious development are lost in the process and religion is depicted as a universal phenomenon despite its changing nature over time (more on this in the next chapter). In addition to methodological imprecision, such theoretical constructions also have political implications, as the common interpretation of sociological "universals" is that such practices and institutions are necessary for the proper functioning of social systems. But abstracting "religion" too broadly and only in a single instance risks creating false knowledge about what it is or is not and can lump too many examples into inappropriate categories. This approach can mislead us as to how its institutions do/do not function and/or what sorts of rules and laws societies have built into them, which of these rules and laws are social and/or historical constructions, and so on. Marx took pains to articulate how previous models of political economy often remained at surface level appearances, did not get behind the realities in question, and/or falsely universalized capitalist forms of labor or value and so on. One could say the same, perhaps, about the models of religion above, the reasons for which I now turn.

While the method of successive abstractions is Marx's, the above discussion is not really yet fully Marxist in character. It is still a general sociology, though one that employs a comparative method via the process of re-abstraction. To differentiate religions based on the categories of animism, polytheism, and monotheism is both to operate at a surface level appearance and to reduce such categorization to simple variables. Moreover, this is an idealist approach that delineates and analyzes religion mainly using the content of their theologies as the dividing line and is thus disconnected from other historical-material variables. Approaches that organize religious development through these familiar religious taxonomies are, according to the view of Marx and Engels ([1846] 1976: 37), simply "a summing-up of the most general results" and only help with "the arrangement of historical material" but are unfit as a "schema... for neatly trimming the epochs of history." While this approach is common in the social sciences, additional considerations are necessary, considerations that reveal the limitations of traditional approaches.

In any outlook that shares a view with Marx's, religion, like all social institutions, must be examined in its interconnections with broader material, social-structural, and historical realities. This concern is one of the particular advantages of the method of successive abstractions, as it allows the analyst to systematically locate changes in one phenomenon—carved at a particular level of abstraction—in association with changes in other phenomena—also carved at a particular level of abstraction. In this approach, the analyst grasps these levels of abstraction in terms of their interconnections with material reality and both broader and narrower levels of generality as the case may be. As such, this method provides an ideal way to synthesize historical, materialist, and structural analyses while employing procedures found in the experimental model. The next chapter addresses such complex, involved models for the study of religion and shows how Marx's approach is both sociological while at the same time different from traditional sociology proper.

Successive Abstractions and Religion (II): A Historical Materialist Approach

1 Introduction[1]

To study sociological objects of knowledge properly—i.e., scientifically—it is necessary to move systematically from observation to conceptualization and from there to analysis, interpretation, and explanation. If an analyst goes forward with conceptualizations that remain too broad, they risk overreaching in applying them to interpretation and explanation. Marx ([1843] 1975a: 16), for example, criticized Hegel because his "abstractions will be applicable to anything and everything actual." What is required is an analytical approach rooted in concrete realities where conceptualization and explanation proceed systematically to the appropriate level of specificity without obscuring the interrelations between objects of inquiry along the way. This is what we saw in Marx's approach to modes of production, as well as the proposed research schedule for studying both slavery and the history of capitalist development. This is equally true for the study of religion, as arguably seen in the limitations of the approaches discussed in the previous chapter. In expanding on that discussion, this chapter develops a historical materialist model for examining religion across multiple levels of socio-historical generality and concludes with proposing a Marxian taxonomy of religion.

2 Marx's Method and Religion

How should a sociological account of religion proceed? Two common and interconnected lines of attack have internal problems in terms of how their conceptualizations connect with both interpretation and explanation. Durkheim's (1915) well-known approach was to examine religion's "elementary forms," extract what he found there for model building, and then extrapolate to religion's overall functions across societies as a whole, including our modern one. The

---

1 An earlier and abbreviated version of this chapter previously came out in *Critical Sociology* (see Paolucci 2018a).

efficaciousness of this approach is limited because it assumes a questionable commensurability between objects of study—or what Marx ([1867] 1992b: 65) defined as things being "qualitatively equal."

Religion in modern society has a more developed coherence and institutionalization. It does not follow, however, that the earliest expressions with which it shares some similarities are identical—in reality and thus in conception—with what it eventually became. As Marx (1973: 103) phrased it, "although the simpler category may have existed historically before the more concrete, it can achieve its full (intensive and extensive) development precisely in a combined form of society" (also see Chapter 1, note 4). This principle suggests that applying a singular and universal theory of religion equally to its present as to its earliest proto-forms is an error in overgeneralization, especially if they have incommensurable features over time and space. Though similarities may exist, that is, we should not assume these are qualitatively equal things. This point will become more apparent as this chapter unfolds.

This problem with traditional functionalist modeling of religion is similar to applying the concept of "the economy" for all historical production forms, especially modern capitalism (as earlier chapters demonstrated). This sort of conceptual over-application fails to capture important interrelations among different levels of generality as well as prematurely or even falsely depicting specific historical forms as sociological universals. With that said, Durkheim's model of how religion distinguishes the sacred from the profane and uses rituals to interconnect them remains useful when analyzing religion in general and is commensurate with some concepts that Marx uses, as we will see.

Another functionalist model posits that religion exists to provide meaning for individuals and as an integrating mechanism for society as a whole. Though religion can and does do these things, there are three central problems with using this approach as an explanatory framework.

First, using meaning and integration to explain religion's genesis is to presuppose a prior society where these functions went unserved, which is self-contradictory. If religion developed to serve these social needs, how did a prior society exist at all if such necessary social functions were previously unfilled?

Second, if we accept this objection but still pursue a functionalist explanation, then we are forced to conclude that the servicing of these functions occurred through repeated happenstance and thus as an unintended consequence. However, if religion arose because it serviced the needs of meaning and social integration as a latent function, then its general historical development across thousands of cultures resulted from a series of coincidences with astronomical odds, which is scientifically unsatisfactory and really does not account for its origins at all.

Thus, third, once we include real human history, the functionalist approach requires that the socio-historical processes accounting for multiple religions' development—including but not limited to purges, conquests, forced conversions, etc.—happened to service the goals of meaning and integration. If one rejects this as implausible, then this leaves vital elements of real history excluded from the model, which means that the resulting explanatory theory rests on airy abstractions separated from the concrete foundations upon which our analysis must rest. Consequently, functionalist approaches that see religion as a source of meaning and social integration are relevant only *after* a religious practice is well established but such a model cannot account for religion's origins and overall development.

Because of these issues, an additional problem arises with functionalist explanations. Over history, as new religious ideas form, morph and/or decline and vanish, all religions are necessarily different than they once were and will later be. However, religious faith rests on the idea that a religion's current endpoint is as intended. Functionalist theory and religious beliefs each thus tend to "regard religion as a *causa sui*" (Marx and Engels [1846] 1976: 154) or its own cause. Because of this, both outlooks rely on a teleological reconstruction of the historical chain of events, inverting outcomes with causes. These forms of explanation—each emblematic of an "inverted world-consciousness" (Marx [1844] 1975b: 175)—either posit "eternal formulas without origin or progress" (Marx 1982: 102) or offer models where "*history*, like *truth*, becomes a person apart, a metaphysical subject of which real human individuals are but the bearers" (Marx and Engels [1845] 1956: 107; emphases in the original). In short, functionalist explanations of religion—as opposed to *descriptions or interpretations* of its potential functions—are fundamentally metaphysical and teleological propositions antithetical to scientific standards.

For Marx and Engels ([1846] 1976: 43), human "needs and their mode of production" determine "a materialist connection of men with one another," which "is ever taking on new forms, and thus presents a 'history' irrespective of...any political or religious nonsense which would especially hold men together." With "the aggregate of productive forces" determining "the condition of society," "the 'history of humanity' must always be studied and treated in relation to the history of industry and exchange" (Marx and Engels [1846] 1976: 43). In place of an "idealist view" that assumes "a category in every period," a Marxian approach "explains the formation of ideas"—such as "forms of consciousness, religion, philosophy, morality, etc."—through "tracing the process of their formation from [their] basis" in "the real ground of history," "from material practice," and from "the reciprocal action of these various sides on one another" (Marx and Engels [1846] 1976: 53–54). Should a study start with these assumptions, then "the only scientific" approach to religion is to build models that "develop from the actual relations of life the corresponding celestialised forms of those relations" in a way that includes "history and its process" (Marx [1867] 1992b: 352, note 2).

Several additional principles guide this Marxian approach. First, "[m]an makes religion, religion does not make man" (Marx [1844] 1975b: 175). This principle is not simply an abstract general assertion or critique but rather one that grounds research. A study of religion must first examine it as a product of humans, their collective activities, and all that stems from these.

Second, "religious sentiment is itself a social product" (Marx 1978: 145). The first point above, if taken on its own terms, could leave a study of religion at the level of human thought, i.e., the ways humans have developed religious theories, debated them, and passed them on (or failed to). For a Marxian approach, on the other hand, "[t]he production of ideas, of conceptions, of consciousness"— including "mental intercourse" and "morality, religion, metaphysics"—is always "interwoven with" and "the direct efflux of [human] material behavior" (Marx and Engels [1846] 1976: 36). This view incorporates how material relations shape the world of ideas, where material forces are broader, deeper, and insert a determining force that is prior to and often accounts for the emergence of beliefs. Such material relations include the influence of geography, technology, class relations, and modes of production in relation to all of these. Any study of ideas—religious or otherwise—that does not consider such material conditions is inherently limited and therefore incomplete.

Third, religion is also a "historical product, the result of the activity of a whole succession of generations...developing its industry and its intercourse, and modifying its social system according to the changed needs" (Marx and Engels [1846] 1976: 39). Examining the history of the changes in religious ideas is not enough. One must place primary focus on the history of changes in the material world, including changes within and between modes of production, the rise and fall of powers and nations, the influence of wars, changes in the division of labor, the ways class systems develop, and so on. In sum, a scientific study of religion must "look for [the 'essence' of religion] neither in the 'essence of man,' nor in the predicates of God, but in the material world which each stage of religious development finds in existence" (Marx and Engels [1846] 1976: 160).

3   Religion, Levels of Generality, and the Method of
       Successive Abstractions

Having outlined some basic principles, what does a general Marxian approach look like? Marx's outlook is interested primarily in understanding our present, which is where our action always takes place. We must get a handle, therefore, on how religion presents itself to us today and how that presentational form came to be without an appeal to a universal theory of religion. Instead, we must locate what happened in the past that accounts for the present while deciphering which identities and differences religion's embryonic stages share or do not share with us and our modern experience.

To do this work, a historical and materialist sociology examines religious development across different interconnected levels of generality: humans as animals, humans in general (including social relations in general), class society, capitalism in general, its historical stages, and its recent history.[2] Starting at the end of this chain and looking backward through it, we abstract into inquiry the most salient elements of the past—including both those within religion as well as external forces that have shaped it—that explain religion's development into the present, while abstracting those elements not relevant to religious development into modernity out of the investigation.[3] Marx's ([1867] 1992c: 28) approach analyzes these "different forms of development" in order to "trace out their inner connexion." Though inquiry starts with the present and looks backward, presentation starts with a broader abstraction of humans in general (as animals and as humans) and works its way through these levels of generality toward the present. This form of analysis goes forward armed with the preconditions and presuppositions that tell the story of religion in general, its origins, its present, and what sort of future might lie ahead.

3.1   *Humans as Animals*

The presumption of a clear-cut division between animals and humans in terms of morality is increasingly hard to uphold. Among the animal world (Table 5.1, Cell A), humans share group-living with many other species (Cell B), as well as certain emotions and behaviors related to that group membership (Cell C)— e.g., empathy (rhesus monkeys), altruism (dogs, primates, dolphins), grieving for the dead (elephants, chimpanzees, monkeys), gift exchange (crows),

---

2   The use of "recent" here does not necessarily mean as close as possible to a timeframe relative to an author's biography. Instead, "recent" is relative to the subject matter under investigation. For instance, should the Industrial Revolution in Britain between 1800–1820 be the subject matter for a historian, then that period would be abstracted as "recent capitalism," with models of production in general, class systems, capitalism in general, and industrial capitalism used for the investigation. With that said, Marx's approach, more often than not, strives to understand the present in which we currently live and, in investigating that, the concept of "recent capitalism" by necessity more closely connects temporally with the world of the analyst.

3   On abstractions of levels of historical generality, vantage point, and the backward study of history, see Ollman (2003: 86–126).

enforcing norms of fairness, reciprocity, and cooperation (chimpanzees, rhesus monkeys, and crows), and even forming political alliances (male chimps). Though some observers claim morality and/or religion are products of this bio-evolutionary heritage, it is clearly reasonable to suppose that some elements of human rules of conduct (Cell D) *are* rooted in biological evolution (see Bekoff and Pierce 2009; Gray 2009; Sapolsky 2009; Ghose 2012; Rowland 2012; Landau 2013; Proctor et al. 2013; Esfahani Smith 2015; Hogenboom 2015; de Waal 2005, 2009, 2013, 2016; Tomasello 2016; Torrey 2017; Mendes et al. 2018, and citations therein).

Such suppositions about the lineage and the gray area between humans and animals are contrary to long-held assumptions among many classical and even not-so-ancient philosophers, biologists, psychologists, and sociologists. Among the latter are those social theorists who argue that humans "socially construct" their notions of morality. While this is often true (as will be discussed more below), such arguments regularly overreach their applicability. If humans wholly and only socially constructed their rules of conduct, this presumes humans as a blank slate species which culture writes its rules on. This assumption is contrary to evolutionary theory. Or, if combined with evolutionary theory, this assumption would mean that at some point in primate evolution humans represented a decreasing sense of awareness and cognitive complexity in comparison to apes, orangutans, chimps, and bonobos and developed more and more with blank slate minds. This is also to assume that evolutionary processes selected out and excluded behavioral rules of their primate cousins as the human branch developed. The implication here is that humans then needed to construct similar rules anew through the power of cognition, a precondition which blank slate theory cannot then explain. This makes little sense, especially in light of our knowledge of the growth of the human cerebral cortex in comparison to our mammalian relatives. Still, if either one is true—humans have biologically inherited some rudimentary rules for social interaction or

TABLE 5.1   From animals in general to human emotions and rules based on group relations

	The general	The specific
The abstract	Animal world (A)	Social animals (B)
The concrete	Emotions and rules based on group relations (C)	Cooperation, fairness, reciprocity, grief for dead (D)

SOURCE: CREATED BY AUTHOR

human morals are simply social constructions—then basic morality cannot originate from religion.

There is, in fact, no clean break between animal world and human world. Humans are not the only animal to make tools and some primates have similar facial expressions—thus, it follows, emotions—as we do. Some primates laugh and elephants and dogs grieve. We share group-living, notions of fairness, empathy, reciprocity, cooperation with certain animals and we have observed animals lying and using deception. With such similarities and thus connections observed, what does seem to be different is that animal rules are not the product of an abstract sense of "right and wrong." These are the realms of "meaning" and this is something that humans construct, makes them what they are, and distinguishes them from the animal world.

3.2 Humans as Humans

The human cerebral cortex facilitates awareness and memory and allows them to create symbolic communities and intentionally organize their social relations (Table 5.2, Cell A). Given that their "instinct is a conscious one" (Marx and Engels [1846] 1976: 44), humans construct meaning for the world and their place in it (Cell B). This meaning structure—or a "nomos"—is a basic need without which humans experience "anomic terror," a fear borne from the prospect of existing in a meaningless world and thus a motive force in human life (for discussion, see Berger 1967). In constructing meaning, human cognition operates in abstractions whose existence seems to transcend the immediate concrete. This results in consciousness of a type where the individual's cultural norms and nomos appear precognitive or even eternal, as these predate them and have origins seemingly lost in the mists of time. Such mental modeling leads humans to conceive of a reality existing outside of sensuous materiality, including what happens after death. Consequently, humans search for and construct meaning through creating forms of knowledge (Cell C), one of those

TABLE 5.2 From humans and their need for meaning to forms of knowledge

	The general	The specific
The abstract	Humans as humans (A)	Need for meaning (B)
The concrete	Search for and construction of knowledge (C)	Lore, history, philosophy, science, religious beliefs (D)

SOURCE: CREATED BY AUTHOR

forms being religious beliefs about both the meaning of life and what happens after it is over (Cell D).

Humans' hardwiring exists within a larger cerebral cortex that houses their symbolic capacity, facility for language, forms of memory and emotional response, and so on. With a more complex mind and its symbolic capacity comes a greater expanse of meaning and a need for creating it. In this sense, humans are unique in constructing abstract principles of "morality" and "justice." Nevertheless, even here the ways human construct such principles are not wholly arbitrary nor freely or infinitely malleable. Some rules of conduct are rooted in biology, some are highly dependent on time, place, relations of power, and even chance, and others still, sitting in between these poles, are rooted in the prerequisites of that thing we call "society."

3.3   *Society in General: Identities*

As humans engage in social behavior (Table 5.3a, Cell A), so arises both "man's consciousness of the necessity of associating with the individuals around him" and an awareness "that he is living in society at all" (Marx and Engels [1846] 1976: 44) (Cell B). As such, societies develop ways to enforce those rules that are necessary for sustaining *any* society (Cell C)—e.g., rules regulating their communications, security in possessions, and personal safety (Cell D).[4] For instance, the Christian Bible (Proverbs 6:16–19, New International Version), lists seven things that are "detestable" to the lord:

> Haughty eyes
> A lying tongue

---

4   This statement does not mean that such social rules reflect complete restrictions on things like violence. Rather, religious dictums have often stated the principles upon which violence is justified. Such regulations often recognize exceptions or contradictions. There are passages in the Koran, for example, that direct believers to use violence on nonbelievers (2:191) but other passages that say there will be no compulsion in belief (2:256). The Old Testament also has rules of violence, ranging from its use on the lord's enemies or other societies worshiping different gods (Deuteronomy 7:16, 20:10–18) to dealing with disobedient children (Deuteronomy 21:18–21) (for overview, see Seibert 2016). Such scriptures were rules for those internal to the religion and their behavior toward their in-group. In the case of Judaism, its rules were for the Hebrew people specifically. While more universalist in outlook, Islam's rules of conduct were written at a time of outward conflict with the not-yet-converted in adjacent societies, a time of military conquest and, as such, its rules reflect those social conditions. Nevertheless, both doctrines contain rules of governing a society internally and this would include prohibitions on interpersonal violence in daily life against members of one's own society, or at least conditions being set down on when, where, and how such violence is justified.

TABLE 5.3A   From humans as social animals to socially requisite rules (I)

	The general	The specific
The abstract	Humans as social animals (A)	Society in general (B)
The concrete	Behavioral rules required by society in general (C)	Regulations on lying, stealing, violence (D)

SOURCE: CREATED BY AUTHOR

> Hands that shed innocent blood
> A heart that devises wicked schemes
> Feet that are quick to rush into evil
> A false witness who pours out lies
> And a person who stirs up conflict in the community

The author(s) probably did not write down such principles just in case some cultural group in a future society adopted their religious beliefs. Rather, in inscribing them into doctrine, religious moral codes address a variety of principles of conduct by necessity. Some of these codes will be culturally specific, while others will be necessary for any society, though religious thinkers usually do not make such distinctions. Instead, they tend to see their social system as natural and normal and write their specific rules at the same level of generality as socially requisite ones. Note how the rules above are not local rules about crops or diet or about a specific deity's history. Rather, they are rules that, if regularly broken, would cause any society to function poorly—i.e., a society where pride and arrogance, deceit, murder of those who have committed no crime, frauds, cons, manipulators, hired guns, amoral people, liars, and gossip all went unchecked.

The rules above relate to social relations and interpersonal interaction. In living in social groups, there are other practical realities that human beings must manage, realities they have no way of getting around. Such realities include diet, parent-child relationships, coupling, sexual behavior, and dealing with the dead. While rules for these things do not originate in biology nor are they general interactional principles like those above, humans in any society must confront these practical concerns. Certain plants or animals might be poison. Forms of authority are necessary for raising children and human beings form family units for this. Sexual behavior must follow some guidelines to maintain other relationships, such as the aforementioned family units and other concerns related to kinship. What should we do with the bodies of the

TABLE 5.3B   From humans as social animals to socially requisite rules (II)

	The general	The specific
The abstract	Humans as social animals (A)	Society in general (B)
The concrete	Behavioral rules required by society in general (C)	Rules on diet, parent–child relationships, coupling, sex, disposal of the dead (D)

SOURCE: CREATED BY AUTHOR

dead? Though unavoidable practical realities of daily life, the rules societies construct for handling them will vary because of a host of other variables (more below).

It is also at this level—i.e., society in general—that Marx's theory of alienation enters the picture. Humans, in "developing their material production and...intercourse, alter...their thinking and the products" thereof (Table 5.4, Cell A), creating "phantoms formed in the human brain" as "sublimates of their material life-process" in the form of "[m]orality, religion, metaphysics...ideology and...corresponding forms of consciousness" (Marx and Engels [1846] 1976: 36–37). Why phantoms? Historically, human "social activity" and their productive relations have been "a material power above [them]," something "not voluntary...but as an alien force existing outside them, the origin and goal of which they are ignorant, which they thus are no longer able to control" (Marx and Engels [1846] 1976: 47–48). In this state of "estrangement," "people make their empirical world into an entity that is only conceived, imagined, that confronts them as something foreign" (Marx and Engels [1846] 1976: 48, 159) (Cell B). With alienation arising from material powers standing over them, forces existing outside of them, and conditions the origins and goals of which they do not understand nor can they control, humans have lived in this state from their earliest existence. The outcome is both estranged social relations and malformed knowledge structures that mislead people as to the reality behind those very relations and the conditions that produce them.

In this sense, religion as a knowledge-form is, in part, a product of alienation. As a "mystical veil" (Marx [1867] 1992b: 84) and "the general theory of this world," religion juxtaposes a human "profane existence of error" with a "heavenly" one (Marx [1844] 1975b: 175). In this worldview, "productions of the human brain appear as independent beings endowed with life, and [enter] into relation both with one another and the human race" (Marx [1867] 1992b: 77)

TABLE 5.4   From humans as thinking social beings to religious beliefs in history

	The general	The specific
The abstract	Humans as thinking social beings (A)	Forms of alienated knowledge (B)
The concrete	Mystical veil of ideas about sacred and profane (C)	Particular religious beliefs and practices in history (D)

SOURCE: CREATED BY AUTHOR

(Table 5.4, Cell C). Similar to Durkheim (1915), then, Marx sees religion as beliefs that connect the profane realm to a perceived sacred one through certain types of interrelations (i.e., rituals), which reflect their social world back to them.[5] As a product of alienation, then, religion as a knowledge-form involves mystical meanings and ritual practices that attempt to gain control of the "spiritless conditions" (Marx [1844] 1975b: 175) that humans neither understand nor control, provides a nomos to a world that does not readily provide one, regulates behavior, and integrates people into a social system (Cell D).

3.4   Society in General: Differences

As a form of alienated knowledge (Table 5.5, Cell B), religion is shaped by "specific form[s] of material production," where "a specific relation of men to nature" determines "their spiritual outlook" (Marx [1963] 1969: 285) (Cell C). Social forces assert themselves once there "emerges the difference between natural instruments of production and those created by civilization" (Marx and Engels [1846] 1976: 63). The level of development of material production "discloses man's mode of dealing with Nature" and "lays bare the mode of formation of his social relations, and of the mental conceptions that flow from them. Every history of religion...that fails to take account of this material basis is uncritical" (Marx [1867] 1992b: 352, note 2).

Material conditions shape the contents of religious beliefs in multiple ways. Geography in relation to technological development provides the animals,

---

5 Jesus at first was a religious personage for a group of Hebrew desert dwellers, i.e., a figure for their time and place. Later, for reasons we will later investigate, he became a non-Jewish totem with symbolic flexibility. Almost everywhere we find Christianity after its spread his depiction resembles the features of people in that culture, e.g., a European feudal Jesus versus an Ethiopian one.

TABLE 5.5   From humans as thinking social beings to material forces that shape religious
            practices

	The general	The specific
The abstract	Humans as thinking social beings (A)	Forms of alienated knowledge (B)
The concrete	Spiritual outlooks shaped by material conditions (C)	Religious beliefs shaped by geography, technology, modes of production, change within and between systems (D)

SOURCE: CREATED BY AUTHOR

plants, rivers, mountains, and so forth that shape multiple social rituals and rules, such as what is available for totems and how to deal with the dead.[6] The structural features of material production—i.e., divisions of labor, property relations, development of productive forces, the subject of production, terms of labor, etc.—shape system-specific conditions—e.g., class hierarchies, social roles, rules, and organizations, forms of authority, forms and contents of knowledge, patterns of exchange, trade, and communication, accessibility of material goods, the ability to defeat rivals, and so on. With changes within or between systems, knowledge-forms adjust to such political-economic power relations, with religion being no exception in these regards (Cell D).

Such relations and processes influence the formation of new ideas or force older ones upon new subject populations. For instance, modes of production have varying levels of trade (and thus exchange of ideas) and/or conflict built into them. After a military conquest, subject populations may be forced to adopt new beliefs—e.g., via a colonial system—or have new beliefs form as a

---

6   In Tibet, where Buddhism dominates, firewood is too scarce to use on pyres and a cold climate often works against an earthen burial. As a result, practices of leaving the dead above ground developed, i.e., 49 days of prayer over the body and sky burial, where people leave the body of the dead on a mountainside as carrion for predatory birds. In warmer, more arid, areas where Judaism, Christianity, and Islam emerged, burial should take place as "soon as possible," a rule still followed by many of Jewish and Islamic faiths. With today's technological developments—e.g., embalming, refrigeration, and so on—in many parts of world rules on the timing of burial (or even cremation) have relaxed, allowing for a longer period before disposal of the dead and for family and friends who might live some distance away to gather.

consequence—e.g., cargo cults.[7] In another example, pre-capitalist modes of production are not as such that surplus-value is systematically reinvested back into productive forces, while capitalism is so structured. This is why capitalist societies experience more technological development and a rapid advancement of knowledge about nature, especially knowledge related to diseases, natural disasters, and/or famines. All of these material relations shape which religious ideas survive, morph, and/or decline, as well as the development of new ones.

4   Summary and Some Implications of the General Model

Before continuing, it will be helpful to summarize the initial model (Table 5.6) and provide an overview of some of its implications. We can consider three of these variables constants, though one of these will vary on material-historical conditions. The remaining two will also vary but more widely and for reasons that need specification during the act of research.

First, humans share several behavioral traits with other group-living species in the animal kingdom, such as emotions like grief or anger and norms about cooperation, fairness, reciprocity. Second, as a specific species with complex cognitive abilities, humans require meaning in both personal life and their social relations and construct forms of knowledge to service these ends. Third, as a social animal, there are rules without which sustaining any society becomes anywhere from difficult to impossible, including rudimentary bonds of trust and faith in one's personal safety and material security. That said, *the actual expressions* of biologically and socially based rules and types of meaning and beliefs in real historical societies tend to vary. The variables here include geography, modes of production—including, but not limited to, their class relations, complexity in the division of labor, and forms of technology—specific historical developments, the extent to which humans are controlled by external forces and/or do not understand them, and the ways in which local rules become socially constructed and passed on. Finally, some religious ideas are

---

7   After World War II, dozens of cargo cults emerged independently of one another in the South Pacific. People living on these islands witnessed American and British military installations receiving goods and materiel from airplanes, while the soldiers there appeared to do no planting, harvesting, herding, fishing, etc. They interpreted military parades and their uniforms (and so on) as a religious ritual that petitioned the gods for gifts. People across many different islands mimicked this behavior striving for similar results and even identified a messiah in the figure of "John Frum."

TABLE 5.6   Broad levels of generality and roots of religious rules and ideas

Level of generality	Root of religious ideas	Types of ideas	Applicability
Humans as animals	Evolutionary inherited emotions and rules based on group dynamics	Exchange, cooperation, fairness, reciprocity, grief for dead	Constant across societies
Humans as humans	Need for meaning	Nomos (cosmological meaning of one's society and individual's place in it)	Constant across societies
Society in general: similarities	Socially necessary rules	Rudimentary bonds of trust General safety of persons and things	Constant across societies
	Contingent social rules based practical realities in all societies	Parent–child relations Diet Coupling and sexuality Dealing with the dead	Addressed in all societies with various resolutions
Society in general: differences	Geography Technology Mode of production Historical developments	Natural features available for totems Knowledge of nature Number and nature of religious roles Exchange of religious ideas Class and political relations	Variable with material relations
Specific societies	Socially constructed rules	Specific rules on forms of authority, acceptable food, sexual regulations, gender roles, sacred totems, and so on	Variable with material relations

SOURCE: CREATED BY AUTHOR

the product of historical happenstance or result from developments in structural power relations.

Several interconnected implications follow from these constants and variables. Religions develop rules believed to be sacred in nature that are, instead, products of the culture in which certain stories are written, e.g., rules about what animals to eat, prayers to say for certain illnesses, and so on. At the same time, religions also develop sayings, writings, inspirational dictums, and so on that, while also written as if "coming from god," are pitched at the general social level, outside of specific time, place, or context. Nevertheless, no matter if rooted in biology, society in general, and/or specific historical-material conditions, all such rules appear in a religious discourse as sacred in origin. Here, the universal level of rules grounded in biology or society in general function as covering apologia for culturally specific socially constructed rules. People interpret prohibitions against killing, for example, as coming from the same realm as sexual mores, rules about which then carry a similar gravitas. Such historically specific beliefs can survive and spread, while others fall away, through material influence or historical contingency. Teachings incompatible with a new world are changed or ignored and those compatible with it are likely to remain. Culturally specific beliefs then can be passed down over generations but detached from their origins and spread by a system's spatial growth, while their origins may be forgotten and appear as given assumptions about the proper order—which is just one indication of malformed knowledge produced by an alienated human existence.[8]

Though Marx's theory of alienation is but one element in his overall theories about social relations, it is an important one. This theory assumes that the profane-sacred construct results from humans confronting their ignorance in conjunction with material forces outside their control, e.g., extracting food and

---

8   In the Old Testament, after Onan's brother Er died, their father, Judah, wanted Onan to enter into a levirate marriage and procreate with Tamar, Er's widow, to produce a son to continue Judah's line (patriarchal lineage). According to custom, such an offspring would get double the share of what a son from Er and Tamar would have received. Should Tamar go childless, Onan would get all of the inheritance. Initially, this story was about Onan's greed, selfishness, and failure in his duty to maintain the patriarch's line when, during sexual congress, he spilled his seed on the ground rather than impregnating Tamar, insulting his father, family, and god and, therefore, committing a sin. A later interpretation was that Onan's sin was wasting his seed and that sex was only for procreation purposes within a family context. As a result, "Onanism" became the name for the masturbatory habits of men, which religious leaders deemed a sinful practice, as was non-marital and/or recreational sex. These ideas animated discourse on sex and sexuality in almost every society touched by the Abrahamic faiths. This set of beliefs was not restricted to only cultural or religious discourse but animated putatively scientific knowledge and practice for centuries.

shelter from nature, vagaries of weather and climate, the threat and actuality of disease, natural disasters, and famine, living under social relations of domination from powers internal or external, and so on. One assumption of the theory is that an alienated existence produces misleading forms of knowledge. In a sort of vicious circle, the existence of this malformed knowledge subjects humans further to alienating social conditions on top of those already produced by the initial alienated state.

This is not, however, a static condition. Religious beliefs should change with changes and advances in knowledge (especially of nature but not only this) as well as with humans' ability to control the forces—social and/or natural—to which they are subject. Or, to phrase it another way, if religious beliefs are shaped, in part, by *the extent to which* humans not only remain subject to forces outside of their control but also to the *extent to which* they do or do not understand those forces, then the quantity and quality of those forces become variables in an overall explanatory model. Advancements in technology, knowledge of nature, of history, and/or of society, improved methods of securing food, dealing with disease and weather, and/or improved social conditions in general—e.g., less inequality, less forced labor, greater political freedom— should produce corresponding changes in both the conditions of alienation and thus the state of religion.

A Marxian model must move from the general theory of alienation to an examination of social structure, especially of how political-economic relations shape religious beliefs and practices. As is commonly understood about Marx's model, ruling class ideas tend to become ruling ideas generally.[9] This means that groups that dominate systems as well as those that overtake others (often the same groups) are in the structural position to have their religion dominate. With this dynamic, changes in power relations within/between modes of production should influence religious growth and decline.

---

9   "The ideas of the ruling class are in every epoch the ruling ideas: i.e., the class which is the ruling material force of society is at the same time its ruling intellectual force. The class which has the means of material production at its disposal, consequently also controls the means of mental production, so that the ideas of those who lack the means of mental production are on the whole subject to it. The ruling ideas are nothing more than the ideal expression of the dominant material relations, the dominant material relations grasped as ideas; hence of the relations which make the one class the ruling one, therefore, the ideas of its dominance. The individuals composing the ruling class possess among other things consciousness, and therefore think. Insofar, therefore, as they rule as a class and determine the extent and compass of an historical epoch, it is self-evident that they do this in its whole range, hence among other things rule also as thinkers, as producers of ideas, and regulate the production and distribution of the ideas of their age: thus their ideas are the ruling ideas of the epoch" (Marx and Engels [1846] 1976: 59).

Beginning with these models and principles in hand, we are ready to begin sorting out the historical evolution of religious beliefs and practices in a way that allows us to organize them into a taxonomy. Here I attempt to do so with several methodological principles in mind (based on what prior chapters have covered).

First, just as Marx did not need to report empirically on every society in order to construct his models for modes of production, it is not necessary for my sample of religious practices to be exhaustive. This would be impossible in any case. An adequate sample should cover a broad enough range of historical practices so that analysis can build a general framework upon them. This I hope to do, though specialists might conclude that my observations have been too narrow. That said, one cannot include everything and I have tried to make my sample sufficiently representative.

Second, in analyses such as this, one must decide on what criteria to use for lumping and splitting of religious practices. Here—just as Marx used variations in the productive relations and economic processes across history to differentiate modes of production (see Chapter 2)—I use variations in religion's constants to differentiate them. In terms of constants across them as a knowledge-form, religions assert that supernatural forces (spirits, gods, etc.) exist outside the observable world and their practices (prayer, rituals, and so on) mediate these realities to target a range of humans whose lives the sacred realm is meant to shape (local group, believers only, citizens of a political state, all humans in general). Special humans (shamans, priests, imams, etc.) have unusual access to the sacred realm through special training (meditation, monasteries, seminaries, etc.) and/or through special tools (revelation, holy books, a talisman, altars, incantations, etc.) to elicit desired effects (healings, blessings, answers to questions about the future, diet, sex, illness, death, and so on). Beliefs relative to these matters can be conservative, liberal, or relativist. For conservative theologies, one sacred realm and one way to mediate it exists and they usually demand exacting adherence to teachings, moral codes, rites, and/or scriptures. A more liberal approach accepts religious pluralism and assumes that specific beliefs can contain partial, evolving truth. The relativist positon holds that all religions contain *some* truth, often with judgment on their overall veracity withheld.

Specific religions in their historical forms will be differentiated along the following variables: (1) what they posit as inhabiting the sacred realm, (2) the nature of ritual and doctrine as mediators between realms (the exacting level of ritual performance that is required to activate the sacred; conservative, liberal, or relativist theological outlooks), (3) to whom beliefs apply (in-groups, anyone, everyone), (4) the terms of belief (required or not), (5) what happens after death (no afterlife, returning to spirit form, reward, punishment, reuniting with loved ones, and so on), (6) knowledge structure (the subject of sacred knowledge as well as its location in lore, canon, and/or individuals), and (7) authority structure (situational, an established priesthood, bottom-up / top-down organizations, individual) (Table 5.7). By first grasping "material production...in its *specific historical* form" in order to "understand what is specific in the spiritual production corresponding to it and the reciprocal influence of one on the other" (Marx 1969 [1963]: 285), comparison of these variables across historical systems allows for constructing a religious taxonomy.

4.1   *Religion and the Earliest Societies*

Hunting-gathering societies have rudimentary technology, common property, and lack classes or permanent authorities. These "ancient social organisms of production" are "extremely simple and transparent" and are "founded either on the immature development of man individually," as in a "primitive tribal community, or upon direct relations of subjection" (Marx [1867] 1992b: 83–84). In such societies, human consciousness is rooted in their "limited connection with other persons and things" and "the immediate sensuous environment... confronts men as a completely alien, all-powerful and unassailable force...by which they are overawed" (Marx and Engels [1846] 1976: 44). For social worlds such as these, "the social relations between man and Nature, are correspondingly narrow" and there arises "the ancient worship of Nature," which sets the preconditions for "elements of the popular religions" (Marx [1867] 1992b: 84).

As this "natural religion" arises "precisely because nature is as yet hardly altered by history" (Marx and Engels [1846] 1976: 44), *nature worship* is less a "religion" one can adopt as would a convert but instead a nomos without a hard distinction between profane and sacred realms. Rudimentary technology translates into celestial bodies, the weather, crops, pregnancy, illness, and/or death often explained by imagined nonmaterial forces, with rituals usually magic-based and requiring an exacting use of chants, charms, burnt offerings, sacrifices, etc. Religious authority is typically a shaman, but this is often a situational authority, not an institutional one. Religious knowledge survives here more through lore, practice, and tradition than through hierarchical authority and enforced dogma.

Though exchange and trade result in exchanges of ideas, the commonality of beliefs found in nature worship rest more in their form than in their contents, which display a wide range of stories, spirits, forces, social rules about sex, marriage, kinship (etc.), and claims about what happens after death—e.g., no afterlife/nonexistence, returning to a spirit form, or joining deceased ancestors. Typically, terms of belief are not as such that one can choose to believe or not

TABLE 5.7   Identifying similarities and differences in specific religions' historical forms

Study of similarities		Study of differences
Religion in general $\longrightarrow$	Religion in specific systems over historical development $\longrightarrow$	Inhabitants of the sacred realm Ritual and doctrine as mediation between realms Application Terms of belief What happens after death Authority structure Knowledge structure

SOURCE: CREATED BY AUTHOR

in the sense that there are few to no other belief systems with which to compare to one's own culture's nomos. As a result, proto-religious beliefs tend to be applicable only to the local in-group, which is usually coterminous with that group's understanding of what modern people would term "human," as true universality is not yet materially possible.[10] While spirits or forces may be simultaneously worldly and otherworldly—thus the common term "animism"—sacred knowledge posits humans and their Earth-bound lived-worlds as the cosmological subject and the ultimate relevance of sacred knowledge.[11]

---

10   Here, I am adopting usage of "proto" through the influence of the work of Bart Ehrman (2003, 2005, 2009). Ehrman often refers to "proto-orthodoxy" to denote the many different Christian sects and cults emergent in the period (a few centuries) after the crucifixion. His goal is to highlight how many views at the time contained beliefs we would not recognize as Christian today. However, he also recognizes that some of these groups *could* have won supremacy and those that did moved from being "proto-orthodox" to "orthodox" and now appear to us as not only established but are taken by believers as the intended faith of divine will.

11   This concept of the "cosmological subject" reflects the idea that the relevance of what humans either observe in the natural world, the traits they attribute to that world, and/or the attributes they instill in their spiritual forces/gods ultimately have human beings as their subject matter. Even in recognizing that early proto-religions may have developed beliefs that posited forces, beings, spirits, gods in the heavens that were not directly involved in human affairs, those stories themselves remained human constructions told

4.2   Religion from Class Societies in General to Feudalism

Compared to the earliest societies, class systems have greater technological complexity, larger populations, and the first forms of landed property and surplus-value appropriation, i.e., slavery, forced labor rents, taxes, and tribute. Exchange and trade increase in class systems and with them so increases the exchange of ideas. These societies develop formal military, religious, and political structures, though most people remain peasants, artisans, traders, serfs, or slaves.[12] With growth in the division of labor, specialization puts religious "consciousness...in a position...to proceed to the formation of 'pure' theory, theology, philosophy, morality, etc." (Marx and Engels [1846] 1976: 45).[13] Knowledge and authority structures also thus shift to ascendant canonical texts, more formalized training, and a priesthood that monopolizes knowledge, such as "the Indian Brahmin who proves the holiness of the Vedas by reserving for himself alone the right to read it" (Marx 1964: 25). Inhabitants of the sacred realm change from forces guiding nature to more coherent god-figures with human-like names, characteristics, biographies, duties, and domains. They also interact with more intention toward the social world—e.g., the polytheist gods in Greece, Rome, India, who often influenced battles or mated with humans to create demigods.

The development of specialists and moral/theological codification are usually associated with the "class which has the means of material production at its disposal, consequently also controls the means of mental production, so that the ideas of those who lack the means of mental production are on the whole subject to it" (Marx and Engels [1846] 1976: 59). As such, stratified class

---

and passed on among them. Thus, the ultimate *relevance* of those stories was their participation in the human construction of the meaning of their own existence.

12   In Chapter 2, the characteristics Marx attributed to "Asiatic mode of production" were addressed. However, a survey of all real societies that fall under that category, such as India, China, Japan, Mongolia, Tibet, Cambodia, and so on, cannot produce a succinct summary of their differences in productive relations and connect these to their various forms of religious development in this short space. This is not to say one could not do such an analysis.

13   "Incidentally, it is quite immaterial what consciousness starts to do on its own: out of all this trash we get only the one inference that these three moments, the productive forces, the state of society and consciousness, can and must come into contradiction with one another, because the division of labour implies the possibility, nay the fact, that intellectual and material activity, that enjoyment and labour, production and consumption, devolve on different individuals, and that the only possibility of their not coming into contradiction lies in negating in its turn the division of labour. It is self-evident, moreover, that 'spectres,' 'bonds,' 'the higher being,' 'concept,' 'scruple,' are merely idealist, speculative, mental expressions, the concepts apparently of the isolated individual, the mere images of very empirical fetters and limitations, within which move the mode of production of life, and the form of intercourse coupled with it" (Marx and Engels [1846] 1976: 45).

relations—e.g., landed property, labor obligations, states and citizens (political subjection), etc.—become encoded into laws. Military duties to the state, duties of slaves to masters, stricter gender rules (patriarchy), and requirements such as taxes and tribute become moral goods. Military victors and political leaders often determine religious practices of favor and sometimes become god-kings, e.g., in Rome and in China, among other places. In class systems as a whole, then, "the 'true religion'...[is] the cult of 'their nationality,' of their 'state'" (Marx 1964: 23), i.e., *state religion*.[14] Such developments set the foundation for officially adopted monotheism in the West after Constantine's conversion to Christianity.[15]

As the consolidation of beliefs into more exacting canons and rituals marginalizes competing proto-forms, mutual contrast with and conflict between other consolidated traditions becomes more likely, a "contradiction, arising not within the national orbit, but between this national consciousness and the practice of other nations" (Marx and Engels [1846] 1976: 45). Canonical consolidation, however, does not eliminate breakaway cults, schisms, purges, or the rise of new nations, political-economic revolutions, demographic shifts, and so on that can eliminate, absorb, and/or produce other traditions. For instance, the consolidation of dynastic regimes in ancient China lifted

---

14   "The truly religious state is the theocratic state; the prince of such states must be either the God of religion, Jehovah himself, as in the Jewish state, God's representative, the Dalai Lama, as in Tibet, or finally...they must all submit to a church which is an 'infallible church.' For if, as in Protestantism, there is no supreme head of the church, the domination of religion is nothing but the religion of domination, the cult of the will of the government" (Marx 1964: 36).

15   In ancient society, Judaism might not have been the first tradition to imagine a singular god (Zoroastrianism is traceable to a similar period in time). In fact, should one go back far enough they would have to categorize Judaism as a form of polytheism. The early tribes of Israel lived side-by-side with others in some places, established their own domains in others, and also migrated to and/or were born in regional cities such as Rome. In different places they were accepted, ignored, persecuted, expelled, or even killed. Adopting an image of god that combined characteristics of other gods and asserting that this god had chosen them for a special mission consolidated their theology. This jealous and angry, powerful and vengeful, demanding and observant god was not only superior to all other gods (the initial stance) but in fact was the only one (a later assertion). This likely facilitated in-group cohesion across time, place, and generation. Christianity began as several disparate movements within Judaism but over time a proto-orthodox belief system won out and transformed the meaning of Jesus and his ministry, which went from a rabbi that was god's anointed messenger of Jewish redemption and liberation—one early view—to both god and a messiah of universal spiritual salvation. Though it took a few centuries, the idea of an official singular religion with a singular god (instead of multiple religions and multiple gods) was probably a tempting maneuver of statecraft for Roman leadership in order to produce a more cohesive social body and thus a way to consolidate political power. Whether this was the intent or not, this did appear to be the outcome.

Confucianism into orthodoxy over earlier local schools of thought. Though both families and larger landowners owned most land, distribution of power in offices and taxes to government were the main locale of political-economic power and, as such, religion was an official state religion.

In state religions, we find a mix of conservative and liberal features. The mode of mediation between realms remains relatively exacting where the proper execution of ritual ranks above faith, with individuals having a duty to social institutions and political-religious authorities. Such conservative beliefs and supplications apply mainly to political subjects, a growth beyond the simpler in-group thinking of the earliest systems and a step toward universality.[16] For example, as one of many tribal religions in ancient Rome, Judaism did not posit its belief system as universally required, though, as a prophetic cult, Christianity did (eventually). As such, in *state religion*'s maturation, terms of belief become required for citizens, as do obligations and devotional exercises, though states often tolerate other local traditions, a feature of liberality. Notions of an afterlife become more solidified but with variations (e.g., Valhalla, Nirvana, Elysium; different Judaic, Buddhist, and Shinto traditions have no afterlife or are agnostic on the subject). In state religion's general concrete history, Earth and humans as cosmological subjects remained, as did appeals to

---

16   "If now in considering the course of history we detach the ideas of the ruling class from the ruling class itself and attribute to them an independent existence, if we confine ourselves to saying that these or those ideas were dominant at a given time, without bothering ourselves about the conditions of production and the producers of these ideas, if we thus ignore the individuals and world conditions which are the source of the ideas, then we can say, for instance, that during the time the aristocracy was dominant, the concepts honour, loyalty, etc., were dominant, during the dominance of the bourgeoisie the concepts freedom, equality, etc. The ruling class itself on the whole imagines this to be so. This conception of history, which is common to all historians, particularly since the eighteenth century, will necessarily come up against the phenomenon that ever more abstract ideas hold sway, i.e., ideas which increasingly take on the form of universality. For each new class which puts itself in the place of one ruling before it is compelled, merely in order to carry through its aim, to present its interest as the common interest of all the members of society, that is, expressed in ideal form: it has to give its ideas the form of universality, and present them as the only rational, universally valid ones. The class making a revolution comes forward from the very start, if only because it is opposed to a class, not as a class but as the representative of the whole of society, as the whole mass of society confronting the one ruling class. It can do this because initially its interest really is as yet mostly connected with the common interest of all other non-ruling classes, because under the pressure of hitherto existing conditions its interest has not yet been able to develop as the particular interest of a particular class. Its victory, therefore, benefits also many individuals of other classes which are not winning a dominant position, but only insofar as it now enables these individuals to raise themselves into the ruling class" (Marx and Engels [1846] 1976: 60–61).

magic for blessings and guidelines on human affairs (both of which persist over time, even into modernity).

After "the downfall of the old states...brought the downfall of the old religions" (Marx 1964: 23), the Catholic Church remained influential on the Continent, out of which European feudalism emerged and to which Christianity adapted.[17] Becoming increasingly centralized, hierarchical, and wealthy in this system, monarchies and the Church dominated most land ownership and serfs were obligated to provide labor rent to landlords and tithes to the Church. While royalty were not gods *per se*, their rule was a "Divine Right." The elaborate cathedrals of Europe—with statues and friezes of the local king, sword in hand, walking next to Jesus—depicted monarchs and lords as god's intermediaries on Earth and elevated both to a standing above everyday people. Christianity—no longer a faith of a downtrodden desert people, nor simply one enjoying more status and influence via the conversion of an emperor—became an arm of feudal class power. Duty to a royal sovereign replaced duty to a culture or a state and political rulers increasingly enjoined with and at times usurped religious authorities over practice, e.g., the schism of the Church of England with the Roman Catholic Church. Specialization continued and increased, as did a monopoly over dogma and practice, e.g., bans on reading the Bible. Rather than a theoretical universality—as in "anyone could participate"—monotheistic religion achieved a required universality corresponding to the new ruling class's vision of its right to rule and ruling groups enforced it as such. Thus developed *ruling class religion*.[18]

Feudalism's nomos was a religious one—i.e., being the children of Abraham and actors in a singular god's earthly plan—and religious regulation of life

---

17   "Christianity was preceded by the total collapse of the ancient 'world conditions' of which Christianity was the mere expression.... ['C]ompletely new world conditions' arose not internally through Christianity but only when the Huns and the Germans fell 'externally' on the corpse of the Roman Empire.... [A]fter the Germanic invasion the 'new world conditions' did not adapt themselves to Christianity but [rather] Christianity itself changed with every new phase of these world conditions. [We cannot think of] an example of the old world conditions changing with a new religion without the mightiest 'external' and abstract political convulsions setting in at the same time" (Marx and Engels [1850] 1978b: 244).

18   A general historical survey of class systems, religion, and monotheism would require placing Islam in a timeline between the fall of the Roman Empire and an analysis of the feudal system that emerged from that decline. However, given our vantage point of the capitalist present as our starting-point, Islam enters the analysis later as an already established religion found in the colonial domain of European expansion. As such, though one could examine its emergence from the Abrahamic tradition in the context of class systems, such an analysis is beyond the scope of this chapter (also see Chapter 2, note 4).

proliferated—e.g., conservative and exacting doctrine (texts on theological minutiae), rituals (church attendance, the elements of the Mass), behavioral requirements (rules on sexuality, diet, prayer), and rules on authority (death for heresy). Heaven was for obedient believers, hell for unrepentant sinners and nonbelievers, purgatory for those needing additional purification, and limbo for unbaptized infants. Political-religious authorities required belief and forced it upon an illiterate people kept ignorant and mystified, e.g., priests said Mass in Latin facing away from their congregations. Those same authorities viewed non-Christian traditions and competitors from paganism to Judaism to Islam as threats and enemies and treated them as such—e.g., the Crusades, the Spanish Inquisition, other religious pogroms—while internecine struggles emerged over political-theological power.[19]

As monarchies aligned with different religious organizations and battled with each other over land and wealth, this connection spilled over into the Catholic Church's accumulation of land, possessions, and money. The Catholic Church then faced challenges in theological form, e.g., disagreements over the Pope's authority and objections to the sale of indulgences. In the subsequent Protestant Reformation, Luther's more individualistic outlook "overcame bondage of *piety* by replacing it by the bondage of conviction...shattered faith in authority because he restored authority of faith...turned priests into lay-men...[and] layman into priests...[and] freed man from outer religiosity because he made religiosity the inner man" (Marx [1844] 1975b: 182). The Refor-mation thus brought into being a new, more individualistic authority structure

---

19   Feudal political leaders ordered Crusades against Islamic apostates, especially those liv-ing in lands upon which Church leaders set their sights. Authorities repressed aspiring scientists and labeled them as heretics subject to inquisitions, excommunication, exile, and even execution. Such a demand for orthodoxy in belief and practice led to a series of schisms. The "Great Schism of 1054" that split Christendom into a Greek East and a Latin West is usually attributed to conflicts over doctrine and authority (e.g., the source of the Holy Spirit, the bread to be used for the Eucharist, the authority of the Bishop of Rome). Gutenberg's advent of the printing press (1440) and the publication of the Gutenberg Bi-ble (1454/55) helped spread both literacy and religious teaching, and this influenced the Protestant Reformation. The Reformation (usually seen as beginning with Martin Luther in 1517 and lasting until the Peace of Westphalia in 1648) produced a schism within Euro-pean Christianity. Issues of contention included the sale of indulgences, the Pope's au-thority over purgatory, and whether the Bible justified the idea of saints. King Henry VIII broke from Rome (1532–1534) over disagreements about rules of marriage and divorce, bringing about the Anglican Church and further consolidating its ties to English political power. In 1534, Parliament passed the Act of Supremacy that declared him Supreme Head on Earth of the Church of England and, by 1559, doctrinal and legal authority rested with the English monarchy (then Elizabeth I) rather than with Rome.

TABLE 5.8   Drivers of religious development in society in general

The general abstract	The specific abstract	The general concrete	The specific concrete
Society in general	Material base	Production and exchange	Population size Trade in goods and ideas Contact (or isolation) with others
		Division of labor	Size and specialization of religious authority (codification, number, and enforcement of religious rules)
		Power-structure transformation	Moral rules shaped by material conditions Moral rules incompatible with new system disappear New moral rules develop
		Technological change	Knowledge of nature Spread of ideas Population growth Advanced systems defeat less advanced
	Ideological conditions	Cultural traditions detached from origins	Rules on marriage, sex, diet, dress
		Knowledge in general, alienated knowledge, and institutionalized beliefs	Lore, tradition Gaps in knowledge filled with supernatural explanations

SOURCE: CREATED BY AUTHOR

as a competitor to Catholicism's hierarchical centralization. After the tele-scope's invention, the work of Galileo, Copernicus, and Kepler overturned the Ptolemaic model during the sixteenth and seventeenth centuries. Still, the

TABLE 5.9   Drivers of religious development in class systems

The general abstract	The specific abstract	The general concrete	The specific concrete
Class systems in general	Material base	Separation of laborers from means of production	Alienating institutions of labor control
		Property systems	Rules about relationships of servitude (property ownership, forced labor, inheritance, control of women, etc.)
	Ideological conditions	Priesthood and ruling class merge	Political leaders deified doctrine, dogma, and beliefs enforced by state
		Ideas of ruling class are ruling ideas	Universality Forms of appropriation and obedience to authority defined as morality

SOURCE: CREATED BY AUTHOR

"only Earth" view of reality and humanity as the cosmological subject remained intact. Should monarchial authority change, those on the wrong side of the political-theological divide were often forced to convert and/or sometimes killed, setting the stage for religious development in modernity, with both Catholicism and Protestantism each positing their own belief system as required and universally applicable.

Above I summarize the factors shaping religion's historical development (previous variables assumed) in *society in general* (Table 5.8) and *in class systems* (Table 5.9). These factors, both as separate forces on their own and in conjunction with those unique to capitalism, have shaped religion's development in modern society, a subject investigated below.

4.3   Religion and Capitalism in General: Contradictions and Changes

The structure of capitalism is based on private ownership of the means of production, the appropriation of surplus-value through the exploitation of wage-labor in commodity production, and the sale of commodities on a free market with the goal of accumulating profits as capital. One "innate necessity of this mode of production, [is] its need for an ever-expanding market" (Marx 1971a: 237), with the world-market as its "basis and vital element" (Marx 1971a: 110). With a structure beset with "polarization," capitalism reproduces "the complete separation of the labourers from all property in the means by which they can realize their labour" "on a continually extending scale" (Marx [1867] 1992b: 668). As a system that "is constantly changing" (Marx [1867] 1992c: 21), capitalism's "characteristic features," such as "mobility of capital and labour and continual revolutions in the method of production, and therefore in the relations of production and commerce and the way of life, leads to great mobility in the habits, modes of thinking, etc., of the people" (Marx 1971b: 444). With these material relations "contain[ing]...contradictory tendencies and phenomena...[that] counteract each other simultaneously" (Marx 1971a: 249), capitalism and religion both promote and undermine one another, which we can see across their mutual historical development.

4.3.1   Religion and Capitalism's Historical Development

In capitalism's period of primitive accumulation, those powers that enjoyed geographical advantage and possessed maritime technology capable of an oceanic reach—e.g., Spain and Portugal, to name two—led in colonizing foreign lands—i.e., Central and South America, the Caribbean, and the Philippines, and Brazil, Indonesia, and southern Africa, respectively—and, once there, set themselves the task of "Christianizing savages."[20] In "destroying the former

---

20   The subsequent conquests of the Spanish (the Caribbean, Central and South America, the Philippines) and the Portuguese (Brazil, Indonesia, southern Africa) initialized Christianity's (i.e., Catholicism) spread under ascendant capitalism, as both suppressed or even stamped out many indigenous religions and proto-religions in the process through either direct violence (colonizers had better military technology) or the predictable spread of disease. For those who survived the period, Christianity was enforced through coerced conversion and, over time, established churches and colonial institutions became socializing agents. As capitalism matured into a period of manufacture, other locales, having experienced the scientific revolution, Calvinist logico-deductive theology brought the masses the doctrine of Predestination and the Protestant work ethic. This branch of Christianity followed the Dutch (South Africa, Indonesia) and British (Canada, North America, the Caribbean, Australia, New Zealand, India, southern and northern Africa) empires, with similar outcomes for indigenous people and religions.

natural exclusiveness of separate nations" (Marx and Engels [1846] 1976: 73), European colonialism forged some religions together—e.g., Santeria and Voodoo in the Caribbean and North and South America.[21] As the Christian god's patronage shifted from monarchies to nation-states, biblical support for modern class relations was found—e.g., "Let every person be subject to the governing authorities. For there is no authority except from god, and those which exist are established by god" (Romans 13:1)—and Christianity was again remade.

In class systems, class structures merge with religious organizations and leaders of each overlap and become figures of reverence. By extension, the same is true in capitalist society, where anthems exalt nation-states and their leaders become a secular priesthood, a residue leftover from both state religion and ruling class religion. Yet this has developed unevenly in modernity's history and with contradictory results.

Given capitalism's relations of private property and the legal individual (as opposed to family, clan, etc.), Christianity's ideas of personal sin and salvation and "its religious *cultus* of abstract man, more especially in its bourgeois developments, Protestantism, Deism, etc., is the most fitting form of religion" (Marx [1867] 1992b: 83). When not so fitting, Christianity adapted its teaching—e.g., endorsing capitalism's terms of labor and forms of appropriation in teaching obedience of slaves (Ephesians 6:5; 1 Peter 2:18–25), cultivating the work ethic as a moral good, and dropping once and for all support of Biblical prohibitions against usury.[22] Unlike Rome's state religion—which required a ritualistic

---

21   "[Large-scale industry universalized competition and] destroyed as far as possible ideology, religion, morality, etc., and, where it could not do this, made them into a palpable lie. It produced world history for the first time, insofar as it made all civilised nations and every individual member of them dependent for the satisfaction of their wants on the whole world, thus destroying the former natural exclusiveness of separate nations" (Marx and Engels [1846] 1976: 73).

22   "The social principles of Christianity justified the slavery of antiquity, glorified serfdom of the Middle Ages and are capable, in case of need, of defending the oppression of the proletariat, even if with somewhat doleful grimaces.... The social principles of Christianity preach the necessity of a ruling and an oppressed class, and for the latter all they have to offer is the pious wish that the former may be charitable.... The social principles of Christianity declare all the vile acts of the oppressors against the oppressed to be either a just punishment for original sin and other sins, or trials which the Lord, in his infinite wisdom, ordains for the redeemed.... The social principles of Christianity preach cowardice, self-contempt, abasement, submissiveness and humbleness" (Marx [1847] 1976a: 231). In "antiquity," usury was at first forbidden and considered "wicked" but later became "lawful and very prevalent"; in the "Christian Middle Ages" it was "sin" and prohibited; in "modern times," because of "the monetary needs of government" and "the development of trade and manufacture," it became "very widespread," beginning with Holland (where it was subordinated to industrial and commercial capital), England (where polemics

gesture or gift to the gods while multiple local traditions were often tolerated—
or in comparison to feudalism's ruling class religion—where belief and practice were required and non-favored practices squelched—Christianity's required universalist monotheism clashed with the political and social pluralisms
(and even non-required belief) of modern nation-states. In Europe, cultures
and politics grew more secular while still referencing god/providence in their
constitutions; the US Constitution referenced not god but "the people" as the
source of its laws and legitimacy, while its culture was one of the most religious
in the modern world and remains so to this day.[23]

Political-religious conflicts among and between ruling groups in feudal Europe set the stage for the later separation of church and state in the United
States.[24] With this historical backdrop and with capital separating production
into competing industries and laborers legally reduced to independent entities,
social organizations—including the family, governance, education, and
religion—similarly divide into distinct institutional spheres. With this separation, "religion develops in its *practical* universality only where there is no *privi-
leged* religion (cf. the North American States).... The [modern] state declares
that religion, like the other elements of civil life, only *begins* to exist in its full
scope when the state declares it to be *non-political* and thus leaves it to itself."
Therefore, after "the abolition of the *state church*," religion "henceforth obeys
its own laws undisturbed and develops to its full scope" (Marx and Engels
[1845] 1956: 156, 158; emphases in the original). This "separation of religion from
all profane content makes it *abstract, absolute* religion" (Marx and Engels [1845]
1956: 130; emphasis in the original) and transforms ruling class religion into

---

against it in principle decreased, though criticisms of its amount and its domination of
credit remained and regulations were imposed), and by the Eighteenth century, "unre-
stricted usury is recognized as an element of capitalist production" (Marx 1971b: 534).

23   One might argue that the Founding Fathers of the United States were not specifically
      Christian and actively tried to keep law and theology, state and religion, separate. While
      this is true to some degree, some US founders did profess a Christian faith and still others
      were Deists. Such variations do not distract from the fact that those who established early
      modern nation-states imbued them with religious overtones, whether viewing them-
      selves as part of god's plan, doing god's work, or otherwise enjoying special favors and/or
      dispensations from providence. Such opinions long remained in the public conscious-
      ness. Both supporters of American slavery and those favoring its abolition each appealed
      to the Bible for their positions, as did the combatants in the American Civil War. After-
      ward, the push west received god's approval with "Manifest Destiny." Belligerents in World
      Wars I and II appealed to god for sacred favors, e.g., Nazi soldiers had *Gott Mit Uns* on
      their belt buckles.

24   "For instance, in an age and in a country where royal power, aristocracy and bourgeoisie
      are contending for domination and where, therefore, domination is shared, the doctrine
      of the separation of powers proves to be the dominant idea and is expressed as an 'eternal
      law'" (Marx and Engels [1846] 1976: 59).

institutional religion. Mirroring the system's "immense accumulation of commodities" (Marx [1867] 1992b: 43), this development leaves room for multiple beliefs, cults, sects, churches, denominations, and even non-participation.

As capitalist organizations grew in size and complexity, they needed a workforce with more education, which states increasingly extended to the wider population. Competition for profits leads to a portion of those profits poured into technology in an attempt to lower the cost of labor. With capitalism's development of productive forces and its growing need for intellectual skills, the populace grows more literate, educated, and mobile, while enhanced understandings of nature constantly emerge. These developments present religion in modernity with new social antagonisms, which it struggles to accommodate. For example, though opposed to free and scientific inquiry for centuries, the Vatican feared that continual refusal to accept new forms of knowledge would lead to a loss in legitimacy (and thus membership) and eventually allowed biblical scholarship (1943), declared that the theory of evolution did not conflict with Catholic principles (1950), and accepted the Big Bang (2011). Even the Dalai Lama (2006) admitted the risks of denying scientific knowledge: "If scientific analysis were conclusively to demonstrate certain claims in Buddhism to be false, then we must accept the findings of science and abandon those claims."

In the industrial period, consolidated European nation-states intensified their expansionary efforts to secure cheaper raw resources and labor, which culminated in the "scramble for Africa" and initiated additional Christian missionary penetration. By the early twentieth century, several societies, including Russia and China, reacted to capitalist expansion and banned religion, though they could not ban the need for meaning and religion went underground. Starting in the late 1950s and early 1960s, postwar powers experienced challenges in their domains. Great Britain withdrew from India and Kenya. China underwent upheaval with the Cultural Revolution. France, humiliated in Algeria, decolonized there. The United States signed a truce in Korea (with Christian missionaries leaving a lasting mark on the southern half of the peninsula) and its war in Vietnam reached its apex (ultimately ending in defeat in the 1970s). Not coincidentally, France, the United States, Japan, and Mexico all experienced cultural transformations as capitalism entered a transnational stage. Across the modern world, feminist movements challenged patriarchal rule. Vatican II's reforms further loosened Catholicism's grip on the requirements of faith. Financial and sex scandals beset innumerable Christian congregations worldwide and Western materialism left people unsatisfied as the postwar euphoria receded. Church attendance almost everywhere in the West declined while new religious movements grew.

As capitalism changed, so did religion and both will continue to do so. In the global period, all but a few modern states prioritize securing the bourgeoisie's need for the ceaseless accumulation of capital to the exclusion of other, wider, social needs. From the vantage point of capital, there arises "not only...alienation and indifference" towards the conditions of labor but with modernity's cultures intermingling, its popular knowledge unreliable, and "[i]n line with its contradictory and antagonistic nature, the capitalist mode of production proceeds to count the prodigious dissipation of the labourer's life and health, and the lowering of his living conditions, as an economy in the use of constant capital and thereby as a means of raising the rate of profit" (Marx 1971a: 86). In short, everyday people have their lives increasingly organized as an extension of capital's thirst for surplus-value, while their connections to community and each other become more precarious and severed. In such conditions, religions today struggle against modernity, each other, and themselves, while people everywhere remain confronted with forces they cannot control or understand.

Three trends are indicative of this struggle: (1) polarization and religious crisis, (2) religion as marketplace consumption, and (3) the emergence of a new "generic" god.

4.3.2 Polarization and Religious Crises

A society where "[a]ll that is solid melts into air" and "all that is holy profaned" (Marx and Engels [1848] 1978a: 476) regularly produces crises of meaning. Religions have responded to this condition with liberal accommodations and reform and conservative reaction to both modernity and such accommodations and reforms.[25] Secular states can no longer compel belief or even require a

---

25   Fundamentalist Christian movements initially emerged among Protestants out of Britain and the United States in the late 19th and early 20th centuries. In the 1800s, English strains of Christianity (e.g., Pietism, Presbyterianism, and Methodism generally) were a background influence of Christian beliefs in America. After the Civil War, Christianity in America witnessed modernists who wanted to update their faith to keep pace with advances in science and societal evolution. Religious conservatives found this movement heretical. In 1910, a series of essays, *The Fundamentals: A Testimony to the Truth*, articulated this rejection of modernism and aspired to return Christianity to its putative roots. From the Englishman, John Nelson Darby, fundamentalism adopted the idea of "Dispensationalism," which divided history into seven stages (or "dispensations") of god's revelation, each ending with god's judgment on humankind. For this view, we live in the last stage, which will witness a final battle with nonbelievers and apostates at Armageddon, after which Christ will return and reign for 1000 years. In the 1930s, they organized as the Independent Fundamentalist Churches of America (IFCA International as of 1996). Their doctrines included the inerrancy of the Bible (from the Princeton Theology of Charles Hodge), its historical accuracy—including the origins of Earth and the miracles of Jesus, his virgin birth and resurrection—and the Second Coming. These tenets are still held by

gesture to practice and culture often mirrors this, even if unevenly. As they are
commanded to convert others, and in relation to their institutional separation
from their moorings in ruling class and state religion, leaders of the required
universalist monotheisms have tried to return religion to its place of socio-
political authority. This is an attempt at remaining societally relevant and even
dominating secular institutions. This is most apparent in trends found amongst
different strands of Christianity and Islam.

Modern Christianity and Islam have maintained their sacred realm's inhabitants (the god of Abraham), application (everyone), and terms of belief (required), while clashing with modernity in multiple ways. Across the Middle
East, parts of Africa, and the Arabian Peninsula, more than one Islamic sect
rebelled against societal secularization, liberalizing trends in religion, and colonial interference.[26] Sometimes these religious movements are nationalist in
nature and endorse radical politics. The Islamic State, an offshoot of these
movements, aspires to create a caliphate across parts of Northern Africa,
Southern Europe, and the Middle East, reminiscent of Rome's state religion.
Both The Islamic State and other Islamic movements resemble ruling class religion in other respects, such as violence against blasphemers, heretics, and
apostates, strict adherence to text, dogma dictated by religious authorities, a
combined power of church and state, and a desire for forcibly confronting enemies. Religious leaders call for Sharia law internally and devout Islamic im-
migrants often demand its establishment in areas where they reach a certain
mass that they feel politically empowered. The institutionalization of Sharia

---

most Christian fundamentalists and those who reject such premises—including Christian modernists, non-fundamentalists, liberals, and non-Christians—are destined for
hell. Christian fundamentalist traditions include Pentecostals, Southern Baptists, some
Methodists, Seventh Day Adventists, and Jehovah's Witnesses, among a multitude of
smaller sects and offshoots.

26   Islam teaches several forms of jihad, or struggle, e.g., personal struggle over the mind, the
body, good works, and so on. Jihad also includes defending the faith, violently if necessary.
As a required universalist monotheism, Islamic belief holds itself not only as returning
purity to the religion of Abraham, but its historical roots spread often through violent
confrontation between regional tribal powers during and after Mohammad's original
ministry. Since that period, struggles against apostates have marked its history. Addition-
ally, being subjected to the powers of external nation-states—Britain in Egypt, Britain
and the United States in Saudi Arabia, the Soviet Union, the United States, and Britain in
Iran, the same three in Afghanistan, and Holland in Nigeria, to name four cases—several
regions of the Islamic world experienced imperial interference and humiliation (as well
as secularizing trends). Such developments produced a backlash—e.g., the radicalism of
the Islamic Brotherhood in Egypt, the Islamic Revolution in Iran, and surging Wahhabism
in Saudi Arabia (including Al Qaeda's attacks against the United States and the West
generally)—against outsiders as well as against local liberalizing trends within Islam.

law moves religious laws into the order of the state, usurping incipient secular authority and replacing it where already established.[27]

Similarly, the West—especially the United States—has witnessed growth in fundamentalist Christian sects, some of which are also radical in their rejection of modernity and its secularizing trends. To name just one instance, Dominion Theology (first emerging in the 1970s) is nationalistic in flavor, wants the US Constitution interpreted on a biblical basis, denies the Enlightenment roots of American democracy, and aspires to limit citizenship to Christians. Though secular systems cannot require Christian faith or practice, Dominion Theology's leaders strive to have themselves and biblical principles instituted among the "seven mountains," i.e., religion, government, the economy, the family, education, media, and arts and entertainment. Dominion Theology is not the first or only fundamentalist current in American Protestantism and all of them tend to believe that modernity is inherently corrupting of religious truth and that religion should play a central role in public policies. Because belief in and the practice of fundamentalist Christianity cannot be enforced in secular systems, efforts to establish dominion over state and cultural institutions are attempts to require belief and practice by proxy.

Both of these fundamentalist religious movements currently rest on a moderate form of hierarchical authority and, unable to successfully harness an army of colonial conquest with their own resources, their strategy is to take over and transform secular institutions into a macro religious authority over

---

27   A general form of Islamic fundamentalism is a search for "pure" belief. However, as with any fundamentalist religion, the road has many forks where believers on any one cul-de-sac see those on others as heretics. In Saudi Arabia, for example, "salafism" is a generally conservative approach to Islamic belief encompassing a more specific version of ultraconservative "Wahhabism" (not all of those thinking of themselves as Salafists would accept a Wahhabi label but the reverse is probably accurate). In any case, these movements emerged in the 1960s as a reaction against European colonialism, with adherents tracing their theological inspirations back several centuries to Muhammad ibn Abd al-Wahhab, who reformed the Islam of his period by purging the veneration of saints, asking for their assistance, and visiting their tombs, which he viewed as forms of idolatry. He eventually made common cause with Muhammad bin Saud, whose successors established the House of Saud and today preside as the royal family of Saudi Arabia. This family-political apparatus, since at least the 1970s, has tried to establish its form of Sunni Islam worldwide, while aligning with several of capitalism's powerful nation-states, including Britain and the United States. One could do a similar sort of historical tracing for the fundamentalist form of Shia Islam and its spread via Iran and its influence. However, neither of these would completely account for the various offshoots of Islamic belief found in Africa, South and Central Asia, Indonesia, and so on.

modern society.[28] The key knowledge structure for both rests on the inerrancy of religious texts and an eschatological vision of their civilization's place in god's cosmological plan (Islam's Last Prophet versus Christianity's End Times). As such, both posit their doctrines apply to everyone and upon death god will punish those who refuse them.

Christian and Islamic fundamentalisms represent a struggle against the gravitational pull of the separation of religion into its own institutional sphere amidst modernity's crisis of meaning. Profoundly rejecting this institutional inertia and modern society's secular social forms, each desires a religion that combines both state religion (their period of origination) and ruling class religion (when they matured to dominance), where authorities are strong, institutions are religiously organized and regulated, belief and participation are required, and religious pluralism suppressed. The idea, it seems, is to firm up and stabilize a meaning-structure that continually threatens to melt into air.

Capitalist society also has secularizing trends pushing in the opposite direction. Increasing numbers of people are leaving religion—e.g., lack of church attendance, no longer affiliating with particular faiths, agnosticism, non-belief, and public expressions of atheism (Bullard 2016; Cooper et al. 2016; Pew Forum 2018; Sahgal 2018).[29]As society liberalizes and secularizes, populations turn away from the dogmatism—as well as the extremism, xenophobia, racism,

---

28   Though different in theology and cultural background, both Islamic and Christian faithful believe god's will and sacred knowledge do not change. Therefore, modernizing trends in religion corrupt its pure (putatively original) intent. In a world beset by this corrupting influence, assuredness can be found in strict adherence to religious texts—i.e., literal reading and interpretation. Modernity encourages individual freedom, including critical biblical scholarship and scientific skepticism fostered by such freedom, which is an anathema to religious orthodoxy. For Islamic fundamentalists, conquest of their lands and peoples by a colonial system left them relatively powerless and humiliated. Fundamentalist Islam provides psychological armor against this humiliation and an ideological justification for the struggle against it (it should be noted here that Islamic radicals have usually first targeted other Muslims they deem heretical or lacking in sufficient faith). Christian fundamentalists, also appalled by how modernity erodes the certainty of faith, live in a society with strong governing bureaucracies, military strength, and a mighty economic engine. As a result, their universalism extends not to the individual's freedom of conscience but rather justifies usurping individual agency through control of modern institutions to shape and control collective consciences or, at the very least, command obedience. These attempts at dominance over ever more people stem from the inherent logic embedded in required universalist monotheisms.

29   As with many macro-variable measures, this issue is complicated. On the one hand, while multiple measures do find that non-belief and atheism are growing worldwide, the *share* of these outlooks might in fact decline between 2015–2060. Population growth in areas of the world where religion remains influential accounts for this (see Lipka and McClendon 2017). In places like the United States, while approximately 90% proclaim a belief in "god,"

sexism, and homophobia—of many traditional religious beliefs. With advances in science, technology, and historical knowledge, many claims upon which religions built themselves are entirely explainable by natural causes—e.g., geo-centrism, natural disasters as god's wrath, illnesses as the result of curses or spiritual forces, and so on—while other ideas just seem outlandish—e.g., talking serpents, virgin births, reanimated corpses, and so on. Consequently, attributing things to an otherworldly source seems less and less plausible to many modern people.

Today, scientific knowledge has radically decentered the Earth to an arm of an average galaxy among a hundred-billion galaxies, none of which we knew about less than 100 years ago. With this new vision of the universe and humanity's relative insignificance within it, religion struggles with and against its prior positing of Earth and humans as the cosmological subject, where a nomos built around being the children of Abraham is difficult to maintain. With the willingness of fundamentalists to use violence against each other, bystanders, and public institutions, it is likely critics of religion will continue to find receptive audiences. It is therefore probable the numbers of those leaving religion will continue to grow with state enforcement of practice disabled and with religions unable to require participation (even though their theologies do).

4.3.3   Religion as Marketplace Consumption

Fundamentalism and leaving religion are not the only responses to modernity's crisis of meaning and/or the internal crises within institutional religions. Without the power to punish available to religious leaders, those who believe in the biblical monotheistic god and in Jesus-as-Christ can ignore aspects of Christianity they find problematic—e.g., miracles, a virgin birth, mandatory church attendance, rules on sex, prohibitions on divorce, homophobia, etc.—and select from it as if in a buffet line, a (pejoratively) so-called "Cafeteria Christianity." Though positing a god that applies to everyone, this trend represents a de-structuring of tradition and this provides space for individuals to accept outside non-doctrinal ideas as personally acceptable beliefs (e.g., astrology, fortune telling, karma) without cognitive dissonance.

Others have discarded specific religious faith while holding on to certain spiritual beliefs and practices. As global political-economic links—e.g., trade, immigration—and improved technologies—e.g., planes, television, and satellites—bring cultural exchanges as well as environmental problems,

---

and with 80% claiming belief in a biblical god, church attendance is nevertheless in decline (Fahmy 2018).

modernity's affluent classes encounter ideas such as Buddhism, Taoism, various pagan traditions, astrology, yoga, and so on (often accompanied by new dietary discipline, such as vegetarianism and veganism). By the late 1970s and early 1980s, a "New Age" movement emerged and persisted, if not always by that name. Here, individuals—now free to ignore required institutional doctrines and organizations that demand obedience—assemble their own rituals and practices from the global marketplace. Today, practices like astrology, Wicca and witchcraft, membership in UFO cults, and paranormal beliefs facilitated by internet communities are all on the increase (Kingsbury 2017; Magee 2017; Paul 2017; Routledge 2017; Squires 2018).

Both Cafeteria Christianity and New Age beliefs represent *individualized conglomerate religion*. While it has not been historically uncommon to combine ideas from different traditions, the degree to which this is self-motivated, nondenominational, and organizationally unstructured is new. Still in need of meaning, many modern people may not embrace specific religious dogmas and institutions but still believe in a god, gods, or spiritual forces. Such people search for and find a variety of them. With the Earth and human life remaining the cosmological subject, beliefs here posit their meanings are universal and apply to everyone, even if only in potential. Given their individual (rather than organizational) orientation, both Cafeteria Christianity and New Age belief are unenforceable by either religious or secular authorities and requiring belief is anywhere from difficult to impossible—thus, the need for constant recruitment and a tendency toward the occasional cult or sect. With no one view on what happens after death, especially reward or punishment, it is hard for conglomerate religious messages to compel people to commit to them. These trends represent the embryonic stages of a new god, one that is more abstract and a further step away from both institutional religion and conglomerate religion.

4.3.4   The New Generic God

With institutional religion represented by aspiring but failed monopolies in a competitive religious market, as individualized conglomerate religion grows as an alternative, and as capitalism integrates people, markets, cultures, and ideas while undergoing constant change, a new god analogous to George Herbert Mead's ([1934] 1962) "generalized other" has emerged. For much of history, gods were like significant others—with names, biographies, and points of view (e.g., Odin, Zeus, Hera). Today, "god" is increasingly detached from tradition and authority and has no name, history, or a specific people. Yahweh, the god of Abraham, is, in a sense, functionally dead after having been slowly but increasingly usurped by the proto-form of this generic god, though in a Christian guise. Instead of a turn towards atheism, for today's non-doctrinally aligned theist, god still exists as "a superhuman being in the fantastic reality of heaven" (Marx [1844] 1975b: 175). This new general, abstract, and nameless god without a history and indifferent toward specific organizations or rites represents *generic belief.* Being generic, this new god-as-totem is more personal than ever as believers base it on their preferences and even in their own image (Epley et al. 2009). This god has escaped the orbit of religious teaching and authority, requires no ritual or specific doctrine, and has believers who usually posit it as universally applicable. Paradoxically, many such believers tend to be relativists on the requirements of theism and agnostic on the afterlife. With belief personally rooted, there is no authority structure per se and knowledge is a patchwork of lore, tradition, and individual proclivity.

5   Discussion

Science isolates objects and their interrelations in order to study laws, regularities, and differences. Since "society" is a broad concept covering all historical periods, we must be able to identify and conceptually capture specific structures and their relevant variables with the combined analytical precision and flexibility required for studying systemic and historical change. However, the study of religion, whether from apologists or critics, usually starts with the nature and number of the gods or remains on the grounds of the history of religious traditions. Marx (1971a: 817), on the other hand, believed that "all science would be superfluous if the outward appearance and the essence of things directly coincided." In a proper scientific modeling of religion, "our difficulties begin only when we set about the observation and the arrangement—the real depiction—of our historical material, whether of a past epoch or of the present" (Marx and Engels [1846] 1976: 37). That material presents us the challenge of piecing together the "concentration of many determinations" (Marx 1973: 101) that make up the concrete, with religion being no exception. For this work, we must train our focus not on what religions tell us about themselves nor on their surface appearance but on their development within and between real historical societies shaped by material forces. The analysis above proposes a model for such an inquiry.

For such work, we first identify religion's forms of development across multiple levels of generality (Figure 5.1). This approach better prepares us to piece together their interrelations. Second, we then locate how the variables used to

FIGURE 5.1 Levels of abstraction for a study of religion from broad to narrow
SOURCE: CREATED BY AUTHOR

differentiate societies in general find expression in capitalist society and use them to isolate religion's corresponding development there (Table 5.10). Third, we similarly isolate variables related to class systems in general and identify how they have influenced religion's development in capitalist history, as it too is a class system (Table 5.11). Fourth, we isolate the unique features of capitalism in general as a system and their influence on modern religious development (Table 5.12). Finally, Table 5.13 breaks this down into the history of religion across stages of capitalism's development (as discussed in Chapter 3).

The analysis above facilitates a Marxian taxonomy of religion. Analysis builds this model upon the comparison of religions and religious beliefs observed across history. Starting with holding constant humans as animals, humans as humans, and society in general, we compare religious practices observed across historical changes within and between modes of production (Table 5.14) and use variations found there to differentiate religious categories (Table 5.15). While all religions make a distinction between the sacred and the profane, they posit different types of sacred realms. All traditions use ritual to

TABLE 5.10   Religion in society in general and religious development in capitalism

The general abstract	The specific abstract	The general concrete	The specific concrete
Religion in society in general and its expressions in capitalism	Division of labor	Size and specialization of priesthood	Proliferation of religious organizations and doctrines, variations in authority structure, enforcement of religion recedes
	Property relations	Prevailing class relations as moral order	Religious nationalism, Private property as sacrosanct law, Nature as resource for exploitation
	Subject of production	Systemic productive relations as moral order	Capital accumulation as social and moral good
	Changes in power-structure within and between systems	Moral rules compatible with new system remain	Rules on premarital sex, homosexuality, monogamy
		Rule incompatible with new system disappear	Prohibition of usury ends
		New moral rules develop	Selling one's labor seen as contribution to society
	Social development of productive forces	Knowledge of nature	Decentering of earth, scientific knowledge about nature, knowledge about disease, continued alienation from nature
		New forms of mass communication	Increasing literacy, cross-cultural knowledge
		Advanced technological systems defeat less advanced	Religious ideas adopted across global cultures
	Terms of labor	Forced labor system endorsed by religious beliefs	Work ethic, profit motive not seen as immoral exploitation

TABLE 5.11 Social forces in class systems and religious development in capitalism

The general abstract	The specific abstract	The general concrete	The specific concrete
Religion in class systems in general and their expressions in capitalism	Systems of labor exploitation and appropriation	Alienating institutions of labor control	Continuation of religion as spirit of spiritless world Increasing susceptibility to religious extremism
	Ruling class relationship with religious organization	Political leaders deified while state secularizes	Nation's leaders as secular priesthood, state sanction of religions declines, ability to force participation ends
	Ruling class ideas become general ideas of society	Appropriation as moral order	Profit motive no longer seen as greed, capitalism as human nature, property relations backed by law, nature as natural resource for exploitation, work ethic
		Legal universality	Social movements for increased freedom for women, ethnicities
		Obedience as morality	Revolution as sin against society

SOURCE: CREATED BY AUTHOR

connect these realms but differ as to its requirements, e.g., exacting and conservative doctrines versus more liberal and relativist ones. Other considerations
include to whom a religious system applies (application), to what extent beliefs
are required (the terms of belief), what awaits humans after death, a religion's
authority structure (top-down, bottom-up, or somewhere in between), and its

TABLE 5.12   Development of religion in capitalism in general

The general abstract	The specific abstract	The general concrete	The specific concrete
Capitalism in general	Abstract individualism	Legal individuality and individual rights	Personal god, individual soul and salvation
	Institutional separation	Secularization	US constitution, secular laws Freedom of religion
		Religion and state as separate institutions	Proliferation of religious organizations, unbelief and declining participation
	Expansion, constant change, contradiction, polarization, alienation	Merging of global religions Liberalizing trends and conservative reaction Crises of meaning	Missionary transmission across cultures Fundamentalism and Atheism New Age beliefs Generic god
	Institutional merger	Capital fetishism Religious support of market principles	Market fundamentalism Political-economic conservatism merges with religious conservatism*

SOURCE: CREATED BY AUTHOR
Note: * See Chapter 6.

knowledge structure (the cosmological subject as related in lore, canon, personal beliefs). This model reveals the historical changes in religion across systems, its development into canon and organizational structure, and its current breaking apart and, perhaps, dissolution.

Marx's approach to religion is often reduced to something a ruling class invents to subdue a working class and thus as "the opiate of the masses." While, true, political-economic powers have and do use religion for their own ends, such assumptions unnecessarily limit the range and utility of both Marx's theories and his methods, which provide us a broader framework to study religion's rise and historical development. Static conceptions of religion—universal definitions that depict it as a historical constant, functionalist apologetics based on this depiction—fail to grasp religion's real development in time, space, and social structure. The method of successive abstractions provides both the conceptual precision and the freedom in empirical matter to do this.

TABLE 5.13   Development of religion across stages of capitalism

Capitalist development in the general abstract	General concrete material conditions	Religious develop- ment in the general concrete	Religion in the specific concrete
From agricul- tural capitalism to manufacture	Colonialism	Christianizing of "savages"	Missionary system and forced conversions
From capitalist manufacture to industrialism capitalism	Rise of the nation- state, increased technological complexity	Rise of fundamentalism Religion as a separate institution	Growth of sects, churches, denominations
From monopoly to transnational capitalism	De-colonialization	Decline of church authority	Spread of Protestant Christianity in Korea and China Salafism,
	Neo-colonialism	Crisis of meaning: backlash against secularization	Wahhabism, Islamic Brotherhood, Christian Nationalist movements
	Emergence of neo-liberal order	Crisis of meaning: religion as market- place consumption, increase in new religious ideas	New Age movement, Cafeteria Christian- ity, the Generic god
From transna- tional to global capitalism	NAFTA, European Union, WTO, TTP, free trade agree- ments in general, privatization, etc.	Crisis of meaning: radicalized fundamen- talism doctrines	Islamic Brother- hood, Taliban, Al Qaeda, ISIS, Dominion Theology and other forms of fanaticism
		Crisis of meaning: withdrawal from religion	The New Atheism

SOURCE: CREATED BY AUTHOR

TABLE 5.14   Comparing religion's variables across historical mode of production

Constants	Variables	Modes of production	Compared to
Humans as animals	Inhabitants of the sacred realm	Earliest societies	Class systems
			Feudalism
			Capitalism in general
Humans as humans	Ritual and doctrine as mediators of realms		Recent capitalism
		Class systems in general	Earliest societies
			Feudalism
Society in general			Capitalism in general
	Application		Recent capitalism
		Feudalism (as precondition of capitalism)	Earliest societies
Religion in general: sacred and profane	Terms of belief		Class systems
			Capitalism in general
	What happens after death		Recent capitalism
		Capitalism in general	Earliest societies
			Class systems
	Authority structure		Feudalism
			Recent capitalism
		Recent capitalism	Earliest societies
	Knowledge structure		Class systems
			Feudalism
			Capitalism in general

SOURCE: CREATED BY AUTHOR

This approach forces upon us a critical eye toward any ideological dogma—religious or political—where "man is governed by the products of his own brain" (Marx [1867] 1992b: 582). Such ideologies—political, economic, religious—return to that same mental home and leave people susceptible to similar methods of influence, often in other spheres of life. This observation reveals why forms of religious and political fanaticism often resemble one another and why we sometimes find such forms of thinking within the same group of individuals. Coming to this conclusion does not necessarily require the use of Marx's overall approach but that approach itself does lead to such conclusions, making Marx's a very political science.

TABLE 5.15   A Marxian religious taxonomy

Variables	Categories						
	Nature worship	State religion	Ruling class religion	Institutional religion	Individualized conglomerate religion	Generic belief	Atheism
Inhabitant of sacred realm	Spirits, ancestors, supernatural forces	Multiple gods and demi-gods rooted in home civilization	God or gods with name, history, personality that reflect image of ruling class	Inherited gods from ruling class religion; spiritual realm increasingly independent of social class and state forces	Combined tradition unbound by culture	General god-figure	None
Ritual and doctrine as mediation between realms	Exacting	Exacting, conservative Tolerance for local traditions	Exacting, conservative Little tolerance for other traditions	Various: exacting and conservative, liberalizing trends	Multiple, liberal Relativist trends	Declining in rituals Relativist trends	None
Application	"Humanity" coterminous with local in-group	Citizens and political subjects of city-states, empires	Universal, kingdom prioritized	Universal, nation-state prioritized	Universal, individual and global	Universal, individual and global	Everyone
Terms of belief	Assumed	Official religion required Secondary tolerated	Required Secondary non-tolerated	Mix of required and not required Varying levels of toleration	Various Pluralism assumed	Various Personalized expectations	Not required
What happens after death	Various	Various	Reward or punishment in afterlife for obedience	Various	Various	Various	Agnostic

Variables	Categories						
	Nature worship	State religion	Ruling class religion	Institutional religion	Individual-ized conglomer-ate religion	Generic belief	Atheism
Authority structure	Situational	High priests, political leaders, god-kings	Organiza-tional	Organizational	Various	Personalized	None
Knowl-edge structure	Lore, tradition	Lore, proto-canon-ical texts	Canon, doctrine, political and religious fiat	Canon, doctrine	Mixture of prior canons, beliefs, practices	Individual but use of myth, lore, history, etc.	Scien-tific N/A
	Earth and humans as subjects of cosmos	Earth and humans as subjects of cosmos	Earth and humans as subjects of cosmos	Earth and humans as subjects of cosmos	Earth and humans as subjects of cosmos	Cosmologi-cal subject vague, shifting, various	

SOURCE: CREATED BY AUTHOR

CHAPTER 6

An Essay on Religion

1   A Provocation

I once lived without a television for several years. This was not a conscious decision, a commitment to a philosophy of life, nor a political statement on my part, but rather the result of living with roommates who also did not own one. One day I happened to watch a few hours of television at a friend's house. Having been away from it for a while, the sophomoric nature of the commercials and their assault on the intelligence really stood out, as if I were seeing them for the first time. By now, sadly, I have grown so accustomed to television again that I have lost that newfound sense of consternation at the medium. Rather than contempt, sometimes familiarity breeds dulled indifference and passivity.

Around this same period, an acquaintance took me to see an exhibition by Buddhist monks. On a mission in the United States to connect with Western audiences, they were visiting several universities and creating sand mandalas on a large platform laid across a floor. The monks, on their hands and knees, would carefully tap small pieces of folded paper that held the sand so that the slightest amount would trickle out just right, allowing them to draw whatever lines or shapes needed and in the color desired. The mandala was about the size of the kickoff circle on a soccer pitch, intricate, and symmetrical. Though this painstaking work normally took two to four days, in a demonstration of the Buddhist principles of impermanence and nonattachment, they would pour the finished mandala into a nearby river or stream, sending its grains back to the Earth from where they came.

As we watched the monks from an elevated deck above them, my acquaintance found the monks and their work as embodiments of "amazing" spiritual devotion. My evaluation was less effusive, based solely on what we were observing. Being a sociology student made me familiar with both Weber's notion of the "routinization of charisma" and Goffman's dramaturgical outlook. This background, combined with my experience in the restaurant business, made me sensitive to the difference between what a front stage audience sees in comparison to actors' back stage behaviors.

Reading the monks' brochure, I noticed that this was not the only university they would visit and, I surmised, the mandalas they would create during their mission were not their first. Even if they were, by the fifth, eighth, or tenth iteration, the activity would only grow easier and increasingly routine. I also pictured the monks as traveling companions and long-term members of the same order, who probably did not think of each other as Lama So-and-So, His Holiness, etc., but rather as "Jim," "Steve," and "Joe." Should they still use them, these formal titles would lose their power of reverence over time, just like when academics or surgeons refer to each other as "Doctor Smith" in everyday interaction. I pictured Lama Steve whispering to Brother Jim (out of earshot) that Monk Joe always "fucks up" this section of the mandala, that he "has to take a piss," and/or that he hopes "there's good food at the commissary" after they finish, as "you cannot trust Americans to make a very good vegetarian dish." "What's the weather forecast for our drive tomorrow?"

When one of my undergraduate sociology professors was a child, his father was a circuit-riding preacher who would go from town to town putting on revivals for Baptist congregations. To make a living on the circuit, a preacher needed to build up a reputation for saving souls, which would produce additional requests for bringing their skills to other churches. His father concluded that to do this he would need to learn and practice successful techniques for getting as many people as possible to respond to the altar call on the last day of the revival, i.e., when the preacher invites congregants who need to be "saved" to the front for blessings, usually involving a baptism.

When he was young, my former professor would often accompany his father during his travels on the circuit, sitting in the car's backseat as his father and his assistant discussed their strategies for success. He remembered his father explaining that the best way to structure a revival is to have a friendly and inviting Friday night service, often accompanied by a meal. This got the congregation familiar with him and built up their trust. Saturday should involve lessons in Bible study, usually sermons related to love, charity, sisterhood and brotherhood, compassion, duty, and so on, demonstrating the social value of the Christian message. On Sunday, it was hell, fire, and brimstone—emphasizing the sacrifice Jesus made for humanity, explaining that faith in that sacrifice was requisite for salvation, and warning that a failure to accept Jesus as one's personal savior would result in an eternal and tortuous damnation.

During this performance, in order to cast the widest net, the sermon should emphasize readings that address common human traits that the Christian Bible says require repentance and thus forgiveness—lust, pride, envy, and so on. Another crucial point of emphasis should be warnings about doubt, insufficient commitment to "giving one's life over to the Lord," and what awaits those who fail to do so. The preaching also should shift in tenor and volume so that it becomes increasingly intense, loud, commanding, threatening, and, thus, fear inducing. At the crescendo, the altar call is announced: "Who is ready to bring Jesus into their heart?!" "I know there are some here who want to be saved, need to be saved! Come now, brothers and sisters, and accept this simple and amazing gift the Lord is offering you!!" Or some such admonishing entreaty. Since it would demystify the performance if congregants discovered that the preacher had preplanned and tested the sequence of messages and events, the front stage action should seem spontaneous and conceal its techniques of audience management, thus facilitating the appearance of authenticity and thus legitimacy. Little that happened there, however, was left to accident or chance.

I have long stopped going to church. My parents gave me and my siblings permission to choose for ourselves whether we would still attend services once we reached adulthood. For a year or so after I turned 18 years-old, I pretended to keep going. As I often worked late on Saturday nights and sometimes on Sunday mornings, I would drive around town instead of attending late Mass on Sunday night. I eventually stopped with the pretense and with it so discarded any personal commitment to or interest in Catholicism. This outlook resulted from years of exposure to that religion and it eventually reflected my lack of attachment to religion in general.

Growing up in church, it seemed doubtful to me that practitioners had the liturgy's specific messages in mind as they recited its prayers, nor could they really know the actual mind frame of the original authors. As penitents, their prayers came across as droning recitations delivered on cue, unified sounds that lost meaning upon decades of weekly repetition. The movements of the Mass (stand, sit, sign of the cross, kneel), too, were rote and had no apparent relevance. Even if someone had explained their meaning to me once, I was likely around 10 years-old and soon forgot the lesson. It seemed to me that most adults probably did so as well, especially to the extent that standing/sitting/kneeling were conditioned responses. So sequenced were these movements that one could use them to mark time until the Mass was over, something I usually did. I strongly suspected that I was not alone in these regards.

As for the Mass itself, there was nothing "spiritual" or "uplifting" about the experience, nor did there seem to be any real point to it. What did these words, gestures, and fancy clothes have to do with "god"? The Church's ornate buildings and vast wealth did not resemble the humility and a preference for the poor Jesus supposedly preached. I also found its constant reminders of its "tradition" unconvincing, as doing something repeatedly for a long period meant nothing to me, regardless of how many centuries back one could trace its origins. I found church members anywhere from arrogant to nice enough, but the judgmental dispositions and pursuit of status and material things I encountered did not seem aligned with Jesus's message. I protested that going to church—in terms of religion generally and Catholicism in particular—surely was not the only way to teach one to be a good person, which was the main lesson Christianity had taught me about its raison d'être up to that point in my life. However, Catholicism also *requires* church attendance on top of internalizing and living out its moral lessons. If participating in religion is not just for learning how to be a good person, then what other reason could there be for requiring that people attend and go through the motions, gestures, and rituals that are required of them?

I sometimes find myself back in church on occasion for a baptism, wedding, or a funeral. When there, I often experience the rituals and prayers as if for the first time, similar to my reintroduction to television several years back. The messages I hear now, in addition to their repetitiousness, are verbalizations of people whose religion teaches that all humans are born fundamentally flawed but that believers should be grateful to be in the presence of the same god who made them and that they need to worship that god thankfully. Words like "sin," "obedience," "forgiveness," and "mercy" juxtaposed to "love," "redemption," "salvation," and "heaven" come off like so many ingredients in a word salad uttered by afraid, submissive, and dutiful sheep—whether layperson, nun, or priest.[1] Catholicism's theology, in other words, requires the petitioner to assume a posture of obsequiousness in exchange for connecting them to the sacred powers it claims to access. It is difficult to avoid concluding that such supplicating rituals demean and humiliate the individual, regardless of whether or not this was the original intent. It is not hard to suspect that it was.

This posture, with the individual making themselves prone before and supplicating to an idol, an object, an altar, or a holy figure, is not specific to any one religion, as it is found in our earliest proto-religious forms, polytheistic traditions, and in Judaism, Buddhism, and Islam as well. According to many religions, human beings *must worship*. This is an activity we mock, ridicule, or judge when done toward non-religious things like money, secular authority figures, celebrities, or even gods other than our religion's own. It is not difficult to conjure up an image of "natives" worshiping at the base of a volcano or some other idol of their own making and sneering at their primitive ignorance and unfounded superstition. But this is just another expression of the same idea, that of worshiping. What does this posture of "worship" mean in a religious context, then? One passage in the Bible (Matthew 8:8) states it outright, "I am not worthy" and only "the Lord" has the power to "heal" me from this state. Humans, in this narrative, are unclean and undignified and require supplicating acts of purification in order to become whole and uncontaminated so that they are qualified to be in the presence of sacred power.

---

1 I am aware of how dismissive this sounds.

Instead of relying on teaching lessons on it, why does religion force its practitioners into a literal posture of humbleness, reminding them to feel honored to participate in the ritual in the first place? In Chapter 5, I addressed the issue of how some human rules of conduct stem from the requisites of society in general, while religious discourse depicts such rules as coming from a sacred realm. Humbleness is the opposite of pride and arrogance—i.e., antisocial attitudes—and helps one get along with others more amicably. It is good for society, in other words. Religious rituals develop in a manner so as not to leave such lessons to chance. Forcing congregants into humbling postures and prayers is a form of deceptive coercion in a sense, as if a scriptural message is not enough. A human dilemma is that in teaching rules of conduct, we often transform valuable social ideas into symbolic acts that smuggle in other messages and even overbearing mechanisms of control. Postures of humility become acts and messages of humiliation.

Let us look at another example, albeit in the abstract. Because stealing from each other results in dysfunctional social relations, religions world over have prohibitions against it. They tell their followers that such rules come from god—or the sacred realm more generally. This gives those rules more gravitas. Think of it like this. What would be a more effective way to teach a child not to steal—telling them rules against theft are sociological requisites for maintaining a functional society, or telling them that an all-powerful deity made this rule and will punish them for breaking it? Religious rules take the latter discursive form and religions established this approach during a time when humans were less sociologically mature—i.e., in the sense of having a historical and scientific species self-awareness. Because of this state, religions encoded such rules in metaphors people could understand, e.g., an eye for an eye—if thy hand offends thee, cut it off—stone the adulterer—and so on. As people sometimes interpret metaphors as instructions, these literal practices still exist in some parts of the world.

Religions only on occasion state outright that they have constructed their messages as metaphors, as doing this consistently would undermine the gravity of those messages. Over time, people forget this basic root tack and use the metaphor as the reality the metaphor tries to get across as a life lesson. And without a warning that any such lesson is in metaphorical form, there is nothing to prevent the religious-minded from treating them literally. Six-day creations of whole universes, talking serpents, arks saving the animal kingdom from global floods, resting on the Sabbath (to the point of immobility), all manner of miracles, and so on can thus become realities in the religious imagination.

This inquiry suggests a way to look at Christianity's theological underpinnings. What claims does it make about how human history was organized and changed via a deity and their intentions for the human world?

I was recently back in church for a funeral and intently listened to the prayers to try to make sense out of them. In generally failing at my task, more than once I whispered in my girlfriend's ear, "What does that even mean?" Her eyes rolled at my impatience, assuming rightly that I already knew what a Mass was like, so why let it bother me? Though she was correct on one measure, I could never shake the idea that if god was the sort of entity its faithful claimed, it is not too much to ask that the knowledge he [sic] revealed to humans be coherent, if not demonstrable.[2] Though this was not a new idea to me, actually following the logic of the prayers carefully was something I now was doing with more intention than I had in my youth.

During this episode, I paid close attention to the Nicene Creed. When I was young, I would repeat it from memory, understanding none of it. There was never any reason to, as congregants said the Creed in unison and a sort of "semantic satiation" absorbed its meaning into a verbal white noise. As I now carefully contemplated its claims, it came across as a jumble of assertions without rhyme or reason. I started to wonder if those who regularly recited the Creed actually understood its basic assertions. Even before this experience, I had pondered what the Christian story would sound like to someone who had never heard it before. Discovering a way to manufacture this scenario mentally was not easy at first, as one learns to treat established religions with reverence or, failing that, a level of deference at least. However, if we unburden ourselves with such expectations, there is a way retell Christianity's story reduced to its basic claims.

By now, Christianity's legitimacy stems in no little part from its longevity and its number of believers. Since its origin story survived through its progressive institutionalization—from the word of mouth proselytizing in the first few

---

2   Evidently, this demand of mine goes back to before my memory of it. My mother used to repeat a story of being in church with our family. I was probably about four years-old (give or take a year or two), as, in her telling, she was holding me in her arms. At the point in the Mass called the "Consecration" (which relates to the story of the Last Supper), the priest blesses a chalice of wine in order to transform it into the blood of Jesus (for Catholic doctrine, this is not metaphorical but a literal transformation). In doing so, the priest states at the end of the prayer (quoting Jesus to his disciples), "This is my blood, which will be given up for you." At this point, I announced to the congregation, "That's not your blood, you poopy head!" To this day I still do not believe anyone possesses magical powers and can use words and gestures to transform the properties of physical objects.

decades after the crucifixion, to encoding followers' beliefs into scriptures, to the Roman leadership's adoption of the faith, to the proliferation of a Christian priesthood and its leaders, councils, synods, and churches—imagine it was not 2000-plus years ago that the events in question took place, but just 20 or so. Change the religious terms, individual names, and locations just a bit, and imagine someone coming up on the street and relating the following story to you.

In 1998, fairies told a young unmarried Peruvian woman named Brittany that she had conceived a child through divine intervention. Mongo, the one and only ruling Supernatural Being, chose her because of her purity in never having broken any sexual or moral rules. She gave birth to a baby boy and named him Larry, who was, in fact, the son of Mongo, creator of all things as imbued by the Sanctified Force. Though we know almost nothing of his childhood and early adult life, Larry became a skilled roofer and a radical shaman who attracted a following of downtrodden people from the Hill Tribes. He preached that the local Andean people should treat each other well, love their neighbors, and pay their taxes. Larry also had special powers—he could feed masses of people on the scantiest provisions, fly without assistance, cure diseases by snapping his fingers, and even raise the dead. He told his people that Mongo would eventually come down from the sky, vanquish their enemies, and rule over them forever in a peaceful world. Moved by his messages and powers, several people soon quit their jobs and followed Larry around, hanging on his every word.

Larry's growing popularity and news of his ministry so threatened the local gurus that they teamed up with a local judge to set him up on charges of heresy, which was punishable by hanging. The Federales carried out the sentence on a highway overpass leading into Lima and left his body there with those of common criminals, a warning to all others not to cross the authorities. Angered by this, Mongo unleashed storms and earthquakes in an unmistakable rebuke. Graves sprung open and several corpses reanimated and walked the city. Even one of the criminals and one of the Federales realized the mistake and openly admitted that Larry truly was Mongo's son.

After a few days, one of his followers took his body down and had it cremated. However, Larry soon came back, visited and talked to some of his disciples, and then eventually flew up to Valhalla, leaving no trace behind. Before he did, however, he promised he would return within their lifetimes and usher in the Empire of Mongo. Though he has not returned yet, the reason all of this happened is because Mongo sent Larry—both his son but also Mongo himself (who was both the only Supernatural Being as well as the Sanctified

Force)—to Peru to absolve his favorite local tribe of the bad karma they inherited at birth from two ancestors who had died thousands of years ago.

Preliterate sheepherders first spread this story by word of mouth and then later city-folk passed it on through text messages. Today, there are entire websites devoted to it and many bloggers believe that ancient long-dead shamans foretold of Larry's presence and that his ministry was not just for the Hill Tribes but, instead, for all of humanity. They claim that if you do not accept this story as true and Larry's ministry and execution as relevant to your soul's destiny, after death Mongo will punish you on a bed of fire ants for eternity. If you do accept these claims, then you will join Larry, Brittany, Mongo, and the Sanctified Force in Valhalla for time without end, along with all your dead friends, relatives, and everyone else who believes this story.

Had you given the person telling you this information—someone who did not witness the events in question—the opportunity to finish, what would you think of them and the potential veracity of their claims? You would probably dismiss them as delusional and dismiss their story as a product of that delusion. Then you would go about your day, losing no sleep whatsoever that night over the matter. What almost *every person* today is *highly unlikely* to conclude is the following:

> I believe in one Supernatural Being,
> Mongo the almighty,
> maker of Valhalla and Earth,
> of all things, even invisible stuff.
>
> I believe in one Lord Larry Christ,
> Mongo's Only Begotten Son,
> born of the Father before all ages.
> Supernatural Being from Supernatural Being, Light from Light,
> true Supernatural Being from true Supernatural Being,
> Produced from that Being's will, not from humans fucking, while being
> Father Mongo at the same time;
> he made everything in existence.
> For all of humanity and to prevent us from being eaten by fire ants for
> eternity
> he came down from Valhalla,
> and by the Sanctified Force was put into the body of Brittany, who never
> had sex before,
> and he became a real person.

Larry's execution under judicial authority was done just for our salvation,
he suffered death and was cremated,
and a month later he came back to life
in accordance with the writings of the ancient shamans.
He ascended to Valhalla
and is seated at the right hand of Mongo.
He will return to Earth again in glory
to judge everyone alive today and all those who have ever lived
and his Empire will go on for eternity.

I believe in the Sanctified Force, the Lord, the giver of life,
who proceeds from Mongo and Larry,
who with Mongo and Larry is adored and glorified,
who has spoken through the bloggers.

There is only one legitimate, divine, all-embracing Church and it was inspired by Larry's closest followers.
I confess one Water Rite for the cleansing of bad karma
and I look forward to the dead coming back to life
and the life of the world to come. Yes, indeed![3]

The story of Larry via the Nicene Creed is the story that Christianity—at least
in its Catholic iteration—requires people accept at eternal risk of their soul for
failure to do so (Protestantism and other versions of Christianity only differ in
minor details). However, these assertions appear so fanciful that it is hard to
imagine anyone believing them today if introduced to that belief system as
reproduced above.

This reconfiguration of the Jesus story tells us much about why religious
authorities often thwart questions from inquirers. In requiring people to believe such a fantastic story at eternal risk of their soul, Christianity's followers
are bound to ask some questions. These questions may be internal to the
theology of the religion or externally related to the practical realities of life and
its troubles. Several such questions internal to Christianity might be:

– If the "fall" of Adam and Eve explains the existence of "sin," then how and/
  or why can god hold anyone else responsible for that? We no longer condone

---

3   The version of the Nicene Creed used in this re-translation comes from the website of The
    United States Conference of Catholic Bishops (retrieved October 13, 2018) at: http://www.us-
    ccb.org/beliefs-and-teachings/what-we-believe/. Not restricted to Catholicism, one could re-
    use this exercise on all religious faiths.

such ancient tribal thinking in secular law today, so why accept it in theology?

- Why would god make humans inherently susceptible to "sin" and then punish them for this normal state? While this set up allows this god to exercise forgiveness, this certainly does not seem to be an exercise in loving.
- Why did god send a universal but singular message for all of humanity to a largely illiterate people in one corner of the world? If humans had free will to spread that message, this seems like a rather risky and untenable strategy. And if belief in this message is required to get into heaven, giving it to such a society seems extremely selective, cruel, and unfair. If belief in this message is not required, then why send it at all?
- How did Jesus's execution 2000 years ago redeem humanity from their "sins" and how and why does believing this today save someone from eternal torment and open heaven up to them?[4]
- If the Christian god is the maker of all things seen and unseen, how does faith in Jesus-as-Christ apply to other intelligent beings (potentially) in the universe? How can any answer other than "it doesn't" make sense? If this is the case, then how does this conclusion reconcile with the "maker of all things" part?
- If a classroom of students cannot keep a simple sentence unchanged in playing the telephone game, it is certain that we have received a transformed version of the events in question, given that the story was passed on only by word of mouth for the first several *decades* after those events are said to have happened. Further, though believers eventually wrote down this oral tradition, we no longer have copies of the first manuscripts, only copies of copies, which came to us already translated into Greek, then later into Latin, and eventually into English, Spanish, German, and so on. Given the multiple changes, interpretations, mistakes, and so on that come with such a transmission of ideas, why should anyone believe any of it?

Questions external to Christianity's specific theology but related to life's daily realities might be:

---

4 I have thought about what Christianity is trying to assert with this claim for years and still do not understand its basic premise. If this idea requires complex theological unpacking to explain, then that is a clumsy, convoluted, and impenetrable message to deliver to a barely literate society. And this is *the key* to all Christian salvation claims. Not all religious doctrines suffer from such incomprehensibleness, however. One can make some sense out of Buddhism's central idea that existence is suffering, suffering comes from desire, and the five-fold path allows one to escape this fate. A person does not have to agree with these assertions, though they can discern a logical argument from them and put them into everyday language.

- If Jesus was a powerful and all-knowing god that came down from heaven to help humanity, why did he not have more actionable information to tell the people of the day, information they could have used with the technology they had available? Would expecting god's representative on Earth to provide information about how bacteria can cause disease be too much to ask? "Leave your families, sell your belongings, and wait faithfully for my return" seems less life-affirming than does, "Boil your water before drinking it. Use some of that hot water not for drinking but for bathing and cleaning your dishes. And wash your hands with it regularly."
- If god is all-powerful and all-knowing, then why does god have such a hard time making his or her message known in a more coherent and consistent matter? Why so many versions of each specific religion? Why so many religions in general?
- What sort of god creates a world where infants are not seldom born with serious birth defects and young children get cancer, inflicting suffering on them and often cutting short the lives of both? What about the heartache of their parents? What sort of "plan" is that?

Christian apologists have no convincing answers for such questions and their appeal to "faith" and "mystery" to smooth over such incongruities suggests that they know that they are asking people to accept something that makes little coherent sense. And Christian apologists are by no means alone in these regards.[5]

To the extent that my rewriting of the Nicene Creed ventures on caricature, by that same measure it also fails to reveal one ingredient of Christianity's longevity. If it is not a convincing narrative, then what has sustained it? Putting aside its adoption by powerful elites, the history of colonialism, repression of dissent, forced conversions and inquisitions, and basic socialization for the moment, Christianity did something no religion before it had done. Recall that Jesus was a rabbi, preaching at a time when Judaism reflected many religions'

---

5   We can ask other questions about religion that are more general and fit for any form of belief. Why would a god that is omnipotent and a perfect being require humans to worship it? How can we reconcile the idea of a "soul" with what we know about evolution? Was there a first soul? What would be the point? Did god get bored? Were souls created for the potential of torturing some for eternity? If spirits and forces are transcendental, why do they always take the form of nearby plants, animals, and geographical features? Where is the landlocked culture that has discovered the god of the seas? If spoken language is simply a set of arbitrary sounds to which humans have ascribed meaning, then how is it possible for specific verbalized prayers to tap into transcendent sacred powers? Such a discovery would have to have astronomical odds.

historical convention, that of being applicable solely to a particular people, a specific tribe, or an otherwise identifiable cultural-ethnic configuration. Jewish prophesies foretold of *their* messiah, a messiah-king that would come to them at the head of an army, liberate them from oppression, and vanquish their enemies. Most Jewish people of the time did not embrace him because Jesus riding on the back of an ass into Jerusalem with his unwashed disciples did not reflect these prophesized expectations. Moreover, faith in this context meant maintaining a belief that the Hebrew messiah eventually would come, not faith that an otherworldly being exists who is the god for all people for all times and in all places. Finally, even the early Christian assumption that Jesus's message applied to the Hebrew people alone continued for a while after his death. In time, however, his followers would change the meaning of his ministry.

When Jesus did not return as promised and his expectant followers were dying off, Paul (mid-first century) transformed Jesus into a universally applicable messiah—not a specific holy figure for a particular place and people but a god-messiah for all of humanity everywhere and always. This transformed Jesus into a culturally fungible figure that believers and proselytizers adjusted for other peoples and times. Though Roman authorities initially repressed Christians—likely because of their refusal to provide sacrifices to official state gods and the emperor (as was normally expected)—the religion continued to spread both through proselytizing and, after Constantine's conversion (about 312 CE), with Rome's empire. In this process, certain messages with wide appeal—such as loving one's neighbor, justice for the downtrodden, the meek inheriting the Earth—were likely not hard for people to embrace. With the later consolidation of the Old and the New Testaments into the Christian Bible (around 400 CE or so), missionaries and proselytizers could select from a plethora of ideas and assert their relevance for other cultures. Ideas about peace, brotherhood, charity, and a future just world came attached with the idea that Jesus was both god and god's son, that belief in this and in his resurrection were requisite for eternal reward, and that failure to believe this would damn one to a torturous fate (that is, a psychological-spiritual element of coercion). With Jesus now almost infinitely malleable, whatever powers found the story compatible, useful, or convenient could reconfigure Christianity as needed.

This sort of required universalist endpoint was not at all how our earliest religious ideas were contextualized and applied. A fungible-cross-cultural-required-theology-as-end-result would not even make sense to an Arunta shaman or an Incan priestess had it been proposed to them as a programmatic goal. It probably would not make sense to Jesus's earliest follows, either. This evolution of Christianity over time produced a new type of religious discourse and practice, where its form of required universalism made it culturally transformable like no other, a discursive model Islam later adopted (absent Jesus-as-messiah).

To have faith is to believe in something despite sufficient evidence to do so—or even requiring no evidence at all. It is therefore instructive that one of the first stories in the Bible is about what happened after Adam and Eve ate from the Tree of Knowledge. This message and its context—ancient religious authorities warning that "original sin" is rooted in the search for knowledge; the Bible's compilers placing such a warning in its earliest pages—reveals much about the *purpose of* religious knowledge and *of* religious authority *according to* religious authorities. In this construct, all human beings start out fundamentally malformed, overcurious, disobedient, and in need of a priesthood to chaperon them properly into God's Truth. Nietzsche depicted this as a morality for slaves, while the Bible uses the idea of "sheep" for the faithful and that of "shepherd" for "the Lord" and/or his [sic] representatives. In this view, people are simple, fearful, ignorant, and need the guidance of an authoritative leader who knows what is best for them, while it is verboten for humans to search for knowledge independently on their own.

In terms of "faith," the story of Abraham and Isaac also tells us a great deal. If you believe that god has commanded you to murder your child, *you do it.* Believers usually do not see this story as one of grotesque cruelty by a capricious god-figure, nor does it move many believers to pause skeptically over the foundational premises of their religion. Instead, believers see it as a lesson on the duties and powers of belief, where one should be so faithful in their god and his will that they would kill one of their children if asked. This is the intended lesson and all Abrahamic traditions celebrate it—i.e., blind obedience to god—as a virtuous one. This knowledge-form has brought all manner of people to justify oppressive and violent actions through claiming divine guidance. If/when a modern person claims god told them to kill their children, we rightly see this as a sign of delusionary mental illness. If the story of Abraham is about a real reason and not a metaphor, then we must wonder how many martyrs are sitting in today's prisons?

Christianity did not construct itself backwards, where theology to which it came was the initial model used by those who wrote the Old Testament's first scriptures. Once a new religious movement emerged from the Hebrew tradition—and with Judaism's previous scriptures as its backdrop—a new message took shape and was eventually consolidated in the New Testament. In combining multiple stories from multiple sources, Christianity developed a worldview where humans are fundamentally flawed, their independent search for knowledge leads to sinfulness, they need authoritative leaders to guide them into god's sacred truth, and obedience to that religious authority is the definition of good and proper conduct. This is an explicitly anti-human discourse, one fundamentally at odds with the principles of freedom, reason, science, and democratic society. It admonishes humans not to seek out truth on their own, with specific questions and general inquisitiveness discouraged as the root of sinfulness. Humans should do what god's authorities tell them to, as exercising their free will only result in transgressions that anger god. In continuing this tradition, Islam literally adopted this premise, where humanity's highest ideal is "submission" to god's will.

Despite these fundamentally worrisome features, an impressive discourse religion is. It drives people to the heights of sacrifice (charity, martyrdom), delusion (self-mutilation, belief in the fantastic), and even achievement (art, temples, cathedrals, mosques, etc.). People devote their lives to stories they have no way of verifying, nor that can be verified. They follow prophets, fakirs, and gurus, sometimes into fits of ecstasy, sometimes into bankruptcy, and sometimes over a cliff. People cut themselves to show their devotion and their children in acts of initiation. We have evidence of massacres, mass sacrifice, and mass suicide attributable to beliefs in gods no one worships anymore. And the graveyard of dead gods is larger than the range of altars at which people bow today, each era convinced about the Truth and the Divinity of the story they have been told and the falsity and corruption of that of others. "Shiva does not live an ascetic life on Mount Kailash, god did not give Joseph Smith golden tablets and seer stones, nor did he whisper revelatory updates to scripture in a merchant's ear, but *my* messiah walked on water and rose from the dead!" Despite the obvious conclusion, religion persists.[6] We cannot explain this persistence solely by the actions of religious institutions, however. There is something fundamental to being human that religion speaks to and this something is our need for meaning.

Because of our need for meaning, we humans have provided it for ourselves in multiple ways that have both benefited and cursed our existence. Filtered through practical daily activity, our need for meaning has produced imaginative art, lore, and literature, the keeping of history, and the ancient pursuit of philosophy. Filtered through science, it has resulted in knowledge of natural forces beyond the imagination of our earliest ancestors. Filtered through religion, we have produced fantastic tales, thousands of gods, and an even greater number of symbolic acts of devotion. Moreover, this need for meaning is the grounds upon which the seeds of religion's continuous rebirth fall and

---

6 "The easy confidence with which I know another man's religion is folly teaches me to suspect that my own is also"—*Mark Twain, a Biography*.

sprout, renewing itself over generations and allowing for both devoted ascetics and the most fanatical demonstrations. This need produces ever-new masses ready to follow charismatic charlatans bent on manipulating people for their own exaltation and/or for the riches they can extract from the flock. With the longevity of a shared meaning structure, religion's institutionalization funnels people's money and energy toward a respected priesthood's life-long comfort.[7] Though this institutionalization enables an appearance of stability, religion is constantly changing and its putative veracity is always unattained (and thus unattainable) while its future is always precarious. Without new initiates, it dies, so religion relies on this human need for meaning for providing it a constant source of new recruits. There is a lesson here, surely.

2   Morality and the Meaning of Life: A Naturalist and Historical Materialist Perspective

People of faith often ask where we will get morals if not from religion? This proposition misconstrues their relationship. Part of morality humans inherited from the animal kingdom, i.e., cooperation, empathy, a sense of fairness, and expectations of reciprocity. Some moral codes are required for sustaining any type of society, i.e., general expectations of honesty, the security of self and possessions. Other codes address practical universal human issues—e.g., rules for diet, coupling, raising children, inheritance, disposal of the dead, etc.—with local variations influenced by geography, social structure, and/or historical events. Human culture develops answers to these social-organizational issues, teaches and enforces them, and sometimes religion has been a vehicle for this. Though religion is not the only possible way to do so, it claims to be the progenitor of these morals and practices as a way of defending itself from criticism and for preserving its monopoly over an area of meaning it has no inherent right to monopolize.[8]

---

7 This practice is not restricted to Jews, Christians, or Muslims as the children of Abraham. Buddhists, too, follow a similar script, where everyday people lack, and therefore need, "enlightenment" and can advance toward that goal with the assistance of monks who provide their services for the alms and monastic security they receive in return. Hindu gurus, too, practice a similar strategy.

8 Many such human social rules escape religion and return to their origins in cultural norms. We teach our children to play nice with others, to respect their elders, and so on. The vast majority of us—the religious and non-religious alike—react with horror when we hear about stories of rape, mayhem, and general human indifference, at least when inflicted upon groups we identify with (extending such concerns becomes more precarious when victims

Even if morality is rooted in material reality, both biological and sociological, this is not to say that religious beliefs cannot become detached from their historical-material roots and maintained on the grounds of ideology. However, religious beliefs never exist disconnected from social conditions completely, either, where material relations have no relevance for what happens in the ideological sphere. Religious beliefs have historical origins and political-economic structures will usually weed out those beliefs incompatible with them. Political-economic structures also produce new social relations and practices to which religious teaching adapts. Those religious beliefs and values without relevance to a political-economic structure may be left untouched and can survive over time (e.g., see the biblical story of Onan as discussed in Chapter 5, note 8). Religious beliefs, still, never simply free float in a system without material realities having their say.

Believers and apologists often argue that without religion, life would have no source of meaning. From the vantage point of a historical materialist perspective, what must an answer to life's meaning both exclude and include? If we are to be as realistic as possible, then we should not construct abstract models outside of real social conditions and then debate their worthiness. Rather, we must draw our meaning from our practical and concrete real life conditions.

Life on Earth has evolved over billions of years and our species shares a branch on life's family tree with many others. While humans as they appear today have existed for about 200,000 years, only in the last 10–15,000 years have we developed settled living arrangements as opposed to nomadic hunting and foraging (which still exists in multiple places in the world). Over 7,500,000,000 people live on our planet today and their numbers increase daily within a political-economic system that cannot distribute resources to all who need them; our modern free market system instead directs resources toward those who can pay for them when profitable for someone else. Our ecosystem's capability to continue functioning for our growing material needs remains in legitimate peril, as modernity's forms of production, technology, consumption, and waste disposal threaten to destroy the natural basis on which all societies

---

are either hated or too far away and thus become more and more abstract and unreal in our consciousness). We encode our shared social norms into law. It is not only believers and the devout who feel violated by certain behaviors. If religion disappeared, we would still have methods of passing on moral codes because the prerequisites of sustaining any society in general will not have disappeared along with it. For instance, most of Europe today finds increasing declines in church attendance but also lower crime rates than similar countries with higher levels of religiosity, such as the United States (see Noise 2011; Zuckerman 2014, 2015, and references therein).

depend. We are sentient beings. We know that we will die. Because we know this, we also know that we must pass on knowledge we have received (and that which we have achieved) to new generations. Nature and technology limit what we can or cannot do on Earth, while we only have one planet on which to live.[9]

During our history, humans have struggled to extract a living from nature, often while being subject to forces they cannot always successfully negotiate. Much human suffering has resulted from ruling classes building states and raising militaries in pursuit of their interests. We have only recently made advances in food production and maintaining health and curing illness. The development of productive forces in capitalist society has outpaced our ability to tame and use them safely. Modernity's growth has been reliant on energy from fossil fuels whose byproducts heat the atmosphere, corrupt the land, and poison our relatively small amount of available potable freshwater. Though new cleaner forms of technology are emerging, we largely remain dependent on carbon-based technologies, whose use is changing our climate in dangerous ways. Weapons industries and agri-businesses seize upon scientific knowledge, producing suicide weapons for the species as a whole and suicide seeds at the level of our daily bread. Today, non-state purveyors of violence, often religiously fanatical, wish to obtain advanced weapons possessed by states and/or strive to infiltrate those state structures themselves. As history has shown, when state power and religious authority unite, the dangers for all grow.

Living in such conditions means that our species' existence is likely more precarious today than at any other time in our history. As we have not yet mastered sustainable, mutually integrated, and coordinated living arrangements, there is no assurance of our long-term survival. Our own practices are the primary determinant of our odds on this matter. In this context, life's meaning depends on whether or not human history proves to be an evolutionary dead end or whether we learn to use our creative capacities and physical energy to organize ourselves in non-self-destructive ways—to seize our history and make it, instead of it seizing and making us. If we do nothing to change our

9   In the 2010s, public figures like Stephen Hawking and Elon Musk openly talked about colonizing the Moon or Mars as a way for humanity to escape ecological destruction. In terms of doing this as a large-scale modern society, such considerations are not only fantasy but also an admittance of defeat. Further, should such an exodus occur, it is highly likely that ability to pay would determine passage, meaning that the very rich could escape an environmental collapse. Moreover, as if kicking dirt in the face of the rest of humanity, it would be the same rich who benefited from a system that produced the very environmental collapse from which they are escaping and that has allowed them to pay for that escape (see Klein 2015; Darby 2018).

current social relations—or continue to aid, abet, and intensify them—then our species will be a brief self-defeating shoot in the tree of evolution and modern society an anomaly in the historical record.

What actions facilitate one outcome over the other will remain part of the human dilemma so long as our social conditions produce and maintain forms of knowledge that mislead us as to the reality of those very same conditions. To grasp these conditions, we need positive knowledge of the world—both our past and our present—and actionable information about the options before us for producing a workable future. Religion has consistently demonstrated traits that are unreliable and misleading for producing that sort of knowledge. Let us take a brief look.

3   Unreliable Narrators, Hostile Witnesses, and Evasive Measures

As one knowledge-form that makes claims about the human experience, tensions exist between religion in general's premises—i.e., (1) an otherworldly realm exists (2) that has spiritual power and sacred knowledge that we can access (3) through special forms of mediation—and those of religion in the specific—i.e., the beliefs, rituals, and rules particular religions proffer based on their own mediations. Can one religion be correct about the relationship between (1), (2), and (3)? Can *all* religions' claims about this relationship have *some* validity? Are there necessary and sufficient reasons for accepting *any* religion's truth-claims about (1), (2), and (3)?

Going back just 100,000 years, geographical dispersion among nomadic hunter-gatherers and relatively simple agricultural/pastoral societies means a lack of direct lineage among most of history's thousands of religions, which were usually in-group directed (even if periodic contact led to some borrowing).[10] The rise of larger, more complex agricultural societies about 10–15,000 years ago brought changes to and growth in political-economic relations, ties, and trade, and thus more exchanges of religious ideas. During the organizational growth of religious practices, an official canon tends to consolidate, none-too-seldom squeezing out groups practicing variations of this canon's proto-form, while also allowing for external juxtaposition to and incompatibility with

---

10   This discussion is cognizant of the current debate over whether a natural catastrophe reduced the global human population to about 15,000 individuals and squeezed them through the bottleneck of northern Africa about 70,000 years ago. If this is the case, the *specific* history of several religions might not follow the outline here, though the general argument should still hold.

other consolidated traditions closer in time, space, and family tree. This consolidation, however, does not halt religious development through prophetic revelations, the rise of new cults, regular schisms, purges of heretics, absorption of other traditions, and a host of wider social changes.

Conservative, relativist, and liberal approaches to this cultural-historical-theological dynamic differ as to the prospective validity of religion's premises. For conservatives, *their version* of the sacred realm and its mediation is singularly correct; other traditions under the same umbrella are, by definition, incorrect and maybe even heretical.[11] Conservative approaches tend toward dogma, demand conformity in belief and behavior, and require obedience to religious authority. But just as it is next to impossible to get six people to agree on what toppings to get on a pizza, when a religion's doctrines are more narrowly carved, the likelihood of disagreements over them increases as its number of adherents grows. This induces a tendency towards methods of enforcing religious norms that can become increasingly draconian—i.e., stricter requirements on when and how practitioners say their prayers and read their scriptures, theocratic control via rules of dress, diet, and association, tests over tenets, methods of exclusion, use of violence for transgressive words and behavior, and even death for heresy, blasphemy, and/or apostasy. This dynamic between conservative theology and methods of control also increases the likelihood of resistance, criticisms, and schisms in response. This condition makes conservative views—i.e., only one religion is true, coherent, and intended by an otherworldly force—inherently contradictory and unsustainable in terms of long-term organizational and theological stability.[12]

---

11   Judaism fundamentally disagrees with Christianity on the meaning of Jesus of Nazareth. Centuries later, Islam emerged from the same Abrahamic tree, claimed itself as a return to a purer form of belief that god intended. Islam accepted Jesus as a prophet (though most Jewish people did not) but not as a messiah (as Christians did). Within Islam, disagreement on Mohammad's rightful heir—a prophet neither Jews nor Christians recognize—led to the split between Sunni and Shia traditions. Within later Christianity, disagreements over the sale of indulgences, the authority of the Pope and a whole slate of grievances produced the Protestant split with Roman Catholicism. Thus, just as Sunni and Shia Muslims fundamentally disagree on Mohammad's true successor, Southern Baptists will never accept Catholics as equals in Christ. We can see similar sectarian divides across all religious traditions, including Hinduism and Buddhism. And so it goes.

12   Conservative forms of Protestantism predominate in the American South. Spearheaded by Southern Baptists, many offshoots, and offshoots from those, become increasingly smaller, fundamentalist, dogmatic, restrictive, and sectarian. I was once driving through Jackson County, Kentucky, a small and impoverished Appalachian area, and saw what looked like a rundown shack or cabin or old building of some sort. Its hand-painted sign read, "One Way Narrow Path Church" (or something similar). A few years later, I had a student from that same county who had experience in such a church (if not that exact

Relativists tend to see religions' truth-values as indeterminable and with-hold judgments about their veracity. Though a *person* can be a relativist toward other belief systems while trying to honor their own faith, the *basic premises* of religion and relativity are incompatible. If sacred knowledge and moral rules for any two religions disagree while each claims special access to an other-worldly realm, then the claims of one or both must be in error. Without intend-ing to undermine the basis of faith, relativity disallows *every* religion's truth-claims given that *any* religion, when viewed from another's vantage point, lacks full and proper access to, knowledge of, and thus mediation with the sa-cred realm. Some religious believers—usually conservatives—accurately diag-nose relativism as a threat for the prospect of their own faith's truth-value.

Liberalism—including inclusiveness to diversity and a willingness for insti-tutional reform—is also incongruent with religion's theological premises. The dietary rules of Hindus, Muslims, and Christians are incompatible. They can-not all be right but they can all be wrong, or neither right nor wrong. If reli-gions differ on basic questions, much less the number and nature of spirits, forces, and/or gods, and if all of them claim access to a sacred realm, then more than one realm must exist. If any two religious doctrines disagree while each claims access to a special realm, then one or both must lack proper access to that realm. On the other hand, if one accepts multiple pathways to multiple sacred realms, why should any one of them enjoy priority? Liberal inclusivity implies a truth to religion in general at the cost of allowing only partial truth to any general tradition, lending even less potential veracity to any specific belief system. Moreover, a liberal religious point of view accepts reform of tenets and practices and this undermines the idea of god's unchanging Truth. Liberality in religion thus begs the questions: Which truths are partial? To what degree? Who is to decide? And how? The likelihood of any widespread agreement on these matters is functionally zero.[13] Further, religion in general and its specific traditions did not found themselves on the prospect of multiple sacred realms nor on claims of partial truth, putting liberal and conservative positions ulti-mately at odds.

---

one, one like it). Brought there by his grandfather, he learned that only the 10–15 people in that room would get into heaven. Not only had Catholics strayed from the correct path to salvation, but *all* other Christian groups besides them had done so as well.

13   I make this statement while cognizant of "Omnism," the belief that *all* religions contain *some* element of truth. Omnism is not internal to religious development as a coherent set of assertions per se but rather an outside intellectual-theological stance attempting to deal with the idea of religion as a whole. As such, it does not play a role in the analysis here, as it has no specific dogma, god-figure, ritual practice, and so on.

Understood as such, the unresolvable tensions that exist between religion in general's premises and those of specific religions produce unreliable, inconsistent, and incoherent claims. To the likely dismay of the liberal and the relativist, it is the conservatives—their own internal contradictions notwithstanding— who come away from such an analysis with the most coherent theological premises, which we saw were theocratic, self-undermining, and contrary to individual freedom. This is one reason why people with conservative religious beliefs have long been at war with both science and modernity.[14]

Our earliest knowledge was forged when Earth-as-one-planet-among-millions was not yet imaginable (its shape and size also unknown), where humans viewed the stars and our sun and moon, just as clouds and streams, as part of a singular and human-centered material reality, i.e., though the stars, constellations, and their gods were "out there," their *meaning* was Earth-bound. With nothing beyond this existence, humans constructed knowledge that focused on their life-experiences and concerns, making themselves the cosmological subject in the process.[15] In their stories, non-corporeal forces/spirits/gods made it all for us. Or, at least, we must negotiate reality in a way that pleases them and/or does not contradict them, as, at minimum, our lives are subject to their principles and/or will. Given the material basis for and the limits of their knowledge, early progenitors of proto-religious ideas forged their stories about nature's mysteries and life's salient problems in an extensively incorrect and necessarily uninformed species-egocentric knowledge. A discourse built on such a misreading of the world and ignorance of modern scientifically verified

---

14   Modernity has won some of these battles, as several variants of conservative religion have become apologists for and embracers of capitalism and its political regimes (more below).

15   Astrology is a similar discourse, though not one with a specific god-figure. As is commonly understood, astrology claims that the position of the Earth relative to the configuration of the stars as we see them in the sky at our birth influences things like our personalities, life histories, and fortunes. This knowledge-form, like that of more formalized religions, constructs the cosmos in a way where what happens to humans is part of its subject matter. This remains true even if a defender of astrology says no intent exists among the stars. The important point is that the truth-claim of astrology is that a force exists "in the heavens," as it were, to which humans are subject. One interesting though unrelated point to this is that astrology, despite what most adherents and skeptics might both believe, is a materialist claim in a way. While a social scientist would accept that geographical realities shape socially constructed beliefs, the astrologer has simply moved the variable farther out in space/time. I once tried to explain this to an academic friend; she was not convinced. This is similar to how the pseudo-science of phrenology missed its target but just barely, with the physical features it posited as relevant for understanding the human psyche not existing on the outside of the head, but just a few inches underneath the skull.

knowledge are incompatible starting-points for understanding humans, their origins, and their place in material existence.[16]

Religious practitioners use several tools to evade both internal criticisms of their faith and their incompatibility with modern knowledge and evidence-based reasoning. One tool is a tautological premise, where a religion's knowledge is true by definition and believers force inconvenient facts into this assumption. Several examples demonstrate the practice.

If one observes that the Bible originated in oral traditions passed on for generations that were written down only later, that from there multiple and incompatible copies of copies were made, and that these were not originally written to be compiled into one book, a believer can simply claim that this was the result of divine guidance. Not restricted to Christianity, believers make similar claims about the Koran and the Bhagavad Gita.

If denial of accumulated facts threatens a faith's legitimacy, believers can change conclusions previously affirmed—e.g., evolutionary theory once undermined doctrinal truth but today is accepted by the Catholic Church (among others)—so that the facts are now evidence of god's plan.[17] Or the work of

---

16   Science has shrunk and de-centered our place in the cosmos. We need higher math and advanced technology to grasp the universe's age and size. "Stars" are distant suns in our galaxy, dwarfed by a universe of trillions upon trillions of stars and billions of galaxies. In fact, relative to human history, we have only recently known that galaxies exist, with the first one discovered outside our own in 1929 by Edwin Hubble. Up until then, what we saw as "the universe" was only the features of our own galaxy. Since then (with help of the Hubble Telescope), we have learned that what appears to us as empty patches of night sky are filled with thousands of galaxies far beyond (see photos and discussions of the "Hubble Deep Field"). Our planet is on an outer arm of a galaxy in a corner of a family of galaxies, one of which is on a collision course with our own. Planets exist in other solar systems. Life on Earth existed long before us and the elements making life up (humans included) came from exploding stars of long, long ago. A microscopic world dominates our mental and physical health in ways we are only beginning to understand. More than a spatial/temporal expansion of early ideas about the world as if a balloon inflating (still leaving us at the center), these are incommensurate models of human history and our surroundings. On the size of the universe, its distribution of matter, the connections of these to the atomic level, and how this knowledge often conflicts with religious knowledge, see physicist Lawrence Krauss's (2009) lecture, "A Universe from Nothing." What would specific religious knowledge look like had religious ideas developed in the context of today's knowledge about the universe and human historical-cultural variability? Whether religion would have developed at all is a reasonable question. If it did develop, that humans and Earth would be the cosmological subject is highly doubtful.

17   This is not always uniformly true, though. Sometimes natural events have shaken the foundations of faith and radically changed society and its forms of knowledge. For instance, on November 1, 1755, an earthquake struck Lisbon, Portugal, destroying much of the city and villages nearby, killing tens of thousands of people and putting to ruin much

nefarious spiritual forces.[18] Or believers can deny the facts. None-too-few conservative Jewish, Christian, and Islamic believers, for example, refuse to entertain the idea that the universe and the Earth are more than 6000 years old—despite geological evidence, despite the fact that light takes longer than that to reach us from many stars, and despite the fact that there are cultures whose histories trace back longer than this timeframe. When confronted with such realities, one common retort is that a "year" is something different to god than it is to humans.[19] An evasive maneuver like this is so infinitely malleable and such a bad faith form argumentation that there is literally way to counter it, as those who use it can change their premises at will to suit any argument they find useful or necessary.

Believers often interpret scripture as convenient, where literalism is for favored rules and troublesome writings are metaphors and/or historically contingent events relative to the culture in the story. For example, Christian fundamentalists proclaim fealty to the Ten Commandments yet do not follow other Old Testament rules, such as stoning disobedient children (Ephesians 6:1–3), planting fields with only one type of seed (Leviticus 19:19), not eating shellfish (Leviticus 11:12), not cutting their hair (Leviticus 19:27), or accepting cash restitution from their daughter's rapist and then allowing him to marry her (Deuteronomy 22:28–29).[20] When fitting their social prejudices, however,

---

of the country's colonial designs. Given that this happened on All Saints Day, a crisis of faith emerged, as a believer would reasonably wonder what a faithful, devout, and practicing Christian people did to invoke god's wrath. Intellectuals such as Voltaire, Rousseau, and Kant used the earthquake and its destruction to demonstrate the fallacies and inconsistencies of religious thought. These thinkers, of course, became foundational to the Enlightenment, which further eroded the authority of Christian theology of the time.

18   Some fundamentalist Christians, when asked about why the Bible makes no mention of dinosaurs—and should it be an accurate account of the animal kingdom, there is good reason to ask why such beasts are not mentioned there—claim that Satan or the devil or some such evil presence put fossils here to test our faith. This sort of evasive end run around logic and evidence is a form of knowledge that not only resists inspection but it is a form of argument one cannot reason with.

19   Another end run around logic and evidence that one cannot reason with.

20   Christians usually do not actually obey the real "Ten Commandments," either. In Exodus, god gives Moses commandants twice. In Chapters 19–20, these are a set of "commandments" that either god or Moses (depending on one's interpretation) spoke. These are the rules with which most people are familiar: (1) Thou shalt have no other gods before me. (2) Thou shalt not make unto thee any graven image, or any likeness of any thing that is in heaven above, or that is in the earth beneath, or that is in the water under the earth. (3) Thou shalt not take the name of the LORD thy God in vain; for the LORD will not hold him guiltless that taketh his name in vain. (4) Remember the Sabbath day, to keep it holy. (5) Honor thy father and thy mother: that thy days may be long upon the land which the LORD thy God giveth thee. (6) Thou shalt not kill. (7) Thou shalt not commit adultery. (8)

many Christians turn to the latter two books to justify their hatred of homo-sexuals and their attempts at socially and legally repressing them.

Religious believers point to gaps in our current scientific knowledge as evi-dence of god's hand in creating our material existence, regardless of the fact that science has regularly overcome and explained such gaps—e.g., the sun's movement, germ theories of disease, and/or plate tectonics.[21]

Finally, when a religion's explanations seem senseless or provide no succor, appeals to "faith," "god's plan," "god's will," or "mysterious ways" remain as last resort stopgaps to explain away incongruities.

Though none of these forms of argument are acceptable in scientific dis-course, religious knowledge engages in both "moving the goal posts" and spe-cial pleading, as if the rules of debate and empirical demonstration all other factual assertions must pass do not apply to religious claims.[22] In tautological

---

Thou shalt not steal. (9) Thou shalt not bear false witness against thy neighbor. (10) Thou shalt not covet thy neighbor's house, thou shalt not covet thy neighbor's wife, nor his manservant, nor his maidservant, nor his ox, nor his ass, nor any thing that is thy neigh-bor's. However, in Exodus, Chapter 34, the story continues with the Lord instructing Moses to bring him two tablets of stone to write on and Moses returning with the "Ten Commandments" (a title that does not appear in Chapters 19–20): (1) For thou shalt wor-ship no other god, for the LORD, whose name is Jealous, is a jealous God. (2) Thou shalt make thee no molten gods. (3) The feast of unleavened bread shalt thou keep. Seven days thou shalt eat unleavened bread, as I commanded thee, in the time of the month Abib: for in the month Abib thou camest out from Egypt. (4) But the firstling of an ass thou shalt redeem with a lamb, and if thou redeem him not, then shalt thou break his neck. All the firstborn of thy sons thou shalt redeem. And none shall appear before me empty. (5) Six days thou shalt work, but on the seventh day thou shalt rest: in earing time and in harvest thou shalt rest. (6) And thou shalt observe the feast of weeks, of the first fruits of wheat harvest, and the feast of ingathering at the year's end. (7) Thrice in the year shall all your male children appear before the LORD God, the God of Israel. (8) Thou shalt not offer the blood of my sacrifice with leaven; neither shall the sacrifice of the feast of the passover be left unto the morning. (9) The first of the first fruits of thy land thou shalt bring unto the house of the LORD thy God. (10) Thou shalt not seethe a kid in his mother's milk.

21   In the "god of the gaps" argument, believers attribute realities that are beyond the ability of current scientific knowledge to explain as god's doing. With science's historical prog-ress, religion has found fewer and fewer areas for which science has yet to develop an explanation and, thus, the domain for religion's deity has constantly shrunk. For a discus-sion on "intelligent design" as well as this "god of the gaps" form of argumentation, see astrophysicist Neil deGrasse Tyson's (2006) lecture, "Beyond Belief: Science, Reason, Reli-gion & Survival."

22   I once had a colleague who was a devout Buddhist. As a sociologist, he held a critical view of religion in general, believing it to be solely a human construction. When we had con-versations about religion, I would sometimes ask how he reconciled his own religiosity with his skepticism of claims religious people make. His two main responses were, first, that his version of Buddhism was of an atheist type and, second, that he found that the

religious discourse, there is *always* an answer to criticism and/or inconvenient facts, and that answer is *almost never* that the specific religion asked to answer such challenges is just a human invention that often gets things wrong. Science, on the other hand, has the effort to prove hypotheses wrong built directly into its methodology. An honest scientist should have no problem if data undermines their favored theory. Moreover, they should embrace it if their work is shown in error, as supporting unfounded and discredited ideas is the opposite of the pursuit of truth as science understands it.

Other religious fallacies are teleological in nature. A religion presents itself to the faithful as a coherent Truth practiced as intended by revelation. By definition, the belief system a person adopts is a version of that religion's ideas as they were knowable in the period in which the individual encountered them. Whether they come to accept this faith through childhood socialization or through later personal discovery is of no matter here. This does bring up a problematic observation, though. If one could traverse world history since (approximately) 30 A.D. in order to find and thus practice "true Christianity" (or "true Buddhism," "true Hinduism," etc.), they would encounter a variety of different and changing criteria from which to choose.[23] This is because in the

----

form of chanting associated with his practice "worked." Prodding him further, he would tell me that his strand of Buddhism was a reformed version, where elitists had corrupted the religion over centuries and it needed to be purified, revitalized, and returned to its roots (I do not recall the name of the person to whom this movement is attributed). He also explained that the chanting used in his practice was a "tool" one could use to align or adjust oneself better with material/spiritual forces that exist and that this could assist a person in their goals, whether those be for peace, romantic endeavors, or even money. Members of his sect believed that their version of Buddhism had discovered a series of verbal sounds one could harness in order to assist an individual in their pursuits. As such, they would often admonish members to use this tool wisely, where many believed pursuing material gain or pleasures of the flesh, while possible through their method, was often contrary to Buddhist principles. One day I again asked him about what I perceived to be a contradiction between his disbelief in religion in general juxtaposed to his particular practice. "What you are telling me, then, is that of all the thousands of beliefs in human history, all of them are simply things humans invented out of whole cloth, *except* your particular set of beliefs? That this *particular set* of verbal sounds your group uses are spiritual practices connected to a real, objective reality outside of human constructions? That your particular belief here relates to something real while all other beliefs are nonsense?" He paused for a second, seemingly in recognition of my question's implications, gathered his response, and, looking me straight in the eye, confidently said, *"Yes."* I concluded at that moment that there would be no point in engaging him again further on the matter and never did.

23   Most of the first one-hundred years of the Jesus story survived as oral tradition among sects that differed in fundamentals—e.g., Was Jesus wholly man, wholly god, or both? We do not have copies of the first scriptures; those who wrote the copies we have (whose

interceding periods between time A and time B that are 100, 500, or 1000 years apart, political powers rise and fall, migrations proceed, wars are fought, different groups ascend to and descent from positions of social influence (including theologians), new technologies develop, and so on. Across such periods, prophesies are made and often rewritten in retrospect, new doctrines form, core beliefs morph or vanish, groups win the battle over orthodoxy only to be later dismissed, and the like. Believers at any one time will tend, nevertheless, to assume that they enjoy a religion's truth-value. If not, then why believe?[24]

---

authors were not eyewitnesses to the events they describe) did so decades after the crucifixion and did not write them for compiling into one book. These copies are irreconcilable in multiple ways and contain forgeries and plagiarisms. Before and during their compilation, believers rewrote the Jesus story to align with Jewish prophesies and he was transformed from the Jewish messiah into a universal god (see Ehrman 2003, 2005, 2009). There were other questions and changes in Christianity's early development as well: Are clergy allowed to become eunuchs, as some had done? The Council of Nicaea decided against it. Should women be clergy? Some had accepted this practice but eventually it was done away with. Was circumcision necessary for converts? The Council of the Apostles and the Elders concluded, no. Where should the seat of power be, Rome or Constantinople? No agreement there, either. Skipping forward several centuries, in 2007, the Catholic Church eliminated limbo from its doctrine. In March 2018, the Pope stated his belief that hell is not a real place of eternal torment but that the unrepentant would simply cease to exist after death (which caused a bit of a kerfuffle among Catholic theologians). Christian sects today also place different emphases on the question of the "Second Coming," which early Christians believed would be in their lifetimes. What will count as "Christian" in the future will no doubt also be different, while believers during that same future will not be subject to beliefs that burden many of today's faithful.

24 "Pascal's Wager" is a famous deductive formula about defending a belief in god. Blaise Pascal (1623–1662), French philosopher, mathematician, and physicist, posited that either god exists or does not. If god does exist and one believes in him [sic], then they are subject to heavenly favor after death. If god exists and one does not believe in him, they risk eternal damnation. If god does not exist but one does believe in him, then they have suffered only a minor loss (e.g., lack of Earthly pleasures and delights, luxury, and so on). If god does not exist and one does not believe in him, one has only marginally gained in comparison to what could be lost or gained if god does exist. The weaknesses of this argument are obvious but not often understood, as many people over time have found the logic convincing. This argument presumes humans as the cosmological subject, a singular god who cares about individual opinions, and an afterlife based on those opinions. In this way, Pascal took several principles specific to the Christian narrative and then generalized them into a more abstract and general idea of god. Such a construction would make little sense to multiple historical religious traditions. However, Pascal argued that he meant his formula to show that logic and deduction alone could not and should not be the foundation of faith. The influence of his "wager," though, suggests that this nuanced part of his argument was lost to none-too-few of his interpreters (myself included, at one point in time).

To view a religious doctrine at any one time—before, during, or after its consolidation—as reflecting the intents of a sacred realm is to accept a backward causal order. Because religious beliefs and practices change doctrinally over time, none can be identical to what they were at their point of origin and/ or all of those times in between up to when an individual encounters them. One period, the other, both, some of those in between, or all periods cannot reflect identical sacred ideas. Facing such dilemmas, shamans, priests, gurus, imams, and yoga instructors often resort to claims about resurrecting the knowledge of "the ancients" or "tradition," a return to an asserted pure form of belief and practice, a claim whose murkiness makes it anywhere from difficult to impossible for their audience to satisfactorily inspect or verify. Given historical development, if a religion is true today, then it was deceptive before this time and will be in the future, making religious truth relative to one's own period. This condition undermines any religion's claim as a coherent and/or unchanging form of sacred knowledge. Moreover, to be true today means that believers must accept a doctrine that required a prior history of error for its later theological veracity. Nevertheless, within that specific theology at any one time, the historical effect (the current endpoint) is the reason for the initial cause (the original ministry) and faith in this backward teleological reconstruction of events makes a believer *a believer*.[25]

What we see, then, is that built into religions' assertions about sacred realms with power and knowledge we can mediate are the use of evasive and impregnable discursive tools—egocentric certainty, false assumptions, selective reading, changing terms of debate, and logical fallacies—to thwart religion's inspection, making science and religion antagonistic magisteria (*contra* Stephen Jay Gould). Conservative, relativist, and liberal outlooks each require these tools all or in part. Be this as it may, religion claims itself to be a special form of knowledge that arrives through divine intervention, prophecy, and/or revelation. From the point of view of religious faith, the discussion above is moot.[26] While religions do not claim to be products of human thought rooted in and shaped by specific historical social relations, given the multiple and often incompatible claims they proffer, reason as well as evidence *are what remain* when sifting through the general plausibility of religion-as-knowledge.

---

25   Researchers have found shared forms of teleological reasoning among those who believe in god, creationists, and conspiracy theorists (Keeley 2007; Wagner-Egger et al. 2018). Similarly, religious fundamentalists have become increasingly susceptible to the "fake news" that targets them for manipulation (see Dolan 2018 and reference therein).

26   For an exception to the principle that religion should not be subject to scientific tests of evidence, see the comment from the Dalai Lama in Chapter 5.

4   On the Religious Proposition of God's Existence

The question of god's existence is not really a scientific question. While science does not dogmatically tell us that god does not exist, it does tell us that evidence should be required before embracing *any* claim about reality, theological claims included. While the proposition of god's existence—by definition invisible, otherworldly, powerful, mysterious—is a hypothesis we can neither falsify nor empirically verify, many specific religious claims—and thus their own historical self-justification—we *can* inspect. If claims about their foundations are fallacious, does it follow that no god or gods exist? This is a non-sequitur, of course. Even if scientists can find little to no archaeological evidence to verify accounts of The Exodus (specific concrete) or modern Christianity (general concrete) is mistaken about Jesus's original ministry (specific concrete), this tells us nothing about the possible existence of god in general (general abstract). Nevertheless, when the historical, logical, and theological foundations of religion are undermined, some conclusions do follow.

First, historically, religions' beliefs center on *their* version of the gods, not a "generic god." So if religions in general have been the historical caretakers of multiple god-concepts, the indemonstrable claims in their knowledge-narratives undermine the fundamental plausibility of their own specific god or gods. Second, if all religions' claims to Truth suffer the same problems (general concrete), then their collective lack of internal validity as specific religions undermines the truth-value of religion in general (general abstract). Third, once we accept that religion has defined a notion of god for us that is impervious to proof or demonstration, then god's existence is a question whose assumptions and terms of debate *leave only two choices: faith or critical analysis.*[27] This is perhaps why Marx argued that the criticism of religion is the basis of all criticism.

Some inquiries into theology in general come from the standpoint of pure logic. The "ontological proof"—which admits that religion lacks the possibility of empirical verification—approaches the proposition of god's existence from

---

27   I recall having a debate with a friend years ago over the claim of god's existence. We were not debating the plausibility of the god of Abraham so much as we were addressing the question of god in general, the "generic god" I referenced in Chapter 5. In trying to explain to him the fallacious foundation of the question, I proposed the following: God is a gigantic centipede on the far side of the moon that controls nature, human actions, and history. However, you cannot see it because it is invisible. Prove me wrong. Though I was trying to demonstrate how the propositions that religions ask us to decide upon cannot be adequately inspected, I could tell from the expression on his face that he did not find my argument convincing.

the standpoint of deductive reasoning. Such proofs begin with a premise that leads to a conclusion—e.g., "If I can conceive of god ... [several deduced principles extending from this] ... then god must exist" (Anselm); or, let us assume a "supremely perfect being ... therefore, god must exist" (Descartes/Leibniz).[28] Prior to these efforts, a similar approach—though one with some descriptive theological content—came from an atheist direction, with the so-called "Epicurean Paradox":

> If God is willing to prevent evil, but is not able to
> Then He is not omnipotent.
> If He is able, but not willing
> Then He is malevolent.
> If He is both able and willing
> Then whence cometh evil.
> If He is neither able nor willing
> Then why call Him God?

In all of these forms of argumentation, the theorist's god is an abstract god akin to the type several religions posit, i.e., masterful, all-knowing, all-powerful, and so on. Why does god have to be all-knowing, all-powerful, all-good, or "a perfect being"? Such approaches lack imagination. Why *could* the god for *this* universe *not* be a child of mega-gods that rule multiverses and our universe the product of this mischievous, petulant, stupid, and capricious child-god toying with its creation? Other than lack of emotional appeal, there is no reason this cannot be the reality of the situation given the discursive terms religions have proposed—from forces the animist imagines, to the Greek and Roman pantheons of gods acting with humor, mischief, and on whim, to the Old Testament's jealous, petty, violent singular supreme being (and so on). Perhaps since positing that god is a spoiled toddler is unlikely to attract many devotees (if any), historical religions have tended not to argue such a thing. God must be impressive, great even.

Reactions against the criticism of religion are really pleas for the special place plaintiffs aspire for their own religion's god. Yet no one panics today at the death of beliefs in Hera, Odin, or Set. Human history has birthed and killed thousands of gods and not once has their vanishing undermined our species'

---

28   These approaches to arguing for god's existence via deduction are of a different order than the argument for having faith as found in Pascal's Wager. The former tries to demonstrate through logic *that something exists*. The latter uses a similar method to argue *why someone should believe in that thing.*

survival. There is no reason to assume any decline in belief in today's deity will have a different outcome.

5   What Is to Be Done?

Given the predicaments for survival we confront today, we spend our time unproductively debating the unverifiable hypotheses of theologians. Religion has been an unreliable narrator from which to extract what we need to know about our real conditions of life. Drawing meaning from religion limits our future to the limits that meaning structure imposes on us. Some religions promise a final reckoning and their adherents are eager for it, hoping to force nonbelievers into the path of an apocalyptic-eschatological destruction they wait for and even aspire to bring about. With environmental collapse and economic crises both real and persistent threats, religion stands somewhere between a diverting clamor when we need concentration and an agent provocateur when coordinated collective action in the opposite direction is necessary.

Sometimes believers ask why nonbelievers cannot leave religion alone and simply let people have their sources of comfort? What harm is religion doing them? In the past, the religious accused the unconvinced of heresy, the wrong word could bring charges of blasphemy, and leaving a religion could result in persecution for apostasy, each often punishable by death (sometimes preceded by torture). This remains true in none-too-few areas of the world. Cults and sects still regularly spring up, sometimes aspiring to mass murder, sometimes disintegrating through suicide pacts, but more often acting to separate their initiates from their families and finances. Modern religious radicals strive to take over governing institutions and to inject them with religious dictates, usurping the power putatively invested in our laws and policies via popular will. Many Christians and Muslims worldwide endorse punishment of nonbelievers, whether in this life and/or the next. The response of the nonbeliever to the positions put forth by the religious—"You have not convinced me"—is taken as an affront and the religious often respond with child-like retorts, including threats to careers, personal well-being, and even of bodily harm. This is truly backward thinking. The religious make claims and then act as if it is the duty of others to accept those claims rather than their responsibility to use reason and evidence to demonstrate why anyone should.

Whether it is for the crime of heresy or simply being a bystander in the sought after Final Days, those who lack the requisite faith cannot leave religion alone because it will not leave them alone. In 2018, Saudi Arabia declared that atheists should be considered terrorists and subject to the death penalty. In

Brazil, support from religious evangelicals was crucial in electing an openly right-wing fascist to its presidency (Polimédio 2018). In the United States, the FBI received a complaint about one State Representative after he proposed killing nonbelievers (see Kovensky 2018). Elsewhere in the United States, Secretary of State under President Donald Trump, Mike Pompeo, said, "We will continue to fight these battles [against multiculturalism and homosexuality], it is a never ending struggle ... until the Rapture." Not coincidentally, this view is similar to one Islamic radicals hold, fanatics who, in fits of extremism, often force conversions at gunpoint and murder those whose sexual practice does not conform to their religious dictates.

Outside the political sphere, a zealous missionary, also from the United States, made news worldwide in 2018 after he three-times tried to force his way onto Sentinel Island and the people there, who are violently protective of their isolation, killed him. In January of 2019, the Brazilian government threatened another zealous US missionary with charges of genocide after he embarked on a similar effort to bring the Christian message to isolated people in the rainforest. In both cases, any outside contact made with these groups could have infected them with pathogens against which they have no natural defense. The imperative for introducing people to Jesus takes precedence over this danger, however.

The very existence of nonbelievers challenges the psychological basis of religion's foundation, for the unconvinced stand as real embodied representations against indemonstrable religious assertions in which believers have emotionally invested. Lack of belief is both an insult and a challenge and the faithful are often itching for a fight. If Christianity and Islam had remained marginal sects and never gained institutional power hooked into the state apparatus, then perhaps today we could simply have a struggle between the forces of reason versus unreason. But this is not where history has taken us, as the theologies of both of these universalist required monotheisms command believers to bring all human beings into their fold. Believers in these proselytizing religions are not content with using personal persuasion but instead have consistently attempted to acquire, dominate, and control the state apparatus, no less today than in the past. For conservative strands of Christianity and Islam, millions of adherents believe their religious books prophesize a final battle between the purveyors of god's Truth and everyone else—atheists and those who practice other religions alike. To bring this endgame about, in their minds, is to act as an agent of god's will, i.e., the story of Abraham and Isaac writ large.

Even if we avoid a global showdown, religion tells us that some otherworldly being exists and watches over us. Should we ever endanger our own existence, then divine intervention will come. This is less an eschatological program than it is a worldview reliant on wishful thinking, implying that humans can go about their reckless and careless ways and an overseeing parent will step in once the danger gets too great. As often applied to the threat of nuclear war, environmental crises, or civilizational collapse, this model (also common with UFO cultists) is also a recipe for disaster.

We must let religion go, refuse to participate in it. Any purpose it once may have served is no longer needed and, given how it has developed into our modern present, today it threatens our very survival. We must not succumb to use of state repression of religion as other societies have done in the past, however. This sort of action is not only undemocratic but also would only create additional conditions of unfreedom that we would later need to undo, which is the opposite direction from the one in which we need to head. Instead, we can, as Marx (1975c: 142) once advocated, embark on a "ruthless criticism" that is not "afraid of the results" nor "conflict with the powers that be." This approach, when based in logic, reason, and evidence, is congruent with the principles of science. A second tactic is simply to stop giving religion our time, attention, money, and/or endorsement. One of the great achievements of modernity is that religious theologies may still require belief but in secular societies they cannot force participation. Paraphrasing one of the great philosophers of the twentieth-century: "If people don't want to come to the ballpark how are you going to stop them?"

6   Capital Worship: The Ascendant Religion

Just as capitalism as a material force broke state religion off and forged it as a separate institution, similar processes push them back together. Marx ([1867] 1992b: 77) depicts the consciousness capitalism cultivates as a "fetish," where "a definite social relation between men" appears in "the fantastic form of a relation between things." In his day, people used the term *fetish* to describe practices of so-called "savages" that imbued physical objects with magical powers. Marx compares our world of commodities to these "mist-enveloped regions of the religious world," where capital has become an object of devotion. He depicts modernity as an "enchanted, perverted, topsy-turvy world" that produces a "religion of everyday life," one where economists treat "the interests of the ruling classes" with "eternal justification" and "dogma" (Marx 1971a: 830). This mutual penetration of capitalist ideology and religiosity finds multiple expressions.

On the side of political economy, we see capital worship in conservative and liberal guises, each elevating it to a status that parallels the treatment of sacred objects in previous societies. Modern society has its high priests (Smith, Keynes, Rand, Hayek, Friedman, Galbraith), bibles (*The Wealth of Nations, The General Theory of Employment, Interest, and Money, Atlas Shrugged*), seminaries (The Chicago School, Harvard Business School, The CATO Institute, the World Economic Forum, dozens of think tanks, and so on), and cathedrals (business districts in Manhattan, London, Frankfurt, Tokyo and the multitude of skyscrapers dotting urban landscapes worldwide, surrounded by so many small businesses appearing more regularly than storefront missions). Human traits religions have always warned against—e.g., pursuit of acquisitions and material affluence, basic greed, and indifference toward others—are planks upon which intellectuals found schools of academic thought and their allied politicians run for office and use in making policy once there. Usury—a forbidden practice in the Abrahamic traditions and condemned in several Hindu and Buddhist teachings—inundates economic institutions from top to bottom. Commentators have observed in some economists a certain "market fundamentalism," which sees unregulated capitalism as human nature in action and an ideal model for social policy and practice. Such dogmatists attribute magical powers to the "wisdom of markets"—i.e., that when left to their own accord, markets produce "the good society" by allocating resources and wealth in a way that is meant to be. These economic clergy express this with an unwavering faith impervious to logic or evidence, a behavior Marx once attributed to religious idealists and philosophers.[29] Social good here does not come from shared morals or higher ideals but from the lack of them.

Though liberal and conservative viewpoints appear to disagree on multiple things, those things are mainly within the same spectrum. Even for liberal economists, the cultivation of profits through exploiting labor and the natural world as "resources" are acceptable practices that, at best, only need "regulation" and are not moral questions or vital issues of survival. More precisely, the average liberal economist does not even have the concepts of "exploitation" and the "appropriation of wealth" within their models of capitalist economics, which they usually conceptualize simply as "market society" and as a normal human condition. To the extent that liberal economists *do* consider these issues vital, their focus remains on taming capital, not moving beyond it. For

---

29   "All idealists, philosophic and religious, ancient and modern, believe in inspirations, in revelations, saviours, miracle-workers; whether their belief takes a crude, religious, or a refined, philosophic, form depends only upon their cultural level, just as the degree of energy which they possess, their character, their social position, etc., determine whether their attitude to a belief in miracles is a passive or an active one, i.e., whether they are shepherds performing miracles or whether they are sheep; they further determine whether the aims they pursue are theoretical or practical" (Marx and Engels [1846] 1976: 532).

both liberals and conservatives, capital's social priority is sacrosanct, a viewpoint similar to the posture of religious liberals and conservatives toward their own favored institutions. Marx's (1847: 121) criticism of economists of his time—i.e., they "resemble the theologians"—equally applies to ours (also see Jouet 2012).

On the side of religion, with the modern laborer's relation to production one of "utter indifference, isolation, and alienation" (Marx 1971a: 85), the working classes in many parts of the world have grown politically and religiously conservative. Conservative Christians in the United States—once seeing politics as something of this world to eschew—became politically active in the 1980s, supported the dismantling of government spending on the poor, embraced supply-side economics, and voted for unleashing capital from government restraints. Like multinational corporations, The Unification Church is but one of many profit-making religious industries that have investments worldwide. With Jesus-the-fungible its servant, a "prosperity gospel"—where, despite Matthew (6:24), god wants people to be rich—enjoys growing audiences in the United States and globally. Once the US Supreme Court granted corporations the legal status of persons, and to the extent that conservatives see the US Constitution as god's inalienable rights made official, its ruling made capital holy in the world's most secular constitution.[30]

Today, capital—an invisible social relation that leaves its mark not only on the structures of society but also on the minds of its members—has ascended to a status once reserved for religious idols. It touches all social institutions, while prioritizing itself over them. Questioning capital's primary role in the world is to court charges of heresy, while serving capital's supremacy opens up professional advancement, just as does pursuing the priesthood. All the while, we sacrifice increasing amounts of nature, bodies, time, and mental energy to appease the demands of a god of our own making and worship.[31] With its

---

30   Adam Smith is a sort of intellectual bridge between these two discursive forms. A common mode of thought in his time was that god governs by general laws and understanding nature's laws is a key to knowing god's will (see Hill 2001 and citations therein). In Smith's logico-deductive view, if god made humans and if human nature unbounded by unnatural interference produces a free market of buying, selling, and accumulating, then capitalist society is, therefore, part of god's plan. It only follows, then, that with capitalism coming into being, history has reached its high point (for discussion, see Alvey 2003).

31   The similarities between religious faith and capitalist ideology reminds me of a friend's reaction to the events of September 11, 2001, as well as those from several economic observers after the financial crisis of 2008. Just like the earthquake that struck Portugal in 1755 (see note 17), both events had wide repercussions politically, economically, intellectually, and religiously. My friend concluded that the proper response to the terrorist attacks was that the world needed *more* religion and religious people. She entered into an

appetite for infinite expansion and ceaseless accumulation, this god is one that we can never sate.

Marx's (1971a: 209) observation that "everything appears reversed in competition" seems as true today as it did in his day. Our political leaders tell us that tax breaks for the rich and for corporations are the keys to economic prosperity and the ever-needed "jobs."[32] The state, one tool in capitalist society that working people can use to press for their interests and well-being, is depicted as the problem and must be dismantled, save its services to the capitalist class. Facing an environmental crisis of global proportions, our leading solutions range from free market incentives to pursue cleaner technology to regulations that attempt to mitigate harm from carbon dioxide and methane by reducing their output to levels just slightly lower than what climate scientists predict for worse case scenarios. The common theme among market apologists is that our environmental policies must be "balanced" with "our" needs for profits, jobs, growth, though our environmental crisis was brought about by those very profits, jobs, and forms of growth in the first place. Finally, the above strategies all exist within a broader era of neo-liberalism and the industrial development of new countries eager to join the capitalist game. Each of these market-based courses are directly the opposite of what we need today if we are to overcome and survive the predicaments the modern world system has produced.

Apologists for religion often proclaim, "Look at the good works! Religious people feed the poor, shelter the needy, and comfort the sick!" True, many religious people do these things, though this has no relevance as to the veracity of

---

Episcopalian seminary, matriculated, and became a priestess in the denomination. About seven years later, the financial crisis hit, causing economic and personal mayhem across global markets. Most observers—Marxist, liberal, and conservative—rightfully targeted many of the deregulatory reforms of the 1980s and 1990s as key pillars of the crisis, including the repeal of Glass-Steagall under Clinton and the later failure to regulate the swaps market. Not everyone saw it this way. I recall reading online—names and articles not particularly relevant here—market apologists claiming what the market really needed was *more* deregulation, not less. Such an attitude reflects a faith impervious to evidence, reason, or logic (even Alan Greenspan openly claimed the crisis had shaken his faith in the self-correcting market to its core). Like a periodic Great Awakening in America, President Trump later granted the deregulatory wish. The parallel between religious faith and market faith is hard to ignore.

32 I recall many years ago seeing an ad in some lefty magazine (I do not recall which one) that was selling a t-shirt that said something like, "No More Jobs Now!" I fear that this sentiment would not make sense to many people today, at least in the so-called "developed" world. Modern politicians are almost required to promise to bring "jobs" to their community, despite the fact that such jobs underpay and overwork their constituents for someone else's enrichment. The promise of "jobs" is like the promise of "salvation." It is the rhetoric used to harvest votes/devotees.

their theological claims, the history of the colonial system and its forced conversions, nor a plethora of ongoing misdeeds of religious institutions. So, too, do apologists point to capitalism's immense accumulation of commodities and declare, "Look at all the abundance and innovation!" Only a fool or a dogmatist would deny this reality. But so, too, only would a fool or a dogmatist look at how capitalism destroys the environment, causes wealth to accumulate to the point of obscenity, undermines hard-fought democratic reforms of the state, impoverishes billions, and drives nations to war and declare that these results are somehow *not* products of the system in which they exist. Instead, capitalism's apologists insist these are products of human failure and/or individual malfeasance.

In the worldviews of both capitalism's and religion's apologists, it is the extremists and fanatics, not the institutions themselves, who are at fault for such unseemly features. Each might admit the existence of greed or dogmatism or charlatans running cults and say in response that capitalism and/or religion are being misused, as these observations do not tell the apologist anything about the inherent nature of their object of worship. Defenders of religion and capitalism deny that these practices are *inherently* dangerous, that death and misery *are part of their design*, designs built *upon and reliant on* exploitation, mind control, domination, and unfreedom. Certainly, the followers of the Hayeks and Friedmans of the world will not admit as much, as they teach their disciples that market liberty is a requirement for modernity's promised freedom. Nor will they admit that slavery and exploitation of the vulnerable are inherent realities in capitalist society. Those holding such an economic faith seem impervious to reason, history, or evidence, as not only are concentrations of wealth, the dominance of monopolies, and the usurpations of democratic states all predictable under the capitalist mode of production—especially in its unregulated free market form—but history has amply demonstrated that such predictions are well-founded.[33]

---

33 Friedrich Hayek, a defender of unregulated free markets, is a leading thinker supported by many conservative economic theorists, especially those of a libertarian bent. For Hayek, the freedom to produce, buy, and sell without government restrictions is an inherent foundation of a free society. Though my point here is not to contrast and criticize his economic theory from a Marxian perspective (i.e., Hayek omits class exploitation from his model), there is an interesting overlap between his view of freedom and that of Marx. This similarity became apparent to me after I had several conversations with a friend who considered himself a libertarian and a Hayek supporter. He and I got along well, though he was somewhat surprised to meet a real defender of Marx, as he only knew the traditional but misleading ideas about what that meant. One of the assumptions my friend held was that Marx and Marxists wanted society reorganized under a government-run economic system, with individual laborers subject to a bureaucratic regime of bosses,

Economic dogmatists come in many stripes, liberal, conservative, and libertarian. These are today's secular theologians and they worship a new and dangerous god.

The god of religion is unreal and invisible. The god of capital is invisible, too, though it is real. However, capital is not a thing, it is a relationship and a process and it produces tangible results we can see and directly experience—skyscrapers and ports, goods for sale on the market, and stocks of private wealth (houses, yachts, jets). We go to jobs where our work produces corporate profits while, absent our own means of production, we give our money back to the ruling class through our need to purchase food, clothing, and shelter. As a relationship and a process centered on the intangible reality of constant accumulation, we cannot overthrow capital as we would an individual king. Nor can we vote capital out of office, as we would a corrupt politician. One cannot leave capital behind as they would a church. Capital is a ubiquitous phenomenon in modern life that only a self-sufficient hermit or an isolated tribe can escape, and even their relative independence is subject to the whims of capitalist developers and their stewards in the state. Moreover, similar to religion, to speak out against capital today is court charges of fanaticism, naivety, and idealistic delusion, only then to risk the marginalization of the blasphemer.

The dilemma runs deeper still. Marx's critique of capital remains our most trenchant and scientifically sound discourse with which to understand the logic of modern society. However, history and his supporters have transformed his ideas into "Marxism," a worldview and political program whose devotees engage in behaviors that at times resemble religiosity and fanaticism, and not without reason. Marx's ideas are powerful and they propose a method for resolving our problems that can inspire. These characteristics, nonetheless, can lead easily to sloganeering, dogmatism, and factionalism and have in fact done so on more than a few occasions. Multiple self-identified Marxist individuals and groups speak of and wait for "The Revolution" just as some Christians speak of and wait for "The Second Coming." More than one Marxist organization has

---

managers, dictates, and so on. While I assured him this was not the case (or not for me and how I understood Marx, at least), I also tried get across to him Marx's basic understanding of individual freedom. I explained that the individual should be able to freely choose the efforts to which their labor is applied, that they should be in possession of the resources (or means of production in Marx's terminology) needed to control their economic well-being and destiny, and that they have the right to reap just rewards from the fruits of their labor. He agreed with all of these points and was a bit nonplussed that these also reflected Marx's point of view. At the time, though, I did not feel it expeditious in our conversation to explain to him in detail why such things were not possible under capitalism.

fallen prey to recruiting initiates similar to Hari Krishna adherents, with similar exclusionary tactics for heretics who utter sacrilegious or fail to follow the party line. Via a reactionary tendency, self-proclaimed Marxist groups splinter off like so many schisms among Baptist congregations in the American South. It is easy to despair at the thought that we need to understand what Marx is telling us about capitalism while, at the same time, mobilizing people through his insights cultivates a path that can so easily go in sect-like directions.

Nevertheless, forward we must go. The need for facing our real life conditions with sober senses is as relevant today as it was when Marx and Engels wrote The Communist Manifesto. And what have our social scientists been doing? Many of them have successfully kept "capital" off their radar and off scientific and public agendas (see the Appendix). The closest mainstream sociology normally gets is a discussion about "inequality" in terms of income and wealth, which, while expressions of capital, are not themselves the root of the matter. Reducing economic inequalities based on income will not fundamentally change the nature of capital, though it may improve lives and alter the balance of forces in the class struggle to some degree and, perhaps, slow down the speed at which we currently are heading toward the cliff—something we learned from our experience with welfare-states. Still, to reduce income inequality is simply to tinker with the details while the system implodes through its self-induced economic and environmental crises.

Inequalities of income and wealth capture less academic attention today than do other inequalities, such as those based on identities of gender, race and ethnicity, and sexuality. While these are important social problems, solving them will do nothing for our ecological crisis nor help us grasp the logic of capital as the ordering principle of modern society. Identity politics is a starting-point for reducing status inequalities but as a political program it will not change the nature of capitalism. That is, eliminating prejudices based on gender, racial/ethnic, and sexual identities will improve people's lives, though eliminating discrimination against such groups will only facilitate their distribution across the class structure and do nothing to transform that class structure into something else. We could replace every heterosexual white male at the top of our corporate pyramids and we would still have capital and capitalists.

The relationship between leftist discourses is neither mutually two-way nor tension free. Today, supporters of Marxian-oriented social critique have become allies to intersectional identity politics to a greater degree than have activists in sexual, gender, and/or racial politics become allies to them. The politics of identity is the predominant motive force among liberal activists today, though as traditional liberals most of them appear oblivious to how liberalism has always deflected attention away from the capitalist man behind the curtain to whom we should pay no attention. In liberal ideology, social reform is the limit of respectable criticism and action. Liberal politics thus unknowingly runs interference for the conservatives, helping keep a radical critique of capital out of public discourse.

For these reasons above, left politics today are splintered and ineffective relative to the structural changes we need to survive and go beyond our current historical moment.

Facing the real life conditions that imperil our immediate survival requires producing positive knowledge rather than entertaining speculative philosophy, prioritizing the internecine battles among status groups (as worthy as those battles might be) to the exclusion of class struggle, or focusing our studies on topics that do not challenge the powers-that-be. Until we rid ourselves of both capital (and the class that sits upon it) and the mystifying world of religious beliefs, we will remain trapped by the fetishes we have created all the while living in a world where both are "becoming senile and ... more and more outlived" (Marx 1971a: 262). It is our task to live in a way so that we may outlive them both.

CHAPTER 7

Reflections and a Critical Evaluation

1 Our Difficulties in Understanding Marx

Despite his intellectual gifts and scientific accomplishments, Marx's scholarly legacy remains mixed. His personal correspondence suggests he overestimated how well his readers would understand him. Even Engels had trouble at times. And though books and articles collectively reference him thousands of times each year—17,640 in 2018 according to Google Scholar—consensus on the meanings of his theories and conclusions in *Capital* remains elusive over 150 years after its original release. Its forms of analysis, array of terminology, and empirical domains are like a multi-layered onion that reveals more the more one peels back. Even after numerous readings, one is still unsure if they have reached its center. As one of Marx's goals was providing the working class both an education and a means of intellectual self-defense, his magnum opus would take on more heft with the scholarly community's endorsement. But getting either or both groups—everyday people and scholars generally—to steadily flock to his camp has seen only marginal success.[1]

---

1 In Marx's day, it was often important to have an established academic position in order for one's work to receive serious scholarly attention. While during Marx's middle-life, he did reach a wider audience through his journalism and gained a level of notoriety from his political activity, the academic community at the time hardly noticed the publication of *Capital*, particularly in Germany. As for today, one could counter the claim about Marx-the-marginal with empirical data to the contrary. For instance, Kaur, Radicchi, and Menczer (2013), in examining whether a scientist had an array of regularly cited work (rather than one big study), created and measured an "h-index" that estimates the degree to which some scholars stand out from all others. Marx's score was 22 times higher than the average for scholars in history and 11 times higher than for the average economist. Relative to 35,000 other high-profile scholars, Marx ranked first, followed by Freud in psychology and Edward Witten in physics. Examination in Google Scholar (January 6, 2019) showed Marx being cited 101,033 times since 2014, and under sociology he ranked second for all measured citations with 315,459, behind Pierre Bourdieu (664,248) and ahead of Max Weber (280,818). Even with that said, one would not mistake sociology's top journals as ones publishing Marxian infused content nor would one find the world's leading sociological associations brimming with Marxist scholars. It is not that Marxist discourse is absent in academia, as this is clearly not the case. However, Marx's domination of citation indices is greatly out of line with the actual content found in social science disciplines in terms of personnel, training, and subject matter (for example, see the discussion and data in the Appendix).

It is no wonder. Reading Marx can be a heady experience, equal parts exhilarating and frustrating, often at the same time. He packed *Capital* with wide-ranging erudition, rhetorical flourishes, revealing insights, and criticisms that are as white-hot as they are trenchant. Unfortunately for the methodologist in search of guidance, Marx's instructions can be overwhelmed by his prose, where the latter grabs one's attention while making the former easily missed. Here is an example from the *Grundrisse*:

> In all forms of society there is one specific kind of production which predominates over the rest, whose relations thus assign rank and influence to the others. It is a general illumination which bathes all the other colours and modifies their particularity. It is a particular ether which determines the specific gravity of every being which has materialized within it.
>
> MARX 1973: 106–107

Chapter Two used the first sentence above as one of Marx's guidelines for considering empirical observations when modeling modes of production. As a methodological statement, it is clear, concise, and informative. Had one read this section quickly, however, trying to absorb the language, cadence, and meaning of the second two sentences could derail their attention away from the meaning of the first. Illumination bathing colors and ether determining specific gravity? No social science methodology class in the world, I dare assert, prepares a student for such phraseology. It should be no mystery, then, why methodology classes in sociology do not usually teach Marx.

These are not the only issues confronting Marx's readers. One none-too-seldom encounters passages that go on and on, leaving them unsure of the narrative's direction and exactly what they are supposed to be learning. *Capital* depicts a world of fluidity, motion, and development. It can be dizzying in a way, as one feels their mind sort of whirl around Marx's words as his exposition unfolds. Once Marx's writing seems to achieve a sense of firmness, his bearings shift yet again and, thus, so do ours. Still, as one becomes more familiar with his approach to communicating his ideas, they become more comfortable and in tune with his cadence, concepts, and theories. Only then does reading Marx become less of a struggle, even as the sense of movement, fluidity, and dynamics remains. Few authors, at least in the nonfiction world, provide this same experience.

Science is not supposed to be this way. Scientific inquiry is supposed to be sober and uninterested. Scientific writing should be calm and strive for solidity in its modeling of reality. We expect a science's presentation to be systematic and, preferably, linear. While *Capital* meets these standards at times, Marx embedded so much within it that is unorthodox, critical, unexpected, perplexing, and in motion. What is one to make of it?

Part of this experience rests in Marx's method of presentation, which often *does not* resemble scientific practice as generally understood. Words are not supposed to change their meanings—especially within the same analytical framework—and the analyst should not apply models during presentation before spelling out their foundations clearly and systematically. In contrast, Marx's words and models unfold before you, revealing new dimensions, new facts, and new dynamics. We cannot reduce this expositional style down to simply Marx's idiosyncratic preferences as if the product of his personality quirks. There is an intent and a purpose here founded on a conception of how to do a social science and the ends to which one should put it. Marx's intends for his language and method of presentation *to teach us something*.

One of Marx's goals is to teach us to see through the world's illusions. One illusion—one common across societies in general—is how people tend to view their own society as a product of human nature, the result of the way the gods, god, or biology meant humans to be. In seeing their own society's social relations as "normal," humans interpret the world in its terms, find their society as one of universal truths, and as having an eternal existence. Marx throws icy water on this view. He assumes society's historical variability, reveals its forces of development and transformation, and shows us our own society's origins, its history, its limitations, and the reasons it is not likely to go on forever. The human mind so rarely encounters this way of approaching knowledge that it rebels against it. The (often strong) negative reactions against his ideas—in his lifetime and since—testifies to this fact.

On top of illusions common across societies in general, there are specific illusions built into our own. Marx repeatedly returns to the idea of how capitalist society "inverts" our consciousness in a way where the world appears backwards to us.[2] We see capital as the producer of wealth rather than labor. We treat competition as the foundation of progress rather than as a coercive force that compels people to insert themselves into an industrial machine that grinds up many of them. Police focus their efforts on the poor robbing each other, while the bourgeoisie robs laborers and society-at-large via wages, prices, and through direct fraud. The only acceptable political ideologies tell us

---

2   For one of my early examinations of this idea in Marx's approach, see Paolucci (2001).

that modern states are seats of democracy instead of vehicles for ruling classes to pursue their interests against everyone else. Everywhere capital's spokespersons remind us that the world it has created is the product of human nature rather than the height of our alienation from it. Capitalist society turns our common sense knowledge against us.

Part of Marx's project is *re-inverting* this consciousness, *un-teaching* us the ideological constructs that inundate our lives and to which we have grown accustomed. With Marx's words, models, and organization of material meant to turn our thinking back around, reading him can *feel* mentally taxing because it *is* mentally taxing. Just as lifting weights to strengthen one's muscles makes them sore, the reader is not imagining what they are experiencing. With more experience, the fogginess does peel away, reading Marx does get easier, and our understanding of things does re-invert, though it takes effort and persistence. Many readers soon give up, too frustrated and/or too impatient to continue until the payoff. Again, the comparison to lifting weights is apt.

Perhaps Marx deserves some of our understanding in these regards. He seems to know that he cannot simply tell us that the world appears backward to us and then expect us to accept him at his word and to figure out the rest for ourselves. Marx meant for the re-inverting effect to take place through the process of reading *Capital* (not to exclude his other writings). And like foretelling a punchline or a plot ruins a joke or a movie, Marx also cannot tell us what exactly he is doing or is going to do before he (and thus we the reader) gets there. He has to bring us along with him and we have to engage his narrative enough to follow him to his destination. With his work unfinished, however, his destination is one at which he never arrived.

Marx's readers do not always arrive at his intended destination, either. Many explanatory gaps in *Capital* need clarification for the average reader to "get it" more easily. Marx does not provide explicit lessons on his philosophy of science. He often does not directly explain how he connects his theories and models together or, when he does, he leaves his explanations spread across different chapters and volumes. He does not tell the reader the strategy behind his use of terms, whether dialectical concepts, traditional scientific ones, those in between, or many of his other theoretically invested principles. The theory of alienation, for example, is crucial to the overall critique of capitalist society offered in *Capital*. However, the concept appears there only a few times and the entire edifice of the theory is absent in terms of a systematic engagement. So seemingly absent is the theory that Althusser's assertion that alienation is not operative in *Capital* at all enjoyed a non-insignificant level of influence (albeit only for a time). Scholars today tend to agree that any interpretation of the book is incomplete without it.

Our terminological and theoretical problems do not end there. In *Capital*, Marx uses concepts like "functions," "quantitative," "ratio," "proportions," "degrees," "mass," and many other terms familiar in science. Words that bridge with these—such as "determines," "conversions," "transformations," "concentration," and so on—also everywhere repeat. Moreover, what is the average reader to do when they encounter dialectical terms like "totality," "appearance" and "essence," "embryonic," "embodiment," "process," "relations," "expressions," "moments," "movement," "immanent," and "contradiction"? Save a few passages in his prefaces to its different editions, Marx does not give the reader a primer on dialectics so that *Capital* might be more intelligible, especially to an audience unschooled in the tradition in which he is working. With readers of his period more familiar with Hegelian language than readers today, time has not been Marx's ally in these regards.

Marx mobilizes all of the terms and strategies just recounted in the context of his method of successive abstractions, which is perhaps the most disguised feature of his masterpiece. In this book, I have emphasized how his use of the doublets "abstract and concrete" and "general and specific" unite both dialectical reason and scientific protocols, something else Marx never makes plain. His narrative gives the reader, often unawares, lessons in both scientific dialectics and a view of the world this outlook facilitates. This was part of his genius and failure. It has taken scholars over one-hundred years to unravel *Capital*'s methodology, and so it is no wonder that, outside of Marxian scholars, the scientific community generally—at his time and ours—failed to embrace it as the groundbreaking work that it was and remains. Only Newton's *Principia Mathematica* and Darwin's *On the Origin of Species* come to mind as comparable works.

I find relating Marx's expositional approach to jazz an appealing analogy. In jazz, each player is not simply riffing improvisational with total freedom, lacking direction or reason. Instead, a piece of jazz music usually has identifiable beats and rhythms, chord progressions, and melodic signatures that need to be played in certain ways and at certain times for the material to hold together. This is its structure. Absent these determining variables a piece would be noise without form or context. At the same time, players—sometimes one at a time, sometimes several, and even, though more rarely, all of them—have the freedom to improvise within that structure. They might stay close to the core melody while changing it somewhat or they might investigate a momentary inspiration while the rest of the band holds the tune together. This produces the possibilities of chance, indeterminacy, contingency, and accident. If the goal of science is to understand reality as much as possible and if societies have both structure and flux, patterns and chaos, determining variables and contingent outcomes, then one's analysis and the presentation of their results must also incorporate similar characteristics if they are to reflect their object of inquiry with a higher degree of fidelity.

We can think of Marx's approach in a similar way. Marx is trying to capture the interrelations between social structures and real history, which requires balancing, synthesizing, and/or playing moments of stability and change off one another. Structural variables (the basic melody of a song in jazz) determine a patterned range of what *should* happen (in terms of probability, not morality), while real historical practice and events shape what actually *does* happen within that framework (improvisation within the structure). One must be able to depict past, present, and potential futures with nimbleness and this requires that they venture into areas that are only partially determined and remain open to potentials and possibilities. This is another reason why Marx's outlook requires merging dialectical and scientific tools to do a proper social science, while our minds struggle to keep up with his direction and cadence.

One example I have returned to several times in this book is Marx's nonlinear method of presentation, something about which we can now perhaps make additional sense. The method of successive abstractions allows him to extract the structure of a system, identify its constants and its variables, and then apply both of these—explanatory structural relations in conjunction with their variable range of possibilities—to real historical observations and other concrete data. Presenting one's results in such an approach will clearly present problems specific to the goal of the investigation as a whole. If Marx was writing on *A Taxonomic History of Economic Formations*, then he might have met readers' expectations of a linear presentation. Such an exposition could first present the variables that cross all modes of production, then develop a model for each mode, and then present an analysis of societies representing those modes using the model so developed for interpreting and explaining their history.

Marx's object of inquiry, however, is "capital" and that means he must select topics and chapters relevant to it. The role of non-capitalist societies is to help him uncover the variables shared across all modes of production, model the specific configuration of these variables for each mode, and compare and contrast each model against the others to identify how each variable influences and is influenced by other variables in that structural context. In this way, the features of other systems function as comparative frameworks that help him come up with a model of capitalism's *differentia specifica*. Understood in this way, *Capital*'s presentation is more "linear" than it might appear, as it works through multiple features—structural and historical—that comprise capital as a social relation. It appears nonlinear because what our assumptions tell us to look for are not the way Marx organized the book.

Given all of these observations, a novice who reads *Capital* can easily get the impression that Marx is just writing off the cuff there, sometimes waxing philosophical and often using data as it suits his whims. "He's no Darwin!" "What's all the fuss about?" True, Marx did not seem to expect that everyday readers would walk away from *Capital* experts in method. Nevertheless, none-too-few mainstream sociologists and economists, much less Marxian aficionados, have worked their way through its volumes only to come away without recognizing more than one scientific convention with which he invested them. One revealing reason for this is that *Capital*'s various prefaces only briefly revisit Marx's preparatory meditations in the *Grundrisse*'s Introduction, and then mainly in two short statements of how the power of abstraction allows him to make experiments and focus on objects of inquiry as if using a microscope. Because it takes an interpretative model like the method of successive abstractions to better illuminate these tools, those engaging *Capital* without such a model are likely to navigate it with less facility than is possible and thus extract less from it than Marx intended.

2   Omissions, Limitations, Mistakes, Objections, and Final Thoughts

It would be hard to cover all of the territory in Marxian scholarship—starting with Marx himself and continuing with his interpreters (including myself)—with omissions, gaps, limitations, mistakes, and reasons to object. That truth notwithstanding, some subjects do warrant addressing in the context of the preceding chapters.

How adequate are the complement of variables Marx used for categorizing modes of production? This question, of course, presumes both that those variables I have identified are exhaustive of Marx's actual criteria and that all of my selections belong in any such account. Those variables I have selected *do* appear in his analyses of all production modes he examines and, though it is possible, I do not believe that I have missed any. If I have, then answering this question would first require adding such a variable (or variables) to the model provided here, at least to the degree that mine is a useful starting-point. That said, I believe that Marx's model is rather satisfactory, though reasonable questions do remain.

Marx left many holes in his work that scholars have tried to fill. For the type of analysis this book represents, the lack of a work on method from him has been the most vexing. This is not the only gap with which we must deal, however. Marx, at one point, planned to write six books for his advanced political economy—capital, landed property, wage-labor, the state, international trade, and the world-market. With only *Capital*'s first volume completed, this work remained vastly unfinished. Related to all of these absences, the models of Marx's modes of production I have developed do not contain the state as a variable within them. I should not let this omission go unaddressed.

Beyond some general statements, *Capital* does not develop models of the state to accompany different modes of production. As such, the relative absence of the state in my presentation is, at first, a product of what is or is not contained in *Capital*'s volumes. This omission by Marx is not an oversight. His base-superstructure framework assumes that modes of production develop state forms that correspond to each mode's class relations (which we saw a passing reference to in Chapter 2, see Marx 1971a: 791). This means that when Marx focuses on what makes a mode of production what it is, his conclusion does not include the state as a taxonomic variable because a state form is not a structural feature of modes of production but rather results from those features.

Within my methodological framework, a Marxian theory of the state would proceed in a systematic fashion similar to what we saw for the analysis of slavery and/or religion. Such an inquiry would start with production in general and establish what functions states play there. Given that this level of abstraction would also include non-class societies, the operative abstraction would probably be something closer to "mode of governance," as "the state" reflects political institutions resting on class relations in Marx's theory. His method would then isolate class societies in the general concrete and mutually compare states across them to extract the commonalities and the differences in the structure and role of states in such systems. Next, drawing from both of these broader levels of abstraction—i.e., society in general, class systems in general and in the specific—focus would move to the features of states founded upon capitalist class relations. Though Marx would do all of this first both mentally and in the acts of research and analysis, given what we saw with *Capital*, it is doubtful that his presentation would proceed in such a step-by-step manner.

The absence of the state is not the only issue subject to questioning in my analyses. Though discussed, I did not include socially necessary labor-time in my catalog of Marx's taxonomic criteria for modes of production. True, socially necessary labor-time exists in all modes of production, while its specific level varies within and between them. However, tools and technology are also constant features of modes of production and Marx does not use these as specific identifiers but instead uses how the configuration of variables of different modes influence the *social development of productive forces*. While this concept includes technological complexity, Marx emphasizes what productive relations and economic processes account for a social structure's overall dynamic—i.e., stagnant, uneven, constant, rapid, and so on—and what type of technological development results from this—i.e., simple, moderately developed, highly complex. In the same way, socially necessary labor-time exists in any production system but without being an identifying *structural* feature. Rather, variations in socially necessary labor-time *result* from the interconnections in a mode of production's class relations, forms of appropriation, development of productive forces, and terms of labor.

I did not afford "abstract labor" a taxonomic role for the capitalist mode of production for similar reasons. Marx states several times in *Capital* that abstract labor is a key to capitalism's law of value. All societies have relationships involving concrete labor—i.e., the actual work, the subject of it, and the terms under which it is done. The capitalist system is unique in that it equates all labor via the ability to do work generally, with labor-power subsequently bought and sold on a labor market. There are reasons, however, to pause in using abstract labor as a taxonomic criterion. First, as it is not applicable to pre-capitalist systems, it does not work as a general criterion along with the other structural variables already identified here. What about as a subcategory, e.g., just as "forced labor" is a subcategory of "terms of labor"? The problem is that abstract labor stems from several of the general categories central to Marx's models rather than being a subcategory of one.

Abstract labor relates to the *terms of labor* in the way an impersonal market forces people to sell themselves as possessors of labor-power. Labor-power has a market price and laborers are free to enter into contractual agreements to sell it, just as capitalists are free to buy it. That purchase is one that capitalists make in conjunction with calculating the average cost of the needed means of production as a whole. This *class relationship* makes labor in capitalist society something abstract. If the laborer were legally forced to work and the cost of buying their labor-power was not part of business calculations in a competitive market, then labor in capitalism would lose its abstract character—and we would not have a "capitalist" system as we know it. By extension, while abstract labor is not the *subject of production*, that subject requires exploiting labor as part of a business model. Abstract labor, therefore, also extends from the *form of appropriation*, though here "wage-labor"—as an abstract category connected to a concrete reality—suffices for the work needed as a taxonomic identifier, particularly in relation to its companion categories in other class systems—e.g., serfdom, peasantry, and slavery. What we see then is that while abstract labor's existence does elucidate capitalism's wider conditions of labor alienation, abstract labor is less an identifying *structural* variable specific to capitalism than it is a product of that structure, just as we saw with the state and with socially necessary labor-time above.

How efficacious were Marx's models in terms of the variables he associated with different modes of production and the different real historical outcomes in societies representing them? Does he apply these variables to specific observations with sufficient precision and explanatory validity? Is it accurate, for example, for Marx to depict the development of productive forces in the Asiatic mode as relatively stagnant? Was he right that merchant's capital everywhere played a historic role in the systemic rise of slavery? Was he correct about usury's effects in Asiatic, ancient, and feudal modes as compared to the capitalist mode? I must admit that I do not have the requisite expertise to answer these questions. That confession notwithstanding, the methodology presented here hopefully clarifies how Marx isolated the variables and observations that he did and thus suggests a method by which one would go about testing his conclusions about them.

Though I do not have the expertise to answer the questions above, I do have experience with using Marx's models for my own sociological inquiries. In those investigations, I have fallen prey to problems resulting from what is and is not contained in his works. For example, in more than one publication I relied solely on the passage in *Capital* where Marx ([1867] 1992b: 209) says the essential difference between class systems is their different modes of appropriation of surplus-value. I once had assumed this was *the* criterion Marx used to differentiate class systems from each other; I did not consider that there may be other criteria, and subsequently I did not look for them. Similarly, I have included slavery as one of Marx's modes of production in previous writings (also found in multiple examples from Marxian scholarship). Though at first this may seem reasonable—given slavery's reality as a form of forced labor in the production of appropriated surplus-value—slavery does not meet Marx's full complement of criteria for modes of production. Rather, slavery is a system of labor exploitation present in multiple modes of production. Moreover, Marx never refers to slavery itself as a mode. Errors such as these are reducible, in part, to what Marx does and does not present to us in his analyses, specifically a clear and exhaustive account of his taxonomic criteria for modes of production, why specific modes he designates meet those criteria, and why other productive relations and economic processes do not.

I hope I have been more thorough in this book than I was in the past, which is also part of the point. A more exhaustive understanding of Marx requires scouring through his writings and carefully sifting out the criteria he consistently uses but never compiles and explicates for us. Without careful reading and an efficacious interpretive framework, it is difficult to keep track of how Marx's modeling proceeds. Though other fruitful approaches exist, it is unlikely I would have made the conclusions I have without having learned Ollman's internal relations approach to dialectics, deciphering Marx's method of successive abstractions, taking him at his word that his abstractive method approximates the experimental model, and painstakingly sifting through his texts with these frameworks in mind. Having pondered the issue several times, I am still unsure if uncovering how Marx used the experimental model and employed sociological microscopes would be possible without this interpretive framework.

In contrast to such an untangling reconstruction, the literature's treatment of alienation and surplus-value—which, by contrast, seem more straightforward in Marx's writing—is both vexing and perplexing. More than a few Marxian scholars have claimed that these concepts are capitalist-specific for Marx—where alienation applies solely to the conditions experienced by wage-laborers and surplus-value is restricted to the exploitation of their labor. In *The German Ideology*, however, Marx and Engels do not limit their focus to the conditions only wage-laborers experience but rather they apply the theory of alienation to human realities prior to (though including) capitalism. Their theory of alienation there relates to the human condition in general, where, thus far historically, humans have been subject to forces—both natural and social—they neither control nor understand. Further, to the extent that the theory of alienation relates to humans not being in control of their own labor, its terms, and its products, this model cannot be capitalist-specific in light of the labor conditions in other class systems. Not only this, viewing alienation as capitalist-specific also stands in contradiction to using the theory for examining religion in any society that is not a modern one. This, too, is inconsistent with what we know about Marx's overall approach. If alienation is capitalist-specific, then what theoretical model is he using when he accounts for religion in pre-capitalist societies?

It is similar with surplus-value. Class societies differ from non-class societies on, among other things, the existence of surplus-value appropriation. Class societies differ from each other on, among other things, the different modes by which this appropriation occurs. While Marx *does* claim that wage-labor is a form of surplus-value appropriation specific to capitalism (on top of the rent and usury also found there), his entire approach to political economy would not make sense if surplus-value as a general phenomenon is capitalist-specific. To wit:

- What does surplus-labor produce in any society if not surplus-value, given that by Marx's definition labor is the source of all value?

– What was, in fact, being produced and appropriated in all other class systems if not surplus-value?
– One core purpose of his comparative analysis is to show how capitalism relies on the exploitation of forced labor for surplus-value appropriation. Once he can show how other systems express this relation, this helps him reveal how a similar process happens within capitalism. If surplus-value did not exist in pre-capitalist class systems, what was his point in analyzing their labor systems, value forms, and modes of appropriation and then comparing them to capitalism in the first place?

While these questions only have nonsensical answers if surplus-value is capitalist-specific, this not-uncommon interpretation cannot be due to Marx's omission of clearly defined terms and the changes in his usage of them. As we have seen here, Marx *does* explicitly state more than once that all surplus-value is the product of surplus-labor and that surplus-labor exists in all modes of production. Moreover, he also explicitly states several times that surplus-value exists in *all other systems*, even in non-class systems. Given their repetition, such instances are unlikely to be analytical mistakes or inconsistencies, slips of the pen, or the result of poor editing on Marx's part.

One possible reason why the idea of surplus-value being capitalist-specific is embedded in the literature is that early scholarship on Marx likely made an error similar to the one I made about forms of appropriation being the singular feature Marx used to distinguish class systems from each other. If a reader of Marx encounters a passage where he writes about surplus-value only in its capitalist context, they might assume it is a capitalist-specific concept for him and thus they do not look for it elsewhere in his writings. When multiple scholars accept and repeat such an interpretation, this acceptance and repetition reinforce one another and a standard reading emerges over time. Once a reading becomes standard, it often becomes unquestioned orthodoxy moving forward. For someone encountering literature that is anywhere from recent to over a century old, it is understandable that they assume the apparent general agreement on the meaning of a concept means it has been well-vetted, even though that general agreement may be the product of an early misinterpretation handed down over time. This pattern is not limited to surplus-value, or alienation for that matter. One can also find it in the literature on Marx's socalled stage theory of history as well as metaphysical approaches to dialectics, e.g., the triadic formula of thesis-antithesis-synthesis.[3]

---

3 Rather than referencing instances of this error about surplus-value in the literature, another personal anecdote will perhaps be indicative of my point. I once encountered an academic at a conference who told me with confidence that Marx's theory of surplus-value was, in fact,

Identifying Marx's variables also provides us a better view of his approach to socialism and communism, two additional areas of regular misunderstandings. Multiple commentators in popular culture and in mainstream social science reduce his ideas on these issues to overly simplistic terms and other terms that are flat incorrect. One misconception sees "socialism" as an overarching state in control of the means of production. Another misconception interprets "communism" in utopian terms, as a theory built on the high ideals of complete equality, harmony, justice, and so on. Despite the fact that Marx rejected these approaches, two corresponding views reflect and repeat them. With the history of Stalinist regimes as a backdrop, one view sees Marx's approach to socialism as an authoritarian program. Though this view is often commonly applied to communism as well, an associated interpretation here comes in the refrain, "Communism sounds good on paper but it is terrible in practice." One often wonders what such commentators believe this vision "on paper" actually is, as we rarely, if ever, find Marx waxing utopian on the topic.

Though he sometimes used socialism and communism interchangeably, we do know that Marx envisioned a transitionary stage between a successful worker revolution (that has seized the means of production and taken over the state) and the long-term development of a communist future.[4] In a socialist transitionary period, proletarians and middle classes become the appropriating class but in a re-inverted way, as they expropriate wealth *back from* the bourgeoisie who had previously appropriated it from them, while any new surplus-value production also remains in their hands. If the (former) ruling class refuses to relinquish the means of production and their accumulated wealth voluntarily (and they are unlikely to), the method of wealth reappropriation is force. That force could come from an armed insurrection, from mobilizing the state's coercive power (party formation, voting blocs, policy changes that transfer wealth, other forms of force), or some combination of both. This transformation of property relations is accompanied by labor that people freely choose for individual (economic) and class (political) purposes, while that labor is directed toward its traditional ends of producing use-values,

---

capitalist-specific. I told him I could provide him multiple instances where Marx says it exists in all societies in general but with different features under different systems. He retorted that he, too, could show me instances of Marx identifying surplus-value as unique to capitalism. I have never found anywhere in *Capital*'s three volumes or the three volumes of *Theories of Surplus-Value* where Marx ever makes such a claim. If the reader is interested, they can find my critique of formulaic dialectic, fallacious assumptions about Marx's theory of surplus-value, and the myth of Marx's so-called stage theory of history elsewhere in my publications (see Paolucci 2007, 2010, 2011, respectively).

4   For my previous discussion on this topic, see Paolucci (2004).

exchange-values, and surplus-values. Exchange proceeds as needed, while surplus-value is used for the social fund (e.g., emergencies, deficits) and for taking care of those too young, too old, or too infirmed to work. As inherited from capitalism, the productive forces remain highly developed. Politically, with more people being able to access the state—which is in a condition of decline as a repressive force over society—democracy increases.[5]

In a communist society, people provide labor according to their ability, which is unforced and done freely. Classes do not exist, so appropriation of surplus-value from one class to another also does not exist. Generalized want will not exist in communist society, either, as people will receive from society according to their needs. The lack of an appropriating social class also means that the state as a repressive apparatus will tend to fade away. There will be inequality in a communist society—at least in its early stages—based on amount of labor inputs, personal skills and endowments, and family structure, each of which would result in some individuals receiving more than others (see Marx's comments in his Critique of the Gotha Program). While means of production held in common exist, the laborer also owns their own personal means. Again, production of use-values, exchange-values, and surplus-values continue, with the latter used in social production and reproduction, for the social fund, for general social needs, and for exchange purposes as needed. As a worldwide worker revolution is the vehicle for these transformations, trade remains a globalized practice. Absent a system based on sales competition, profits, and reducing labor costs, technology—as adopted from the prior capitalist system—remains complex and developed further as needed, especially for arduous and/or dangerous work. Or so goes the general theory (Table 7.1).

A few things are noteworthy when thinking about socialism and communism in this way. First, putting aside whether or not these programs are possible, likely, or desirable, Marx did not build his understanding of these possible futures upon abstract moral principles nor visions of a hypothetical society that could only exist in the imagination. Rather, Marx's realist approach is based upon what political-economies in general look like and how capitalism is likely to develop. A guiding question is that in transforming capitalism into communism by going through socialism first, what must the theorist take into consideration to remain on the grounds of the requisites of *any* system, no matter its form?

---

5   How the state will fade as a repressive force while and/or after it appropriates wealth from the former ruling class does not appear to be adequately addressed in many Marxian political writings. The customary approach seems, more than anything, a matter of faith.

TABLE 7.1   Socialist and communist societies in Marx's outlook[a]

	Socialist transitionary period	Future communist society
Appropriating class	Proletarians, middle classes	None
Laboring class	Proletarians, middle classes	Everyone
Property relations	In transformation	Means of production held in common, laborers own their own means of production
Terms of labor	Unforced	Unforced
Subject of production	Use-value Exchange-value Surplus-value (Social fund, exchange)	Use-value Exchange-value Surplus-value (Social fund, exchange)
Form of appropriation	Forced redistribution of wealth away from ruling class to working and middle classes	None
Role of exchange and trade	Exchange as needed	World trade, free associations
Social development of productive forces	Complex	Complex
State form	More democratic, increasingly less hierarchical	No repressive state apparatus

SOURCE: CREATED BY AUTHOR

a   Note that the bottom row here includes "the state," even though I previously mentioned how
    the state is not part of Marx's taxonomic criteria of what makes a mode of production what
    it is. This table, however, depicts not only these modes of production but also reflects a wider
    model of their political-economic structure, which would include the state. Even the model
    presented here is not a complete image of what a socialist or a communist "society" might
    look like.

Second, Marx's lack of systematic writing about and modeling of socialism and
communism makes it easy for his interpreters to impugn a false utopianism to

him and ignore those policies that he actually supported. In the Europe of his period, communists emphasized voting rights for all adult men and women, freedom of the press, and general access to education. These were radical views at the time, given that many parts of Europe still struggled under monarchial rule. Today, we take these principles for granted and do not see them as "communist" at all. By that same measure, which of Marx's programmatic positions seem controversial and/or implausible today that people in the future will take for granted? Perhaps no class of capitalists and their managerial overseers? Perhaps worker ownership of the means of production? Perhaps a state that is both minimal and non-repressive or even its non-existence? Perhaps a system where the generalized threat of privation is not what drives people to contribute labor to society? It never hurts to remind oneself that proposing a world without god-kings, emperors, feudal lords, and slave-owners also once seemed controversial, implausible, and/or utopian.

Marx did not base his vision of communism on a rigid, starting-from-scratch, bottom-up formula common to the utopian approaches like those of Owen or Fourier. Instead, Marx envisioned that communism would be built on the structure capitalism had put in place but that had been overcome, transcended, and brought to a new level of development.[6] So communism at first would look visually a lot like what capitalism has produced, with its roads, ports, housing, and other infrastructure but without people divorced from the means of production. In Marx's approach, people would not be subject to forced labor nor ruled by a system of bankers, CEOs, multinational corporations, and oppressive management, while being coerced into a lifetime of office drudgery or dangerous industrial work. Instead of hypothesizing a perfect society conceived in the abstract, Marx asks us to envision a society where the social dysfunctions that class relations bring about—including forced labor, surplus-value appropriation, and a concentration of wealth—no long exist. While often supporting a variety of practical activities for his present, he also did not

---

6 "Capital comes more and more to the fore as a social power, whose agent is the capitalist. This social power no longer stands in any possible relation to that which the labour of a single individual can create. It becomes an alienated, independent, social power, which stands opposed to society as an object, and as an object that is the capitalist's source of power. The contradiction between the general social power into which capital develops, on the one hand, and the private power of the individual capitalists over these social conditions of production, on the other, becomes ever more irreconcilable, and yet contains the solution of the problem, because it implies at the same time the transformation of the conditions of production into general, common, social, conditions. This transformation stems from the development of the productive forces under capitalist production, and from the ways and means by which this development takes place" (Marx 1971a: 264).

provide a full-fledged schematic on how to get there beyond general ideas about worker control of their own productive lives. The further into the future his statements on communism were the vaguer and more indeterminate they became. It was not, he once said, the theorist's role to write recipes for the cookshops of the future.

Third, we can also use this model to assess self-labeled communist regimes as well as current political programs of self-identified radical groups. What would an evaluation of the Soviet Bloc, the regimes of Vietnam, Cambodia, and North Korea, or those of Cuba or China look like through the model above? Though these were/are not identical systems, their practical realities clearly do not reflect Marx's views on class relations, the terms of labor, freedom of the press, increasing levels of democracy, workers owning their own means of production, and so on. It is not so much that we must dogmatically adhere to his words, but rather to the extent such regimes veer from Marx's approach is the extent that those ventures are more "Marxist" in word than in deed. By extension, to the extent that they do veer from Marx's vision is the extent to which criticisms levied at them are not applicable to Marx's views. One result is that when some people criticize "Marxism," they often are not really addressing Marx's ideas at all.

We could also take a similar tack toward self-identifying "Marxist" political groups today. Marx consistently held that the liberation of the working class is a task for the working class itself, not one for an elite revolutionary leadership—a role he refused on more than one occasion. His model further requires that access to the state expands to include more people and, as an organization, it becomes less hierarchical. Both of these are stands from which he never wavered. Marx was not, that is, a Leninist.

For the contemporary social scientist, understanding Marx remains difficult, whether they are from the Marxian tradition or from a more mainstream approach. For the latter, social science disciplines developed in a different trajectory than Marx's way of going about things. Operational definitions, systematization of static models, mathematical and/or individualistic reductionism, and abstract theorizing outside of historical development are the prevailing trends. When not the case, the social sciences have embraced the ethnography as the preferred alternative. Such sociological investigations are not bereft of any methodological lessons or important information, but these approaches do little to engage in the type of discourse one needs for better understanding Marx's research practice and its justifications within scientific conventions.

This lack of connection or interaction between mainstream social science and Marx's type of analysis works its way back into Marxian social science as well. It is highly likely that a student schooled in conventional social science today receives training in advanced statistical modeling and presenting data through new computing platforms and programs. Though it is quite probable that were Marx alive today he would master such techniques of collating and presenting data, contemporary social science students who use such tools are unlikely to receive lessons in Marx's methodology. And students interested in Marx are unlikely to receive exposure on how to employ an experimental model in historical-structural analysis. Such concerns notwithstanding, with its synthesis of dialectics and conventional scientific methods, Marx's *Capital* remains fruitful grounds for developing new dynamic analyses of the era in which we live, many of which we can develop through approaches social scientists are already investigating. Network analysis, capital flows, core-periphery relations, broader Kondratieff cycles, statistical models I have no familiarity with, and new variables we are yet to imagine all await an engagement with Marx's masterpiece and its method of successive abstractions. What are we waiting for? We are on the clock and have a world to win.

Appendix to Chapter 6

In a previous work, I noted how, generally speaking, mainstream American sociology keeps a critical analysis of capital off its overall agenda (see Paolucci 2011: 7, note 6):

> In 2008, the *American Sociological Review* (Volume 73) published six issues containing 43 Articles, one Presidential Address, and one Research Note. The following list presents the most frequently used terms or subjects in titles and the number of times they appear that year: 'gender,' 'sex,' 'men/women' (10), 'ethnic/ity,' 'race,' (and derivative usages), (7), 'labor,' 'worker/s,' 'employment' (5), 'earnings,' 'income,' 'wage/s' (4), 'education' (4), 'inequality,' 'inequalities' (4), 'identity' (3), 'market/s' (3), 'corporate,' 'corporations' (3), 'immigrants,' 'migration' (3), 'religion,' 'religious' (3), 'delinquency,' 'crime,' 'social control' (3). 'Capitalism' (1) appears in an examination of debates on transitions in China (issue Number 4). In the same issue, 'capital' appears the only time in the whole yearly volume but in reference to 'ethnographic capital,' a topic that has nothing to do with capital as such (note: if a term appeared in both the main title and the subtitle, it was only counted once here; this list is not exhaustive of all the terms used in this volume).

After criticizing trends in sociology at the end of this chapter, I decided to revisit my examination of the leading American journal in the field. To better portray the material covered in the *American Sociological Review*, this time I expand both the time range for my sample and my categorizations (see Table A.1).[1] While the outcome generally reflects the pattern I previously found

---

1   The manner of data collection and analysis here differs from my 2008 sample. This time I first examined the article titles in the journal for each year and made notes on the topics that I found. I then organized them into general themes and placed other topics into subcategories under those themes as made substantive sense on their surface content. With this general framework in hand, I then returned to each article for each issue over the ten-year period of interest (2009–2018). Every topic or subtopic contained in a title or subtitle resulted in a "point" scored for a category, so that each article could be scored in as many categories that were reflected in their title and in my list. Thus, the total numbers here reflect not the total number of articles but rather an estimated total number of topics and their representation across 10 years of the journal's publications. Some articles were clearly within the main category (left column of Table A.1). Other article topics were more clearly within subcategories related to those main categories. Some could be scored under either and, in such cases, a judgment was made on what category was most fitting. Finally, some subcategories could

TABLE A.1   Terms and topics in *American Sociological Review* articles, 2009–2018

General category (#)	Subcategories, associated topics (#)	Total / %
Labor Issues (30)	Class/Income Inequality (48), Work/Workplace/Workforce (16), Welfare States (12), Unions/Unionization (9), Labor Markets (7), Mobility (6), Poverty (3), Un/employment (3), Elite Incomes (1)	135/ 16.7
Gender Issues (65)		65 / 8.0
Marriage & The Family (37)	Motherhood (12), Intimate Partner Violence (4), Domestic Labor (3), Divorce (1), Households (1)	58 / 7.2
Class & Race (22)	Race/Ethnicity and Racism (17), Ethnic Conflict (7), Segregation (4), Discrimination (1), Racial Attitudes (1)	52 / 6.4
Education (48)		48 / 5.9
Social Organizations (10)	Occupations (16), Management (6), Bureaucracy (5), Businesses/Firms (2), Non-Profits (2), Advocacy Organizations (1), Civil Society Organizations (1), Voluntary Associations (1)	44 / 5.5
Crime/Deviance (37)	Surveillance (4), Hate Crimes (1), Law (1)	43 / 5.3
Political Economy (1)	Democracy (9), Capitalism (4)/ Capital (1), Financial Capital (1)/Crisis (4), Nation-State (3), Class Struggles (1), Class Power (1), Colonialism (2), Classes (1), Core-Periphery (1), Corporate Restructuring (1), Corporations (1), Downsizing (1), Elites (1), Geo-Politics (1), Global Economy (1), Interlocks (1),	42 / 5.2

General category (#)	Subcategories, associated topics (#)	Total / %
Political Economy (1)	Military Industrial Complex (1), Neo-Liberalism (1), Privatization (1), Speculation/Bubbles (1), Super Rich (1), US Corporate Political Activity (1)	
Health & Medical Sociology (20)	Life Course (6), Mental Health (3), Demography (2), Gerontology (2), Suicide (2), Social Isolation (1), Elderly Care (1)	38 / 4.7
Economic Sociology (26)	Cultural/Social Capital (2), Firms/Business (2), Bank Panics (1), Downsizing (1), Economic Exchange (1), Foreclosure Crisis (1), Modernization (1), Professions (1), Response to Great Recession (1)	37 / 4.6
Social Movements (8)	Activism (11), Political Struggles (6), Collective Violence/Rebellion (3), Collective Action (2), Protests (2), Nationalist Movements (1)	33 / 4.1
Social Networks (23)	Group Dynamics (3), Exchange Networks (1)	27 / 3.3
Migration, Immigration & Citizenship (24)	National Identity (1), Assimilation (1)	26 / 3.2
Miscellaneous	Sociology of Science (11), Art (2), Music (2), Olfaction (2), Food (1), Comedy (1), Entertainment (1), Military Sociology (1), Sociology of Disasters (1), Social Environment (1)	23 / 2.9
Theory/Methods (18)	Exchange Theory (4)	22 / 2.7
Cultural Analysis (21)	Cultural Appropriation (1)	22 / 2.7
Political Sociology (17)	Human Rights Organizations (1), Red Scare (1)	19 / 2.4

TABLE A.1   Terms and topics in *American Sociological Review* articles, 2009–2018 (*cont.*)

General category (#)	Subcategories, associated topics (#)	Total / %
Sex/Sexuality (10)	Same-Sex Relations (2), Heteronormativity (1), Sexual Harassment (1), Sexual Orientation (1), Sex Work (1)	16 / 2.0
Sociology of Religion (15)		15 / 1.9
Status (9)	Socioeconomic Status (4), Social Inequality (1)	14 / 1.7
Community	Neighborhood (6), Housing (4), Community Politics (2)	12 / 1.5
Intersections (2)	Diversity (4), Identity (3), Gender and Race (1), Multiple Categorical Memberships (1)	11 / 1.4
Media (5)	Online Activity (6)	11 / 1.4
Uncategorized (9)		9 / 1.1
Urban Soc, Rural Soc (6)		6 / .7
Environment (1)	Environmentalism (1)	2 / .2
	Total	807 / 101.2

SOURCE: CREATED BY AUTHOR

above, here I will parse my recent results in more detail and with more nuance than before.

I will start with some general comments.

First, note that the categories and subcategories in the table are not necessarily mutually exclusive for the act of sociological inquiry. One could use data and other relevant information from an article not directly related to one's research agenda to inform their investigation. For instance, there may be

---

possibly fit under more than one general category and here, too, judgment was necessary. Note that a score in a subcategory did not also translate into a score in the general category. Instead, an article could score in a general category and more than one of the *other* subcategories, though not usually its own. In addition, an article could score in multiple subcategories without scoring in a general category. The result was that each article received 1–4 points across all general categories and subcategories. Comments and Replies related to articles published in previous issues were not included in this data set.

information from an article on art that might inform research on occupations, or a political-economist might find an article on welfare states useful for their interests. This is a testimony to sociology's wide range of inquiry and, as such, my general categories and subcategories do not *necessarily* reflect constraints mainstream outlets place on the discipline's practitioners.

Second, for matters more directly related to the themes of this book, an obvious question is why isolate topics categorized under "Labor Issues" from those for "Political Economy"? Why did I not categorize the former under the latter? One concern in my categorization was the extent to which an article appeared to come from a more "liberal" approach to sociological analysis than from a more critical one. Here I tried to make such distinctions as fairly as I could. For example, take two articles published in Issue 3: "Firm Turnover and the Return of Racial Establishment Segregation" and "Income Inequality and Class Divides in Parental Investments." The first one scored in "Labor Issues," "Economic Sociology," and "Class & Race." The second scored in "Class/Income Inequality" and "The Family." Neither appears particularly Marxist or political-economic in character in that each deals with forms of inequality in general, labor markets, race issues, and familial issues. Again, all relevant and worthwhile questions but, as presented here, these articles really do not seem focused on the logic of capital itself, capitalist class dynamics, or political economy generally.

Third, why do some general categories have no subcategories, such as "Gender"? The issue of gender was similar to "Education," "Religion," and even "Crime/Deviance" in that articles related to all of these also usually had subcategories somewhere else in the table. For instance, articles on gender often connected with income inequality, or motherhood, or occupations, and so on. As we will later see, "Gender" had the second highest representation of all general categories, even though it did not receive subcategories associated with it.

When we combine all general categories and related subcategories, we find that articles I connected to "Political Economy" as a whole made up 5.2% of all articles published in the journal from 2009 to 2018. Whether this level of representation is "high" or "low" or "just about right" depends on one's outlook, interests, and priorities, at least when viewed through a lens carved from mainstream sociology's point of view. From this more conventional perspective, concerns that might interest a "Marxist" sociologist probably received sufficient attention, especially in juxtaposition to issues such as "Sex/Sexuality" (2.0%) or "Religion" (1.9%) or even "Media" (1.4%). Given how I have criticized mainstream sociology for sidelining traditional Marxian concerns, scholars of sexuality, religion, and mass media could realistically respond that their marginalization is even greater. According to my data, that argument would be valid. Complaints about marginalization from advocates of rural and/or urban sociology would be valid even more so.

This result of 5.2% for "Political Economy," however, came from subsuming several categories underneath it, some more squarely and clearly fitting there than others. As you can see from the table, it took 24 subcategories to add up to the final score for "Political Economy" (the highest set of subcategories related to any general category). One can interpret this one of two ways, even partially as both. First, more critically, one must bring in multiple subcategories into the "Political Economy" general category for the set of issues it collectively represents to match a level represented by mainstream issues, e.g., gender, race, the family, crime/deviance, and so on. Second, more positively, one could interpret the same data as reflecting how the journal pays attention to a wide array of topics, including those related to Marxian scholars' interests. Still, if one reviews the article titles, then even those scored for "Political Economy" are not always clearly and obviously from a political-economic perspective. To reduce my biases toward my preconceptions as much as I could, I tried to be generous but fair in these regards.

One related point on this issue before continuing. Whether the articles scored for "Political Economy" came from an *actual* Marxian framework is one that I did not examine. For example, not all articles under the subcategory of "Democracy" were necessarily political-economic in nature. I added them under "Political Economy" because political-economists are usually interested in the growth or decline of democratic processes that occur within a capitalist framework, even if they are not the only ones so interested. Nevertheless, note that "Democracy" contributed the most to the score for "Political Economy," without which its overall representation is considerably lower (3.8%).[2]

---

2   This list above is also a bit misleading. For instance, "Political Economy" as a main general category here only has a score of 1, while "Economic Sociology" is at 26 and "Political Sociology" scored 17. The latter two received scores for topics that seemed rather mainstream in orientation, though often not directly referring to themselves as "Economic" or "Political" sociology, while the score for "Political Economy" reflected a title more closely associated with that term. Returning to Issue 3, take the following two titles as examples: "Policy Generosity, Employer Heterogeneity, and Women's Employment Opportunities: The Welfare State Paradox Reexamined" and "Unemployment, Temporary Work, and Subjective Well-Being: The Gendered Effect of Spousal Labor Market Insecurity." I did not score these as "Political Economy," as I found "Political" or "Economic" sociology more fitting. By contrast, two articles published in Issue 6—"The Social Ecology of Speculation: Community Organization and Non-occupancy Investment in the U.S. Housing Bubble" and "The Social Sources of Geopolitical Power: French and British Diplomacy and the Politics of Interstate Recognition, 1689 to 1789"—represent examples more fit for concerns that political-economic research addresses.

'There are other ways to interpret the table, as this data set is not one with simple or obvious results. Approaching the question from the more clearly articulated general categories, things look decidedly different (see below).[3] Using this approach (excluding both Miscellaneous and Uncategorized), "Political Economy" ranks at the bottom with "Environment." Recall that I constructed this set of categories to reflect the more general themes found in the discipline as a whole. This result brings up two critical points. First, many sociologists appear to analyze their objects of inquiry from a vantage point that does not specify the type of society in which those objects exist, something an anthropologist would never do. Second, in a world in which the business class and its demands increasingly dominate the state—which subsequently is ceding its regulatory powers—and in which capital attacks the natural foundations upon which all societies rest, publishing so few articles specific to political economy and to environmental concerns is highly telling about the state of the discipline.

Gender Issues (65)
Education (48)
Marriage & The Family (37)
Crime/Deviance (37)
Labor Issues (30)
Economic Sociology (26)
Migration, Immigration & Citizenship (24)
Social Networks (23)
Class & Race (22)
Cultural Analysis (21)
Health & Medical Sociology (20)
Theory/Methods (18)
Political Sociology (17)
Sociology of Religion (15)
Sex/Sexuality (10)
Social Organizations (10)
Status (9)
Social Movements (8)
Urban Soc, Rural Soc (6)

---

3   Note that the scores reproduced here are the same as presented in Table A.1. As such, these scores do not represent totals that include the scores for subcategories related to any of these general themes.

Media (5)
Intersections (2)
Environment (1)
Political Economy (1)

Several possible reasons—not necessarily mutually exclusive—could account for this outcome:

- In comparison to gender, education, the family, crime/deviance, etc., fewer scholars studying political-economic issues submit articles to the journal.
- By extension, fewer scholars studying political-economic issues submit *quality* articles to the journal.
- Some reviewers on the editorial board are not friendly to Marxian / political-economic topics.
- Even if some reviewers are friendly to such topics, the editors often decide against publishing an extensive number of articles addressing that subject matter.

Clearly, the data presented here does not provide necessary and sufficient evidence for any of these possible explanations, which must remain at the level of conjecture. What is clear, however, is that for a journal that bills itself as the discipline's "leader," it does not give one the impression that "capital" must be at the center of one's analysis in order to adequately understand modern society. To the extent that this journal is representative of the discipline's practitioners, it is difficult not to conclude that sociologists as a whole hold a similar view.

The *American Sociological Review* is not alone in these regards. The *American Journal of Sociology* and the *British Journal of Sociology* have similar priorities, though examination of their 2009–2018 articles does, admittedly, reveal a more modest level of interest in the modern capitalist system and its social relations (though just in a few instances, too). To ignore such overbearing social realities in a social science requires discipline, and it is a credit to their editors, readers, reviewers, and authors that they embrace the idea that some attention to capital and capitalism are vital issues of sociological import. Nevertheless, it is possible that when challenged on their dominant subject matter, the editors of "top" journals would reply that they tend to leave the study of capitalist society—as well as research on Marx—to the more Marx-oriented journals. Though this would seem reasonable on the surface, it does not really justify their general lack of focus on the real social conditions produced by a system where capital is the central organizing force.

Before closing, I will provide another small example of this pattern. As I was finishing this book, I was also preparing a talk on Marx for the Southern

TABLE A.2   Keywords found in the Preliminary Program for the Southern Sociological
Society's Annual Meeting (April 10–13, 2019, Atlanta, Georgia)

Category	Total
Intersectionality (25), Intersectional (16), Intersection (4)	45
Identity (50), Identities (9)	59
Race (40), Racial (58), Racialization (1), Ethnicity (8), Ethnic (6), African-American (15), Black (70), Blackness (2), Latina (2), Latino (2), Latinx (7), Asia (4), Asian (7), Indigenous (1), Native (4), White (25), Whiteness (11)	263
Gender (89), Women (53), Men (13), Transgender (9), Female (10), Male (6), NonBinary (3)	183
Sexuality (13), Sexualities (9), Gay (20), Queer (15), Homosexuality (1)	58
Inequality (31), Inequalities (10), Stratification (6)	47
Class (12), Income (12), Wealth (6), Poverty (4)	34
Capital (2; 2 others where about social or cultural capital and not counted here), Capitalism (3), Capitalist (2)	7
Marx (1), Marxism (1), Marxist (0)	2

SOURCE: CREATED BY AUTHOR BASED ON THE PRELIMINARY PROGRAM, (RETRIEVED FEBRUARY 11, 2019): HTTPS://WWW.SOUTHERNSOCIOLOGICALSOCIETY. ORG/2019MEETING/SSS2019PRELIMINARYPROGRAM.PDF

Sociological Society's Annual Conference (Atlanta, Georgia, 2019). I had a moment to look over their Preliminary Program that listed presentations scheduled for delivery there (prior to the release of the Final Program). The Program stated the theme of the conference as, "The Challenge of Intersectionality: Who and What are Missing?" It is likely that organizers did not choose this theme with a sense of irony over the type and amount of proposals that scholars would submit and reviewers would accept. Intersectional sociology is, ostensibly, an investigation of how inequalities intersect, especially those of race, class, gender, and sexuality. I downloaded the program, converted it into a Word document, and searched for common terms related to such studies. I then arranged and counted them categorically through several general groupings. I present my results above without additional analysis or comment.

In Chapter 6, I argued that economists have come to treat capital as if a sacred reality of religious devotion. Given the relative absence of capital, capitalists, and capitalism from their analytical frameworks, one might conclude that sociologists are not guilty of this practice. There is at least one good reason to pause before accepting that conclusion. Multiple religious belief systems—especially our earliest forms—forbid people from speaking the name of their god and/or otherwise depicting it in some fashion. In this construct, to speak god's name is to claim knowledge of the deity. To claim such knowledge is also to deny one's submission to that god. For more than one set of ideas in social science, capital is the god whose name one shall not speak and knowledge about which one must studiously avoid. To examine many realities of modern society and omit capital from one's framework becomes an act of mystification, one analogous to religious behaviors of old. This is a form of knowledge preventing us from ever getting to the root of the matter. Science, whether or not animated by Marx's approach, requires that we do better.

References

Alvey, James. 2003. "Adam Smith's View of History: Consistent or Paradoxical?" *History of the Human Sciences* 16(2): 1–25.

Ambrose, Stephen E. 2000. *Nothing Like It in The World; The men who built the Transcontinental Railroad 1863–1869*. New York: Simon & Schuster.

Bain, David Haward. 1999. *Empire Express: Building the First Transcontinental Railroad*. New York: Viking Penguin.

Bekoff, Marc, and Jessica Pierce. 2009. *Wild Justice: The Moral Lives of Animals*. Chicago: University of Chicago Press.

Berger, Peter. 1967. *The Sacred Canopy: Elements of a Sociological Theory of Religion*. Garden City, New York: Doubleday.

Bullard, Gabe. 2016. "The World's Newest Major Religion: No Religion." *National Geographic*, April 22. Retrieved November 6, 2018: http://news.nationalgeographic.com/2016/04/160422-atheism-agnostic-secular-nones-rising-religion/.

Burawoy, Michael. 1990. "Marxism as Science: Historical Challenges and Theoretical Growth." *American Sociological Review* 55(6): 775–793.

Cooper, Betsy, Daniel Cox, Rachel Lienesch, and Robert P. Jones. 2016. "Exodus: Why Americans Are Leaving Religion—and Why They're Unlikely to Come Back." PRRI. September 22. Retrieved December 6, 2018: https://www.prri.org/research/prri-rns-poll-nones-atheist-leaving-religion/.

Dalai Lama XIV. 2006. *The Universe in a Single Atom: The Convergence of Science and Spirituality*. New York: Broadway Books.

Darby, Luke. 2018. "Billionaires Are the Leading Cause of Climate Change." GQ.com. October 11. Retrieved December 16, 2018: https://www.gq.com/story/billionaires-climate-change.

David, Kumar. 2018. "Is Marxism Science? Part 1: Darwin, Marx and the Scientific Method." The Island. March 10. Retrieved October 15, 2018: http://island.lk/index.php?page_cat=article-details&page=article-details&code_title=181248.

deGrasse Tyson, Neil. 2006. "Beyond Belief: Science, Reason, Religion & Survival." Salk Institute. November 5–7, 2006. Retrieved July 5, 2017: https://www.youtube.com/watch?v=N7rR8stuQfk.

de Waal, Frans. 2005. *Our Inner Ape: The Best and Worst of Human Nature*. London: Granta Books.

de Waal, Frans. 2009. *The Age of Empathy: Nature's Lessons for a Kinder Society*. New York: Harmony Books.

de Waal, Frans. 2013. *The Bonobo and the Atheist: In Search of Humanism Among the Primates*. New York: W.W. Norton & Company.

de Waal, Frans. 2016. *Are We Smart Enough to Know How Smart Animals Are?* New York: W.W. Norton & Company.

Dolan, Eric W. 2018. "Study: Religious Fundamentalists and Dogmatic Individuals Are More Likely to Believe Fake News." *PsyPost*. October 28. Retrieved December 6, 2018: https://www.psypost.org/2018/10/study-religious-fundamentalists-and-dogmatic-individuals-are-more-likely-to-believe-fake-news-52426.

Durkheim, Emile. 1915. *The Elementary Forms of the Religious Life*. New York: Free Press/ Macmillan.

Eastman, Max. 1935. "Marxism: Science or Philosophy?" *New International* (August): 159–163. Retrieved October 15, 2018: https://www.marxists.org/archive/eastman/1935/science-philosophy.htm.

Ehrman, Bart. 2003. *Lost Christianities: The Battle for Scripture and the Faiths We Never Knew*. New York: Oxford University Press.

Ehrman, Bart. 2005. *Misquoting Jesus: The Story Behind Who Changed the Bible and Why*. San Francisco: Harper San Francisco.

Ehrman, Bart. 2009. *Jesus, Interrupted: Revealing the Hidden Contradictions in the Bible (and Why We Don't Know About them)*. New York: HarperOne.

Engels, Frederick. 1941 [1888]. *Ludwig Feuerbach and the Outcome of Classical German Philosophy*. New York: International Publishers.

Epley, Nicholas, Benjamin A. Converse, Alexa Delbosc, George A. Monteleone, and John T. Cacioppo. 2009. "Believers' Estimates of God's Beliefs are More Egocentric than Estimates of Other People's Beliefs." *Proceedings of the National Academy of Sciences of the United States of America*. Retrieved October 2, 2018: http://www.pnas.org/content/106/51/21533.full.

Esfahani Smith, Emily. 2015. "Is Human Morality a Product of Evolution?" *The Atlantic*. December 2. Retrieved December 2, 2018: https://www.theatlantic.com/health/archive/2015/12/evolution-of-morality-social-humans-and-apes/418371/.

Fahmy, Dalia. 2018. "Key Findings About Americans' Belief in God." Pew Research Center. April 25. Retrieved December 6, 2018: http://www.pewresearch.org/fact-tank/2018/04/25/key-findings-about-americans-belief-in-god/.

Fuchs, Chris. 2017. "150 Years Ago, Chinese Railroad Workers Staged the Era's Largest Labor Strike." *NBC News*. June 21. Retrieved March 30, 2019: https://www.nbcnews.com/news/asian-america/150-years-ago-chinese-railroad-workers-staged-era-s-largest-n774901.

Ghose, Tia. 2012. "Animals Are Moral Creatures, Scientist Argues." *Live Science*. November 15. Retrieved December 2, 2018: https://www.livescience.com/24802-animals-have-morals-book.html.

Gray, Richard. 2009. "Animals Can Tell Right From Wrong." *The Telegraph*. May 23. Retrieved December 2, 2018: https://www.telegraph.co.uk/news/earth/wildlife/5373379/Animals-can-tell-right-from-wrong.html.

Harvey, David. 2005. *A Brief History of Neoliberalism*. New York: Oxford University Press.

Hill, Lisa. 2001. "The Hidden Theology of Adam Smith." *The European Journal of the History of Economic Thought* 8(1): 1–29.

Hogenboom, Melissa. 2015. "Humans Are Nowhere Near as Special as We Like to Think." BBC | Earth. July 3. Retrieved December 2, 2018: http://www.bbc.com/earth/story/20150706-humans-are-not-unique-or-special.

Jouet, Mugambi. 2012. "Religious and Free-Market Fundamentalism Have More in Common than the Tea Party." Truthout | News Analysis. July 21. Retrieved December 3, 2018: http://www.truth-out.org/news/item/10079-religious-and-free-market-fundamentalism-have-more-in-common-than-the-tea-party.

Kaur, Jasleen, Filippo Radicchi, and Filippo Menczer. 2013. "Universality of Scholarly Impact Metrics." *Journal of Informetrics* 7(4): 924–932. https://doi.org/10.1016/j.joi.2013.09.002.

Keeley, Brian L. 2007. "God as the Ultimate Conspiracy Theory." *Episteme* 4: 135–149.

Kingsbury, Paul. 2017. "Has Paranormal Belief Gone Mainstream?" Live Science. November 3. Retrieved December 6, 2018: https://www.livescience.com/60854-has-paranormal-belief-gone-mainstream.html.

Kitching, Gavin. 1994. *Marxism and Science: Analysis of an Obsession*. University Park: University of Pennsylvania Press.

Klein, Herbert S. 1978. "The English Slave Trade to Jamaica, 1782–1808." *The Economic History Review* 31(1): 25–45.

Klein, Naomi. 2015. *This Changes Everything: Capitalism versus the Climate*. New York: Simon & Schuster Paperbacks.

Kovensky, Josh. 2018. "State Rep's Outline for Killing Non-Believers in Holy War is Referred to the FBI." Talking Points Memo. November 2. Retrieved December 6, 2018: https://talkingpointsmemo.com/news/washington-state-legislator-circulates-proposal-on-exterminating-liberals.

Krauss, Lawrence. 2009. "A Universe from Nothing." AAI, The Richard Dawkins Foundation. Retrieved July 5, 2017: https://richarddawkins.net/2009/10/a-universe-from-nothing-by-lawrence-krauss-aai-2009-2/.

Landau, Elizabeth. 2013. "Morality: It's Not Just for Humans." CNN. January 19. Retrieved December 2, 2018: https://www.cnn.com/2013/01/19/health/chimpanzee-fairness-morality/index.html.

Lenski, Gerhard, Patrick Nolan, and Jean Lenski. 1970. *Human Societies: An Introduction to Macrosociology*. New York: McGraw-Hill.

Lipka, Michael, and David McClendon. 2017. "Why People with No Religion are Projected to Decline as a Share of the World's Population." Pew Research Center, April 7, 2017. Retrieved November 6, 2018: http://www.pewresearch.org/fact-tank/2017/04/07/why-people-with-no-religion-are-projected-to-decline-as-a-share-of-the-worlds population/.

Little, Daniel. 1986. *The Scientific Marx*. Minneapolis: University of Minnesota Press.

Magee, Anna. 2017. "Meet the Astrology to the Stars Making Horoscopes Cool Again."
The Telegraph. November 11. Retrieved December 6, 2018: https://www.telegraph.
co.uk/women/life/meet-astrologer-stars-making-horoscopes-cool/.

Marx, Karl. 1847. *The Poverty of Philosophy*. Moscow, USSR: Foreign Languages Publishing House.

Marx, Karl. 1911. "Preface." *A Contribution to the Critique of Political Economy*. Chicago:
Charles Kerr.

Marx, Karl. 1936. "Marx to Engels, July 7, 1866." In *The Correspondence of Karl Marx and
Friedrich Engels*, pp. 209–210. New York: International Publishers.

Marx, Karl. 1964. "The Leading Article in No. 179 of the *Kölnische Zeitung*." In *Karl Marx
and Friedrich Engels, On Religion*, pp. 16–40. Chico, California: Scholars Press, The
American Academy of Religion.

Marx, Karl. 1968. *Theories of Surplus-Value*, Part 2. Moscow, USSR: Progress Publishers.

Marx, Karl. 1969 [1963]. *Theories of Surplus-Value*, Part 1. Moscow, USSR: Progress
Publishers.

Marx, Karl. 1971a. *Capital, Volume III*. Moscow: Progress Publishers.

Marx, Karl. 1971b. *Theories of Surplus-Value*, Part 3. Moscow: Progress Publishers.

Marx, Karl. 1973. *Grundrisse*. New York: Vintage.

Marx, Karl. 1975a [1843]. "Contribution to the Critique of Hegel's Philosophy of Law." In
Karl Marx Frederick Engels: Collected Works, Volume 3, pp. 3–129. New York: International Publishers.

Marx, Karl. 1975b [1844]. "Contribution to the Critique of Hegel's Philosophy of Law:
Introduction." In *Karl Marx Frederick Engels: Collected Works*, Volume 3, pp. 175–187.
New York: Progress Publishers.

Marx, Karl. 1975c [1844]. "Letters from the *Deutsch-Franzosische Jahrbucher*." In *Karl
Marx and Frederick Engels: Collected Works*, Volume 3, pp. 133–145. New York: Progress Publishers.

Marx, Karl. 1976a [1847]. "The Communism of the Rheinischer Beobachter." In *Karl
Marx Frederick Engels: Collected Works*, Volume 6, pp. 220–234. New York: International Publishers.

Marx, Karl. 1976b [1847]. "Moralising Criticism and Critical Morality." In *Karl Marx and
Frederick Engels: Collected Works*, Volume 6, pp. 312–340. New York: Progress
Publishers.

Marx, Karl. 1978. "Theses on Feuerbach." In *The Marx-Engels Reader*, edited by Robert
C. Tucker. 2nd ed., pp. 143–145. New York: W.W. Norton & Company.

Marx, Karl. 1979 [1877]. From Letter to the Editor of the Petersberg Literary-Political
Journal, Otechestvennye Zapiski, [Homeland Notes], November 1877, in Reply to
Nicolai K. Mikhailovski's Article, "Karl Marx Before the Tribunal of Mr. J. Zhukovski,"
Published in the October, 1877, issue of that journal. In *The Letters of Karl Marx*,

edited and translated by Saul Padover, pp. 321–322. Engelwood Cliffs, New Jersey: Prentice-Hall, Inc.

Marx, Karl. 1982. "Marx to Pavel Vasilyevich Annenkov, December 28, 1846." In *Karl Marx Frederick Engels: Collected Works*, Volume 38, pp. 95–106. New York: International Publishers.

Marx, Karl. 1983. "Marx to Ferdinand Lassalle, November 12, 1858." In *Karl Marx and Frederick Engels: Collective Works*, Volume 40, pp. 353–355. New York: International Publishers.

Marx, Karl 1984 [1861]. "The London *Times* on the Orleans Princes in America." In *Karl Marx and Frederick Engels: Collected Works*, Volume 19, pp. 27–31. New York: International Publishers.

Marx, Karl. 1985. "On Proudhon [Letter to J.B. Schweitzer], January 24, 1865." In *Karl Marx and Frederick Engels: Collected Works*, Volume 20, pp. 26–33. New York: International Publishers.

Marx, Karl. 1988. "Letter to Ludwig Kugelmann, June 27, 1870." In *Karl Marx and Frederick Engels: Collected Works*, Volume 43, pp. 527–528. New York: Progress Publishers.

Marx, Karl. 1989. "Marginal Notes on Adolph Wagner's *Lehrbuch Der Politischen Oekonomie*" (Second Edition, Volume I, 1879). In *Karl Marx Frederick Engels: Collected Works*, Volume 24, pp. 531–559. New York: International Publishers.

Marx, Karl. 1992a [1873]. "Das Kapital," in *European Messenger*, May, 1872: pp. 427–436. In *Capital, Volume I: A Critical Analysis of Capitalist Production*, pp. 27–28. New York: International Publishers.

Marx, Karl. 1992b [1867]. *Capital, Volume I: A Critical Analysis of Capitalist Production*. New York: International Publishers.

Marx, Karl. 1992c [1867]. "Preface" to First German Edition. In *Capital, Volume I: A Critical Analysis of Capitalist Production*, pp. 18–21. New York: International Publishers.

Marx, Karl, and Frederick Engels. 1956 [1845]. *The Holy Family*. Moscow, USSR: Foreign Languages Publishing House.

Marx, Karl, and Frederick Engels. 1976 [1846]. "*The German Ideology*." In *Karl Marx Frederick Engels: Collected Works*, Volume 5. Moscow/New York: International Publishers.

Marx, Karl, and Frederick Engels. 1978a [1848]. "The Manifesto of the Communist Party." In *The Marx-Engels Reader*, edited by Robert C. Tucker, 2nd ed., pp. 469–500. New York: W.W. Norton & Company.

Marx, Karl, and Frederick Engels. 1978b [1850]. "Reviews from the *Neue Rheinische Zeitung. Politisch-Ökonomische Revue* No. 2." In *Karl Marx Frederick Engels: Collected Works*, Volume 10, pp. 241–256. New York: International Publishers.

Mead, George H. 1962 [1934]. *Mind, Self, and Society*. Chicago, Illinois: University of Chicago Press.

Mendes, Natacha, Nikolaus Steinbeis, Nereida Bueno-Guerra, Josep Call, and Tania Singer. 2018. "Preschool Children and Chimpanzees Incur Costs to Watch Punishment of Antisocial Others." *Nature Human Behavior* 2: 45–51.

Noise, Dave. 2011. "Misinformation and Facts about Secularism and Religion." *Psychology Today*. March 30. Retrieved December 10, 2018: https://www.psychologytoday.com/us/blog/our-humanity-naturally/201103/misinformation-and-facts-about-secularism-and-religion.

Ollman, Bertell. 1976 [1971]. *Alienation: Marx's Conception of Man in Capitalist Society*. New York: Cambridge University Press.

Ollman, Bertell. 2003. *Dance of the Dialectic: Steps in Marx's Method*. Urbana, Illinois: University of Illinois Press.

Paolucci, Paul. 2001. "Classical Sociological Theory and Modern Social Problems: Marx's Concept of the Camera Obscura and the Fallacy of Individual Reductionism." *Critical Sociology* 27(1): 77–120.

Paolucci, Paul. 2003. "The Scientific Method and the Dialectical Method." *Historical Materialism* 11(1): 75–106.

Paolucci, Paul. 2004. "The Discursive Transformation of Marx's Communism into Soviet Diamat." *Critical Sociology* 30(3): 617–667.

Paolucci, Paul. 2007. *Marx's Scientific Dialectics*. Leiden, The Netherlands: Brill Academic Publishers.

Paolucci, Paul. 2010. "The Labor-Value Relation and Its Transformations: Revisiting Marx's Value Theory." *Current Perspectives in Social Theory* 27: 163–211.

Paolucci, Paul. 2011. *Marx and the Politics of Abstraction*. Leiden, The Netherlands: Brill Academic Publishers.

Paolucci, Paul. 2018a. "Marx's Method of Successive Abstractions and a Historical-materialist Sociology of Religion." *Critical Sociology* (December): https://doi.org/10.1177/0896920518809843.

Paolucci, Paul. 2018b. "Marx's Method of Successive Abstractions and his Analysis of Modes of Production." *Critical Sociology* (December): https://doi.org/10.1177/0896920518809829.

Paul, Kari. 2017. "Merry Christmas! Why Millennials Are Ditching Religion for Witchcraft and Astrology." *MarketWatch*. December 19. Retrieved December 6, 2018: https://www.marketwatch.com/story/why-millennials-are-ditching-religion-for-witchcraft-and-astrology-2017-10-20.

Pew Forum. 2018. "Being Christian in Western Europe." Pew Research Center. Retrieved December 6, 2018: http://www.pewforum.org/2018/05/29/being-christian-in-western-europe/.

Polimédio, Chayenne. 2018. "The Rise of Brazilian Evangelicals." *The Atlantic*. January 24. Retrieved December 6, 2018: https://www.theatlantic.com/international/archive/2018/01/the-evangelical-takeover-of-brazilian-politics/551423/.

Popper, Karl. 1963. *Conjectures and Refutations: The Growth of Scientific Knowledge.* London: Routledge & Kegan Paul.

Proctor, Darby, Rebecca A. Williamson, Frans B.M. de Waal, and Sara F. Bronson. 2013. "Chimpanzees Play the Ultimatum Game." *Proceedings of the National Academy of Sciences.* February 5, 2013. https://doi.org/10.1073/pnas.1220806110.

Routledge, Clay. 2017. "Don't Belief in God? Maybe You'll Try U.F.O.s." *New York Times.* July 21. Retrieved December 6, 2018: https://www.nytimes.com/2017/07/21/opinion/sunday/dont-believe-in-god-maybe-youll-try-ufos.html.

Rowland, Mark. 2012. *Can Animals Be Moral?* New York: Oxford University Press.

Sahgal, Neha. 2018. "Key Findings About Religion in Western Europe." Pew Research Center. May 29. Retrieved December 6, 2018: http://www.pewresearch.org/fact-tank/2018/05/29/10-key-findings-about-religion-in-western-europe/.

Sapolsky, Robert. 2009. "The Uniqueness of Humans. TED: Ideas Worth Spreading." Stanford University, September. Retrieved October 2 2018: http://www.ted.com/talks/robert_sapolsky_the_uniqueness_of_humans.html.

Seibert, Eric A. 2016. "Recent Research on Divine Violence in the Old Testament (with Special Attention to Christian Theological Perspectives)." *Currents in Biblical Research* 15(1): 8–40. https://doi.org/10.1177/1476993X15600588.

Sheehan, Helena. 2017. "Marxism and Science." *Culture Matters | Technology and Science.* April 21. Retrieved October 15, 2018: https://culturematters.org.uk/index.php/culture/science/item/2509-marxism-and-science.

Squires, Nick. 2018. "Exorcisms Booming as Christian Faith Declines and Internet Offers Easy Access to Black Magic, Priests Told." *The Telegraph.* April 16. Retrieved December 6, 2018: https://www.telegraph.co.uk/news/2018/04/16/casting-demons-catholic-priests-perform-exorcisms-phone-demand/.

Sweezy, Paul. 1964. *The Theory of Capitalist Development: Principles in Marxian Political Economy.* New York: Monthly Review Press.

Sweezy, Paul (with Paul Baran). 1966. *Monopoly Capital: An Essay on the American Economic System.* New York: Monthly Review Press.

Tomasello, Michael. 2016. *A Natural History of Human Morality.* Cambridge, Massachusetts: Harvard University Press.

Torrey, E. Fuller. 2017. *Evolving Brains, Emerging Gods: Early Humans and the Origins of Religion.* New York: Columbia University Press.

Wagner-Egger, Pascal, Sylvain Delouvée, Nicolas Gauvrit, and Sebastian Dieguez. 2018. "Creationism and Conspiracism Share a Common Teleological Bias." *Current Biology* 28(16) PR867–R868. DOI: https://doi.org/10.1016/j.cub.2018.06.072.

Wallerstein, Immanuel. 1974. "The Rise and Future Demise of the World Capitalist System: Concepts for Comparative Analysis." *Comparative Studies in Society and History* 16(4): 387–415.

Zuckerman, Phil. 2014. "Secular Societies Fare Better Than Religious Societies." *Psychology Today*. October 13. Retrieved December 10, 2018: https://www.psychologytoday.com/us/blog/the-secular-life/201410/secular-societies-fare-better-religious-societies.

Zuckerman, Phil. 2015. "Think Religion Makes Society Less Violent? Think Again." *Los Angeles Times*. October 30. Retrieved December 10, 2018: https://www.latimes.com/opinion/op-ed/la-oe-1101-zuckerman-violence-secularism-20151101-story.html.

Index

www.ingramcontent.com/pod-product-compliance
Lightning Source LLC
Chambersburg PA
CBHW070908030426
42336CB00014BA/2329

* 9 7 8 1 6 4 2 5 9 3 6 8 6 *